A Thousand Years
Over a Hot Stove

A Thousand Years
Over a Hot Stove

A History of American Women
Told Through Food, Recipes,
and Remembrances

Laura Schenone

W. W. NORTON & COMPANY
New York • London

Since this page cannot legibly accommodate all the copyright notices, pages 387–90 constitute an extension of the copyright page.

For information about permission to reproduce selections from this book, write to Permissions, W. W. Norton & Company, Inc., 500 Fifth Avenue, New York, NY 10110

Manufacturing by The Maple-Vail Book Manufacturing Group
Book design by BTD NYC
Production manager: Andrew Marasia

Library of Congress Cataloging-in-Publication Data

Schenone, Laura.
    A thousand years over a hot stove : a history of American women told through food, recipes, and remembrances / Laura Schenone.—1st ed.
        p. cm.
Includes bibliographical references and index.
    ISBN 0-393-01671-4
    1. Cookery—United States—History. 2. Women cooks—United States—History. I. Title.
    TX645.S34 2003
    641.5'0973—dc21

                                                                                        2003010418

W. W. Norton & Company, Inc., 500 Fifth Avenue, New York, N.Y. 10110
www.wwnorton.com

W. W. Norton & Company Ltd., Castle House, 75/76 Wells Street, London W1T 3QT

2 3 4 5 6 7 8 9 0

For Herb and all his faith

Contents

Haunted by Kitchen Ghosts

For a brief period, I was a vegetable goddess. I had been an urban creature much of my life, but a twist of fate brought two pastoral years on an isolated farm amid sixty-five acres of soybeans, with an immense garden plot behind my back door. On many a dawn, I'd wake up thinking immediately of my vegetables. In only my nightgown and bare feet, I'd walk straight from bed to garden to woo my tomatoes and string beans, pull a few weeds, and rejoice at the miracle of growing my own food. In the evening I'd return, colander and shovel in hand, to collect muddy potatoes and carrots for dinner.

It was then—living in that house—that I began to look over my shoulder for the ghosts of women before me.

The house was more than a 150 years old, and while I wandered the grounds by the barn and silo and tread across old wide-plank floors, I wondered who had been the very first woman to preside over this place when the paint was still fresh, just before the Civil War. Where had her root cellar been? Where was the wood pile for her stove? Had she preserved pears from this very tree, or baked apples from those across the way? Had she pulled vegetables from this same soil?

I suppose I looked for her through food because that was the only aspect of her work and her life to which I could relate. Like most women of my era, I had no interest in sewing, quilting, cleaning, laundering clothes, or raising seven or eight

Harvesting, 1938. BY JOSEPH SCHARL. *(Print Collection, Miriam and Ira D. Wallach Division of Art, Prints, and Photographs, The New York Public Library, Astor, Lenox and Tilden Foundations.)*

children. But cooking—well, that was different. My mother had been a devoted cook, so too my grandmother and great-grandmother. Even in the late twentieth century, it was something women were still raised to pay mind to.

And so I imagined her, the ghost of the farmhouse, in her crinoline dresses leaning over the collard greens, gathering eggs from hens, baking breads, slaughtering chickens, and throwing rabbits into her pot. I counted the bedrooms on the top floor and calculated that she faced as many as ten hungry mouths each morning when she woke. For her, growing and producing food each and every day was a mandate of life, as necessary and unquestioned as breathing air.

What a contrast to my own cookery. For my husband and me, that brief tenure at a rented farmhouse was a lark, an impulsive move in search of pastoral beauty—something like buying a new pair of shoes to walk in for a couple of years and then discard. Life in my era, obviously, affords such experiments for women. I was thirty years old and still childless. Indeed, my immersion in vegetables was a lovely sort of experiment, a form of recreation my city friends envied. With an undemanding husband, there were few real requirements of me to cook, no less manufacture food. And yet I grew pumpkins and baked pumpkin pie, made marinara sauce from my own tomatoes, baked eggplant, and stirred up various dressings for my freshly picked cucumbers. Cooking this way (the long and hard way from fruits and vegetables I grew myself) was secondary to my real work as a freelance writer, earning money for my labor—a task far more valued by my society than keeping a cold cellar stocked with vegetables for the long winter.

One day, while I was steaming the skins off some tomatoes in that hot August kitchen, it dawned on me that I could tell my life's story through food. Since food is such an eternal thread through women's lives, I wondered, perhaps naively, if I could tell other women's stories that way too.

First I examined the women of my own family line. From the stench of grapes fermenting in the living room (homemade wine, of course) to bread lunches, excessive holiday tables, first-communion feasts, Crock-Pot dinners, and take-out foods, I could trace immigration, poverty, marriage, children, work, love, and death. But beyond these pieces of personal history, I saw a larger scope of history. I saw women changing over time, both creating and responding to the world around them. Almost always these changes showed up on their dinner tables. Through the path of food, I easily found my way back into the nineteenth century, and I realized that I could just keep on going further and further into the past.

History—as we have been told a million times—helps us to understand who we are. Through history, we look back and ask important questions like, How did we get to this place? Was it by choice or necessity? What compromises had to be made?

Much as I love history, I have never found much of it that reflects my own experience of American life in general and women's lives in particular. The women I grew up with spent an awful lot of time in the kitchen—day in, day out, year after year—and in terms of "real" written history, they seemed of no obvious consequence.

Fruit Picking, Fruit Selling, 1953. SOUTHERN UTAH MORMON TOWNS SERIES. PHOTO BY DOROTHEA LANGE. *(Copyright the Dorothea Lange Collection, Oakland Museum of California, City of Oakland. Gift of Paul S. Taylor.)*

And yet food—that centerpiece of women's work—is essential to life itself, biologically, culturally, and for many people, spiritually. From the beginning of time, women have been the caretakers of our stomachs. Men may have cooked for aristocrats and kings, but it was women who devoted extraordinary energy to finding, growing, preparing, and serving food to the better part of the human race. We are born into this world as hungry infants, and until we die, we must eat to survive. This human necessity has helped shape the very nature of women's lives since the days we lived in caves. And in turn, women have shaped the very nature of food. Through creativity, they discovered alchemies to transform raw materials into edible, even beloved, human sustenance. In the modern world, women's choices have swayed—and in some cases, created—the fortunes of billion-dollar food industries. And through food, women have made life simply better: more delicious, more lovely, more beautiful, not to mention more bearable during dark hours. Even without wanting to, women respond with their bodies to that first infant cry of tiny lips asking for milk.

Of course, there are problems in lumping all women together in a single experience or a single anything. And there are problems in writing a book that may seem to suggest, on first glance anyway, that women can best be studied from their "place" in the kitchen. Perhaps rightly so, historians in the academic world are trained nowadays to recognize differences more than those traits we all have in common. Yet I cannot help but see that the majority of women in every race, culture, and time have shared a certain set of concerns that go with the task of cooking.

Maybe this would at least explain why I sometimes feel that the act of cooking is an archetypal code in the dark parts of my brain, and if no one had ever taught me to do it, I would know how anyway, in the same way birds mysteriously find their way to the same tree year after year. If I were cast out into a field with no memory of my life, I would figure out a way to gather roots and herbs, kill what I needed, make a clay pot, and find a big stick for stirring.

Am I suggesting that women are all secretly connected by underground tunnels of recipes? Who can know? Though the majority of American women may no longer slaughter pigs, preserve peaches, or make their own tortillas, the effort of cooking continues to be largely women's work, a major force in the rhythm of our lives, keeping us alive, and bringing us together around the table with those we like, those we love, and those we need.

Perhaps this is why cooking still matters to women. In the thousands of years that this book covers, our world has changed almost beyond recognition. And yet despite all these changes, women still cook and still care deeply about cooking. While they may have less time to do so, they buy cookbooks, watch cooking

Linda Neal cooking chicken for a church banquet. Apostolic Church of God, Chicago.
PHOTO BY ERIC FUTRAN.

shows, share recipes with one another, make potluck dishes, and find time to bake. For all its associations with oppression and drudgery, some of the most "feminist" women I know love to cook and boast that they are the proud owners of their grandmothers' cookbooks. Through food, we search for the elusive past.

This is not to say that food and cooking should be seen as a defining aspect of women's lives, their place in history, the key to their souls, or any such thing. Rather, food opens a window that we can look through. When we sit at their tables, look at their recipes, and consider how they cooked, we get a chance to ask larger questions about who American women were, how they felt about their lives, and what their place has been in society.

In some ways, cooking helps us find a secret language of women because it has been communicated entirely outside of the usual accounts of history—wars and great men—and outside the usual realms of historians and universities, though this is just beginning to change. For generations, women's ways of cooking were never even put into written words but rather were passed on largely through action, from mother to daughter, friend to friend, and only recently, via diaries and cookbooks and the faded ink of recipe cards.

The earliest cookbooks of Western society stand dramatically apart from the cookbooks of today. Right alongside recipes for pig and turtle, you'll find instructions for herbal healing remedies to cure life-threatening fevers. Clearly, women wielded almost mystical strength in their kitchens. And yet in those very same, ancient cookbooks—woven among the recipes, magic potions, and herbal cures—was an unending stream of labor and propaganda to restrict women's lives. Cookbooks dictated proper demeanor, attitude, purity, and obedience to men.

What a consistent paradox this has been. Throughout history, cooking reveals itself as a source of power and magic, and, at the same time, a source of oppression in women's lives. It has helped them win lovers, social standing, admiration, and money, too. And cooking has also helped limit women's lives, by tying up their days with endless chores, too long in the kitchen and out of the arenas of "public" life and business.

I have days in my very own kitchen when I am a high priestess of life. Steam rises up from my bubbling pots. Spices dance in their jars like spirits yearning to be set free. Garlic smells as alive as sex. I wield knives. Outside my kitchen door people clamor with hunger, and I am the only one who can make things right.

Also true: On some days I detest cooking, for it makes me a wretched woman. I cannot believe that I am chopping yet another onion, yet another garlic clove. The repetition. The boredom. A toddler wrapped around my leg so I can barely walk to the refrigerator. Hours in the sweaty kitchen when I could be out in the world supping from life's real table—so I think. How I curse that Susie Homemaker plastic oven I loved as a child and the cooking badge I labored for as a Girl Scout—raised to be a kitchen slave by my culture, my mother—tricked into this bondage.

Long before the farmhouse ghost began to haunt me, I was haunted by other ghost women who slaved over the stoves of history.

As a young girl, I took to heart a story—part real, part dream—about a man from the Old World who took a long journey by boat to America in search of his fortune. He came from a faraway country we then called Yugoslavia, but what is now once again known by its former name Croatia. When he finally reached America, he got a job in New York City, working as a janitor at the Woolworth Building, then the tallest skyscraper in the world and a symbol of America's promise. Each month, he sent back a few crumpled American dollar bills to his wife and two daughters.

His women back in Croatia lived in a Mediterranean paradise on the Dalmatian Coast. They grew lemons and lavender in their backyards. Into their cooking pots went olive oil and fresh octopus that had been caught by the local fishermen and hung out to dry by the bright blue sea and sky—or so I always imagined with romantic yearnings. In the evenings, the women practiced their embroidery, sewing red, yellow, and purple flowers into white linen—the tradition of that faraway place.

Then one day, the dream was broken. The father sent word that he required a daughter to come take care of him and keep house in America. Most importantly, he was hungry. He needed a daughter to cook. After much despair, it was decided that the younger girl would go, though she was heartbroken by the prospect. Of course, there was no choice: He was her father, and what a father said was law. And so, after many nights of crying, this sixteen-year-old girl said goodbye to her sister and mother and boarded a ship, alone, for America and a new life in the gray tenements of Hoboken, New Jersey. She would not return home for almost fifty years.

The girl's name was Katherine, and as you may have guessed, she was my great-grandmother. The lesson I learned early on from this tale was that if men had been able to cook—if there had been microwaves or even take-out food—then my great-great-grandfather never would have needed his daughter. Because she came to America, Katherine's life was, in many ways, ruined. Yet my life was made possible—and that of my mother's family line. I exist simply because

Katherine was a woman who had no choice. I exist because Katherine was a woman and therefore was expected and required to cook.

How many other women in America can trace their roots through such creation myths of cooking? I wonder.

After Katherine had been in the United States a year or perhaps two, the Croatian father repaid his daughter for her loyal services by arranging her marriage to a man she did not love. Once again, she did her womanly duty. She complied with her father's wishes, bore three children, took good care of their domestic existence, and learned to cook American foods. Then after ten years or so, she did something most shocking and undutiful: she ran off with a lover, leaving her three children in the hands of a father who was gone more often than not, working on ships or drinking at the tavern.

Almost immediately, the younger daughter—a girl named Frances—recognized that in this household of alcoholism, negligence, and shame, there was work to be done. Someone, after all, had to step up and take care of the family's nutritional needs. "Instead of going to school, I stayed home and took care of the house," explains my grandmother. "My mother was gone, of course, so I did the cooking."

I ask her what she cooked, and with a sigh she answers, "A lot of potatoes—potatoes, potatoes. I cooked for my sister and my brother. We ate a lot of sandwiches, too." She pauses. Regret of this haunts her some seventy years later. "More than anything, I wish I had gone to school." From her tone, I know she traces the path of her life back to that defining moment. And in my mind's eye, I strain to see her, ten years old, wearing button shoes, putting on her mother's apron, stirring the pots her mother had left cold.

As she grew through womanhood, my grandmother came to embrace food as her realm of expertise, devotion, and even love. By the time I came into her life, she was making double and triple batches of everything—Hungarian goulash, stuffed peppers, pot roast, and a carrot cake so heavy you could barely lift it from the table. Sometimes her cooking was wonderful. But more often, it was just good simple food meant to keep you well and keep you going. The extras went to her daughters, her beautician, her neighbors—basically anyone who would take them. There she was, walking into the gas station with a Quiche Lorraine neatly wrapped in tin foil for that nice mechanic, Mr. Brody, who had done such a good job on her Ford LTD.

Cooking was something my grandmother needed to do. Like everyone, she wanted to excel at something. Growing up poor at the beginning of this century, where else could a respectable woman in her circumstances shine, if not in the arena of housekeeping? Cooking set her on higher ground—not just as a child, but through the deaths of three husbands. The sharp smell of onion sizzling at the bottom of her pan, the loud clattering of her pots, the incessant steps of her feet beating a path in the linoleum—she cooked down every bad emotion until she wilted it under the heat and rendered it under control.

Like so many women, the queen of all my influences in the kitchen is my mother, an incomparable woman named Marcia, who is forever clinging about my skin as I cook. Sometimes, this is a comfort beyond words. Other times, I desperately want to shake her loose, like when I am standing over the marinara sauce and feel the urge to throw granulated sugar into the pot. She always had that desire to please, to transform life's natural bitterness into something easier for the palate. Sometimes, I feel her worries in my own body, as I move quickly from stove to refrigerator, a script I absorbed into my cells, a script taught me by a woman who had lost her father by age eight, was abused by relatives, became pregnant (with me), and then married at nineteen. For my mother, cooking was part of a great improvisation to move ahead with life as a mother and a wife even though she was uncertain, afraid. A traditional role of womanhood was not what she'd had in mind for herself, and yet there she was navigating this very path.

With great effort, my mother threw herself into cooking and food. She learned the Italian-American classics to please her husband and affirm his heritage. She exchanged recipes with friends. And for years, she pored through cookbooks, always trying new recipes as though in endless pursuit of just the right formulas that would make us a happy, healthy family. In many ways, she was successful. Food—particularly her carefully planned dinners each night—helped to hold us together, forcing us to talk to one another, at least for a while. So too her parties, which brought hundreds of relatives and friends to our home, making it the center of a small universe through my child's eyes. Though we lived a modest family life on the salary of a foreman plumber, my mother managed, through food, to create lavishness. In doing so, she gave my sisters and me new possibilities with which to see our own lives.

During an era we now recall with clichés of women's lib, my mother distinguished herself as an odd sort of throwback. During the 1970s, her friends were

Cutting carrots for canning, 1978. Allegheny County, North Carolina. PHOTO BY LYNTHA SCOTT EILER. *(Library of Congress.)*

getting divorced, getting jobs, and even finding feminism—or some version of it—while their kids made their own ham sandwiches for dinner. And yet my mother continued on pounding flank steak for Italian-American *roulades*, stuffing hens, and carrying forth some dubious home economics–style recipes such as pork chops and canned peaches. Even when she finally got a job (as it seems every other mother during the seventies did), she made sure to provide dinner, relying much on advance planning, devotion, and the occasional services of a Crock-Pot.

I was particularly proud of her homemade cakes. When someone dropped by our house (as people then did), coffee cups and saucers instantly appeared, along with neatly folded napkins and teaspoons placed just so, followed by the theatrical clink of the cake tin being lifted. She exceeded ordinary expectations with yellow pound cakes, blueberry crumble, and my favorite, her coffee toffee pie. Even as a young child, I could see that she had taken what life had given her and found a way to create grace. And I adored her for it.

As my mother's culinary efforts grew, our family parties grew larger and grander. One Christmas Eve, my father and I looked at one another with worried eyes as we felt the floors shake beneath us. At least a hundred people had come to eat her sausage and peppers, her lasagne, her special dips, her cookies, cakes, and pies—all of which took weeks of preparation. We could hardly move through the crowds. But there, across the room, was my mother, in her thirties, lit by the candles she insisted upon for these events, wearing a shimmery blue dress, beads jingling against a plate as she leaned forward to serve one of her creations. I was certain that every guest admired her. Everyone wanted what she had to give.

This was all long ago, and things are much different now. The passing of time, the change of eras, and our own individual losses have shaped us in new ways. But even back in those glory days, my mother did not worry much about bequeathing her skills.

"You don't teach these girls how to cook," my father observed of his three daughters one day when we were all in the kitchen. "They don't do things like you."

"I don't want to teach them how to cook," said my mother. "If they can read, they can learn to cook. That's all. I don't want them to do things like me. I want them to be able to do other things."

In many ways, her wishes came true. Among the three of us, my sisters and I have done many "other things."

But to rid ourselves forever of cooking would be to renounce a heritage—one that I have no desire to let go of. What would our lives be without the lessons those women taught us? Through food, my two sisters and I learned about generosity, strength, and love. We learned the brutal realities of a world dominated by men. We learned, too, the *bon vivant* side of life: to eat, drink, and be merry despite our sorrows.

For years, I have been overwhelmed by the ephemeral quality of food. I read accounts of women who risked their lives and overcame immense obstacles to feed and nourish children who have since lived and died, and whose own children are long gone. And yet their efforts matter immensely, for without them we would not exist. Food gives life, and life is fleeting. More food is cooked, and then life begins again. It is true that through history, we understand ourselves. And that is why I still want to be in the kitchen, haunted by those old ghosts.

A patriotic celebration. Southern California, circa 1900.
(Shades of L.A. Archive/Los Angeles Public Library.)

From Her Head Grew Pumpkin Vines: A Few Ideas about the Nature of Women and Food

Most of us had a mother who cooked for us. If not, we had a grandmother who did the job. Or a stepmother. Or an aunt. Or a kindly female neighbor who stepped in during a pinch. It's hard to imagine growing up loved and not being lovingly fed at some time or another. More often than not, it was a woman who did the job and did her best, however uneven the culinary results may have been. Throughout the world, throughout families, and throughout cultures, an invisible food safety net seems to spread under us, ensuring that children are nourished and that the human race can move forward. Usually, this safety net has been woven by the female half of humanity. When it has not been possible to eat as we wish, as in times of great famines, we suspect that it is the women who clutch hungry babies to their breasts and suffer the greatest despair.

If we go beyond these private acts of eating and the love and bitter disappointments entailed, if we step outside of the kitchen and into the world a bit, it's still hard to separate women and food—more specifically, the perpetual image of women offering us something to eat, be it good, bad, or mediocre. In my own life I recall a long single-file procession of cafeteria ladies (as they were called) dishing up mashed potatoes at school, church mothers presiding over neat rows of sticky cakes at bake sales, Girl Scouts selling cookies, waitresses balancing plates of eggs, and aunts who came to family celebrations bearing covered dishes. Like

many girls, the first money I ever earned had to do with food. In my first job at age fourteen, I found myself standing behind a glass bakery counter, handing out bread, cake, and smiles.

Has it always been so? Have women always been the primary cooks and feeders of the human race?

No one can know for sure how people lived in ancient societies that left behind no written records. There is no consensus among researchers. Estimates range from 200,000 to 1.9 million years ago that women (or their pre–*Homo sapien* ancestors) made the discovery that seeds, nuts, vegetables, and meats could be improved with the addition of fire.

But perhaps deep academic inquiry is not necessary to answer my simple question of whether women have always been cooks or not. If I stopped ten ordinary people on the street, they would surely tell me the same as any scholarly social scientists: Of course women have always cooked. Isn't it obvious?

Far less obvious is why.

Why have women always been the ones to gather, cook, and share food with those around them? Were they programmed by their biological natures to serve? Was cooking a burden put on them by men, god, or society? Or did they take on the task willingly, with intelligence and creativity?

Bread dough rising. Amana, Iowa, 1941. PHOTO BY DOROTHEA LANGE. *(Copyright the Dorothea Lange Collection, Oakland Museum of California, City of Oakland. Gift of Paul S. Taylor.)*

Anthropologists say that women have been preparing and serving food for hundreds of thousands of years because it was logical for them to do so. Home-bound by the "burdens" of childbearing, it simply made sense for them to stay at the campsite and tend the cooking fires. In this way, cooking became a woman's job out of a simple concern for practicality; it fit nicely with the needs of her clan and her biological job as a mother. It's hard to argue with the fundamental logic here—which may explain why this theory has long held a favored status.

If we turn to the Bible, we will find another explanation entirely, pointing perhaps to that first damning gesture of Eve and her tempting hand offering Adam a sweet crunchy apple. Though Eve may have led Adam astray, she was still acting according to her nature, for—as the Bible suggests not just in Genesis but in numerous places—God put woman on earth to be man's helpmate. Feeding a man is definitely a great help to him. Therefore, women cook because it is God's will for them to do so.

If these notions don't suit us, we can seek out yet another point of view—that of an evolutionary biologist. Here we learn that women evolved over hundreds of thousands of years to feed others because the survival of each individual human baby depended on whether his or her mom was a good nurturer, which as everyone surely knows involves a good deal of cooking and feeding. Women with good nurturing traits flourished and multiplied, permanently altering the female gene pool and the destiny of the female half of the species. Hence, women cook because it has been programmed into their hardwiring, their very biological code. If we think this way, then the kitchen is nothing short of evolutionary destiny for all women.

In each of these far-ranging perspectives, the fundamental idea is the same: A woman cooks because it is her societal fate. She cooks because it is her religious fate. She cooks because it is her evolutionary and biological fate. In all cases, some higher power—be it the needs of clan, the edicts of God, or the imperatives of biology—hands over the job. In short, women cooked because they had to, because someone told them to—because they had no choice.

I cannot let the matter rest here, for all these views give us an incomplete, if not a paltry, view of women and a paltry understanding of food—of the necessity and complexity of its role in human life, and the goodness it brings to people. Though these well-circulated theories may hold some truth, they don't begin to explain the immense culture of growing, producing, and serving food that has surrounded women's lives from the dawn of human existence to this present moment.

Is it possible to see the origins of women and food in a different way?

I suggest we suspend some of our usual thinking and travel back to the beginning of time in search of the mythic first woman. Let's call her All Woman, the very first female who emerged from ice glaciers, fog, ocean, Adam's rib, the sky, primate lineage, or whatever you wish. Did she walk across the Bering Strait? Arrive on a canoe down a river in Africa? No matter. Somehow, she is here on earth, and others have joined her.

Consider the task before her. Consider all that she must learn if she is to put dinner on the table. Being opportunistic, she first turns to all the plant life growing about her: free food for the taking. But she must figure out which of those pretty berries and roots and leaves and seeds are edible and which ones will kill her (or more likely, her children who by now are clamoring for food). In time, she will learn that a wild gourd eaten from the desert will give intense stomach cramps but can be a highly effective medicine when used in proper doses. She will learn that pumpkin seeds are excellent to eat, but that apple seeds can be poisonous.

With fire, she makes new varieties of roots and seeds digestible. They taste better, too. One day she looks up and sees that a crowd of people have gathered, drawn by the aromas wafting from her cooking fire. They set up permanent camps. The most virile men begin competing for her attention. (She feels some flutterings of delight at this.) A handsome one starts hanging around her, acting protectively. She rewards him with some extra food.

In the evenings around the orange flames, the people begin to search for a way to communicate with one another, and they develop a common language. They create dance and music. In this way, All Woman's cookery gives rise to the very things we call human civilization—the desire to express ourselves, to share, to be creative, to live and work cooperatively.

Over time, All Woman will refine her knowledge. Because she is a gatherer, she will notice that small shells at the edges of rivers and oceans contain sweet-tasting meat and that there are times of day and year when the supply is best and the tides low enough to get at them. She'll also learn which trees have edible nuts, when they are ripe, and which of them are delicious but only if you leach out the acids by rinsing again and again to flush the bitterness away. She will discover

Because of their roles in preparing food, women turned their attention to food-related inventions, including pottery, basket weaving, and preservation techniques. Excavated from Casa Grande Ruins, Arizona. *(Library of Congress.)*

wild grains that can add texture and heartiness to stews of wild beans. She will offer her children scrubby cactus and muddy cattail bulbs as delicious crudités. She will learn to enhance states of mind, transforming coffee beans into energizing drinks and mint leaves into calming fragrant tea. When men bring home animals, she will skin, butcher, and put flesh and bone to fire (not too little, but not too much). First, she achieves palatability. Later, she will strive for flavor, searing the outer layers of meat into a smoky crust and then pushing it away from the high flames to cook more slowly, giving the interior a tender juicy contrast.

Surely the endeavor of cookery will occupy much of All Woman's time and thought and will lead to other kinds of discoveries and technologies. She will use dried gourd shells and bark as bowls, and seashells for spoons, and she will make baskets woven so tightly that they can hold water. She will use animal stomachs or hides as containers, too. Eventually she will figure out how to turn clay into sturdy containers, which she may embellish later with decorations. The invention of pottery will create all sorts of new cooking and storage possibilities such as boiling and braising. Most importantly, she will discover how to save for the future and for barren times, eventually replanting seeds and preserving meats and vegetables. But even this is not so simple now that All Woman is in search of not just survival but also good flavor whenever possible. All foods do not taste as good preserved by the same methods. Some, like pumpkin rings and beans, are best when dried in the sun; other items, like fish, do best in a smoke house; yet others, like buffalo meat, are good when first roasted over a fire and then dried and soaked when needed. Yes, an enormous task lies before All Woman, impossible for one lifetime or even several, and so her daughters and granddaughters will have to carry on, discovering new knowledge over the course of generations.

Although the words *change*, *innovation*, and *technology* are conventionally associated with men in history, it's quite apparent that by inventing and refining the art and science of cookery, women have altered the course of history and all of human civilization. They have done this by constantly developing new ways to grow, obtain, process, and perfect the cooking of foods on which entire cultures, economies, and religious systems are based.

Wilderness Cooking Tip: Boiling Water When You Have No Pot

Before the invention of pottery, women used "stone heating" to heat liquids in their baskets or cooking boxes. Materials needed: fire, stones, cooking container such as a basket or redwood box, tongs long enough to reach into the fire.

1. Get a pile of clean stones ready near your cooking fire and your cooking basket or box. Put the stones in your fire.
2. Prepare the corn or meat—whatever you intend to boil—and put it in your basket or box, filled with water.
3. When the stones are red hot, use your tongs to pick them up and drop into your water. Do this successively with a number of stones until the water begins to boil. Remove stones that have cooled and add hot ones from the fire as needed.

Once we become aware of All Woman, we can find her influence in many unexpected places. In the region we now call Mexico, for example, a woman first kneaded cornmeal into sticky dough and created new possibilities for human wanderings. Her fragrant tortillas made it possible for people to travel distances, carrying their food wrapped in a sandwich, not needing to return to the soup pot every few hours for a meal. The same could be said of the prehistoric woman who first decided to cut meat into thin strips and dry it into lightweight jerky—perfect for long trips. Or the wife who, some thousand years ago, sent her hunter packing with a dry mixture of ground corn and nuts that he could make into a

Ancient Fruit Preserves

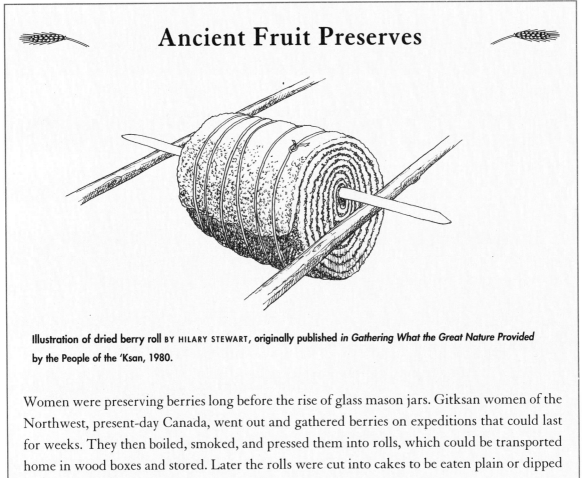

Illustration of dried berry roll BY HILARY STEWART, originally published *in Gathering What the Great Nature Provided by the People of the 'Ksan, 1980.*

Women were preserving berries long before the rise of glass mason jars. Gitksan women of the Northwest, present-day Canada, went out and gathered berries on expeditions that could last for weeks. They then boiled, smoked, and pressed them into rolls, which could be transported home in wood boxes and stored. Later the rolls were cut into cakes to be eaten plain or dipped in grease—perfect for traveling while hunting.

cereal by adding water at his hunting camp. These sorts of convenience products were first invented not by commercial food companies but by prehistoric women.

Consider maize (corn), towering grain of the Americas, a native food that would ultimately feed billions all over the world. True, this golden kernel has a wonderful taste, fantastic yields, and incredible adaptability to extreme climates. But, as food historian Sophie Coe has explained, what really made it a superior item was *nixtamalization,* a process developed by women somewhere in Central America, long before the time of Jesus. To make *nixtamal,* women soaked their corn grains in water with lime or wood ashes from their cooking fires, loosening the tough hulls that were characteristic of ancient strains of corn. The soaking made the kernels easier to grind into meal for tortillas. Or the cook might boil the nixtamal into a puffy ricelike dish called *hominy* (also called *posole* in the Southwest). Though these techniques made for good eating, much of the brilliance lay in the nutritional chemistry: alkali from the wood ashes enhanced the protein of the maize.

How much did this process really matter? Nixtamalized maize was so much better than the unprocessed kind, wrote Coe, that "it is tempting to see the rise of Mesoamerican civilization as a consequence of this invention, without which the peoples of Mexico and their southern neighbors would have remained forever on the village level."

Some millennia later, Europeans would adopt corn without nixtamalization, contributing to widespread malnourishment and vitamin deficiencies such as pellagra.

What gave our foremothers the audacity to try such things? Was it boredom? Starvation? Curiosity? And to think that at these early breaths of ancient human life, when the world was raw and new, All Woman began with no tools but stones and sticks. With intelligence, creativity, and some luck, she transformed the earth's rough surfaces into nourishment. It would seem that she must have also had powers of a sacred nature to take on the task of satisfying the endless hungers of humanity.

Women in Central America soaked corn in water mixed with lime or wood ashes. This made it easier to grind into meal and also boosted the nutritional qualities of the grain. Illustration published in 1780. Original caption: "Method of Making Bread. (1) Woman peeling the grain, (2) Woman grinding it, (3) Woman forming and cooking the bread." From *Storia Antica del Messico* by Francisco Javier Clavijero.

NATIVE ROOTS

When we speak about native women and food, we find a story that is inextricably connected with the natural abundance of this continent, its native animals, fish, plants, roots, and herbs.

As the Hurons tell it, the origins of earth go back to a divine woman who came falling from the sky, long ago when there was no land and no humans, only a chaotic watery world inhabited by animals and sea creatures. She fell to the world pregnant, pushed by her husband Sky Father.

Two loons saw her falling and flew to her rescue, catching her in their con-nected beaks. They carried the woman in safety to a turtle, who agreed to take her on his back. Then, using their great loon cries, they called a meeting of all the creatures. Desperate measures were required to save the woman who could not survive in water, and the animals frantically dove way down to the bottom of the ocean in a fruitless search for land. They exhausted themselves. Some drowned. Finally, a frog emerged with a bit of earth in his mouth. He gave this morsel to the divine woman, who placed it on the back of a turtle. With her touch, this bit of dirt grew and grew into a great expanse of land that would become earth, for-ever known as "turtle island."

Shortly after, it was time for the divine woman to give birth. She had twin sons inside her, one good, the other evil. The good son was willing to be born the usual way, but the bad son insisted on pushing out of his mother's side, tearing her apart and killing her.

The woman was buried. Later, on the same spot where her body had been interred, a bounty of food sprang from the earth. From her head grew pumpkin vines; from her breasts, maize; from her arms and leg came beans and other foods. There would be enough to eat for the world's first peoples and those ever after.

This idea that a woman's very body brings forth edible plants to the world was quite popular among agricultural tribes of the eastern woodlands of North America. Here, women were the chief farmers of their tribes, presiding over the seeds, the fields, and the crops. According to the Seneca, the first potatoes of the world sprang from a woman's feet; beans came from her fingers, squash from her abdomen, tobacco from her head, maize from her breasts. The Creek say that a woman created the first corn by rubbing her feet. The Cherokee tell us of Selu, who rubbed her stomach to fill her basket half with corn, and then her armpits to fill it to the top with beans.

Selu, whose name in Cherokee means "corn," offers an archetype for Corn Mother, one of the greatest deities of North America whose legacy exists, in one form or another, from present-day Maine to the Southwest. In all these sacred stories, it is women who bring the most sacred food—corn—to the world and its people.

If we listen to the ancients, we learn that life-giving powers are part of woman's very organic matter and that, ultimately, she is made of food. Food is a part of her skin, her bones, her blood.

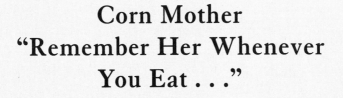

Corn Mother
"Remember Her Whenever
You Eat . . ."

The way the Penobscot tell it, she was First Woman, born of a plant, mixed with dew and the warm life-giving power of the sun. From this potent mixture, she came to life, announcing herself with these words: "I am love. I am a strength giver, the nourisher, a provider of men and animals. They all love me."

The first man on earth, who had been born of sea foam, watched her come forth, amazed at her beauty. The two married and soon conceived, bringing forth many children.

In time, the population grew and grew, living mainly from hunting. But they were so successful that after some years, they killed off all the game. There was nothing left to eat, and great starvation came.

First Mother pitied the children with all her

Corn Mothers have been central to religious beliefs in agricultural societies of Native North America. Inherent is the idea that a primordial woman brought forth the sacred grain that would feed the world. *The Corn Maiden,* 1945.
HARRY SAKYESVA, HOPI, B. 1921, WATERCOLOR ON PAPER.
(Philbrook Museum of Art, Tulsa, Oklahoma.)

If we roam farther, beyond agricultural groups, we continue to find female gods who hold sway over food and life itself. Among cultures dominated by hunting and male brawn, we find divinities like Sedna, the "she down there" goddess who lives in the cold forbidding oceans of the Innuit, presiding over salmon, whale, and other sea creatures vital to the old fishing societies.

heart. They came to her, begging for food. "Feed us," they cried. "We are hungry." She wept so hard that her husband was desperate to help her.

"What can I do to stop your crying?" he pleaded.

"Only one thing will stop my tears," she replied.

"What is that?"

"You must kill me, or I will be crying and grieving forever."

The husband, bereft because of this unbearable prospect, traveled to the far end of the earth seeking divine guidance. There, he found his uncle, the Great Instructor.

"You must kill her," the Great Instructor said. "You must do what she has asked."

And so, when he returned, the wife gave him instructions on how to slay her. "Tomorrow at noon, you must kill me," she said and then advised him to drag her body over an empty patch of earth, back and forth, back and forth, and afterward bury her bones in a particular spot.

So the heartbreaking task was done. The husband killed his beloved wife and dragged her body over the earth, weeping loudly.

Seven moons later, the husband and children and some grandchildren came back to the place. There before them, the earth was covered with tall, green, tasseled plants bearing corn that was so sweet and beautiful, it was beyond imagining. No one had ever tasted such a wonderful food before.

Exactly as First Mother had instructed, they saved some kernels and planted them back in the earth. In this way, her flesh and spirit continued to renew them. And so she saved her people from starvation.

"Remember her and think of her whenever you eat," said her husband. "She has given her life so that you may live. Yet she is not dead. She lives in undying love as she renews herself again and again."

Among the Sioux—known as a great warrior tribe—it is a female, White Buffalo Calf Woman, who is the holiest of deities. When the Sioux people were starving, White Buffalo Calf Woman appeared and brought the sacred pipe and seven sacred ceremonies. She taught the Sioux how to pray, how to live, and how to cook, and she advised the women that it was the work of their hands and the fruit of their bodies that kept the people alive. "You are from the mother earth," she said. "What you are doing is as great as what the warriors do." Finally, she turned into a white buffalo calf, the most sacred living creature. As she disappeared into the horizon, great herds of buffalo suddenly appeared, allowing themselves to be killed so that the people could eat.

Can those of us who are not natives feel the presence of these deities?

I believe we can in our own private ways. All people today, male or female, can share this connection to All Woman and her daughters who wove that first invisible food safety net for humanity, a net that many of us continue to hold. No matter how simple the meal, we can almost always find her ghost in the shadows of our kitchen. Her influence is in the heat of the oven, the bread, the knife and cutting board, the box of berries we bought at the store, the lettuce for salad. Even if we are unaware of All Woman, the truth of our kinship with her remains real, true, and enduring.

A Thousand Years Over a Hot Stove

Chapter 1

Gathering Up the Earth

WHO DID WHAT TO THE MASTODON?

Where and when did cooking actually begin on this continent? Most archaeologists believe that the first people in North America were "big-game hunters." They entered present-day America by walking across the Bering land bridge that connected the Ice Age worlds of Asia and Alaska some 12,000 years ago when sea levels were 300 feet lower than today. Clad in fur coats, great stoic adventurers they were—men in pursuit of a hunter's dream: the wooly mammoth, the immense mastodon, the great stags. These "paleopeople" chased the legendary beasts through the Rocky Mountains, some of them migrated down to South America, traveling between ice glaciers along melted passageways. In time, the theory goes, they slowly migrated east.

In this manner, all human life and culinary adventures on this continent began with a hunger for meat—a hunger pursued by men. Of so little concern are women in these theories, we might conclude that these hunters single-handedly brought forth a race of men. Instead of sacred women, such as the Native American Corn Mother, our greatest archaeologists have given us a sportsman progenitor, the great hunter father who conquered the wild beasts of a rugged frozen world.

Traditional Indians have long rejected these notions in favor of their own tribal histories and beliefs. Some trace their origins in America back to "time immemorial." Interestingly even some scientists are now willing to consider new theories that place humans in North America further and further in the past, though it is a source of ongoing debate.

The archaeologist Carole Mandryk tells me that theoretically, people could have come here from the Russian Far East as early as 24,000 to 26,000 years ago, though we still have no physical evidence to prove it. And so while the mastodon hunters were real, they may not have been the first people here.

A new generation of archaeologists now supports the idea that a mixed group of Asiatic men, women, and children may have arrived by boats along the Pacific coast—not bands of hunters but family and tribal groups of seafaring people. The men may have hunted; more likely they focused their efforts on fishing. The women gathered shellfish, in addition to plants and seaweeds. They probably built fires for roasting and dug underground earth ovens for baking. Perhaps these first coastal peoples are ancestors of the Northwest Indian nations who, without agriculture, built elaborate economies based on the sea, its salmon, seals, and shellfish, plus plants and berries growing inland of the temperate shore.

I have neither the desire nor the ability to resolve the difficult questions of who were the first Americans and when or why they came. Far more interesting to me is the mystery of what those ancient women cooked in a world that was still raw and new.

The earliest physical evidence we have (so far) of women cooking may be the charred remains of hearth fires found in Alaska and dated at 12,000 years old. Or perhaps the enormous mammoth bones dug up at a campsite in New Mexico and dated from the same time. If we study the ghostly hack marks of a butcher who struggled to pull meat away from bone, we may have before us the work of a woman's hands, considering that in most hunting cultures women did the butchering. In fact, we can be fairly certain that the camp itself was a place run by women. Archaeologists believe that paleomen and paleowomen probably went their separate ways in order to get their work done. The hunters set up male-only camps where they prepared arrowheads and devised strategies for chasing, cornering, and killing the giant animals. Meanwhile, women prepared meat-processing centers. They built drying racks from branches, gathered kindling, and dug roasting pits. They set up their tools for butchering and scraping hides. They also went out and gathered wild plants and roots, which they sorted and cleaned. When the hunters finally returned with the kill, the women swung into action, running out to greet them and perhaps helping to drag back the carcasses. They butchered, roasted, and hung mastodon meat to dry. They processed the hides into blankets and cloth.

Our paleo-foremothers left us no written records, and so we will never know as much about them as we'd like. Did they use herbs to marinate their meats? Did they stand over their meat to catch the juices and baste it? Did they rejoice at the sound of the hunters' triumphant return? These are the mysteries old bones can never tell.

We do know that after 10,000 B.C., the Ice Age receded, and the physical world began changing rapidly beneath the feet of these early people. Between the lives of grandmother and granddaughter, rivers dried up and disappeared, coastlines sank, and the air grew warmer. The Haida people of the Northwest tell of "flood tide woman" who forced them to move their villages to higher ground. Inland, the great mega-animals of prehistory became extinct, and along with them the epic culture of hunters and preparers of mammoth and mastodon. To survive, Mandryk tells me that men and women probably had to be extremely adaptable. They had to find new ways to live and eat; they needed to hunt smaller game and gather different foods.

In the least fertile parts of the Southwest, a "desert culture" rose up around 7000 B.C., and women went out to search the landscape for edible plants, wild grains, seeds, and beans. They used stones we call *metates* and *manos* to pound tough grains and beans and nuts into life-sustaining nourishment. The grinding of grain against these stones would provide a central feature of work and culture and daily rhythm to women's lives for thousands of years.

As the world slowly thawed, ancient people migrated eastward. As early as 8000 B.C., women were gathering new delicacies in the eastern forests—hickory nuts, acorns, walnuts, chestnuts, and hazelnuts. In places like Kentucky and Tennessee, they also spent a good deal of time in the shallows of freshwater lakes and rivers, combing for clams and other mollusks. Not far from the waters, on the muddy green shores, we can imagine them working together to build drying stages made of twigs and placing their shellfish on hot coals in underground ovens. Perhaps they sang as they worked. Thinking ahead, they pulled meats from the shells and dried them for the spare cold winter days to come. They gath-

Pinyon nuts on *metate* and *mano*. Ancient women used grinding stones to make grains, beans, and nuts digestible. PHOTO BY MARGARET WHEAT. *(University of Nevada Press.)*

ered herbs and used digging sticks to collect tubers and roots. In the summer, they cooked fish caught by their men; in the fall, they butchered, roasted, and dried venison and other wild meats and birds of the hunt.

WHY AMERICA'S FIRST FARMERS WERE PROBABLY WOMEN

Man the hunter. Woman the gatherer.

See them there, in your mind's eye: Men, bursting with speed across the ice tundra, the Great Plains, the leafy green forests of the East. See the women searching for jewels amid the thicket, salal berries in the Northwest, sweet

How to Build an Earth Oven

The earth oven was a popular tool among many native cooks in North America, used to bake fish, corn, bread, and vegetables.

1. Dig a hole or pit large enough for the fish, roots, or corn you want to bake. Fill it with stones about the size and shape of large baking potatoes.
2. Now put some kindling (brush, twigs, wood, etc.) in the pit and start a big fire. Let it burn down until hot coals remain. Remove any extra kindling that might be in your way. (Another method is to heat your stones in a fire and transfer them to the baking pit with wooden tongs.)
3. For insulation, cover your hot stones with a thin layer of earth and then a layer of greens, like ferns, skunk cabbage leaves, or tree boughs.
4. Place the food you want to bake on the bed of greens. If you are cooking meat or fish, you may wish to wrap it in additional leaves or bark (make sure you can identify and stay away from any poisonous ones) to keep it clean and seal in the juices and flavor.
5. Now, place another layer of greens over the food, and then more soil. Let it cook until nicely done.

Only experience and judgment (or the help of a more accomplished cook) can tell you how long to leave the food in the pit or how much soil and leaves you need, but you can always check on its progress by scooping a corner of the earth away and taking a peek.

prickly pear cactus in the desert, wild onions in the South. Yes, we are confident of this. Men hunted. Women gathered. However, if we remain strongly committed to this idea, then we'd have little choice but to conclude that women probably were America's first farmers.

Before we consider the beginning of horticulture, let's explore a bit further this idea of woman the gatherer. Plenty of Indian men gathered foods. Plenty of women hunted. In fact, stories persist of women going on big-game hunts along with men for caribou and other great creatures. Still, despite these variations our original idea holds up in most cases. And so we come back to it: Man the hunter. Woman the gatherer.

> *I*mpatient for fresh green food, naked women waded into the marshes, reaching arm-deep into the chilly water to search in the mud. The shoots were covered with soggy brown leaves that the mothers peeled off with their thumbnails before passing the white spears to the hungry children who sat huddled in their blankets on the banks.
>
> —MARGARET M. WHEAT'S
> description of cattail gatherers
> *Survival Arts of the Primitive Paiutes*, 1967

Let's have a look at her again, a woman moving light-footedly through brambles, gathering berries. To our modern perceptions, the image seems somehow innocent and trivial. In fact, the ancient gatherer women were nothing short of botanists with extensive knowledge far beyond the scope of berries for dessert. This knowledge could only be built up over generations through careful judgment, skill, and yes, even some poisonous trial and error along the way. By the time the Europeans came, Indians from coast to coast were gathering almost two thousand types of edible roots, nuts, vegetable plants, greens, fruits, and herbs, as well as insects and shellfish. In the arid climates of present-day Arizona and Mexico, women of more than a dozen nations collected cactus, cholla buds, mesquite beans, acorn, pinyon nuts, agave, wild currant, dandelions, purslane, and a wide array of berries, such as juniper, elderberry, and desert hackberries—to name just a few of their wild foods.

Spend one week (even one day) in the wilderness with no food, and you'll quickly realize that without know-how, you'll starve or poison yourself. And it's not just knowing what you can eat, but where to find it and when it will be ripe or available. If you get to the nut trees or fruits even a few days late, more enterprising animals will have beat you to them, or you'll find yourself left with the taste of overripe or rotten fruit in your mouth, opportunity so closely missed.

And so who was in the best position to develop horticulture and farming? The men who spent their time tracking wild animals every day or the women who devoted their lives to botany?

While we can never be entirely sure, many experts believe that women "discovered" horticulture and were probably America's first farmers. The rise of farming was most likely a gradual process. Perhaps one woman decided to help along the wild plants and bushes she liked best. First, she began to weed away competing plants or give water to her favorites. Maybe she noticed that a basket of dropped seeds had sprouted in the loosened soil where she'd built an earthen

oven. It was only a matter of time before she thought, *Why not plant seeds ourselves?*

Natives of Mexico farmed corn as early as 5000 B.C., and shortly after, beans and squash. The spread of farming traveled northward over millennia. The oldest-known cobs of maize (corn), smaller than a pinky finger, were discovered in Bat Cave, New Mexico, in the 1940s. Many scientists believe they had lain there since 3600 B.C., give or take a few centuries. At the time the Europeans came, more than a hundred local varieties of maize, including red, black, and blue corn, were farmed all over America.

Pine Nut Soup

- Put your pine nuts in a winnowing basket (one you've woven yourself). Rinse to clean pitch* and needles from your nuts.

- Shovel hot coals from your fire onto the nuts in your basket. Immediately toss and shake, keeping the nuts and coals in constant motion to keep from scorching the basket.

- When nuts are roasted, skillfully flip coals out of the basket (but not the nuts—this takes practice). Carefully remove the remaining bits of charcoal by hand, quickly so as not to burn your fingers.

- Take your stone huller and rub gently over your stone metate, using just the right pressure so as to crack the shells but not the kernels. Put the nuts back in your winnowing basket and separate shell from nut. Call on the wind to help. If the wind fails, use your own breath to blow the last of the shells away.

- Do a second roasting, putting more fresh coals on the nutmeats, again shaking the basket constantly to avoid scorching. Grind a few of the nuts into a paste by mixing with water. Use this paste as a cleaning agent, rolling it over the remaining pine nuts to remove all charcoal and ashes.

- When your twice-roasted nuts are clean, grind between mano and metate, a few at a time, converting them into flour. Transfer to a bowl. Slowly add mountain spring water to the soup to thin it to the right consistency. Stir it with a stick. Serve heated if desired.

—Adapted from MARGARET M. WHEAT
Survival Arts of the Primitive Paiutes, 1967

*Women coated their baskets with pitch from trees to make them waterproof.

OPPOSITE: Wuzzie George, a Paiute Indian, demonstrates how to make pine nut soup "in the manner of old ones." Here she roasts the nuts by tossing them with the hot coals. Nevada 1957. PHOTO BY MARGARET WHEAT. *(University of Nevada Press.)*

In the Southwest pueblos, men ultimately did the farming (some suspect that men may have taken over the job from women). But in midwestern, eastern, and southeastern North America, farming was female work. Women probably planted gardens as early as 2000 B.C. in the fertile soil of what we now call Illinois and Missouri. As paleoethnobotanist Gail Wagner points out, most American schoolchildren learn that the Indians of the East grew the "three sisters" of corn, beans, and squash. But actually, women had been tending gardens for thousands of year before this, and their earliest gardens were quite different from what the first colonists found. Long before corn traveled to them from Mexico, women grew gourds and grasses that yielded fatty seeds, like sumpweed, sunflowers, chenopod, and maygrass.

New archaeological treasures are being unearthed each year, but as of now, we believe that maize kernels reached our women farmers in Illinois as early as A.D.

100. But it was not until around A.D. 700 or 800 that people began to fall in love with maize, and the plant began spreading rapidly from village to village. Not long after this, in the area we now call Pennsylvania, women farmers developed a distinctly northeastern variety that could withstand the colder climates. By the year A.D. 1000, the resulting "Northern Flint" corn reached Ohio, Indiana, Kentucky, and West Virginia. Northern Flint was a monumental success and the basis for all modern varieties of "Corn Belt Dent," a strain that would revolutionize agriculture and is eaten all around the world today.

Brilliant as this invention may have been, few people munching on a golden cob of Fourth-of-July corn in Harrisburg would guess that this beloved grain was originally grown by native female farmers. If we wish to reach out to one of those curious farmers of the past, perhaps we can imagine her like this:

She keeps the maize seeds in a pouch made of deer skin. The spring rains have let up, and now many days of sun create the perfect soil for planting—moist, with light crumbs, not soaked and muddy. The sharp winds off the Great Lakes are gentler now. The woman sets off with her daughter, her sisters, her mother, and aunts for planting time. The corn kernels she holds are something new and special that have come to her village via trading trips from the Plains—corn kernels, along with obsidian stones, grizzly bear teeth, and other coveted goods. She has heard from the shaman in her tribe that these seeds have special power.

By midsummer, an odd-looking plant grows tall as a pillar, gaining the attention and interest of all the planters. No one has ever seen such a tall human-like plant before. Its tassels seem like hair. Its leaves like arms. It sways in the breeze as though it is dancing. At first, the yields are meager—small ears with few kernels. But the taste of this grain holds great promise, so the women continue trying, plucking seeds from the most vigorous plants and saving them for next year. Each growing season, experimentation continues: One season the women try planting deeper; the next spring, more shallowly. Some years, earlier in the season; some years, later. Sometimes in hills patted lightly with hands; other times in furrows.

The corn grows in a garden plot, along with the weedy plants the women have been growing all their lives—sumpweed, bottle gourds, maygrass, sunflowers—all of which they learned to plant from their grandmothers and they from their grandmothers before them. Finally, these gardeners have success, producing the tight rows of sweet grain that are strong and delicious. Over time, the farmers and their daughters and granddaughters discover many ways of cooking corn. They roast it over fire, bake it in ashes, dry it in the sun, boil it in water, soak it and grind it into flour, add it to stews and meat broths, and bake it as bread sweetened with berries and maple syrup tapped from the trees.

BUFFALO BIRD WOMAN'S GARDEN

"We cared for our corn in those days, as we would care for a child; for we Indian people loved our fields as mothers love their children," said Buffalo Bird Woman. "We thought that the corn plants had souls, as children have souls, and that the growing corn liked to hear us sing, as children like to hear their mothers sing to them."

Buffalo Bird Woman was a Hidatsa Indian born around 1839 in an earth lodge in present-day North Dakota. The Hidatsas are a Siouan tribe and speak a language akin to that of the Crows. A supremely skilled farmer, Buffalo Bird Woman devoted her heart, soul, and formidable skills to the old agricultural ways. At age sixty-seven, she met Gilbert Wilson, a minister and anthropologist, with whom she began an unlikely friendship. Buffalo Bird Woman told Wilson about her life and the traditional farming methods of Hidatsa Indians. He recorded her stories in extraordinary detail in his book *Buffalo Bird Woman's Garden*.

Turtle (Buffalo Bird Woman's grandmother) working among her corn hills. The blade of her hoe is made from a buffalo shoulder. Illustration from *Waheenee: An Indian Girl's Story.*

Growing up in a traditional matrilineal society under the care of her aunts (whom she collectively called "mothers"), Buffalo Bird Woman spent her youth sleeping on buffalo skins in a circular earth lodge, working the earth in communal fields with her female clan members, listening to the stories of her elders. She sewed with an awl and sinew. She built her own boats, followed her husband on buffalo-hunting trips, and made blood puddings stirred with a choke cherry stick to give it a "pleasant flavor." She wrapped her baby in a papoose filled with cattail down and earned from her clan the honorable woman's belt for her industriousness.

And yet, so much of this world would change in her lifetime. When Buffalo Bird Woman was thirty-three, she was forced out of her earth lodge into a cabin. The U.S. government plowed up the women's communal fields and gave each family a land allotment and seeds for watermelons, large squashes, potatoes, turnips, and other foreign vegetables that the Hidatsa women took little interest in.

By the nineteenth century, the Hidatsas had already confronted the iron tools and imports of white culture. "I was not quite twenty yet when we bought an iron pot for cooking," she explains. "Before that we used only earthen pots for cooking in our family." But their farming methods, with a few exceptions, clearly had been handed down from mother to daughter, long before the coming of the plow—perhaps as far back as A.D. 1100. They used rakes of wood or the antler of black-tailed deer. The women knew it was corn-planting time "by observing the leaves of the wild gooseberry bushes." To prepare squash for the earth, they wet the seeds, wrapped them in sage leaves and buffalo skins, and then hung the whole bundle on a drying pole. On the third day, the seeds had sprouted "nearly an inch" and were ready to plant.

Buffalo Bird Woman relied on one-pot meals of dried buffalo meat in broth and morning breakfasts made of squash, beans, and corn eaten with horn spoons or mussel shells. She made sticky sunflower-seed balls using ground sunflower seeds and water—a treat that a warrior could carry in his bag while hunting.

At age seventy-two, after winning a prize for her corn at a reservation agricultural fair, she noted, "I raised it on new ground; the ground had been plowed, but aside from that, I cultivated the corn exactly as in old times, with a hoe."

ANCIENT RECIPES

Because Indian cultures were based entirely on oral traditions, no written records exist to tell us exactly what women cooked a thousand years ago. Instead, to find recipes, we must interpret from a combination of sources. Today there are hundreds of native communities all over North America in which many Indians cherish and carry out the old ways—collecting wild foods and medicines from the natural environment and recording recipes from their elders. Some California women continue to make acorn bread. Hominy stew remains a classic pueblo dish. In Alaska grandmothers and granddaughters still string and hang herring to dry in the sun as they have for generations. Native women also live in cities, work in professions, and shop at the grocery store for wheat bread, steaks, potato chips, and everything else that Americans eat.

We can consult the records of anthropologists who studied Indians' rapidly changing cultures during the nineteenth century. We also have many accounts written by the first missionaries and explorers who arrived in the seventeenth century. These outsiders often had little understanding of the cultures they were witnessing, but their records are valuable and sometimes startling because they remind us how far human beings have come from living intimately with nature.

The recipes in this chapter come from a variety of these sources. They are not meant to offer a representative sampling of native cookery or the complexity of native cultures over the vast expanse of time before European contact. My intention is simply to present the larger traditions and techniques of people who had access to absolutely no manufactured goods—nearly inconceivable in our postindustrial world. Here I am interested in how women used skills accumulated over centuries to prepare simple wholesome food each day from the rivers, lakes, oceans, forests, and earth.

TAKING CARE OF THE SACRED

As cooks, Native American women lay the first claim to some of the greatest ingredients in the history of the world. Tomatoes, corn, potatoes, cacao, manioc, chile peppers, squash, and peanuts all originate in the Americas. It's hard for the modern American to imagine, but before Columbus's fateful voyage, Ireland was without potatoes, Italy had no tomatoes or polenta, Africans had no peanuts or hot chiles for groundnut stews. These wonderful foods were all first identified, cultivated, and cooked by women in North, Central, and South America.

By the time the Europeans came, more than five hundred Indian nations lived in North America. In each region, women had developed extensive recipes and

"She's Got to Be Patient"

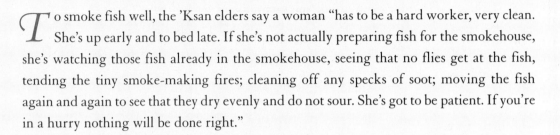

To smoke fish well, the 'Ksan elders say a woman "has to be a hard worker, very clean. She's up early and to bed late. If she's not actually preparing fish for the smokehouse, she's watching those fish already in the smokehouse, seeing that no flies get at the fish, tending the tiny smoke-making fires; cleaning off any specks of soot; moving the fish again and again to see that they dry evenly and do not sour. She's got to be patient. If you're in a hurry nothing will be done right."

The old smokehouses at Kisgegas. *(Canadian Museum of Civilization.)*

Because of their remote location, the people of the 'Ksan River in North-Central British Columbia were not engulfed by traders and settlers at an early date. In the twentieth century, old ways were preserved and written down from the memories of elders, in a collective tribal book *Gathering What the Great Nature Provided*. Farming was of little interest to the 'Ksan people because greens and roots were prolific. Men hunted goats, caribou, deer, groundhog, and porcupine. Fish were abundant in their river. Ducks, geese, and swans could easily be trapped. Not to mention that there were berries, "just tons" every year.

Above all, fish was the supreme staple of life, eaten at each meal. This meant that the 'Ksan "worked like slaves," as they describe it, during spring and summer so they could eat all year. For flavoring, the most important condiment was oolichan grease derived from the small silvery oolichan, also known as the candlefish. To preserve foods, they wrapped them in birch bark cut into neat squares because it was perfectly watertight and airtight and worked well in their earth storage cellars.

Boiled Fully Dried Salmon (*Jamksxw*)

Take some dried fish and soak it overnight. Boil it plain or with onions in the water. Serve with boiled potatoes.

—PEOPLE OF THE 'KSAN
Gathering What the Great Nature Provided, 1980

Toasted Seaweed (*Sa Xulgwa*)

Warm the seaweed for a few minutes over a fire—not very long. Crumble it up and serve it on top of fish soup or herring eggs or just nibble on it. Anyone who enjoys seafood will enjoy seaweed.

—PEOPLE OF THE 'KSAN
Gathering What the Great Nature Provided, 1980

techniques for preparing their staple foods. Eskimo women knew how to adeptly butcher a thirty-foot-long whale and then boil and smoke the blubber into jerky. Kwakiutl women strung hundreds of scarlet-red salmon to dry in their smoke-houses each spring and summer—enough to last the whole year. Illinois women roasted, boiled, and dried buffalo meat. Seneca women served corn three times a day, often along with squash and beans. All over California, women collected and transported immense quantities of acorns, which they ground and then mixed into nutritious breads, soups, and porridge.

Food was not just about nutrition or taste. Food was inseparable from religion. At the center of all was the staple food eaten at each and every meal—a sacred

Harvest Dance. Virtually every native culture in America held spiritual rituals to give thanks for food. PAINTING BY ALFONSO ROYBAL (AWA TSIREH) OF THE SAN ILDEFONSO PUEBLO. *(Denver Art Museum.)*

item that bound people together. Virtually each native culture held regular celebrations and religious rituals to give thanks for the foods that sustained them—the salmon, the corn, the strawberries, the buffalo, the acorns. When a woman cooked, she was a custodian of the sacred. It was her practical and spiritual responsibility to take good care of what nature had given because food was both symbolically and literally full of life.

The Gitksan people of British Columbia reassembled fish bones and sent them back to the water so that a fish would reincarnate and come back again. Before cooking a dead rabbit, a Tewa woman might drop cornmeal on the creature to first "feed it." When a Sioux butchered a buffalo, she saw not just four legs of the animal but also four directions of the universe. On the Pacific coast, a woman cut a salmon with her knife of stone or mussel shell, knowing that fish were "spirit people" sent upriver each summer merely disguised as fish to feed the human race. The Hopi believed that seeds and plants were brought from the underworld by deities.

Divinity was also in the corn and nuts at the grinding stone, in the berries from the gathering fields, in the cooking pots and baskets, and in the ashes of the fire. Divinity was in the cook's hands, which turned the raw gifts of nature into sustenance.

In the Great Lakes region, the staple was wild rice, called *manoomin* or "sacred gift." In fact, the high-protein manoomin is not rice at all but the only grain native to North America. When Europeans first encountered the black sticklike spears of manoomin, they incorrectly called it rice. Today, most of the commercial "wild" rice sold in supermarkets is not wild at all, but comes from mechanically farmed paddies never touched by human hands. For natives on the tribal lakes of Wisconsin, Minnesota, and Canada, however, hand-harvested naturally growing grain remains an essential source of identity.

The gathering and preparation of the rice was traditionally a woman's job. At the end of August, about two weeks before the rice was ready to harvest, Ojibwa women would pole their canoes among the green rice stalks. The purpose of this first trip was to tie the stalks in bundles (long ago they used basswood twine) and prevent them from sinking into the water. When the rice was ready, the women returned in their boats and beat the bundled stalks using a "knocker" made of cedar. The ripe kernels fell down into their canoes. When women's boats

When harvesting wild rice, Ojibwa women used cedar "knockers" to beat the plants and make the ripe kernels fall down into their canoes. Engraving, 1884. *(Library of Congress.)*

were full, they'd return to the shore to cure, roast, hull, winnow, cook, and store the rice.

European dinner guests as early as the seventeenth century tell us that Ojibwa women cooked their wild rice with bear fat and added it to meat stews of venison, or made a sweet rice dish by mixing it with corn or berries and maple syrup. In Wisconsin and Ontario, women added it to stews of bear, fish, and fowl. Explorer James W. Biddle recalled, "The Indian women used to make a favorite dish of wild rice, corn, and fish boiled together, and called Tassimanonny. I remember it to this day as an object of early love."

"There Was Scarcely an Idle Person Around the Place"

In the 1920s, anthropologist Frances Densmore gathered this firsthand account from Nodinens, a Chippewa (Ojibwa). A combination of hunting, gathering, and agriculture created an astoundingly diverse and rich tradition for the Ojibwa. In addition to the complex seasonal rounds, Nodinens also gives us a flavor for the shared jobs of subsistence divided between men and women and the interdependence of clan members, based on a life almost entirely shaped by the need for food.

*I*n the spring we had pigeons to eat. They came in flocks and the men put up long fish nets on poles, just the same as in the water, and caught the pigeons that way. We boiled them with potatoes and with meat. We went to get wild potatoes in the spring, and a little later the blueberries, gooseberries, and June berries were ripe along the lake shore. The previous fall the women had tied green rice in long bundles and at this time, they took it out, parched and pounded it, and we had that for food. There was scarcely an idle person around the place. . . . We dried berries and put them in bags for winter use. During the summer we frequently slept in the open.

Next came the rice season. The rice fields were quite a distance away and we went there and camped while we gathered rice. Then we returned to our summer camp and harvested our potatoes, corn, pumpkins, and squash, putting them in caches which were not far from the gardens.

By this time the men had gone away for the fall trapping. When the harvest was over and colder weather came, the women began their fall fishing, often working at this until after the snow came. When the men returned from fall trapping we started for the winter camp.

—as told by Nodinens to FRANCES DENSMORE

Chippewa Customs, 1929

By the sixteenth century, the great empires of Europe began casting their eyes covetously on the New World. In 1513, Spanish explorer Juan Ponce de León first sighted present-day Florida and claimed the land for Spain. Over the next fifty years, six expeditions failed to achieve a permanent colony, but in 1565 Spain finally succeeded in founding Saint Augustine. It was not a secure position. The British and French settled not far away, and competition was bitter all along the southern Atlantic coast.

In the more distant reaches of the new country, however, the story was different. The Rocky Mountains and deserts of the West proved too remote for the French and British. But for the Spaniards, who had already plundered the Aztecs and Incas in Central and South America, the journey to the north was much more feasible.

The Zuni "eat the best cakes that ever I saw. . . . They have the finest order and way to grind that we ever saw anyplace, and one Indian woman of this country will grind as much as four women of Mexico," observed Francisco Vásquez de Coronado in 1540. Coronado had reason to be impressed by the culinary skills of Pueblo women who each day made breads of cornmeal that the Spanish called *tortillas* (translated as "cakes"). But of course, it was not bread the Spaniards were after. They arrived in present-day New Mexico in search of the fabled "Seven Cities of Cibola." What they found instead was some ninety pueblo villages and fifty thousand diverse Indian peoples who had no great material riches but cultural and spiritual wealth that few of the Spanish adventurers could comprehend. It was a peaceful farming life following the cyclical rhythms of the seasons.

Corn, not gold, sprouted from the sandy soil. Corn was the mother of the people, their spiritual power, the center of all life. When a Hopi child was born, he or she received a "corn mother," an ear of perfect corn kept at the baby's side for twenty days. During the naming ritual, mother and grandmother made a path for the child—a trail of cornmeal leading to the sun. The child belonged not only to his or her family but also to the earth.

This earth was precisely what the Europeans were searching for. Virgin land,

Tortillas de Maize

2 cups fine white or blue cornmeal*
1½ cups warm water

Mix meal and water until dough is not sticky. Form into balls about one and three quarters inches in diameter and roll out between wax paper or pat with hands until about six inches in diameter. Cook on moderately hot dry stove lid or griddle, turning frequently until flecked with brown.

—PHYLLIS HUGHES
Pueblo Indian Cookbook, 1977

The basic premise behind this recipe is at least a thousand years old and still works, though I must warn other novices like myself that without a tortilla press, this is not so easy as it looks. It takes some practice to get the feel of the dough as well as the level of the heat just right so that your tortillas don't break. If you have no tortilla press, use a rolling pin or two paper plates fitted together to press out the dough into thin disks. The wax paper is essential. I suggest letting the water and cornmeal soak for up to an hour before you begin. You may wish to add a teaspoon of salt.

*Ordinary coarse supermarket cornmeal absolutely will not work. Use finely hand-ground cornmeal or masa harina (found in specialty stores). White meal should be made from dried lime-hominy (nixtamal) and blue meal, from toasted native blue corn (See Resources for Historic Cooking section at the end of the book for mail order.)

as they called it, was the key in their drive for revenue and profit. But because land was the source of Indian food, it is impossible to tell the story of native cookery without telling the story of access to land—and the story of how the Spanish, English, Dutch, and French took native-occupied lands and brought death to millions of Indians.

If we look at the chiles and tomatoes in the hands of the Pueblo, Comanche,

dibeˊbici•n bi beˊ•ž
Boiled Mutton

Cut meat from the bones, break up the bones, add salt and boil, well covered with water, until done. Green corn may be added if desired.

—FLORA L. BAILEY
"Navaho Foods and Cooking Methods," 1940

Locusts

Remove legs, wings, and head of insect. Brown the rest in the ashes and eat. It tastes like peanuts. Used to be eaten in the old days but now mostly by children. Used as medicine to cure stomach ache and prevent measles, smallpox or other contagious diseases.

—FLORA L. BAILEY
"Navaho Foods and Cooking Methods," 1940

Though the recipe for mutton was recorded in 1940, it's quite likely that southwestern women began making this sort of simple dish (though without salt) when the Spanish arrived, bringing sheep. Navajo women, who had migrated to New Mexico from the Northwest not long before the Spanish came, were particularly successful at sheep farming.

The recipe for locusts is rooted in ancient history, although the calamity of smallpox—a scourge that killed millions of natives whose bodies were defenseless against these foreign germs—came with the Europeans.

Apache, and Navajo women who found themselves working in colonial kitchens as slaves, servants, or wives of the Spanish, we find this story. The conquerors had brought these delicacies on their quest northward from the valleys of Mexico, along with pork, mutton, peaches, and wheat—products from Europe. In their cooking bowls, on their tortilla griddles, and out in their vegetable gardens, native women mingled the worlds of the Spanish with the recipes of their grandmothers. They used Spanish-style bricks to transform their own earth ovens into adobe *hornos*, the clay beehive structures that would become an icon of Pueblo life.

The Spanish took control of the Pueblos and squeezed each village for "tributes" in the form of food. Men and women had to process enough corn and pinyon nuts not just for their own families but also to feed the colonizers. When drought or crop failures hit, the villages still had to pay up. If they did not comply, the price could be steep: The Spanish were known to cut off the feet of Pueblo men in the public squares. Women could be shipped off to Spain indefinitely as servants.

Not surprisingly, the Pueblos finally revolted in 1680. What could be a more potent symbol of the enemy than his foods? As part of the massacre, the Indian warriors destroyed all Spanish wheat, sheep, and pigs. They pulled up peach trees from the roots.

Twenty years later, the Spanish once again conquered the Pueblo people. Women permanently added wheat to their bread and tortilla recipes, but they continued to grind and worship corn. They adopted Jesus into their centuries-old religions and celebrated the Catholic Christmas and Easter, in addition to their Green Corn Harvest Dance. In Pueblo churches today, we find statues of the Virgin Mary with a bounty of corn about her feet, looking remarkably like a corn mother, a fertile and generous goddess who presides over the abundant earth.

FOOD AND LOVE

If there is love between a man and woman, food is sure to follow. When a girl is facing the prospect of marriage, what more precious gift is there than the promise to nourish? When a Hopi girl wanted to marry a boy, it was her job to propose, which she did by presenting her suitor with a gift of blue *piki* bread. Along with her mother and maternal uncle, she went to her betrothed's home and left

the piki on his doorstep. If the boy and his family accepted the gift, then they accepted the girl. If not, they left the bread on the doorstep, and the girl's family quickly went to retrieve it to spare her embarrassment. Long ago, it was said that a man would not marry a woman who could not make good piki bread.

Piki making takes years of practice, preferably under the tutelage of a master, such as one's grandmother. In the Hopi Nation of Old Oraibi, grandmothers still teach daughters and granddaughters how to make the blue-corn wafer bread using a one-thousand-year-old method. Recipes vary, but the main ingredients are very fine blue Indian cornmeal, ashes, and water, which are mixed together. After the ash water is strained, the prospective bride mixes the batter with a stick until it is smooth as pancake batter. Simple enough. The real test comes at the smoothly polished flat piki stone, about the size of a serving tray, which is raised on four stone legs. A fire is built beneath it using cedar or juniper wood until the stone is scalding hot. Then, with fast hands, the girl must swipe a thin rectangle of batter on the stone and lift it up within seconds so the cooked bread—now thin and paperlike—doesn't burn. If she is skillful, she will have a beautiful pile of thin wafers rolled up like scrolls.

The gift of piki reminds us that the nature and spirit of marriage—from ancient times until the very recent present—organizes men's and women's labor into separate but complementary lives. In native America, men generally did the hunting, warring, and diplomacy. Women generally did the butchering, the cooking, and textile making. However, it would be going too far to say that

> *I* had cut a green stick with prongs, on which I spread slices of fresh buffalo steak, and held them over the fire to broil. I had three juicy steaks, steaming hot, lying on a little pile of clean grass, when my husband came in. "Sukkeets—good!" he cried; and he had eaten all three steaks before I had the fourth well warmed through.
>
> —WAHEENEE,
> *A Young Girl's Story told by herself to Gilbert L. Wilson*, 1921

OPPOSITE: *The Piki Maker,* 1906. When a Hopi girl wanted to marry, it was her job to propose, which she did by presenting her suitor with a gift of blue piki bread. PHOTO BY EDWARD S. CURTIS. *(Library of Congress.)*

"We Call It Moose Butter . . ."

*T*he work of the women was to go fetch the animal after it was killed, to skin it, and cut it into pieces for cooking. To accomplish this they made the rocks red hot, placed them in and took them out of the kettle, collected all the bones of the Moose, pounded them with rocks upon another of larger size [and] reduced them to a powder; then they placed them in their kettle and made them boil well. This brought out a grease which rose to the top of the water, and they collected it with a wooden spoon. . . . From the bones of one Moose, without counting the marrow, they obtained five to six pounds of grease as white as snow, and firm as wax. It was this which they used as their entire provision for living when they went hunting. We call it Moose butter; and they Cacamo.

—PAUL LE JEUNE,
describing the Montagnais and Algonquins
in *The Jesuit Relations and Allied Documents,* 1634

women were equal to men. On the whole, it seems that many Indian women were treated more fairly than women in the white societies that would come and conquer them. Navajo girls had the puberty ritual of *kinalda* to emphasize the pride of female life. Sioux women earned respect as herbalists and healers and carried knives so they could defend themselves against attack. In the plateau nations of present-day Washington State, women's gathering activities provided half their peoples' subsistence and were considered equally as important as hunting and fishing. And though shaman and chiefs were usually men, it was possible for women to attain these positions.

With shock and sometimes horror, early explorers and missionaries noted the independence of native women who lived their daily lives without much interference from their husbands. Women were usually in full control of their households. In most tribes, women "owned" the homes they lived in, the fields they planted, and the stored caches of food their clans ate. Family members usually traced their lineage through mothers, not fathers. In the Southwest and Northeast, when a man married a woman, he often went to live with her clan.

Throughout North America, the far-reaching influence of clan and tribal life was perhaps the most striking characteristic of traditional Indian life. The clan and tribe—more than the family—bound people together through life. The idea of private landownership was rare if nonexistent. Without the drive for personal profit, all clan members shared the right to the bounty of nature and shared in the hunt and harvest.

Living within the sphere of the clan meant that a woman was not entirely dependent on a husband. After all, the home was hers, and her mother and siblings and aunts were probably nearby. If the husband turned out to be a poor provider or abusive, she usually could instigate divorce. If her husband died, she'd never have to worry about becoming destitute or being unable to care for her children. No such possibilities or freedoms existed for women in England and France.

By the late 1500s, the Iroquois Confederacy was a sophisticated political organization of five different nations—the Mohawk, Oneida, Onondaga, Cayuga, and Seneca—living from the Adirondacks to the Great Lakes in what is now Pennsylvania and upper New York. In this confederacy, women could initiate policies, vote, remove chiefs from office, and even prevent warfare. According to the Iroquois constitution, "Women shall be considered the progenitors of the Nation. They shall own the land and the soil. Men and women shall follow the status of the mother. It is of them that the nation really consists; and it is through them that the nobility of the blood, the genealogical tree and the families are perpetuated."

If the highly skilled techniques of food preparation gave women power, what happened when imported ready-made foods arrived on French ships? In eastern Canada, by the winter of 1633–34, some of the Montagnais Indians were eating French imports of "sea biscuit, bread, prunes, peas, roots, figs, and the like," according to the records of the Jesuit missionary Paul Le Jeune. Copper kettles began replacing wooden troughs. Instead of spending their days gathering and preparing food to provide nourishment to their clans, women suddenly found themselves stretching, scraping, and preparing animal hides—almost like factory workers—to make merchandise for Europeans an ocean away.

Taos Indian women hold their baskets up to the wind to help winnow grain, 1929.
PHOTO BY ORVILLE L. SNIDER. *(Library of Congress.)*

THE TRANSFORMATIVE POWER OF FOOD

We cannot imagine walking two miles for water or having the skill and strength to butcher dozens of buffalo after a successful hunt. The prospect of leaning over a grinding stone hour upon hour, day after day, now seems overwhelmingly arduous to most of us.

And yet, if we prayed to the wind to help us winnow a basket of shelled pinyon nuts, does this change the act? If we returned with the first strawberries or corn of the season and found our labors celebrated with song and dance, would this lift us, despite our aching arms and back? Or for that matter, how would any laborious chore be transformed by working side by side with our aunts and

Seminole women pound corn in mortar and pestle. (National Anthropological Archives, Smithsonian Institution.)

friends, singing songs as we worked, be it out in the fields or on a long journey to gather food under the hot sun?

Many of us like to believe that food comes from greater forces than mere humanity. Consider the energy locked in the dry dormant seed, released by water and sun and heat. Where does that energy come from?

American Indians were not the only ones to pay homage to the divinity of food. The ancient Greeks, Africans, and Asians all held similar faith in the histories and mythologies they once considered truth. By the time the Europeans came to America, goddesses of classical antiquity such as Demeter (goddess of the harvest) and Artemis (goddess of the hunt) were a distant memory. Villagers and peasants still lived close to the earth through farming but could not recall the ancient past when they, like American Indians, had once shared communal claims to land. The cities of London and Paris were crowded and filled with

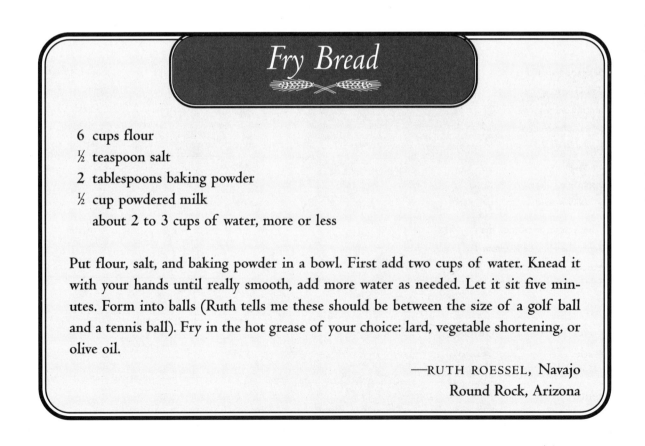

Fry Bread

6 cups flour
½ teaspoon salt
2 tablespoons baking powder
½ cup powdered milk
    about 2 to 3 cups of water, more or less

Put flour, salt, and baking powder in a bowl. First add two cups of water. Knead it with your hands until really smooth, add more water as needed. Let it sit five minutes. Form into balls (Ruth tells me these should be between the size of a golf ball and a tennis ball). Fry in the hot grease of your choice: lard, vegetable shortening, or olive oil.

—RUTH ROESSEL, Navajo
Round Rock, Arizona

What's more important, the food itself or the meaning we give it? *Making Fry Bread—Crown Point,*
September 30, 1956. From *The Enduring Navaho,* 1968. PHOTO BY LAURA GILPIN. (*Amon Carter*
Museum, Fort Worth, Texas. Bequest of the Artist.)

poverty, and a growing merchant class was shaping a new world of international
trade.

Wherever they arrived in America, Europeans brought dramatic changes to
centuries-old native foodways, first indirectly via trade. Later, the colonists took
control of land and waters, and ultimately the U.S. government forced Indians

onto remote reservations where they no longer had access to the traditional game, plants, fish, and hunting that had sustained and defined their lives for centuries.

The wanton extermination of the buffalo is well known. Less well known is that salmon—a symbol of the abundant Northwest—is now an endangered species owing to pollution. That the once abundant Atlantic is overfished and low on cod. That the Ojibwa have lost rights to gather rice and hunt on much of the lands in their own reservations. That walleye in the Great Lakes are filled with mercury.

In this chapter of American history, we learn a crucial lesson of conquest. If you want to destroy your enemies, destroy their food. And yet, not all native cultures were destroyed—they continue on, often in spite of hundreds of years of assault.

Adaptation is at the core of all human survival—and at the core of cooking. Indian women kept traditions and cultural identity alive during the seventeenth century and beyond, while adapting, as necessary, to constant change and making new ingredients their own. The hominy stew may call for pork. The gathered greens may be boiled in an iron pot. The Zuni corn soup may be made with lamb. But the essential Indian identity is at the base of these dishes and triumphs when a woman cooks them. This is the sensual aspect of history, usually left untold—a history arising from the tastebuds, whether we know it or not.

Perhaps this is what Rayna Green means when she tells me that I must understand the "transformative power of food" in Indian cultures, something that transcends even the specific ingredients. Rayna is a Cherokee and head of the Native American Program for the Smithsonian Institution. According to her, this transformative power is something like religious faith. You can't see it or prove it. You've just got to believe.

She points to the modern Indian fry bread served in native communities across the nation. Women take great pride in their recipes and compete over who makes the best. They sell it to tourists as an authentic specialty and prepare huge quantities of it for pow wows. Yet, the ingredients are entirely European—wheat flour, yeast, sugar, lard. This does not seem to matter. It is not the point. Fry bread is a symbol of Indian power and unity, just the same.

"When a twentieth-century Mohawk woman opens a can of corn," says Rayna, "she keeps this transformative power alive if she thinks of Selu, the god of corn, or the three sisters. And if you pray in the morning at a pueblo, as women have done for a thousand years, maybe you toss cornmeal you got from the super-market instead of some you ground yourself. That's okay. It still works. That's the transformative power of food."

Not everyone can still believe in this. Not all Indians or anyone else. But it is worth a try.

To make A Frykecy

ken, or a hare, kill & f

& wipe them withm, cut

ible they A pestle, y^n p

ing pan, & fry it till it

ue it a walme or two, y^n

well seasoned with pepp

full o^f parsley, & time,

together till they be enoug

into ye pan ye youlks of

little wine vineger or sa

least it curdle, y^n dish

Chapter 2

She Cooked in a New Land

We could begin this chapter with a journey across a vast ocean. But I say we start with a recipe instead. Countless stories begin on boats embarking on momentous voyages to unknown shores. Few stories, however, begin with recipes, and so here is one for *samp,* a common breakfast dish enjoyed by pilgrims in the northern and southern colonies.

Gather a pound or two of hominy ("Indian" corn carved off the cob, hulls removed by soaking and rinsing). Pound hominy in a mortar either by yourself or employ a human "pounder" if you can afford one. The resulting coarsely ground grain is "samp." Put samp in kettle and cover with water several inches. Bring to boil then simmer until tender. Stir occasionally. Add milk gotten from the cow you milked this morning. Add butter and sugar if you have it.

Such a humble breakfast porridge may seem a simplistic way to tell the life-and-death drama of colonial women in America. And yet, if we look a bit closer at the corn kernels and the milk before lifting the spoon to our mouths, we find the collision of two universes. When the English housewife could not have her oats, she substituted the sacred grain of native Americans, mingling it with her

Europeans introduced cows to the New World, and along with them, the job of dairying—generally women's work. A Massachusetts farm scene, first published in 1796. *(Library of Congress.)*

beloved English cow's milk. In doing so, she created a radical pairing of two cultures within the same bowl. Each morning all the billions of cornflakes in the world made soggy by milk trace back to this original confrontation almost four hundred years ago between Indian and English women on the American continent.

Milk and corn. In both, we find the labor of women's hands. In England, the rote morning milkings belonged to the country housewife, as did the highly skilled crafts of cheesemaking and butter churning and preservation that occurred in the dairy barns behind her farmhouse. Just as corn sustained millions of native Americans, so too did the housewife's dairy products make all the difference between health and malnutrition among the rural English. One respected husbandry writer of the 1600s believed dairying knowledge so universal that he omitted it from his guide, writing, "I shall not mention anything about the making of Butter and Cheese, because most good Housewives are acquainted with the way of doing it."

And yet without corn, the original society we now call the English colonies may never have existed. In both Virginia and Massachusetts, the colonists came pathetically prepared for life in the wilderness, unskilled at hunting, clueless about fishing hooks, and equipped with the wrong seeds for American soil. Corn was their only salvation. Without it, they probably would have died or gone home. And so they borrowed it, traded for it, stole it from the Indians, and killed them for it. To look at corn porridge mixed with milk by a colonial woman's hand is to consider the infinite questions about human beings. Their determination for survival. Their capacity to steal and kill.

Corn belonged to Indian women, who for centuries grew it, cooked it dozens of ways, and preserved it for winter. In Jamestown, Virginia, the English arrived in 1606 and soon were demanding "tribute" in corn from the local Powhatans. In time, they burned the Indians' cornfields as punishment for not readily complying, and pushed them off their lands. Similarly, one of the first acts of the *Mayflower* pilgrims on arriving in Massachusetts in 1620 was to dig up and steal corn they found in an underground cache prepared by Wampanoag women— though they later paid back the natives. These pilgrims selected land for their first settlement based on the fact that it offered many abandoned cornfields already cleared by Patuxet natives who had formerly lived there. Why was the village abandoned? Three or four years earlier, European fishermen had unwittingly brought a plague that had decimated the Patuxet natives. This fact the pilgrims took as a sign of God's will for them to settle in Massachusetts.

The early New England pioneer woman found herself pushing the weight of her body against the pestle and mortar hour after hour to produce samp—an anglization of a Narragansett word. The English loved wheat and looked down on the native grain as a "more convenient food for swine than for man," as English writer John Gerard noted in 1597. But the colonists ultimately grew corn themselves. Corn simply made more sense—at least in the beginning—because it was far less labor intensive and each acre wrought much larger yields. Without wheat, without oats, and without a mill, the pioneer woman was stuck with it. The drumbeat of mortar meeting pestle constantly filled the air of the early settlements.

Not surprisingly, the colonial cook reinterpreted corn into her existing repertoire of cooking. She used it where she wished she had wheat or oats, substituting it in breads and puddings. She enclosed the Native American pompion (pumpkin) with her English-style pastry. She forced the implausible combinations of corn and rye and molasses together, giving birth to Boston brown bread. Beyond the appropriation of corn, colonial women adopted native foods like cranberries and maple syrup. From the beaches and marshes, they gathered clams, mussels, and lobsters, though these were derided as nourishment for the poor back home in England.

Some prophetic scenes must have taken place between Indian and English women throughout the colonies, in spite of language barriers, distrust, mutual distaste for one another, and fear. I envision a wary meeting of an Indian woman dressed in deerskins and an English housewife wearing her heavy linen skirts and long sleeves. They stand over a kettle inside an English hut, trading wild blueberries for English pudding, raccoon meat for English biscuit, dried pumpkin rings and pounded corn for an iron pot. The Indian woman uses hand gestures to demonstrate the making of a bread called *pone*. She takes dried corn powder, enlivens it with water, molds it into cakes, and then boils and bakes it on the hot stones of a fire.

The willingness of Indians to share their cooking methods and foods helped ensure the Europeans' survival, but ultimately this generosity proved to be greatly against their own interests. Relations generally began with a spirit of fair diplomacy on both sides. But during the twenty-five years following the *Mayflower*'s arrival, twenty thousand English people would come to New England, outnumbering the Indians and killing them through disease, wars, and massacres.

> *W*e entertain them familiarly in our houses, and they as friendly bestowing their venison upon us.
>
> —*Mourt's Relation: A Journal of the Pilgrims at Plymouth*, 1622

The traditional histories never tell us of the early meetings between women. Instead, most amazingly, legend and textbooks have immortalized Squanto, a Patuxet Indian man, as the great food hero to the Massachusetts colonists. While Squanto certainly did teach the English the basics about corn and pumpkin growing, eel fishing, and hunting, it's wrong to give him exclusive credit for the transfer of culinary knowledge between the Massachusetts natives and the English. Wampanoag people "came very often" to Plymouth colony and usually brought "their wives and children with them, they were welcome," wrote one Puritan in what is now called *Mourt's Relation*, a collective journal kept by several of the first Englishmen at Plymouth. "We entertain them familiarly in our houses, and they as friendly bestowing their venison on us."

Of course women used these opportunities to barter and trade and share techniques. How else did they learn the preparations and the words for Indian dishes such as *hominy, no-cake, pone, succotash, suppawn,* and *samp?* All this from Squanto? I think not.

But I can't prove any of this because no one bothered to write down much of anything that Englishwomen did—other than give birth and die. Under English law, wives simply did not exist as individuals. Upon marriage, a woman was officially transformed into the legal status of *feme covert,* translated as "covered" or "hidden" by her husband. She was not even "Mrs. Goodman Brown." Rather, she was "Goodman Brown his wife." She had few individual rights and could not own property, bring lawsuits, or make contracts. It is humbling to read the early documents of the Puritans in Massachusetts who describe their dizzying experiences with thrilling detail and yet barely mention their female companions except in connection with births and deaths, such as "this morning goodwife Allerton was delivered of a son, but dead born." That is all we find of her.

Churning butter. From *The Vertuose Boke of Distillacyon,* by Laurence Andrewe.

What She Packed for the Wilderness

In 1630, Francis Higginson published New England's Plantation, *recommending that immigrants pack the following provisions. What woman wouldn't spend many a late night worrying about what to pack for the journey?*

Victuals for a whole yeere for a man, and so after the rate for more

8 Bushels of meale

2 Bushels of pease

2 bushels of otemeale

1 Gallon of Aquavitae [spirits]

1 Gallon of Oyle

2 Gallons of Vineger

1 Firkin of Butter

Spices

Sugar   Cinnamon

Pepper   Nutmegs

Cloves   Fruit

Mace

Household Implements

1 Iron pot

1 Kettell

1 Frying pan

1 Gridiron

2 Skellets

1 Spit

Wooden Platters

Dishes

Spoones [forks were not yet in
     common use]

Trenchers [rough wooden "plates"]

REMEDIES FOR THE JOURNEY

The earliest voyages from England to America lasted anywhere from six weeks to several months. Gale winds blew hard, sometimes knocking people into the sea. Dampness was everywhere. Passengers drank rainwater that fell on the deck, though it tasted of tar. Choppy Atlantic waters and rotten food brought sickness, weakness, and death. A housewife of any means at all would be sure to pack medicinals, lemon juice to prevent scurvy and other concoctions such as a stomach-settling drink for her nauseous children being tossed about on the rocky seas.

During the seventeenth century, food and medicine did not reside in the separate spheres they do today. Before the rise of professional medical schools (exclusively for men) during the nineteenth century, the job of healing, or "physic," naturally belonged to women. Most doctoring came from the kitchen and its gardens, and you were as likely to eat or drink something for your ailment as to take a specialized medicine. Cookbooks of the era contain hundreds of healing remedies that relied on thistle, borage, peppermint, licorice, rosemary, lavender, sage, anise, fennel, clove, elder, garlic, and ginger. Nutmeg was as likely to be grated into a minced pie as it was to be mixed into a curative drink. If we rifled through the bags of, say, *Mayflower* passenger Dorothy Bradford—wife of the prominent puritan William—we'd probably find garlic, ginger, and an array of other herbs for medicinal use, packed alongside her pots, pans, food provisions, and spices.

Tarragon, from John Gerard's popular *Herball*, 1636 edition. "Tarragon is not to be eaten alone in sallades, but joyned with other herbs, as Lettuce, Purslain, and such like, that it may also temper the coldness of them. . . ."

Like all the rest of the *Mayflower* women, Dorothy Bradford must have rejoiced at seeing that dark bit of land take shape on the horizon after twelve weeks at sea. When the sailor loudly called out, "Land ho!" we can be sure there was a scramble as the passengers gathered on the main deck to see. As wife of a visionary Puritan leader, perhaps Dorothy had an added responsibility to put on a face of hopefulness and strength amidst her beleaguered companions—to show that faith in God would be sufficient sustenance. But as the ship blew in closer to the forest-edged shore, her joy must have sunk with each sharpening glimpse of the austere coast staring back at her, bare, brown, and dead for winter, with little hope of food in sight.

Numerous frustrations had delayed the "pilgrims" during the summer of 1620. It was not until September that the poorly provisioned *Mayflower* was finally ready to set sail. Amazingly, the pilgrims insisted on departing at this late

For Seasickness

To make wormwood water take two gallons of good ale, a pound of aniseed, half a pound of liquorice, and beat them very fine; and then take two good handfuls of the corps of wormwood, and put them into the ale and let them stand all night, and then distill them in a limbeck [still] with moderate fire.

—GERVASE MARKHAM
The English Housewife, 1615

For Heart Sickness

Take rosemary and sage, of each a handful, and seethe them in white wine or strong ale, and then let the patient drink it lukewarm.

—GERVASE MARKHAM
The English Housewife, 1615

Please do not try the seasickness recipe. Wormwood is currently discouraged because of potentially dangerous side effects, though licorice has proved an enduring remedy for upset stomachs. As for the heart sickness remedy, I say it can't hurt to try.

time of year. Arriving in November, their fates were sealed. It was too late to plant anything, and their moldy supplies of biscuit, cheese, and peas would never last the whole winter. Meanwhile, they lived aboard their badly beaten boat, wading back and forth through the frigid sea to the shore while building their first shelter. Rain and sleet seeped into their already drenched clothes, beds, skins, and lungs. By January, they began watching one another die by the dozens from hypothermia, pneumonia, and scurvy.

Within three months, roughly half of the 102 original passengers were dead.

Among the lost was Dorothy Bradford, who accidentally went overboard and drowned. Accidentally, perhaps, but many have suggested it was a suicide. Did Dorothy choose death rather than the bleak life before her?

Indeed what an overwhelming prospect it must have been for those first women. Many of them had come from the busy urban center of London. Now here was nature beyond their imaginations. There were no markets, no fairs, no butchers, no bakers—and certainly no homes that they could fathom. Without provisions or experience as hunters and gatherers, starvation nearly broke them. When sixty new settlers arrived in 1623, some immediately "fell a-weeping" at the sight of the Plymouth folks in ragged clothes and waxen faces. All they had on hand to offer the newcomers was some lobster meat and a cup of water.

Starvation was a constant threat in the first frontier societies. To survive, women went out to search the woods for anything edible, and as records tell us, they found wild strawberries, leeks, sorrel, watercresses, nuts, onions, greens, and grapes. As their husbands became skilled at hunting and fishing, they boiled and roasted wild geese, ducks, venison, salted cods and herrings caught from the sea. They worked in the fields planting corn. They dug on the beach for clams. In short, the pilgrims, by necessity, lived a hunting-and-gathering life, supplemented by the growing of corn. It was a life much like that of the natives—but such a life would never suit them for the long term.

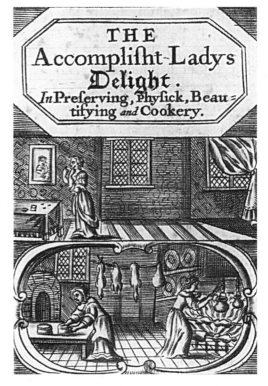

From the title page of *The Accomplished Lady's Delight in Preserving, Physick, Beautifying and Cookery,* 1675. On the left, a pie crust is being made. On the right, a servant prepares meat over a hearth. Above, the lady of the house beautifies.

We postindustrial people may idolize nature and the virtues of land lost, but the English of the seventeenth century were hardly wilderness lovers. In fact, they dreaded the wilderness as a place of isolation and treachery. The devil lurked in the forests and dark pine-needled groves. Not surprisingly, the colonists had no desire to live permanently like the Wampanoags or Massachusetts or Narragansetts who had been there for centuries before them. As soon as possible, they

The First Thanksgiving

Few women survived the first winter at Plymouth. Of the eighteen married women who came on the *Mayflower,* only four of them—Elinor Billington, Mary Brewster, Elizabeth Hopkins, and Susanna Winslow—survived to see the fall of 1621 at Plymouth. These women were most certainly the cooks who prepared what has become designated the "first Thanksgiving."

Before the English came to Plymouth, native tribes all over the continent had held annual celebrations to give thanks for their foods. Similarly, the English had their harvest days—notably Michaelmas, traditionally celebrated September 29, when villagers gathered together for a simple feast of bread, beer, and cheese.

As far as the first Thanksgiving is concerned, we know little, except that some sort of event—part celebration, part diplomatic meeting—did occur in the fall of 1621 at Plymouth for fifty-five surviving English colonists (half of whom were under age twenty-one) and about ninety Wampanoag Indians.

Only two paragraphs of documentary evidence remain to tell us about the three-day festival. The women cooked corn, fowl (perhaps geese or maybe even turkey), and cod. The only dessert they may have had was steamed pudding in the English tradition, using goat's milk because there were not yet cows. Interestingly, the Indians wound up bringing the majority of the food—five venison—perhaps out of charity or graciousness.

We can be reasonably sure that the surviving five teenage girls and one maidservant went to work as the helpers of Elinor, Mary, Elizabeth, and Susanna. I imagine at least a couple of them must have been assigned the job of supervising the ten young children, including several motherless little ones and babies. This was no small concern to the female cook and mother. Children needed to be kept from wandering into hearthfires, the woods, and the ocean itself. Indeed the ocean was quite near the first settlement, almost always within view, vast and blue. I imagine it was a constant source of yearning, the source of so many deaths, always reminding them of the impossibly long trail from where they'd come. Here, with gratitude for survival and grief for those lost, those four women prepared "thanksgiving."

strove to build a world that was "civilized" in their view—a new England in the likeness of the old. This would be gradual but of course never fully realized, because America was not England. Progress, in both northern and southern colonies, was often measured by how English things were becoming. "There are already all sorts of English fruit and garden herbs," bragged one South Carolina adventurer in a letter home to his father in 1682. And so the English systematically set about to clear land and enclose it into privately owned family farming plots.

Native foods enabled the English to survive. But in their hearts, they yearned for loaves of leavened wheat, apple tarts, puddings, pickles, jams, marmalades, minced pies, and omelettes with herbs. They wanted domesticated animals at dinner—roast mutton and veal, boiled chickens stuffed with parsley, the delectable pig roasted and put in brine or made into "links." Above all, life simply wouldn't be life without cows. The English had to have their beef, and they needed their milk, fresh each morning, their soured curds and sweetened custards, their steamed puddings and cream churned into butter, their hard cheeses pressed and aged for winter. In short: they wanted their own culture.

Only women could give this to them.

Memory—that endless human yearning for what has been lost—lives in our bellies. Always, it is the job of immigrant women to transport their culture to a new land, to re-create beloved foods, adapted to whatever conditions they find. Wave upon wave of women have come to this country with pots and pans from the Old World, spices in their bags, and recipes in their heads. In doing so, they helped set up life itself, a system of values, and countless economic exchanges. We see this continuing today as new immigrant women come to this country bringing with them hot peppers from Africa, curries from India, olive oil from Italy, coconut milk from Thailand. English immigrant women were among the first in this chain of millions to bring such imports, and in doing so they helped shape the basis of modern American culture and eating.

We rightly celebrate the nutritional and environmental nature of Native American cooking. But many Englishwomen brought vivid culinary traditions to America as well. If you were to leaf through cookbooks of the 1600s, you might be taken aback by dishes like stewed sparrows, mutton baked in blood, or liver puddings. But you would also be impressed by the well-roasted meats; the

As American as . . . Pippin Pie

Take of the fairest and best pippins, and pare them, and make a hole in the top of them; then prick each in hole a clove or two, then put them into the coffin, then break in whole sticks of cinnamon, and slices of orange peels and dates, and on the top of every pippin a little piece of sweet butter: then fill the coffin, and cover the pippins over with sugar; then close up the pie, and bake it, as you bake pies of like nature, and when it is baked anoint the lid over with a store of sweet butter, and then strew sugar upon it a good thickness, and set it into the oven again for a little space, as whilst the meat is in dishing up, and then serve it.

—GERVASE MARKHAM
The English Housewife, 1615

Who would have thought that the English housewife's favorite fruit pie would become an enduring symbol of all that's good in American life? In fact, apple pie was a traditional and beloved English dessert. By 1629, Massachusetts colonists had begun planting the apple trees they considered essential to life.

omelettes prepared with spinach, marigold flowers, and strawberry leaves; the cakes scented by anise and caraway seeds; the fresh sorrel grabbed from the garden; and the great variety of fowls and meats flavored with nutmeg, mace, and cinnamon. You would find the tang of vinegar brightening soups and custards scented with rosewater, an ancient Middle Eastern flavor lovely enough to make you swoon.

OPPOSITE: "To make a Frykecy," from Martha Washington's cookbook. This compilation of handwritten recipes came from her first husband, Daniel Custis, who received it from his female ancestors. It probably goes back to Stuart England of the early 1600s. *(Historical Society of Pennsylvania.)*

To Make a Frykecy

Take 2 Chicken, or a hare, kill & flaw [skin] them hot. take out theyr intrills & wipe them within, cut them in pieces & break theyr bones with A pestle. y^n [Then] put halfe a pound of butter into y^e [the] frying pan & fry it till it be browne, y^n [then] put in y^e [the] Chiken & give it a walme [bubble] or two. y^n [Then] put in halfe a pinte of faire water well seasoned with pepper & salt & a little after put in a hand-full of parsely & time, & an ounion shread all smal[l]. fry all these together till they be enough, & when it is ready to be dished up, put into y^e [the] pan y^e [the] youlks of 5 or 6 eggs, well beaten & mixed wth A little wine vinegar or juice of leamons. stir thes[e] well together least it Curdle, y^n [then] dish it up without any more frying.

—*Martha Washington's Booke of Cookery,*
circa mid-1600s or earlier
transcribed by Karen Hess

Unlike the populist pippin pie, which was within reach of any middling or rural housewife, this fine fricasse recipe unmistakably comes from an aristocratic lady's kitchen. It is extremely rich but very good. As Karen Hess suggests, don't let the butter fry beyond the golden-brown stage. Use chicken or veal stock instead of water. Since eggs were smaller then, use two yolks for each cup of cooking juices for a beautiful sauce. Stir quickly. Lemon is lovely.

What was a housewife in colonial America?

Just as women brought their foodways to America, they brought with them their expectations for culture, life, and law of the countries they'd left behind—whether this was the Netherlands, Germany, France, or England.

In 1615 English farming expert Gervase Markham tried to pin down the essence of a housewife in his magnum opus, *The English Housewife: Containing the inward and outward virtues which ought to be in a complete woman; as her skill in physic, cookery, banqueting-stuff, distillation, perfumes, wool, hemp, flax, dairies, brewing, baking, and all other things belonging to a household.* Markham's book was wildly popular in both England and the colonies and reflects the skills and ideas that Englishwomen took with them on their journey into the wilderness. (For those wondering why a man was such an authority on cooking, Markham confesses early on in his book that he pilfered all he knew from a woman he left anonymous.)

Let's consider the English housewife's extraordinary abilities:

1. She was a healer who, from her nearby kitchen garden, could concoct all sorts of herbal remedies and medicinal waters for the curing and prevention of sickness.

2. She was a butcher and preserver of meat who could transform all animal innards, flesh, and organs into roasts and bacon, salted meats, stews and minced pies. She was comfortable sawing

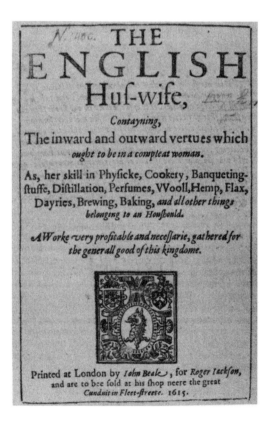

The English Housewife, by Gervase Markham, published in 1615, was a popular household guide in the British colonies. Markham wrote that the country housewife was responsible for her family's health and "soundness of body."

apart bones, reaching in for the treasured suet fat near the kidneys, and making good culinary use of all animal parts, such as brains and intestines.

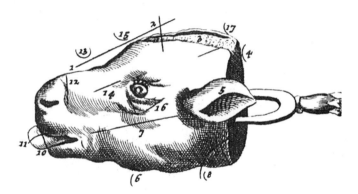

Useful parts of a calf's head.
From *Le vrai cuisinier françois*, 1712.

3. She was a dairy manufacturer who could milk the cows each morning, churn butter, and transform cream and milk into cheeses—including fresh curd dishes, as well as hard aged cheeses that would preserve treasured nutrients for winter.)

4. She was a brewer who quenched her family's thirst with ale. Before the arrival of coffee and tea, the English drank a weak alcoholic beer as their primary beverage—even for breakfast. (Some have speculated that the alcohol killed harmful bacteria, making the water safer to drink.)

5. She was a baker. In those days, brewing and baking went hand in hand. The "barm," or foam of beer, was the chief leavening agent of bread. Weekly, the housewife used the by-product of her brewing to make wheat, barley, and oats into risen loaves called *manchets*.

6. She was an excellent gardener.

7. She was a notable cook. A wife could love and obey, but if she didn't know how to cook, she could perform only "half her vow." Her repertoire encompassed boiling, roasting, and preserving all types of meat, fowl, and fish, from mutton and pig to goose and mallard to pike, carp, and trout. She knew how to make a wide variety of sauces for these meats. She knew how to make

The art of brewing beer. From *Dictionarium Domesticum*,
by Nathan Baily, published in London, 1736.
(Indiana State University.)

pies, puddings, and marvelously interesting salads. She "conserved" berries and other fruits into jams. She pickled cucumbers for winter.

The English Housewife provided a model of pie-in-the-sky perfection for women to follow (not unlike twentieth-century women's magazines). In the tradition of many cookbooks of the era and the eras that would follow, *The English Housewife* assigned women with vast and intriguing powers, while at the same time limiting them with strict prescriptions for proper demeanor and attitude. Markham told his housewives to be "chaste of thought, stout of courage, patient, untired, watchful, diligent, . . . witty, pleasant, constant in friendship, full of good neighbourhood." Housewives were to be "wise in discourse, but not frequent herein, sharp and quick of speech, but not bitter or talkative." Or simply put, it was best for them to leave most of the talking to their husbands.

How and what a woman cooked revealed not only the nature of her labor but

"Know Your Herbes"

In March, the moon new, sow garlic, borage, bugloss, chervil, coriander, gourds, marjoram, white poppy, purslane, radish, sorrel, double marigolds, thyme, violets. At the full moon, aniseed, bleets, skirrets, succory, fennel, apples of love, and marvellous apples. At the wane, artichokes, basil, blessed thistle, cole cabage, white cole, green cole, citrons, cucumbers, hartshorn, samphire, spinache, gillyflowers, hyssop, cabbage-lettuce, melons, muggets, onions, flower-gentle. . . . In the month of April, the Moon being new, sow Marjoram, Flowre-gentle, time, Violets; in the full Moon Apples of Love, and marvellous apples; and in the Wain, Hartichokes, Holy thistle, Cabage, Cole, Citrons, Hartshorn, Samphire, Gillyflowres and Parsnips.

—GERVASE MARKHAM,
The English Housewife, 1615

also her place in the world—a place most definitely beneath men. The husband's domain was his fields, the market where he sold his crops, and the land at large. He was the head of household and acted on the family's behalf in the outside world, including the church and any local government. Considering the amount of production and manufacturing that the housewife had to do, it comes as no surprise that she spent most of her time in and around the homelot. She may have gone to market to sell her extra butter on Wednesdays and Saturdays. Perhaps in spring, she walked to a neighbor's to trade some of her freshly killed veal for some eggs. In fall, she might be down at her husband's orchards pressing cider. But generally, the housewife's domain was the garden, the dairy, the outbuildings, the livestock pens, and of course the kitchen and house.

The seventeenth-century English housewife spent most of her time around the homelot and dairy but ventured out to sell her extra produce at the local market. From *Civitates Orbis Terrarum*, vol. 5, by Georgius Braun and Franz Hohenberg.

Under English law, women were socially and legally inferior to their husbands. But during this pre–individual rights era, this fact was hardly a source of outrage. Women might complain of their drudgery, but after all, everyone had to answer to someone. Servants and slaves obeyed their masters and mistresses. Children obeyed their mothers. Wives obeyed their husbands. Husbands obeyed their betters. Betters obeyed the crown. All obeyed God.

And yet, what was acceptable then confounds our modern minds now. As cook, baker, brewer, dairyer, butcher, gardener, and healer, wasn't the English housewife a paragon of accomplishment? Obviously her roles in sustaining life and health were immense. How could she not be powerful if she were so essential?

Historian Laurel Ulrich describes colonial New England life and its "tolerance for contradiction." It was true that colonial women held inferior roles, but this did not mean they were helpless. Ulrich argues that they were effective, valued for their skills, and could even be quite powerful.

"Man cow provides. Wife dairy guides." This little gem from Thomas Tusser's 1573 book of husbandry beautifully sums up the interdependence of English yeoman farmer and wife. He owned everything, but he was also responsible for providing his wife with the tools of her trade. She, in return, supplied cheeses and pigs in brine, her minced pies, and baked loaves. Without one another, they could not survive—or at least, they could not thrive.

Still, I wonder what those adventurous women thought about when they left the safety of their British homelots and sailed on boats to America. How much of a stake did they have in this enormous undertaking of relocating themselves to a foreign country across the sea? Were they simply following the wishes of their husbands? It was a bold new adventure, but what did women reap from the new religious freedom or the economic advantages of taking land and profit?

"Your obedient wife," signed Margaret Winthrop at the end of her letters to her husband John, the first mayor of Boston. In addition to this obedience, Margaret expressed passionate religious faith as zealously as any leading Puritan might: "I will cleave to my Husband Crist as neere as I can." Encouraging her husband on his venture she wrote, "Chere up thy hart in God and in the expectation of his favors and blessings in this thy charge, with assurance of his love."

With her husband as first governor of Massachusetts Bay Colony, Margaret surely believed he was destined to carry out a mission of God—founding the "city on a hill," as he described it in his famous speech aboard the *Arbella*. Though no famous Puritan speeches have gone down in Margaret's name, her letters suggest that she saw herself not just as helpmeet but also as a partner in John's spiritual and political quest to build a morally better civilization in America. Did she see herself, too, as a protester against the worldly greed of the English church, the corruption of the monarchy and English society? As an aristocrat, perhaps, she was afforded this role. Had she been an indentured servant on a journey to America, such lofty philosophy would have been unlikely.

Puritan doctrines allowed women no formal office in the church but held forth that the love of God was equally open to men and women. Women were encouraged to read their Bibles, go to church, and seek God. And yet, the Bible itself was filled with contradictions about the essentialness of women and the beauty and value of their work—contrasted with dictates for their inferior lives, prone to weakness and the influence of the devil. In Corinthians, Paul declared, "Let the women learn in silence with all subjection." And yet in the proverbs, women are praised for their great efforts to feed their families, their essentialness to life, their strength—and most of all, the products of housewifery, the "fruit of their hands." When colonial ministers prayed at funeral sermons for notable housewives, they frequently chose these words from Proverbs 31.

THE MISFORTUNE OF WANTING WIVES

Considering the substantial virtues and immensely practical skills of the English housewife as just outlined, the necessity of women in the colonies would seem quite obvious. But this was a lesson that had to be bitterly learned in the southern colonies, more than a dozen years before the *Mayflower* came.

Men and boys exclusively had composed the first 105 adventurers who set sail for Jamestown, Virginia, in 1606 for what would become the first permanent

English colony in America. They were hired and organized under the sage guidance of the Virginia Company. Eight months later, only thirty-eight were alive.

It is hardly possible to fathom the degree of death and disaster of the Jamestown colony. From 1606 to 1624 (the years of the Virginia Company's rule) about six thousand out of seven thousand English immigrants died, mainly from malaria and starvation in the overbearing heat and harsh wilderness of the Chesapeake Bay.

The Virginia Company was not terribly interested in the health and welfare of its employees. The goal was to get rich fast by exporting wilderness products such as precious metals and furs and medicinals like the abundant sassafras. The company could not have cared less about building a long-term settlement and had no lofty ideas like the Puritans about creating an ideal society founded on the will of God. In this first southern colony, the goal was a "sevenfold return" on the shareholders' investment. They hoped to make their money and go back to England. And so, they believed, women would *not* be needed.

They were sorely mistaken. It didn't take long for the colonists to "grow very sinsible of the Misfortune of Wanting Wives." They were hungry and wanted women to cook for them. They were lonely and wanted women to comfort them. They were overworked and needed children to help them grow tobacco. Quickly, the Virginia Company changed its tune. In 1611, the ruling governor abolished the "common kettle" and tried to lure families by offering all sorts of incentives—acreage, tools, garden, cows, goats, and a start of poultry and swine, the essentials needed for family farming life in a wilderness.

To speed along conjugal matters, the Virginia Company got the brilliant idea of simply importing women who, more or less, were put up for sale to become wives. And so for a short period between 1620 and 1621, the company lured 147 "maids," a good number of them young orphans and widows with "no natural protectors," to go to Virginia and become the first southern colonial women. By 1622, all these imported women were married to planters and other wealthy men who could afford the 120 to 150 pounds of "the best leaf tobacco" for a wife. By

OPPOSITE: **A reconstructed interior of a planter's home, circa 1660, Maryland frontier. Most southern colonial women did not have slaves and led extremely difficult existences.** *(Courtesy Historic St. Mary's City.)*

the end of 1622, most of the population was killed during a brutal Indian massacre.

Popular culture has given us many mythologies of southern life and southern women. We envision the huge plantation home with its colonnades, many out-buildings, and slaves waiting on pampered women. Indeed, a small lavish aristocracy did quickly rise up on the backs of slaves and servants. But most of the men and women in the southern colonies worked their own land and lived an incredibly difficult existence. In the early years, planters and servants alike often lived in one-room shacks on remote plantations. Most of the women who went to the early Chesapeake colonies of Maryland and Virginia in the 1600s did not come as wives but as indentured servants.

The shortage of women helped shape a notoriously harsh culture of tobacco planting. But the wildness of the rough-and-tumble life of the South also put fewer restraints on women than the more rigidly structured early societies of New England.

Indentured servants gambled with their lives that after four or five years of "hard usage," they would "marry up" in status and have a better existence than what was possible back home in Britain. An indentured servant could hope some day to be a mistress with servants of her own helping her in the dairy, the bake-house, and the kitchen. No such upward mobility was possible in England.

Still, outliving one's indenture was no small task. In the forbidding marshy climate of the Chesapeake, malaria struck regularly. For women who survived this constant pestilence, there was still the ever-present risks of death during childbirth or from diseases like dysentery, scurvy, and influenza. Even under a fair master with the best of luck and other circumstances, most indentured women faced brutal lives of work, bending over the soil planting tobacco in the hot sun, in addition to carrying out domestic chores indoors. Few butter churns or cheese-making pans have been found in the remains of the early southern colonies because wives and indentured servants (and later slaves) of tobacco planters worked out in the fields and had little time for such a refined, labor-intensive craft. Most spent their time on the more basic skills of food preparation such as pounding corn in a mortar, which before mills were built, took many hours each and every day for the ordinary planter's family.

The one-pot meal offered the best solution for midday dinner on the

To Dress Beans and Bacon

WHEN you dress beans and bacon, boil the bacon by itself, and the beans by themselves, for the bacon will spoil the colour of the beans. Always throw some salt into the water, and some parsley, nicely picked. When the beans are enough (which you will know by their being tender,) throw them into a cullender to drain. Take up the bacon and skin it; throw some raspings of bread over the top, and if you have an iron, make it red hot and hold over it, to brown the top of the bacon; if you have not one, hold it to the fire to brown, put the bacon in the middle of the dish and the beans all around, close up to the bacon, and send them to the table, with parsley and butter in a bason.

—MRS. HANNAH GLASSE

The Art of Cookery Made Plain and Easy, 1805 edition
originally published, 1757

seventeenth-century frontier. Southern cooking would someday reach great heights, but during the earliest years, a planter's wife or indentured maid needed to put dinner on the fire quickly and be done with it so she could promptly get back to the tobacco fields. A pot of beans would do nicely. Though the accompanying recipe for beans and bacon is a bit fancy for such occasions, it bears the distinction of coming from *The Art of Cookery Made Plain and Easy* by Mrs. Hannah Glasse, the most popular cookbook in the English colonies during the eighteenth century.

PARSNEP PUDDING FOR PENNSYLVANIA

In 1702 a cookbook containing a curious note arrived in the Pennsylvania colony: "In great hast transcribed." The title was "My Mother's Recaipts for cookerys Presarving and Chrurgery—William Penn."

The particular Penn in possession of it was not the one of Quaker fame who founded Pennsylvania, but his son. The cookbook had been transcribed from an original belonging to Gulielma Penn, at this point dead eight years. Evidently, the young Penn wanted the memory and comforts of his mother's cookery to accompany him on a journey to America. The book was rapidly copied in time to make the ship—a vivid testament to a mother's cooking if ever there was one.

Gulielma was deeply devoted to the Quaker faith and its followers. Her sizable fortune went toward the establishment of Pennsylvania, which was to be a refuge for Quakers persecuted in England. It is worth noting that Quaker women differed considerably from Puritans because they were allowed to hold public roles in church leadership. George Fox, founder of the Quaker faith, and his wife Margaret were close friends of the Penns and professed equality for women.

With all this in mind, it certainly seems logical that history would place Gulielma at the side of her beloved husband William Penn when he first departed England for Pennsylvania in 1682. Alas, this was not the case. Traditional womanly duties kept her at home: she was pregnant, had several young children to care for, and was also nursing her frail mother. William hoped she would join him in Pennsylvania later when her load was lighter, but her loads never did lighten, and she never set foot in the colony. She lost several children to illness, continued to nurse her mother, was in frequent ill health herself, and we can only guess, was probably in some deep state of grief over her continual losses. It was not until Will returned to London on business that the couple reunited.

As wife to a famous preacher, rebel, and politician, Gulielma's job required that she do a good deal of hostessing. Quakers frequently gathered—though to do so meant risk of imprisonment—in her home to chart their spiritual revolution and rally plans for a colony. Perhaps she made this parsnip pudding for them one evening.

GETTING DINNER ON THE TABLE

As colonial society grew, getting a meal to the table could mean many different things depending on where you lived and what you had at hand. Historian Laurel Ulrich tell us that in an expanding urban center, a woman's cookery skills might rely more on wise trading and knowing the coming and going of ships than her dairying equipment or butchering skills.

Parsnep Pudding

Take sum parsneps and
boyle them till thay bee very soft,
then mash them very small
and picke out the hard peces,
then put to it sum grated breed or flouer,
and a good many Corrants
sum nuttmeggs and a Litell suger,
and when you have mixed them together
putt too an Indeferett quantaty
the yeolks of 4 or 5 eggs;
Wett it with Creme till it bee as thin as batter,
and then fry them quick,
if you will boyle it you must not make it so thin
and boyle it in a Cloath spred with butter,
when it is boyled melt sum butter with sack [wine] and shuger
for the sam—

—GULIELMA PENN
cooking recipes, mid-1600s, from *Penn Family Recipes*, edited
by Evelyn Abraham Benson, 1966

The English loved their puddings and engendered this love in early America. Here is a rather typical preparation—and a small piece of Gulielma Penn that did arrive in America. Note the lyrical way the recipe is written, with line breaks that resemble poetry.

In the busy port of Salem in the 1690s, a shopkeeper's wife might keep her own garden and perhaps a cow at the back door. But beyond this bit of self-sufficiency, she'd purchase the rest of her larder. To get her butter and cheese, she'd go to a farmer's wife who had a reputation for quality (and for providing an honest sixteen ounces to the pound). To get sugar or wine or spices, she'd walk down to the wharves to see the local merchants. To get meat, she'd go to the

KEEP WITHIN COMPASS.

KEEP WITHIN COMPASS AND YOU SHALL BE SURE, TO AVOID MANY TROUBLES WHICH OTHERS ENDURE.

FEAR GOD.

Domestic Happiness

PRUDENCE

PRODUCETH ESTEEM.

Published as the Act directs, 16 Aug 1785.

Printed for & Sold by CARINGTON BOWLES.

N.º 69 in S.ª Pauls Church Yard, LONDON

Instead of Cards my Fair one look,
(I beg you'll take it kind)
Into some learned Author's Book,
And cultivate your mind.

To drown dull thoughts which now
She hastily applies [surrounds,
The direfull'st cordial to the wounds,
Of which she quickly dies.

If lewdness once your Soul alarms,
There's not so bad an evil,
To prostitute those lovely charms,
Must drive you to the Devil

When Women once o'erstep the bounds
Of decency and cares, —
A crowd of folly quick surrounds,
And nought but woes she shares.

slaughterhouse on Main Street. Before refrigeration, freshness was a constant concern, and the merchant's wife would have to know how to recognize tainted cheese and meat to be sure she was getting wholesome safe goods. If she wanted bread or pies, she'd go to the miller for flour, or perhaps she'd just buy them at the bakery, for one was available in Salem at that time, within walking distance.

By the eighteenth century, all sorts of imported products were flowing into colonial America, available to those who had the means to buy them—anchovies and macaroons, whortleberry brandy, English cheeses and breads, not to mention candlesticks and damask table linens.

Some women had success as retailers of food, and a handful started trading businesses with English companies. They often worked as helpers and even partners in their husbands' baking, grocery, and trading businesses. When husbands died, the widows took over. Widows, interestingly, had more rights than wives to run their own businesses and to own property.

Women advertised their food wares in colonial newspapers—some rather frequently. In the *Boston Newsletter* of the 1730s,

> *M*rs. Hannah Boydell Sells all sorts of Grocerys as before Advertised. Also sweet Oyl, and all Sorts of Corks, over, against the Bunch of Grapes in King Street, Boston.
>
> —*Boston Newsletter*, May 4–11, 1732

Mrs. Elizabeth Barrick announced "Choice Cheshire Cheese" for sale at her shop. In the *South Carolina Gazette* of the 1730s and 1740s, Widow Fisher offered "brown middling, and milk Bisket, Gammons, Coffee, Teas, and Sugar"; Margaret Warden advertised "choice brown and middling bread." In Savannah of the 1760s, Margaret Cresswell advertised pastry, Elinor Bolton offered confection imports, and Margaret Nelson sold her homemade delicacies of "Rich plumb cake at 10s; per pound," in addition to biscuits, jellies, custards, puddings, and tarts.

OPPOSITE: *Keep Within Compass: Prudence Produceth Esteem.* Published some time after 1785. At the woman's feet: "the rewards of virtue," a chest full of money. The four corners show the disasters that befall women who lapse: poverty, drunkenness, maternal negligence, and a life of hard labor. (Colonial Williamsburg Foundation, Abby Aldrich Rockefeller Folk Art Museum, Williamsburg, Virginia.)

Before industrialism, before the cast-iron cookstove, before Fannie Farmer saved the world with standard measurements, cooking was an earthier and far more intuitive experience. Preparing a meal required a good deal of instinct, judgment, individuality, and pure skill. Recipes offered a mere concept of a dish rather than step-by-step instructions, and it was up to the cook to draw on her experience and personal opinion as to how much broth or wine or spice would make a dish right, how much vinegar or lemon would brighten the dull richness of cream or butter. When instructions called for "sweet herbs," the cook decided which ones.

Cooking also had everything to do with fire—the main source of heat and light. Fire held an important place in the colonial view of the world. Along with water, earth, and air, it was one of the four basic elements to be balanced in life and cooking.

On a purely practical level, the colonial woman needed to know what she was doing so she wouldn't burn down the house. Hearth cooking is not to be confused with grilling hamburgers over a campfire. A serious cooking hearth could run six- to eight-feet long. At the top, a lug pole ran its length, and the cook hung trammels (hooks) at different heights from which she suspended her heavy (sometimes thirty- to forty-pound) iron pots—some closer to the flame, some higher and farther away. To make a multidish meal, she had to keep her "back log" constantly hot and build a series of smaller fires within reach—one for each dish—some fast and hot "to give it a bubble," others slow for simmering. All this doesn't even begin to touch on the "art, craft, and mystery" of bread baking in an outdoor wood-burning oven.

I confess that I wanted my own fire and wondered if there were still places in the world where one could preside over a hearth and dangle pots from a lug pole. Searching for this rare opportunity, I found Alice Ross, culinary historian, who operates Alice Ross Studios out of a carriage house in her Long Island backyard.

With an eighteenth-century hearth and every matter of America's cooking relics hanging about, Alice has created an alternative universe in the midst of a congested suburban town. Authentic colonial earthenware, pewter salt dishes, clay pipkins, iron pots, fire pokers, and waffle irons fill the room from floor to

Fire, the essential element. *(Courtesy Historic St Mary's City.)*

ceiling. She even has a water pump. It is May when I arrive, and outside her cooking studio is an astounding garden, enveloping us with lush beds of herbs, flowers, and everything green. This is the sort of place one surrenders to with childlike and helpless awe.

Alice guided the way, helping me cook rabbit and cracklings (fried pork fat). She offered delicately spiced dough for frying Dutch *olykoek* (crullers), and showed me how to make cornbread in a spider pan, using her hands to mix the molasses, milk, and eggs. She sent me to gather firewood and later to grab big handfuls of sage, marjoram, and chives from her copious gardens.

"You needed to use your senses back then," says Alice. "You determined heat with the touch of hand not a dial. You knew the oil was ready for frying by listening to it sizzle. You got exercise by making something—not by riding a machine at the gym."

But what lingered with me most of all was that hearth fire and its orange flames lighting up the dark brick floor. As I carried the heavy, splintery logs to the hearth, absorbing the smell of smoke in my clothes and hair, I was overcome by the physical power of the fire, the sudden bursts of flames and smoldering coals. At one point, my eyebrows felt on the verge of singeing, and my hand became so burning hot, I nearly dropped a pot of water, letting out a primitive screech of fear.

The first iron cookstove was cast in 1765, and throughout the 1800s hearth cooking slowly disappeared, replaced by a nostalgia for things lost. Around this time, the "hearth" was transformed in the public imagination from a hard-driving workplace into a soft and romantic ideal of woman's virtue—"hearth and home," tame and demure. I see now the falseness of these Victorian ideas. To cook over an open fire is in fact a vigorous athletic experience. A true hearth fire seems to me a powerful, dangerous, and sensual place.

Alice tossed heavy logs into the flickering flames using a confident hurling motion, ending with a loud thwonk and a splash of sparks. She loved throwing the logs this way, I could tell. I tried it too. By day's end, I was using my booted foot to kick hot coals where I wanted them—I was suddenly in love with the heavy iron pots, the spider pan, even the humble whisk (a beautiful simple thing Alice hands me, made of twigs bound together). How much better I would sleep at night if I did this all day. I began wondering if it was possible to build a hearth in my home too, or in the backyard as Alice has.

Like the nineteenth-century nostalgists, we contemporary people bring our yearnings when we look backward. But this is a tricky pitfall. In the preindustrial age, a woman saw her hearth as simply part of life and a place of hard sweaty labor. Pitfall number two: to imagine that it was all relentlessly horrible. What would a *Mayflower* goodwife have thought if she could have seen me sitting at my computer all day wearing shorts, tapping on keys, rushing to get a Federal Express package in the mail, driving my kids to school, shopping at a supermarket? Probably she would think it horrible—and that she never could do any of it herself. But she could do all these things if that's what she had been raised to do.

Whether people make history or history makes people remains an ever elusive question. If called on, we could salt a pig or kill a chicken or even forage for berries and clams. We could pack our bags with pots and pans and begin again. We could jump at the dream of going to a vast, natural wilderness, even at mortal cost, all for the hope of being part of something big, bold, and new.

Slavery at Her Table

Wedon't know that much about the early life of Charity "Duchess" Quamino except that she was born in Africa and probably learned to cook at her mother's side. At about fifteen years old, she was captured by slave traders, bound, and packed in the bottom of an airless ship to make the journey to America.

In 1753, she arrived brokenhearted in what must have seemed the miserable and cold climate of Newport, Rhode Island. She was soon taken to the residence of John Channing, the aristocratic shipowner and financer of slave expeditions. Perhaps Channing had told his captain to be on the lookout for a slave who would make a good cook, as this is what he got. At the Channing residence, Duchess was put to work in the kitchen. Four decades later, she was still there, cooking day in and day out.

For many slaves, this would have been the end of the record. But Duchess has left us a bit more, according to the Reverend Frank Carpenter, a Unitarian minister who has researched Duchess's life in Newport. After John Channing died, she worked for his son, William. Evidentally, at nights and on weekends, with his indulgence, she launched her own successful catering business and in time earned a reputation as Newport's best pastry chef, especially known for her frosted plum

cakes for events such as "Washington's birthnight ball." When the wealthy people of Newport held their big parties, Duchess was in high demand.

Despite this high standing, she remained a slave until old age. Her husband, John Quamino, had perished aboard a revolutionary ship while trying to earn enough money to buy his wife's freedom. By 1800, census records tell us Duchess was finally free. Had she used the profits from her baking business to buy freedom for the last ten years or so of her life? Quite possibly. She died in 1804 at sixty-five years old. An inscription on her grave, written by William Ellery Channing, founder of the American Unitarian Church, gave this homage: "In memory of Duchess Quamino, a free black of distinguished excellence. Intelligent, industrious, affectionate, honest and of exemplary piety."

During the years that Duchess lived and cooked, there was much public discussion about the meaning of freedom. A spirit of rebellion was spreading throughout the colonies, as merchants, businessmen, and artisans agitated against Britain. Revolutionary leaders were calling for the end of bondage by the king and were bold enough to accuse the monarchy of "enslaving" the colonies with unfair taxation. How far would the fever spread? Would all this talk of freedom ever reach the kitchens of slave women like Duchess?

On the eve of the Revolution, blacks comprised 20 percent of the American population. Though both black and white women were excluded from democracy and shared a lack of legal rights, their possibilities in life were gravely different. The very poorest of white women or indentured servants might have worked as hard as some slaves, but they could at least strive to have a family of their own and ultimately a better life. Enslaved black women could not harbor such hopes. In the northern colonies, most farm families purchased only one or two workers. Slaves, therefore, often lived isolated from one another, without hopes of finding a marriage partner. On the large plantations in the southern colonies, marriage and family life became more common (once plantation owners realized that reproduction was profitable), but the threat of the auction block was constant. With little warning, children and family members might be taken away and sold, never to be seen again.

OPPOSITE: A woman sells chicken legs and rolls at the train station in Richmond, Virginia, 1860. She may have been free or a slave. ILLUSTRATION BY SIR HENRY WENTWORTH ACLAND. (National Archives of Canada.)

When the American Revolution broke out, the British promised slaves that if they fought the loyalist cause, they'd be rewarded with freedom and relocation to Nova Scotia after the war. This was merely a strategic matter. England still allowed slavery at home and put little stock in the ideals of freedom for blacks. On the other hand, the American rebels offered no such rewards to slaves but articulated an irresistible ideology of freedom and a heart-stirring vision of equal rights. To choose loyalties was wrenching. Which side was the true enslaver? The freedom-promising British or the slaveholding colonial rulers? The answer was uncertain.

After the war, the rights of white landowning men and slaveholders were upheld in the final version of the Constitution. This was not surprising considering that the most prominent "revolutionary fathers"—Thomas Jefferson, George Washington, and James Madison—were slaveholders from Virginia, the state where slavery began. For these men the sight of female slaves spreading manure over vegetable gardens was a common and perfectly acceptable vision. John Adams, the future president, told his wife Abigail that he got a big laugh out of her suggestion to "remember the ladies" when doling out freedoms and rights at the Constitutional Convention. In an early draft of the Declaration of Independence, Thomas Jefferson (himself the owner of hundreds of slaves) included some negative analysis of slavery, but this was later deleted. The final version of the Declaration of Independence stated that "all men are created equal," but the Constitutional Convention made it clear that equality did not apply to more than half of the American population: white men who did not own property, blacks, women, and slaves.

> To be sold very reasonably, A Negroe woman, about 40 years of age, well acquainted with all sorts of house work, and is an excellent good cook. Enquire at the Post Office.
>
> —*The Pennsylvania Gazette,* June 7, 1750

African-American women and food had been deeply implicated on this continent from the very beginning, starting with the first black female who survived the heartbreaking trip from Africa to Jamestown, Virginia, in 1619. As slaves, black women were expected to grow crops that would enrich white people, to cook for white people and nurture their children, to serve white people at their tables, and in some rare cases to stand there and shoo flies while white people ate.

Women Cooking at Fireplace. African-American women cooked for and served whites since the first slave woman arrived on this continent in 1619. DRAWING BY EDWARD PENFIELD. *(Print Collection, Miriam and Ira D. Wallach Division of Art, Prints, and The Photographs New York Public Library Astor, Lenox and Tilden Foundations.)*

At the end of long shifts, they were expected to cook for themselves and their families as well.

Black women did far more than cook in the "big house" or the plantation cabin. And though the majority lived and worked on southern plantations up until the Civil War, generalizations can never tell the whole story. From the first arrival of slaves, African-American women led a great variety of lives in America. Social class, ethnicity, time period, and region—not only race—gave shape to who they were and how they lived.

In eighteenth-century New Orleans, for example, a small cadre of free upper-class women of color held slaves themselves. These elite women enjoyed a cuisine far more akin to that of white aristocratic ladies than field slaves. Similarly, the life and culinary methods of a slave cook in revolutionary Philadelphia differed greatly from that of the slave who worked as a dairy maid on a yeoman's farm in Massachusetts. Their cooking differed still further from the recently arrived African women sent to raise rice in the swamps of South Carolina or the free black woman in Ohio who ran her own catering business.

And so the influences of slavery cannot be the only way to understand the cooking of African-American women. As historian Ira Berlin contends, slaveholders severely limited the lives of Africans, but they did not fully define them. "The slaves' history," writes Berlin, "like all human history—was made not only by what was done to them, but also by what they did for themselves."

Food gave African-American women an arena in which they could do for themselves, define themselves, and take some control of their lives, despite the enormous challenges they were up against. Many women retained the memory of Africa and affirmed their heritage by re-creating dishes from their homelands. Others excelled in white kitchens, earning prestige and privilege as cooks. Still

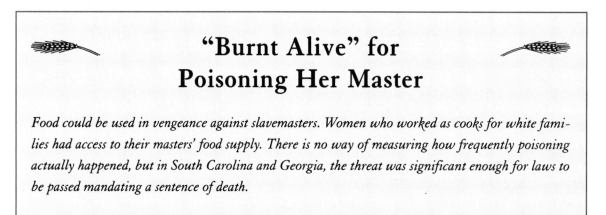

"Burnt Alive" for Poisoning Her Master

Food could be used in vengeance against slavemasters. Women who worked as cooks for white families had access to their masters' food supply. There is no way of measuring how frequently poisoning actually happened, but in South Carolina and Georgia, the threat was significant enough for laws to be passed mandating a sentence of death.

Friday last a negro man belonging to Mssrs. Price, Hest, and Head, and a negro woman belonging to Mr. James Sands, merchant, were burnt alive on the Work-House Green, having been tried some short time before, agreeable to the Negro Act and convicted of administering poison to the said Mr. Sands, his wife, and child, of which the last died.

—*South Carolina Gazette,* August 1, 1769

THE SEPARATION OF THE MOTHER AND CHILD.

" The old men of the company, partly by persuasion and partly by force, loosed the poor creature's last despairing hold, and, as they led her off to hei
new master's waggon, strove to comfort her."—Page 105.

Cooking for and caring for loved ones could be a form of resistance against a system that constantly threatened to destroy family. This 1852 illustration shows a child being torn from his mother to be sold at an auction. (Library of Congress.)

others sold food as vendors and truckers in public marketplaces, earning money that would improve their prospects and the prospects of their children.

But for the majority, cooking gave women something that was far less public, far less "visible." It gave them the chance to nurture and feed those they loved. In this came an expression of freedom—freedom of a different kind from that articulated by Thomas Jefferson. As historian Jacqueline Jones has written, black women—whether enslaved or not—largely saw freedom through the prism of family life.

When a slave woman cooked for her family, she claimed the human right to love and care for whom she wished—to nurture the growing bodies of children, sisters, friends, or husband. In the steaming food on the table of the slave quarters, there was a certain courage. It was the sort of courage hidden in the unspoken phrase "in spite of."

I do not mean to romanticize here. I do not mean to suggest that food could take away any of slavery's oppression. Slave narratives tell us of pregnant women whipped till they bled, of black cooks forced to wear muzzles while they worked in the kitchen (to prevent tasting), of women beaten for burning bread, not to mention endless accounts of sexual abuse by masters who preyed on house servants. After working twelve-hour shifts in the heat of the fields or toiling under the constant eye of mistresses, coming home to cook at night was an exhausting prospect and an extra burden.

But cooking offered a woman the chance to use her labor toward what she cared about and valued, rather than what the slavemaster valued. As the writer Angela Davis has noted, tending the hearth and family was nothing short of an act of resistance on the part of black women. It was resistance against slavery. It was resistance against a money-hungry system that broke families apart and sold babies as chattel. When a slave woman cooked for her own clan or family, she reclaimed a certain possession of what was hers, in spite of what happened yesterday and in spite of what might happen tomorrow.

THE MEMORY OF AFRICA

The story of African-American women and food is a complex one with many twists and turns. To find the true beginning, we must travel across the oceans back to the African continent and consider the cultures of the people who would become slaves in North America.

At the time of Columbus's journey, Africa had a population of about 80 to 100 million people—roughly the same as Europe—and a stunning diversity of cultures, languages, and economies. There were urban centers, a significant coastal export economy, and a population that included consummate craft workers, scholars, artists, and priests, as well as agricultural farmers, hunters, and gatherers.

To enter the vibrant food mosaic of Africa, we must look to the millet cultivated by women in Mali, the yams cooked by the Yoruba, the ginger and aromatic spices of North Africa, the fried plantains of Senegal, the rice kitchens of Sierra Leone, the gumbo stews of Angolans, and the smoked fish stirred into iron pots all along the West Coast.

By the time Africans were sold in the North American slave trade, they had already imported and adopted a number of New World food influences. Ground nuts (peanuts), chile peppers, corn, and tomatoes were not native to Africa but had been introduced by European traders, exported from the Americas by the seventeenth century. In a strange twist of history, African women developed culinary knowledge of these foods and then as slaves, carried this knowledge back to the continent from which the foods originated. They taught European-American mistresses what to do with tomatoes or peanuts.

> *M*u gran hestuh say she kin membuh de house she lib in in Africa. She say it wuz cubbuh wid palmetto an grass fu roof, an duh walls wuz made of mud. She membuh wut de eat in Africa too. Dey et yam an shuguh cane an peanut an bananas. Dey eat Okra too.
>
> —SHAD HALL, interviewed by
> Georgia Writers' Project
> *Drums and Shadows*, 1940

Slaves and free blacks who lived and worked in close contact with white people were more likely to cook in the European tradition, adopt white culture, and join Christian churches. Assimilation often was a matter of survival. In the North, it was common for free black women to establish food businesses. These were women like Nancy Lenox Remond (1788–1867), a fancy cake maker who ran a catering business with her husband in Boston. She passed on the trade to one of her daughters, Susan Remond, whose bakery became a famous salon for abolitionists, female suffragists, and fugitive slaves during the nineteenth century.

In the South, life was very different. The connection to Africa remained stronger—particularly among slaves on plantations and in southern cities where blacks outnumbered whites and maintained greater cultural independence from them. Here, slaves retained a deeper sense of Africanism—in language, in music, in storytelling, in medicine, and in food. Because slaves found themselves thrust amid all sorts of Africans from various countries, it was difficult to re-create the community life of Ghana or Angola or Sierra Leone, or even find others who could speak the same language. Despite the ropes of bondage, the slaves made a new world for themselves. Throughout the South, they invented a creolized culture that drew on many African, European, and Indian influences. In this new culture was a lifeline, a thread of identity, and hope.

In southern food, we find this creativity rising up from the tragedy of slavery. In the high and mighty southern kitchen, black hands take much credit for creating and perfecting what would be perhaps the most distinct and flavorful cookery of the United States. As writer John Egerton has observed in his opus

Woman with a bucket balanced on her head in front of the Hermitage, a plantation in Savannah, Georgia, 1870s. STEREO-GRAPH BY WILSON AND HAVENS. *(Photographs and Prints Division, Schomburg Center for Research in Black Culture, The New York Public Library, Astor, Lenox and Tilden Foundations.)*

Southern Food, "The kitchen was one of the few places where their imagination and skill could have free reign and full expression, and there they often excelled."

Most often when slave women excelled, they did so by mingling the techniques, flavors, and ingredients of three continents: Europe, North America, and Africa. Two features of southern cooking—the heat of the red pepper and sauces made with smoked meats—can be traced directly to Africa. In addition, slaves brought important new ingredients to the Americas, namely, cowpeas, benne (sesame) seeds, and the important okra—all native to West Africa. They also brought well-honed African cooking techniques such as deep frying in oil. But there were transformations too. African women in Louisiana mastered gumbos, thickened with file powder of sassafras leaves, learned from neighboring Indians.

All over the colonies, their cooking shined, using European techniques for roasting, pickling, and baking custards, pies, and yeasted bread.

For their own families, inside the slave quarters, slave women made simpler meals, using the corn and pork of slave rations combined with their garden-grown vegetables (gardens tended at night after long day shifts or on Sundays) and whatever hunted, gathered, or fished items they could manage on their free time. Hoecake, chitterlings, and greens cooked in smoked pig's feet represented the memories of a lost continent combined with the realities of bondage. Hundreds of years later during the political 1960s and 1970s, this food would be renamed "soul food," a political term for the food of the diaspora, raised up as a symbol of the African-American experience.

Hoppin' John

One pound of bacon, one pint of red peas, one pint of rice. First put on the peas, and when half boiled, add the bacon. When the peas are well boiled, throw in the rice, which must be first washed and gravelled. When the rice has been boiling half an hour, take the pot off the fire and put it on coals to steam, as in boiling rice alone. Put a quart of water on the peas at first, and if it boils way too much, add a little more hot water. Season with salt and pepper, and if liked a sprig of green mint. In serving up, put the rice and peas first in the dish, and the bacon on the top.

—*The Carolina Housewife,* 1847

For many African Americans, the dish is a New Year's Day ritual, said to bring good luck for the coming year. This recipe is written, obviously, for the hearth. But it need not be so complicated. Take 1 cup of black-eyed peas and wash and sort. Cover with 5 to 6 cups of water, two or three slices of cut-up bacon (or a ham hock), a chopped onion, and salt and pepper as you wish. Boil gently uncovered until tender, about 1½ hours, maybe more. You should have about 2 cups of liquid left in your pot. (Use your judgment or measure if you must.) If you don't, add some boiling water to make this much. Now add 1 cup of washed basmati rice (shaken or patted dry), cover and simmer on very low heat about 20 minutes or so until done. Remove from heat and let it sit a little longer with the lid on.

Calas

A cup of rice boiled soft in water and allowed to cool; add a big spoonful of yeast and a half a cup of water, then beat it well together; the following morning add an egg, a bit of salt, a small spoonful of sugar, a big spoonful of ordinary flour—rice flour is preferable, but difficult to obtain—beat it all well together; then drop this mixture by spoonfuls, one at a time, into lots of very hot lard, turning them until they are nice and brown . . . and place them close to the fire on a plate covered with a warm napkin. They are eaten with *café au lait*.

—CÉLESTINE EUSTIS

Cooking in Old Créole Days, La cuisine créole à l'usage des petits ménages, 1904

In New Orleans, rice cakes, also known as calas, *were a famous food sold on the street. "Bel calas tout chaus!"—Beautiful calas, piping hot!—was the cry of the black woman who sold them in the outdoor market. She carried her calas in a wooden bowl, which she balanced on her head.*

Though the one-pot family meals differed greatly from the multicourse aristocratic fare in the big house, a number of African dishes crossed over the line and became embraced by whites and even celebrated in the earliest southern cookbooks. Hoppin' John is one such dish—a rice-and-bean preparation indigenous to Africa but one that appears in the cookbooks kept by southern white ladies. Another is Pepper Pot, which traveled with slaves from the Caribbean to North America.

In addition to the actual cookery, African women brought many other food-related skills with them to the Americas. For one thing, slave women excelled as entrepreneurs of food, a role that harkened back to their work as hawkers and truckers in the markets of West Africa. This was particularly true—no, make that legendary—in cities like Charleston, Savannah, and New Orleans that had large populations of African Americans (in some cases larger than the white population) during colonial days. Slave women could be seen each day out of doors, selling surplus items from their gardens and kitchens as well as baked goods such as pralines, ground nut cakes, and *calas*—sweetened rice cakes.

By the early eighteenth century, African-American women developed significant power as food sellers and brokers in these public marketplaces. In 1778, one Charleston observer "counted in the market and different corners of this town, sixty-four Negro wenches selling cakes, nuts, and so forth."

At first, slaveholders tolerated the setup—the women generally paid their owners for their time or shared a percentage of their profits. But in time, slave women began to control prices—much to the discontent of white customers—and generally began to rule the marketplace. Local government tried to crack down on the women numerous times, at least as early as 1739, as historian Robert Olwell has noted, when the "official" marketplace was established in Charleston to "prevent the injurious and illegal Practice of . . . Negro-huckstering." But complaints of slave women's "loose and disorderly" conduct and general incorrigibility were repeatedly noted in the laws and newspapers throughout the eighteenth century. Evidently, there was little to be done to stop the market women.

African-American women worked in public markets as entrepreneurs of garden produce, baked goods, and other foods. It was a practice they'd brought from Africa. *(Library of Congress.)*

"A Fund to Purchase Her Children"

In some unusual cases, entrepreneurial women used their cooking and baking skills to try to buy freedom for themselves or their children. In Harriet Jacobs's 1861 narrative of her life in slavery, she describes her grandmother's valiant effort to set up a baking business that would earn money to purchase her five children out of slavery. (The effort was later thwarted by her mistress.)

She became an indispensable personage in the household, officiating in all capacities, from cook and wet nurse to seamstress. She was much praised for her cooking; and her nice crackers became so famous in the neighborhood that many people were desirous of obtaining them. In consequence of numerous requests of this kind, she asked permission of her mistress to bake crackers at night, after all the household work was done; and she obtained leave to do it, provided she would clothe herself and her children from the profits. Upon these terms, after working hard all day for her mistress, she began her midnight bakings, assisted by her two oldest children. The business proved profitable; and each year she laid by a little, which was saved for a fund to purchase her children.

—HARRIET JACOBS
Incidents in the Life of a Slave Girl. Written by Herself, 1861

THE AFRICAN-AMERICAN COOKBOOK

When would African Americans get credit for their legacy and skill of cooking? When would the slave woman have a voice to articulate her own vision of food?

In 1881, a woman named Abby Fisher authored *What Mrs. Fisher Knows About Southern Cooking*, leaving us with a compendium of recipes deeply imprinted with the South.

Like every cookbook author, she must have thought long and hard about which dish should appear first in her cookbook. The first recipe, after all, would be the door to her culinary world, the welcome to her readers. It was this Maryland Beat Biscuit that she chose to herald forth on page one.

It was an interesting choice.

Read the recipe and let your eyes rest on the words: "Beat until perfectly moist and light." There is an entire universe in that phrase. As southerners know, we are not talking about ordinary bread here. We are talking about a recipe that is bound up with the ghosts of female slaves standing outside in the humid heat of summer, whacking that dough with all possible human strength for some thirty minutes until it was blistered, elastic, and smooth. The beating was a chemical trick, transforming the dough so it needed no yeast or other leavening. To do the job, a heavy mallet or the side of a rolling pin was needed. To spare the kitchen table of wear and tear (and possible destruction), a "biscuit table" made of a felled tree trunk, waist high and planed smooth, was customary. Only with these ingredients do the original Maryland Beat Biscuits become possible, evoking mythic status in the South. Beat Biscuits were not light fluffy breads but delectable crisp darlings, the pride of the plantation mistress's table.

This is not to say that women of all kinds haven't done lots of pounding and sweating in their kitchens throughout history. Surely they have. But those without slaves gave up backbreaking techniques as soon as they could, when alternatives (such as chemical leavenings) became available. The gentry of the American South, however, held on much longer to the likes of beaten biscuits and other

Maryland Beat Biscuit

Take one quart of flour, add one teaspoonful of salt, one tablespoonful of lard, half tablespoonful of butter. Dry rub the lard and butter into the flour until well creamed; add your water gradually in mixing board and beat until perfectly moist and light. Roll out the dough to the thickness of third of an inch. Have your stove hot and bake quickly. To make more add twice the quantity.

—ABBY FISHER
What Mrs. Fisher Knows About Southern Cooking, 1881

This recipe is inseparable from the story of slavery.

elaborate culinary traditions because they could. They held on because they had slaves to do the work. (After slavery ended, a biscuit-beating machine was finally invented.)

Abby Fisher knew the rigors of beating biscuits perfectly well because she herself was a former slave. Considering the legacy of black southern cooks in this country, *What Mrs. Fisher Knows About Southern Cooking* is a momentous work of American literature, women's history, and the African-American experience.

In addition to being an elegant, highly skilled cook, Abby was one of those people whose life was caught amidst a dizzying array of monumental historic forces. She was born in South Carolina during the 1830s. Her mother was a slave and her father a Frenchman. In keeping with the laws of her era, Abby was given the status of her mother and was a slave. She almost certainly lived and learned to cook on a plantation, and judging by the European quality of many of her recipes, she most likely cooked in the big house of the master, perhaps one of those baronial plantation homes owned by French Huguenots not far from Charleston, where fine cooking and opulence reigned.

In 1870, we can locate her in Mobile, Alabama, with her husband. Having survived chattel slavery and the Civil War, she and her family then took the risk of heading for the Western frontier in search of a better life. We can imagine they had little money and could only rely on the strength of their bodies and huge reserves of hope to get them through the hazards of overland migration. Considering that Abby was pregnant, her own chance for difficulties greatly increased. Abby successfully gave birth at a pit stop in Missouri, after which the family moved on. In California, she and her husband set up a pickle-and-preserve business, inspired in no small part by Abby's talents and skills. There, Abby reached some social fame, winning awards for her cooking at various fairs along with the esteem of several white ladies who insisted on helping her publish her cookbook, though she could not read or write sufficiently to do it herself. What an extraordinary life. From plantation slave to entrepreneur, to prize-winning cook, to notable author. I should mention, Abby was also a mother who raised and fed eleven children.

Abby Fisher appears today as a larger-than-life figure—a gift that history gives us as inspiration to the possibility of human potential against oppression. But her voice did not rise up until tens of thousands of black hands had transformed the preceding 250 years of culture, economy, and food. Though the ghosts of most black slave women remain voiceless, their imprint remains indelibly on us forever.

Because her cooking was so very fine, I think we should have another one of her recipes before we move on. I recommend this sweet potato pie to one and all:

Sweet Potato Pie

Two pounds of potatoes will make two pies. Boil the potatoes soft; peel and mash fine through a colander while hot; one tablespoonful of butter to be mashed in with the potato. Take five eggs and beat the yelks [yolks] and whites separate and add one gill [one half cup] of milk; sweeten to taste; squeeze the juice of one orange, and grate one half of the peel into the liquid. One half teaspoonful of salt in the potatoes. Have only one crust and that at the bottom of the plate. Bake quickly.

—ABBY FISHER
What Mrs. Fisher Knows About Southern Cooking, 1881

Blacks in America adopted the sweet potato. They praised it, raised it up, and transformed its sweet orange self into beautiful dishes, no doubt because it reminded them of the yam, a tuberous starchy vegetable that is a staple in Africa. In their affection for the sweet potato, they even sometimes called it a yam, but it is not.

This is a lovely recipe, though I find it barely fills two pie shells, and usually increase it. Note that to save time, you can microwave the sweet potatoes, scoop out the flesh, and then mash them well with a fork or electric beater. Abby says five eggs, but remember that today's eggs are bred to be larger, so three will do. Be careful only to use the outer rind of the orange peel—don't go down to the white.

Use your favorite pie crust recipe, but consider Abby's approach, which calls for equal portions of butter and lard to achieve a good buttery taste as well as flakiness: "One pound of flour nicely sifted to quarter pound of butter and one quarter pound of lard, one teaspoonful of salt, fine, mixed in flour while dry; then with your hands rub the butter and lard into the flour."

She also gives what was for me a revelatory tip for pastry making: "roll pastry out to the thickness of an egg-shell for the top of fruit, and that for the bottom of fruit must be thin as paper." As always, be sure to have your pastry cold. Bake about 40 minutes at 400 degrees.

Planting sweet potatoes, 1862, Edisto Island, South Carolina. *(New Hampshire Historical Society.)*

Legend has it that the first rice seed in America was planted by a black woman—or perhaps even carried on a ship from Africa to America in the care of a black woman. It is doubtful that such a legend will ever be proved, but it contains at least a glimmer of truth. If we could travel back in time to a spring day on the Waccamaw River in South Carolina during the eighteenth century, we might behold a vision something like this:

The women walk across the rice fields in rows, barefooted. As they walk, they use their bare heels to dig a slight depression in the earth. Into this, they drop the rice seed. Quickly, the foot brushes the dirt back over. Walk on. Next hole. Next seed. Brush over. Walk on. Their families did it this way in Africa. When the air cools finally in the fall and the rice is harvested, they will pound it in a mortar and pestle, the African way. Then they will fan the rice in winnowing baskets they have woven themselves in the clockwise weave of Africa. They will carry the baskets of the finished grain on their heads, singing work songs with rhythms from their homelands.

The story of American rice goes back to 1663, when a group of English proprietors with strong connections to Barbados got permission from King Charles II to settle in South Carolina. They were looking for a big cash crop. They tried tobacco, grapes, cotton, indigo, rice, ginger, and olives. But they had little luck, and so they turned their efforts to a surer thing and raised livestock for the ready markets of the British West Indies, a short boat ride away.

In the meantime, they kept experimenting with rice agriculture. The swampy wilderness and semitropical heat offered much promise for rice, but success continued to evade them. The problem was that English people had no experience in growing rice. For years they struggled—first to find good seed, then to get decent yields, then to figure out even the simplest procedures, like the best way to clean the rice. It was a very slow start for the grain that would later be known around the world as the precious South Carolina Gold.

What so dramatically changed the fortunes of the rice planters?

Women pounding rice in Georgia, 1920s. Rice had been abundantly farmed in West Africa. Slaves brought technical knowledge and skills to the rice-growing regions of Georgia and South Carolina. *(Courtesy Georgia Department of Archives and History.)*

The English may not have known much about the ancient grain, but Africans knew quite a bit. Rice was farmed abundantly on the West African coast, and slaves from these countries had a great deal of agricultural knowledge about it. Not surprisingly, between 1720 and 1740, the moment that rice production sky-rocketed in South Carolina, so did the import of slaves. Rice planters were quite particular about where their human cargo came from and sought Africans from the rice lands of Senegal-Gambia and the Gold Coast. These slaves provided not just labor but technical know-how on the best way to clear the swamps; flood the fields; drain them as necessary; hoe, plant, reap, thresh, and winnow the rice; and of course, how to cook it.

By 1740, rice had become king in the low country. Soon after, the golden grain spread to Georgia and Florida, and so did the tremendous imports of slaves. In South Carolina the number of blacks exceeded whites.

It was a wet world. Ricing slaves spent much of their life in stagnant, putrid water and muck, under semitropical sun and in high humidity, beleaguered by reptiles, mosquitoes, and other swamp insects—it was work only fit for slaves, in the planters' eyes. In this way, black men and women produced some of the greatest riches of colonial America. With their fabulous profits, the rice planters built an aristocracy in Charleston that studiously imitated European royalty. They lived in mansions extravagant beyond imagination and served grand multicourse meals at long mahogany tables, covered with candles and cooled by the breezes of their open piazzas. Naturally, such an aristocracy built a great cuisine—one that fused English, French Huguenot, and African foodways with the lavish bounty of the warm southern soil and the abundant creatures of the sea. In this cuisine, rice was the holy grail—worshipped and beloved, served each and every day. The early recipe books of Charlestonians give us enormous assortments of rice dishes: rice pilaus, rice casseroles, rice pies, rice soups, rice breads, rice fritters, not to mention all sorts of stews to be served with rice, prepared exactingly in the South Carolina way—cooked until dry so each grain was separate on the plate, rather than sticky. Though black women did not write these books, their influence is abundant.

The following recipe for Red Rice is an example of a low-country rice beloved to this day. There are many ways to prepare it. Some cooks use other kinds of smoked meat or sausage rather than bacon, and water instead of stock.

Red Rice

½ pound bacon

1 small can tomatoes

1 pound rice

Salt and pepper to taste

4 cups chicken broth

Have the bacon sliced and cut in small pieces. Fry it until crisp and remove the bits of bacon. Leave about four tablespoons of the drippings and in this brown the rice, stirring constantly to see that it does not burn. Then add the tomatoes, a teaspoon of salt and the chicken stock. Cover closely and cook for half an hour or until the rice is tender. Add the bacon bits and serve, seasoning to taste with salt and pepper.

—BLANCH S. RHETT, LETTIE GAY,

HELEN WOODWARD, ELIZABETH HAMILTON

200 Years of Charleston Cooking, 1930

200 Years of Charleston Cooking was written by upper-class Charleston ladies who thought it would be great if people up north could have a chance to try the wonderful cooking of Charleston. In writing this book, they greatly relied on the knowledge of their black cooks.

This requires some important adjustments. Try 3 slices of bacon, 1 cup of chopped tomatoes (fresh are best but canned are okay), 1 cup of long-grain rice, and 1¼ cups of chicken broth. Reduce to 1 cup of broth if you use canned tomatoes.). From here on, you can follow the ladies' advice, though I'd suggest only keeping 1 tablespoon of the bacon fat. Also, with this smaller quantity, it may be ready in 15 minutes—don't let it burn!

The lavish culture of the planters tells but one part of the rice story. The other part is the distinct African-American culture that grew up in the swamps, in the rows of slave cabins, and beneath the palmettos. More than any other group of slaves, low-country ricing slaves were left to themselves. The extreme heat and stagnant water of the swamps brought disease and death during the summer months. To spare their wives and children, rice planters set up town homes far from the plantations. They left their overseers or drivers to manage the farming. And so, in the mid and late 1700s, you could find large numbers of slaves living on coastal sea islands who did not speak any English and who had very little contact with white people.

Low-country planters did not adopt the "gang system" of labor that was common in the rest of the South. Under such a system, a driver or overseer would push the slaves twelve or more hours each day. Instead, low-country slaves worked under the "task system." They had certain jobs to be completed each day. During peak worktimes, this entailed brutally long hours and hard work, but during slower times of the ricing cycle, once the slaves finished their tasks, the rest of the day was their own.

Because of their relative isolation, and because of the relative amount of free time they had, low-country slaves of rural South Carolina and Georgia had more control over their lives than many slaves in other regions. They were able to re-create and reinvent their lives with more African influences than slaves living under other circumstances. They built their cabins with walls of "tabby" (sea shell), as was done in West Africa, and pursued crafts in African traditions. They wore their hair in plaits. They cooked with roots and herbs and palmetto and wove sweet-grass baskets. As a result, a distinctive new African-American culture grew and thrived in the low country, which was like no place else in the United States. The culture was rich with memories of the Old World but adapted to fit their new lives.

The most striking feature of these slaves—later known as Gullahs or Geechees—was their language. It differed from English, but it was not any single African language either. Rather, it was a combination of English and African languages, at first a pidgin tongue cobbled together so the first generation of diverse Africans could communicate. Later however, Gullah was passed on to new generations and became a bona fide native tongue, what linguists call a creole language. At the turn of the century, one writer observed that it took outsiders years to learn Gullah.

After the Civil War, whites abandoned the plantations of the sea islands. On some of these islands, blacks essentially took over and continued their subsistence farming and culture into the twentieth century. In the 1930s, writers for the fed-

"N'yam"

Gullah	English
n'yam	To eat (Note the word "yam" embedded in the word. Some have speculated that this may be the origin of "yum")
baddle cake	batter cake; pancake
"De bread mek wid benny een'um."	The bread is made with benny seed.
bittle	food
"E tell de chile ms'nya de bittle."	She told the child he must eat the food.
"Uh berry lub fuy nym brekwus'-swimp en' hom'ny."	I very much like to eat shrimp cooked in gravy and hominy.
"Bile de crab so dey yent was'e."	Boil the crabs so they are not wasted.

—VIRGINIA MIXSON GERATY

Gullah Fuh Oonu (Gullah for You): A Guide to the Gullah Language, 1997

eral Work Progress Administration interviewed Georgian islanders who still practiced old foodways, made "saraka cakes" (based on African rice recipes), practiced healing arts, remembered stories of ancestors being captured, and generally held their connection to Africa in high regard. Some still recalled the folklore about blacks who could fly back to Africa.

Marylou Linyard, Annie Ruth Smalls, and Eleanor Howard grew up on St. Helena Island, a little more than an hour north of Savannah. To get there, you pass through the waterfront town of Beaufort, where the antebellum mansions still stand in architectural beauty and contemporary galleries and restaurants dot the main boulevards. Cross the bridge, however, and you suddenly enter another landscape entirely. After just a small stretch of highway, you're on St. Helena, a quiet island with an old rural soul. There is little development except for one

Annie Ruth's Okra and Tomato Soup

Okra
Pigs Feet, Smoked Neck Bones, or Ham Hocks
Tomato Paste and Sauce
Celery
Onion
Garlic Powder
Garlic Salt
Black Pepper

- Boil okra separately and drain well to get the slime off.
- Boil meat in plenty of water until tender.
- Combine okra, meat, tomato sauce and tomato paste, reserving some of the water from the meat to use later to thin the soup.
- Combine all other ingredients and let simmer down.
- Use "juice" from the meat "to make stew soupier."
- Season to taste with garlic, sugar, salt, and pepper.

—ANNIE RUTH SMALLS
Coosaw Island, South Carolina

restaurant, a gas station, and a few stores. Many of the back roads remain unpaved, and car wheels easily get stuck in the thick sandy dirt, spinning and sliding as if in snow. Many people live in trailers and modular homes. They sit outside in the evening next to their potted flowers to take in the air, which always smells of salt. Air, water, and land seem barely distinguishable here, blending into one another where the swampy marshes rise up. Egrets and herons wing by overhead. A crab scuttles across the parking lot. It was here on these coastal sea islands

Marylou's Deviled Crab

- First boil your crabs in a pot of water with seafood seasoning in it (such as "Old Bay" crab boil). Boil 15 to 20 minutes or until done (you just have to know when this is).
- Pick the crab.
- Add to your crab meat:

  bread crumbs
  parsley
  sage
  green pepper
  onion
  mayonnaise
  ketchup
  salt
  pepper
  hot sauce or red pepper—whatever you think will add some flavor

- Stuff the crab shells with the crab meat mixture or shape into crab cakes.
- Bake until brown in a 350 oven—about 15 minutes.

—MARYLOU LINYARD
St. Helena Island, South Carolina

up and down the coast of South Carolina that slaves lived and worked, building the fabulous wealth of rice, indigo, and cotton. It is a world where blacks have dominated for hundreds of years.

The Okra and Tomato Soup and Deviled Crab recipes speak of this place. Notice that there are no exact measurements. They are not needed. Annie Ruth Smalls and Marylou Linyard have cooked these specialties since girlhood—

recipes of oral traditions learned from their mother. Their sister, Eleanor, who runs a catering business, is known for her excellent red rice.

These three sisters were born in a family of thirteen children. They are Gullahs, though when you ask them, they don't answer that question. Marylou says

Shaking the Rice from the Straw After Threshing, from the Rice Plantation Series, 1936. WATERCOLOR BY ALICE RAVENEL HUGER SMITH. Memories of her family's plantation, Smithfield, as it was in the 1850s. (Gibbes Museum of Art/Carolina Art Association.)

instead, "We are native St. Heleners." They eat rice every day and have done so all their lives. Though Carolina Gold has long been gone from the fields there, the people still worship it. At the supermarket, forty-pound bags are the common fare.

I guess the sisters to be in their late fifties, but they can remember a life that just as well might come from a hundred years ago. As children, they lived very much from the land and the sea around them. Behind their house, they grew cotton, corn, peas, beans, tomatoes, and potatoes. Before going to school in the morning, they milked cows and worked the crops. They also had to gather eggs and clean out chicken coops. They brought their cotton to market to sell, and took their corn to the public mill, where they turned it into grits.

Eleanor, the oldest, tells me, "I kept the children. That's what the oldest did. We worked hard. We had to." Their father worked in the water. From September to April, he'd stand in the bays, wearing waders to harvest oysters. From May to September, it would be crabs. Their mother worked in a shellfish factory.

On the island, everyone knows everyone, and these sisters are reputed for their warmth and hospitality, their good food at parties and celebrations. Marylou also cooks for events at the Ebenezer Baptist Church, where she is a member. Eleanor is a caterer who makes lunches for the Beaufort County government. For their own everyday meals, they make collards, lima beans, rice, potatoes, and red peas. Annie Ruth is very clear that the key seasoning in her pot is meat—the hamhocks, the pigs feet, or hogs jowls—or, she concedes, smoked turkey wings for the health conscious. She tells me she loves cabbage cooked with bacon and sweet potato pone (pronounced "poon"), a low-country, pudding-type dish. "But you've got to grate the potatoes by hand," she tells me. "A food processor won't work."

Gullah heritage is an inescapable theme of life on St. Helena and other sea islands. But since the boom time of the 1980s, developers have been buying up land, creating tourist resorts like the nearby Hilton Head. Fertilizer runoff from golf courses (and other forms of water pollution) have greatly diminished the oysters and shrimp that formed the livelihood of the Gullah people for decades. Outsiders are buying up real estate. Though the Gullah culture and food traditions remain strong on St. Helena and a few other sea islands along the South Carolina and Georgia coast, the link between past and future remains uncertain.

The rice fields around the sea islands have long been abandoned. But you can still visit swamps that once were alive with the bent-over backs of men and women and the ricing songs from Africa. These places are silent now, except for the screeches and trills of birds, the buzz of insects, the almost audible burning glare of the sun. The indigo, which long ago stopped being farmed on St. Helena, still scatters its seed randomly in the wind, persistently taking root in people's backyards, whether they like it or not. And for the Geechees who live here and the ones who have moved elsewhere, the rice kitchen lives on, forging endless trails around the world.

Chapter 4

Virtuous Cookery: From Drudgery to Sacred Profession

Amelia Simmons was in a difficult position. "A poor solitary orphan," she had no father or brothers to protect her. No dowry. And she could not read or write—at least not well. With no guardian, no money, and no familial connections, there was little else she could do (respectably at least) except to hire herself out to labor in someone else's kitchen.

Despite the odds, this orphaned girl would do something so special that history would not forget her. In 1796, she authored and published *American Cookery*—the first cookbook ever written by an American and published in the United States. It sold out almost immediately.

How nearly magical that a woman of such humble circumstances could do such a significant thing. Horatio Alger couldn't have told it better.

To be single and struggling alone was no easy situation for a woman during the eighteenth century. Simmons tells us plainly that she strove to be a good girl—or to put it in her own words, to adhere to the "rules and maxims that have stood the test of ages, and will forever establish the *female character,* a virtuous character." With this swift brush of her quill (or more accurately, her transcriber's quill), Simmons summed up what would become an American obsession into the nineteenth century and beyond: female virtue.

The idea of virtue may well have been timeless, as Amelia Simmons noted.

But during the early years of the new American republic, virtue seemed to become an especially potent commodity. Looking back, it seemed incomprehensible that a ragtag army of patriots beat an ancient and powerful monarchy. There could be only one explanation: goodness clearly had been on their side, and corruption on the other.

An obsession with purity and morality came to the forefront of politics, religion, and culture in the new nation. By the early nineteenth century, American theology shifted away from Calvinism, which held that humans should submit to the will of God, and moved toward a new strain of Protestantism that stressed the power of individuals to determine their own salvation. With this new ideology came a certain miraculousness of American life—an unbound optimism in the power of ordinary human beings to improve and even re-create themselves, and a faith that they could save others, too.

By the turn of the nineteenth century, Americans became rampant reformers with a certain righteous pride. Hadn't they created the first largest-scale democracy since the Roman Empire? American politics would be fairer than those of England. American people would be superior. Even the food in the new republic would taste better.

With these ideas in mind, Amelia Simmons offered recipes like Federal Pan Cake, Election Cake, and Independence Cake, with a flourish of optimism for the values that were unfolding around her. Today, these may seem like hokey names slapped on some basic old recipes, but in fact here was a woman singing forth with optimism and high ideals about the extraordinary time during which she lived. With this also came her own act of personal re-creation from anonymous poor orphan to mother of American cookbooks.

OPPOSITE: *Liberty. In the form of the Goddess of Youth; giving Support to the Bald Eagle*, 1796. Liberty, a woman, offers a cup to an eagle. Her right foot treads on chains, a scepter, a key, and other tools of tyrannical England. PAINTING BY EDWARD SAVAGE. *(Library of Congress.)*

AMERICAN COOKERY,

OR THE ART OF DRESSING

VIANDS, FISH, POULTRY and VEGETABLES,

AND THE BEST MODES OF MAKING

PASTES, PUFFS, PIES, TARTS, PUDDINGS,
CUSTARDS AND PRESERVES,

AND ALL KINDS OF

CAKES,

FROM THE IMPERIAL PLUMB TO PLAIN CAKE.

ADAPTED TO THIS COUNTRY,

AND ALL GRADES OF LIFE.

By Amelia Simmons,

AN AMERICAN ORPHAN.

PUBLISHED ACCORDING TO ACT OF CONGRESS.

HARTFORD

PRINTED BY HUDSON & GOODWIN,

FOR THE AUTHOR.

1796

The first American cookbook—a declaration of independence. Though the recipes in Amelia Simmons's book were still heavily British, she also featured American specialties like pumpkin pudding, cranberry pie, and hoe cakes. In some recipes, she also called for chemical leaveners instead of time-consuming yeast. Then as now, Americans were in more of a rush than Europeans.

Federal Pan Cake

Take one quart boulted rye flour, one quart of boulted Indian meal, mix it well, and stir it with a little salt into three pints milk, to the proper consistence of pancakes; fry in lard, and serve up warm.

—AMELIA SIMMONS
American Cookery, 1796 (second edition)

Modern tastes differ from those of the eighteenth century. Most of us are likely to find this a bit too dense and gritty, as well as too large in quantity. Here's an adaptation that brings in all the common luxuries of modern American life: white flour, eggs, sugar, and chemical leavening. These additions will make your pancakes sweeter and lighter, but you'll still get to taste the rye and cornmeal combination, once so essential in New England.

¾ cup rye flour	1 teaspoon baking powder
¾ cup cornmeal	½ teaspoon baking soda
½ cup white flour	2 eggs
2 to 3 tablespoons sugar	1½ cups milk
¼ teaspoon salt	

Mix the dry ingredients well. In a separate bowl, beat the eggs well and add milk. Stir this into your dry ingredients until smooth. Fry on a greased griddle until light brown. Serve with stewed apples, pears, or warm maple syrup. Makes about 12 small pancakes.

HOMEMADE TEA FOR THE REVOLUTION

In the new American republic, white women would win a new social status for themselves as the feeders and nurterers of a growing nation. It was something they had to work hard to earn.

> *I*f I have neither Sugar, molasses, coffee nor Tea I have no right to complain. I can live without any of them and if what I enjoy I can share with my partner and with Liberty, I can sing o be joyfull and sit down content.
>
> —ABIGAIL ADAMS to her husband, John

During the long years of the Revolution, they endured fighting, hunger, and death of the people they loved. They organized themselves to spin linen and sewed shirts for soldiers. They raised large sums of money to help the cause. They debated the issues of independence, and they rioted in the streets against greedy merchants who hoarded food and price gouged. In addition to going without countless necessities, women ran farms and businesses while their husbands were fighting. They followed battalions of soldiers, ministering to and feeding the sick and wounded. They were competent, strong, and highly involved.

"I cooked and carried in beef, and bread, and coffee," wrote Sarah Osborne, a servant for a blacksmith's family in Albany. Sarah's husband, Aaron, joined the Continental army without her knowledge and insisted she join him. She agreed and became one of thousands of women (both black and white) who attached themselves to military battalions, following husbands into war. Like soldiers, women marched for days on end, carrying water to battlefields, washing laundry cooking large quantities of food—and risking death.

Early on in the conflict, one of the most effective tools against England had been a long sustained boycott of all imported British goods. For this, women had been not just important but absolutely essential. There would have been no resistance without them. England was at this time an overextended empire, squeezing the colonies through taxation. The best way to fight back was to hit hard in the pocketbook.

Men like Thomas Jefferson, John Adams, and Thomas Paine had turned to their wives, mothers, and sisters and asked them to get involved in the fight—to give up those fine English teas and sugars, molasses, biscuits, and wines for the sake of liberty and justice. They asked housewives and servants to be frugal and industrious, to manufacture substitutes from their own homes, to spin their own linens, to make their own local teas. They asked them to reject all those lovely British things, and in doing so to define themselves as "Americans" rather than English.

In cities and towns, American women had embraced the challenge with zeal, manufacturing goods they previously had bought from British ships. Under the banner of the "Daughters of Liberty," they organized tea boycotts with amazing effectiveness. Foreign tea consumption plummeted from 900,000 pounds in 1769 to 237,000 pounds just three years later. The *Boston Evening Post* reported that the "industry and frugality of American ladies" would contribute to the "political salvation of the whole Continent."

Tea helped women find their determination. Tea helped women find their first political language. Tea helped form the United States. Here was proof, if ever there was, that boycotts are a special form of female politics,

*I*t also appeared, that a Female Patriotism was predominant in their Conduct, when the Tea Table was introduced; for instead of making use of any foreign Tea, (which is become more nauseous since loaded with an unconstitutional Tax,) they substituted a Tea the Growth of that Town, called Ever-Green, which for its pleasant Flavor, and many excellent Qualities, is prefered by many to the best Green Tea.

—*New York Journal*, May 11, 1769
Huntington, Long Island

a fact that American women today would be wise to remember. Though our individual influence may be little, collectively it can add up to a lot in the form of purchasing power. With this in mind, a brew made of strawberry leaves or bergamot plants takes on a more meaningful and enduring flavor.

Homemade Tea

Gather leaves from any of the following plants that grow in your local area: bergamot plants (bee balm), raspberry bushes, strawberry bushes, or peppermint. Hang upside down to dry. After a day or two, store in glass jar to keep flavor. Lightly crush leaves and place into tea ball. Steep in boiling water, and enjoy.

Note: Eighteenth-century housewives made it their business to know their herbs and plants. Do not attempt this recipe without being secure in your botanical knowledge.

In colonial times, the goodwife had been considered morally inferior to her husband, a weaker vessel more prone to the lure of evil and frivolities. Husbands and fathers were the spiritual leaders of their families. Now, after the Revolution, a new more "modern" woman was born: "the Republican Mother," as historian Linda Kerber has called her. The Republican Mother's main job was to build the morals of the nation by building righteous homes and raising good sons who would lead America to greatness. It became common for clergymen and writers

Ladies at a Tea Party. Women drink tea and make a strong stand in favor of temperance, circa 1840, ceremoniously pouring alcohol out of the window. Religious zealotry brought women together. It also erased the flavors of wine and other liquors from many American recipes, bringing forth an era of plain food, especially in the Northeast. WOODCUT BY ALBERT ALDEN. *(Courtesy American Antiquarian Society.)*

to denigrate ladies of the wrong kind—those caught obsessing over fashions and fancy silks, chasing after husbands, or turning French phrases at society balls. As Kerber explains, "The republic did not need fashion plates; it needed citizens—women as well as men—of self discipline and of strong mind."

Some people worried that American women were not quite up to the job, and the improvement of the female species came into wide debate. Did women deserve to be educated and if so, how? Should they be formally schooled in the arts of housewifery so they would run better homes? Or would they actually benefit from studying academic subjects as well? Previously, only wealthy girls had received schooling, but now after the Revolution, academies for women began springing up—some even offering mathematics and liberal arts. Within a few decades, the number of white women who could read, particularly in the North, leapt dramatically.

The road to literacy—an uneven and slow road for sure—provided nothing short of a revolution for American women. It was a revolution that would ultimately lead women to university education and careers. But at this early moment, the literacy movement found its bedrock in the kitchen, as cookbooks, domestic guides, women's novels, and magazines flooded the marketplace. The publishing industry was taking off, and for the first time ever, a single cookbook could rapidly indoctrinate tens of thousands of women.

A select group of educated women seized the fast-rising tide of American publishing, developing themselves into national culinary celebrities and powerful shapers of American culture. With best-selling cookbooks in tow, these authoresses, as they were called, used their culinary platform to try to improve the status and condition of women's lives. In this way, the American cookbook itself became a new vehicle for women who wanted to politely call for social reforms, ranging from labor-saving kitchens to women's education, temperance, suffrage, and the politics of civil war.

Though the cliché lives in our hearts that cookery and feminism are not natural allies, the truth is that they are estranged cousins on a distant limb of the family tree. Cookbooks gave many women their first public voice and for some, such as Amelia Simmons, a "respectable" profession they desperately needed in order to survive. Through cookbooks, women would help define the values of the growing nation.

No other culinary woman embraced the hopes of the new republic so comprehensively as did Lydia Maria Child, the first of many American culinary powerhouses. As a young woman still in her twenties, Lydia embarked on a writing career of high ideals. Her first novel created a sensation by empathizing with the plight of American Indians in New England. Later in her life she took a strong stand for abolition.

A true woman of letters, Lydia wrote fiction, history, and memoir and also founded *Juvenile Miscellany*, the first children's magazine in America. But then, as now, cookbooks sold better than literature, and Lydia was usually in one financial crisis or another. She'd married a human rights lawyer whose promising career took a swift dive soon after their wedding. In 1829, not yet thirty, Lydia published her *Frugal Housewife* (later renamed *American Frugal Housewife*) hoping to make some money. To her delight, she had a national best-seller on her hands.

Lydia was different from any cookbook author before her: she openly proclaimed that she was "writing for the poor, not the rich" and "those who are not ashamed of economy." Evidently, there were a great many unashamed ones in early America, for her book was reprinted thirty-two times within twenty years.

The Frugal Housewife built on women's wartime legacy by painting a frill-free picture of the "Republican Cook"—a dynamo of industry and simplicity. The Republican Cook had a sensible head for economy. She was an earthy rural woman, deeply practical, and not afraid of getting her hands in the pig's feed. "Look to the pails, to see that nothing is thrown to the pigs which

Lydia Maria Child in midlife. In her 1829 *Frugal Housewife,* Child presented recipes along with appeals for female education. She would later become a famous abolitionist. *(The Schlesinger Library, Radcliffe Institute, Harvard University.)*

A Chowder

Four pounds of fish are enough to make a chowder for four or five people; half a dozen slices of salt pork in the bottom of the pot; hang it high [from a crane above the fire], so that the pork may not burn; take it out when done very brown; put in a layer of crackers, small or sliced onions, and potatoes sliced as thin as a four-pence, mixed with pieces of pork you have fried; then a layer of fish again, and so on. Six crackers are enough. Strew a little salt and pepper over each layer; over the whole pour a bowl-full of flour and water, enough to come up even with the surface of what you have in the pot. A sliced lemon adds to the flavor. A cup of tomato catsup is very excellent. Some people put in a cup of beer. A few clams are a pleasant addition. It should be covered so as not to let a particle of steam escape, if possible. Do not open it, except when nearly done, to taste if it be well seasoned.

—LYDIA MARIA CHILD
The American Frugal Housewife, 1833 edition

Codfish was an essential item in New England's colonial and nineteenth-century economy. Perhaps Lydia Maria Child, a great abolitionist, was unaware that New England traded its salt cod for goods produced by slaves (sugar from the West Indies, and rice and tobacco from the South). The economy of the abolitionist North was deeply linked to the "peculiar institution" of slavery she so abhorred.

Variations for chowder are endless. This recipe is interesting to make and taste because . . . well, it belonged to Lydia. Also it has an intriguing mix of beer, tomato ketchup, and lemon. It tastes like the past—that is to say, heavy on pork flavor and the wet dough of crackers. It works well with bacon if you can't get or don't like salt pork. I think you need about half the fish she calls for. I also advise layering with fish first, unless you want all those crackers stuck to the bottom of your pot. (I personally prefer to sprinkle my crackers on top at the end. That's up to you.) For a more familiar New England chowder, you're perfectly within your rights and historical authenticity to substitute milk for the catsup, beer, and lemons.

should have been in the grease-pot. Look to the grease-pot and see that nothing is there which might have served to feed your family, or a poorer one," Lydia counseled.

Despite this severe tone, much of her book offers rather good, though simple New England–style home cooking. Her penny-pinching dishes like bullock's heart, calf's head, and mutton neck do not stand the test of time, but she also suggests some lovely items like currant wine, cranberry pudding, chicken curry, and that Yankee staple, cod chowder made with salt pork.

Like many distinguished women in the new nation, Lydia called for improvement of the female race and the world itself. She felt perfectly comfortable using her cookbook to do so, mingling recipes with her passion for reform. Female education was one of her greatest passions. "There is no subject so much connected with individual happiness and national prosperity as the education of daughters," Lydia wrote in a chapter called "Hints to Persons of Modest Fortune" (placed near an old-fashioned recipe for beer that begins with, "Beer is a good family drink.)"

Lydia's book gives us a clue as to what daily life was like for ordinary rural women before commercial foods and electric refrigeration changed the world. "See that the beef and pork are always *under* brine," Lydia advised. "See that the vegetables are neither sprouting nor decaying: if they are so, remove them to a drier place, and spread them. Examine preserves, to see that they are not contracting mould." According to her guidelines, eggs, properly prepared in salted water and slacked lime, were expected to last "up to three years."

The American Frugal Housewife offered many penny-saving tips. Among them: Make your own soap. Make your own lemon syrup. Make your own bread and cake if you're not rich. Salt your own beef and pork. Make your own tea from young leaves of currant bush.

In Lydia's vision, frugality was a political equalizer. If a wife was constantly vigilant about her food supply, she could make all the difference between poverty and respectability in her family. Frugality was also a civic responsibility. It was in the "interest of our country," Lydia wrote, for women not to be wasteful.

The tremendous success of *The American Frugal Housewife* brought Lydia financial stability for a short while. But her down-to-earth egalitarianism would later get her into trouble. In 1833, she published *An Appeal in Favor of That Class of Americans Called Africans*. The book brought immediate scandal. While it was acceptable for women to write about social issues in imaginative works such as novels (like *Uncle Tom's Cabin* by Harriet Beecher Stowe), Lydia's book was different. Hers was a fact-filled textbook that analyzed the world history of slavery and appealed for nationwide abolishment of the institution. She intentionally targeted men as her audience—the nation's congressmen and political leaders—and this was taboo. Well-bred, credible women simply did not appeal to men as intellectual equals, nor did they debate political issues in such an overt and public manner.

Lydia's rebuke was swift and sudden. The editors and intellectuals of Boston slammed doors in her face. Readers cancelled their subscriptions to her juvenile magazine, and ultimately Lydia was forced to endure a long period of isolation and poverty. After some years, her career recovered. But she permanently fell from grace as a culinary lady and journalist and instead became a nationally known leader of the abolitionist cause.

IN CHARGE OF THE HOME

By midcentury, the rural and practical ways of the frugal housewife began to seem terribly old-fashioned and out-of-date.

The family home was slowly ceasing to be the center of the family economy as industrialism arrived and factory jobs began to replace farm life. A new middle class was rising based on white-collar jobs of trade and commerce. Money was beginning to take over the economy and the world. At the store, you needed cold hard cash—not homemade butter with which to barter. "Man cow provides. Dairy wife guides" was replaced by a different model. Man now earned money, and then gave his wife this money to buy milk from the milkman. If she belonged to the growing urban middle class, she might also buy her cheese, pickles, butter, bread, and bacon rather than make these herself.

A hundred years earlier, the daily life and work of the yeoman and his wife had overlapped considerably. Now, men were suddenly absent from home as they went off to earn money. And while the sense of "progress," technology, and rapid democratization of society had a thrilling aspect, many people were worried. It seemed as though this new world order was spinning civilization out of control.

Love in a cottage. "Never mind; don't cry pet. I'll do the cooking." *Harper's Weekly,* April 3, 1875. Criticism that American women were not very good cooks began to build during the nineteenth century. In a highly mobile society, women often did not live near home and lost opportunities to learn from mothers.

To help keep the social fabric from tearing apart, American women and men began to recast American marriage into a new model to accommodate the new economy and its emerging middle class. In this new arrangement—now called the doctrine of "separate spheres"—men would exist in the public realm of commerce and women would be put in full charge of the home.

In this way, industrialism radically transformed the very idea of home from a messy workplace and economic unit headed by the father into something very different—a safe haven in a heartless, money-driven world. A glorified place. Women would make it so by doing a better job of mothering, housekeeping, and cooking.

The impact on food would be profound.

Before industrialism, most people of the Western world ate with the simple goal of getting enough calories to fill their bellies and enjoy the experience along the way. A skilled cook strove for as much variety as possible. If medically minded, she might consciously try to balance the four humors—earth, air, water, and fire—which then were believed to govern the universe. She'd balance cool-producing foods (like cucumbers and vinegars) with heat-producing ones (like meats).

Now, cookbook authors told American women that food should be able to achieve much more. Through proper cooking, women could encourage better health and better morality. They could prevent infants from dying. They could fight the adulterations of commercial food products. They could prevent greedy desires in their husbands and sons. They could end alcoholism. They could help their families gain upward mobility, higher status, and more comfort by securing appropriate table manners and etiquette.

In this way, women transformed the act of cooking to fit the new economy and their own aspirations. The womanly job of cooking became a social act rather than one of biological need. In the process, women created a more authoritative role for themselves and for the home. And in many ways, they made industrialism itself possible. How else would men find the strength to go to dehumanizing jobs if it weren't for the comfort of home at the end of the day? Middle-class domesticity was not a result of industrialism but a necessary factor for it. The only problem was that once women set themselves to orchestrating perfection within those four walls, it would become terribly difficult to ever leave.

GUARDIANS OF THE DIET AND THE SOUL

"The prevalence of *intemperance in eating, of* luxury in living, is more the fault of woman than that of man," wrote Sarah Josepha Hale, the enormously influential editor of the most popular nineteenth-century magazine, *Godey's Lady's Book.* "She is guardian of the home; she can regulate the arrangement of her household: she can form the habits of her children; she does form them."

In the emerging Victorian home, restraint became a symbol of good morals. Women eliminated alcohol and seasonings from recipes. They strove to make food taste adequate but not too delicious lest it tempt their husbands or children into overindulgence or the dark sensual side of human nature.

Cookbooks advised women that proper meals could keep men from going astray. "Many a day-laborer, on his return at evening from his hard toil is repelled by the sight of a disorderly house and a comfortless supper . . . and he makes his escape to the grogshop or the underground gambling room," warned Mrs. M. H. Cornelius in *The Young Housekeeper's Friend* in 1868.

"There is no more prolific,—indeed, there is no *such* prolific cause of bad morals as abuses of diet,—not merely by excessive drinking of injurious beverages, but excessive eating, and by eating unhealthful food," observed Mrs. Horace Mann in her notable *Christianity in the Kitchen*. "Compounds like wedding cake, suet plum-puddings, and rich turtle soup, are masses of indigestible material, which should never find their way to any Christian table."

People since ancient times have always believed that the right diet creates good health, right morals, and mental strength. Each generation puts forth its own ideals about what the right diet should be—which foods are the good ones and which foods are the bad. This generation would be no different, except now with the aid of cookbooks the news could spread far and wide, reaching more people. An immense wave of dietary reform and healthfoodism spread across the young nation. Cookbook writers and editors routinely admonished their female readers to stop serving fried foods and pastry crust and to cut down on cake. Extremists of the day, led by the nationally famous Sylvester Graham, gained a fair amount of followers by calling for the downright heretical: whole-grain flours and vegetarianism. (If this sounds familiar dear reader, you would be right.)

Dietary reform was greatly aided and abetted by another factor—the great national stomach ache, which was evidently plaguing America. *Dyspepsia*—that curious-sounding word used to describe indigestion and a whole host of other mysterious stomach disorders—was, by all accounts, a rampant scourge of the time. We can presume the national metabolism was being slowed dramatically as many North Americans shifted from physical labor to more sedentary jobs and factory life. The old diet of minced pies, fried meats, and lots of cheese and butter was proving quite binding and indigestible. There also can be no doubt that America's natural abundance of food led to much overeating, which many observers found rather troubling (and still do). In addition, Americans seemed to be in quite a rush at the dinner table—perhaps the burdens of building a new nation can account for the quick-paced culture that began at the outset. In any case, hurried eating was also a source of concern and further indigestion.

Shake Hands?, 1854. Lilly Martin Spencer often painted kitchen scenes that poked fun at the restrained middle-class values of her era. Here, the sensuality is unmistakable, as our cook, with flushed cheeks, offers her messy hands to the viewer. *(Ohio Historical Society.)*

"The cook exercises a greater power over the public health and welfare than the physician," wrote Mrs. Lee in her 1854 *Cook's Own Book*. "After insanity, the most grievous affliction of Providence, or rather of improvidence and imprudence, is Dyspepsia: a malady that under different names has decimated the inhabitants of civilized countries."

Despite the moralizing, there were some good recipes worth keeping, like the one for Cold Fruit Pudding that appeared in *Christianity in the Kitchen*.

THE SACRED PROFESSION OF DOMESTIC SCIENCE

As women became more educated, they wanted to bring greater intellect to cooking and a more "modern" understanding of how food affected the body and health. Americans were in love with science and believed their new country would be a world center for its advancement. (And so it indeed has been.) Many people believed that through science, human beings would be able to improve all aspects of civilization.

By midcentury, cookbooks began appearing with scientific charts of food nutrients and descriptions on the interior workings of the body. Lengthy prefaces educated women on the nutritional aspects of food—with great concern for phosphorus, nitrogen, oxygen, and the nature of gastric juices. Countless misguided rules for correct eating were put forth as great law. Hence, our culinary authorities began a long track record of putting forth one nutritional theory after the next, only to be disproved by the following generation, whose science and nutritional research would evolve more fully and reveal more findings. It is a practice that continues to this day.

> *A*s soon as the food enters the stomach, the muscles are excited by the nerves, and the *peristaltic motion* commences.
>
> —CATHARINE ESTHER BEECHER
> *A Treatise on Domestic Economy,* 1841

"Fish is much less nutritious than flesh," wrote Sarah Josepha Hale in her 1841 *The Good Housekeeper*. "The white kinds of fish, cod, haddock, flounders, white fish &C., are the least nutritious." She also noted that "no kind of beverage should be taken hot—it injures the teeth and impairs digestion."

"*Bathing* should never follow a meal," wrote Catharine Beecher in her *Ameri-*

A Cold Fruit Pudding

Stew together one quart each whortleberries, raspberries, blackberries, a pint of currants, and a pound of brown sugar.

Cut a brick loaf into thin slices, and line with them a deep bowl. Pour a layer of the fruit, then a layer of thin bread, and so alternately until the bowl is full. Lay a plate upon the bowl, which will go easily within the circumference of it. Lay a heavy weight upon it and let it stand several hours, perhaps all night.

Serve with cream or cream sauce. Any sweet and acid fruit combined will answer.

—MRS. HORACE MANN
Christianity in the Kitchen, 1857

This fat-free dessert may be virtuous, but its bright red colors and beautiful flavor make it flagrantly sensual, and perhaps that accounts for its timelessness. It takes some practice to get the layering of bread and berries down, but you'll enjoy the results on the first try—even if they are not so pretty.

The whortleberries that Mrs. Mann called for are a European cousin to American blueberries. Use any berry mixture you like but choose the best quality you can get. I prefer strawberries, blueberries, raspberries, and blackberries. For 6 to 8 servings, 8 to 9 cups of fruit will do, with ⅓ cup of sugar (more or less according to the sweetness of the fruit and your taste).

- *Cook berries and sugar about 5 minutes, until juices are released. Taste. If you like more zing, add a squeeze of lemon.*

- *Choose a dense white bread, such as potato bread, challah, or a pullman loaf that will stand up to the fruit juice. It must be stale, sliced a quarter-inch thick. (Trim the crusts if you are fussy.)*

- *Cut bread into shapes that will line a 5- to 6-cup bowl, beginning with a circle of bread at the bottom. Or take the easier route and use an 8½ x 4½ loaf pan, which is a snap to line with square slices.*

- *Grease the bowl or pan with butter.*

- *Now go ahead and layer your fruit and bread. Though Mrs. Mann doesn't mention this, I suggest dunking each bread slice in the fruit mixture to coat with juice before layering in your bowl. When you've finished, pour any remaining juices on top.*

- *Cover with wax paper, and weight it with a heavy object (this is a must) such as a can or two of tomatoes. Ideally, refrigerate 8 hours then serve, though I have made this ahead and left it in the refrigerator as long as 20 hours with very good, though not perfect results.*

- *Invert on a plate and serve. It's great with vanilla ice cream.*

Sarah Josepha Hale,
Mother of Thanksgiving

*T*hanksgiving as we celebrate it today hardly pays tribute to the "first" Thanksgiving we claim to esteem. Unlike the 1621 event at Plymouth, where politics, venison, and shooting demonstrations reigned, our present national Thanksgiving holiday is largely the product of Victorian ideals that celebrated the virtues of women, home, and hearth.

We have Sarah Josepha Hale to thank for this.

Until Sarah came along, Thanksgiving was an erratic event under local jurisdiction and mainly one of "New England manners." From state to state, it was held according to the whims of reigning governors, sometimes in October or November, but also in December or January. In the South, the holiday was largely unknown. Though some early presidents called for national days of prayer, others, such as Jefferson, believed that the Constitution did not grant a president the power to order people to be thankful.

In 1846, Sarah Josepha Hale, editor of *Godey's Lady's Book,* began a seventeen-year crusade to establish a single national holiday that all states would cele-

Sarah Josepha Hale, cookbook author and editor. She led a relentless campaign to make Thanksgiving a national holiday of food and family values.

can *Woman's Home*, "as it withdraws the blood and nervous vigor demanded for digestion from the stomach to the skin."

The search for legitimacy and authority is unmistakable in their voices. But the existence of vitamins had not been discovered, and for that matter neither had germ theory. Fruits and vegetables were sorely misunderstood. (It was widely believed they should be boiled for hours to be safe and good.) Butter was sinful, but cream was considered okay. Cold drinks, such as ice water, were thought to brate on the same day. It was the culmination of her lifelong faith in the power of food, women, and home. Her ideal of Thanksgiving put the holiday squarely into the woman's sphere—the kitchen and parlor of home, the circle of family life.

So powerful were these forces that Sarah believed a single Thanksgiving Day could have a unifying effect on the North and South. She argued that Thanksgiving could even prevent a Civil War. She did this despite the express policy at *Godey's* magazine that politics were off limits to the "fairest portion of creation" (as publisher Louis Godey put it).

From the editorial pulpit of *Godey's*, Sarah admonished the nation's governors, year after year, to proclaim the last Thursday in November as Thanksgiving Day. She wrote, with her own hand, hundreds of beseeching letters.

In addition to her passionate editorials, she offered her women readers Thanksgiving recipes for turkeys and pumpkin pies, sentimental poems, pictures, and tear-rending sketches of "old-fashioned" Thanksgivings, in which families triumphed over adversity—sometimes death itself—to come together at the Thanksgiving table.

After first targeting the governors of each state to voluntarily agree on a national day, Sarah turned her attention to writing letters to each of the nation's presidents and staff members from 1850 onward. She also reached out to various secretaries of state—and at least one writer mentions that she may have even personally visited with President Lincoln on the matter.

In 1863, amidst the Civil War, Lincoln proclaimed a national Thanksgiving Day. He asked the nation to be thankful for the bounties of nature and to come together, North and South, for a single unifying day. The holiday that Sarah envisioned became an icon of American life.

disrupt digestion and injure the stomach. Five hours should always elapse between meals. Children were to be strictly limited in their fluid intake. Most often repeated: hot bread was bad for the stomach, and sour dough perilous.

Formal training would now be necessary for women to keep up with all the latest health information pertaining to diet and cooking. Old-fashioned mothers and grandmothers with their misguided folklore and intuitive ways were hardly equipped for the job. Anyway, many women found themselves living at a dis-

Catharine Beecher, 1848, a hugely popular public speaker, educator, and author of domestic manuals. She promoted female education but not suffrage, believing women's natural place was in the home. *(The Schlesinger Library, Radcliffe Institute, Harvard University.)*

tance from their mothers. America had become a highly mobile society in which striving men and women constantly moved in search of economic opportunity. A more professional approach to cooking became key to upward mobility.

Catharine Beecher, of the renowned Beecher family, was the greatest proponent of women's formal and scientific education in good housekeeping. In her landmark 1841 *Treatise on Domestic Economy* and later her 1869 *American Woman's Home* (written with her famous sister Harriet Beecher Stowe), she put forth a vision for the home economics movement, a movement that would not come to fruition until the turn of the twentieth century. In doing so, she lay the groundwork for some of our most coveted ideas of home, women's work, and the very nature of what the middle class was supposed to be. Her most fervent cause was education for women, and she started many schools for women where "domestic science" was a formal branch of study. With education and professionalization, Catharine believed housework could be transformed from drudgery into a sacred job on equal footing with the professions of men.

Catharine was a pure American product. Piety and evangelism ran through her blood. She was daughter to the powerful New England minister Lyman Beecher, a staunch defender of Calvinism, and her brother was the Reverend Henry Ward Beecher, whose Brooklyn sermons drew thousands. Catharine's sister, Harriet Beecher Stowe, authored the controversial *Uncle Tom's Cabin*, which initially sold 300,000 copies.

Appropriate to the Beecher clan, Catharine wanted to change the world. When her fiancé was killed in a shipwreck, she decided to never marry and instead dedicate her life to the improvement of society. In her view, an improved society was founded on domesticity and well-ordered homes—all under the guiding force of women. "The family state," Catharine wrote, "is the aptest earthly illustration of the heavenly kingdom, and in it woman is its chief minister."

Catharine Beecher's popular household guides spoke to the concerns of a new generation of modern Christian women, a generation that wanted higher standards of cleanliness, order, and beauty in their homes. These were women who wanted to understand the plumbing and architecture of their houses, the skeletal infrastructure of the body, the chemical breakdown of foods. In short, women who wanted perfection in every aspect of the domestic landscape that was to define their lives. For those females seeking to get the farm mud off their boots and enter the parlors of the middle class, here was an invaluable field guide.

Catharine especially wanted to see improvement among the lower classes migrating to cities and across the chaotic Western frontier. Here, she believed there was much shoddy cooking and housekeeping. Daughters were being raised amid sloth and ignorance and thus were ill prepared to meet their wifely duties. They would pull the nation down, Catharine warned. And so she strove in her schools and her guides to teach these less fortunate how to run a proper home. Efficiency and order were key.

In her domestic manuals, she tended to scold her readers with a voice that I find unbearable and far too similar to admonitions I absorbed early in my life on the importance of strict housekeeping. In Catharine Beecher, we find domestic perfection done in such precise detail that we could never forget it. Here is the dream of an immaculate, perfect home: each drawer and corner ready for inspection, never a dirty dish in the sink, mattresses turned on a monthly schedule. To achieve this dream, Catharine insisted that the mother should become "a self-sacrificing laborer" in her home, and that a woman's "great mission is self-denial."

She was particularly strident on matters of food. "The great object in life to us is not *enjoyment*, but the *formation of right character*," wrote Catharine Beecher in her 1846 *Miss Beecher's Domestic Receipt-Book*. Catharine railed against American

"Proprieties of the Table"

To persons of good-breeding, nothing is more annoying than violations of the conventional proprieties of the table. Reaching over another person's plate; standing up, to reach distant articles, instead of asking to have them passed; using one's own knife and spoon for butter, salt or sugar, when it is the custom of the family to provide separate utensils for the purpose; setting cups with the tea dripping from them, on the table-cloth, instead of the mats or small plates furnished; using the table-cloth instead of the napkins; eating fast, and in a noisy manner; putting large pieces in the mouth; look and eating as if very hungry, or as if anxious to get at certain dishes; sitting at too great a distance from the table, and dropping food; laying the knife and fork on the table-cloth, instead of on the edge of the plate; picking the teeth at the table: all these particulars children should be taught to avoid.

—CATHARINE ESTHER BEECHER and HARRIET BEECHER STOWE
The American Woman's Home, 1869

women for being rotten cooks, for serving sour stringy breads, meats soaked in fat, rancid butter, potatoes that came to the table "like lumps of yellow wax," and indigestible plum puddings that are "boiled into a cannon-ball."

Her receipt book went through fifteen printings, and I have spent many hours wondering why thousands of women spent good money on her writings. Did they suffer from low self-esteem and therefore didn't mind being scolded? Were they, during this reform-minded era, accustomed to being chided into self-improvement? Or did her books sell so well simply because her domestic dream was irresistible? For sure, she had many wonderful tricks. Catharine's guides told women how to build nifty "earth closets" (the predecessor of the modern toilet), how to ingeniously partition their homes for the best use of space, how to organize their kitchens scientifically to save steps and waste (here she was miles ahead of her time), how to make their own picture frames and attractive plant stands, how to build secret storage spaces, how to grow fruit trees, etiquette for the dining room, and how to properly serve fish when the boss came over for dinner.

She was a visionary, but like many visionaries she was obsessed and therefore not always a likable character. Unlike her sister Harriet, Catharine would not stand up against slavery, nor did she support the vote for women. She believed the subordination of women to men was essential to a well-run society. On the other hand, she strove to reduce women's household drudgery and developed new designs for American kitchens that for the first time offered ample workspace and storage. She helped sound alarms about the adulteration of American foods, in particular, the unsanitary state of city milk supplies. She encouraged women to get fresh air, exercise, and use their bodies. She tirelessly promoted women's education and championed the teaching profession to women.

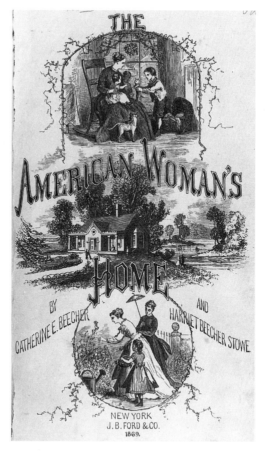

Heavenly home under the Christian woman's care. Title page from the enormously popular domestic manual.

Ironically, though Catharine was a paragon of domesticity, she herself never had a home of her own and probably did not cook much herself. She was the kind of woman who was happiest on the road, lecturing to audiences, traveling from city to city to raise funds for her schools. We can imagine her not in the kitchen but at society parties, cornering the wealthiest industrialist and talking nonstop until he promised a nice big check for her newest school where he pledged to send his eldest daughter as the first pupil. Many believed her a heroine for women.

THE SOUTH AND OTHER FAILINGS OF VIRTUE

The reform-minded cooks—the trailblazing ones anyway—tended to be northern women with firm footing on Yankee soil, usually in New York, Philadelphia, or, even better yet, Boston, that hallowed ground of plain food, righteous morality, and publishing.

Though the northeastern literary ladies may have dominated the cookbook market, their vision was certainly not the prevailing reality in the United States at large. In the epicurean South, for example, cooking, and for that matter most social institutions were shaped by slavery. In the homes of wealthy whites, women in the kitchen were not idealized mothers and wives but black slaves. Intrinsic to the famed "southern hospitality" were groaning tables of savory food—cooked by someone whose freedom had been stolen. The ideal image of womanhood, for the slaveholding plantation wife, was hostess—not cook. Her center of power rested not in the kitchen but in the parlor and the dining room and in her authority over slaves. As mistress, it was her prerogative to be ignorant of cookery if she chose. In contrast to the North, southern food was better and more interesting, as everyone knew. The three first "southern" cookbooks of the nineteenth century—*The Virginia Housewife, The Kentucky Housewife,* and *The Carolina Housewife*—featured nary a word of moral advice, but instead, wonderful recipes for exotic items like gazpacho soup, ice creams, barbecued shotes, and spicy seafood.

All this was rather objectionable to the northern domestic ladies who believed that cookery (preferably plain) was essential to white Christian womanhood. That southern mistresses did not do their own cooking proved beyond a doubt that slavery had corrupted white families. When Harriet Beecher Stowe rocked the

From *The American Woman's Home,* 1869, authored by Catharine Beecher and her sister, Harriet Beecher Stowe. To relieve women's burdens, these famous sisters called for well-organized kitchens—in addition to female self-sacrifice.

To Salt Down Beef to Keep the Year Round

To one hundred pounds of beef, take four quarts of rock salt pounded very fine, four ounces of saltpetre made very fine, four pounds of brown sugar, all well mixed.

Scatter some over the bottom of the barrel, lay down one layer, and over that scatter the proportion of salt belonging to such a portion of the meat, allowing rather the most to top layers. Pack all down very close, and if any scum should rise, sprinkle a pint or more of salt over the top.

—CATHARINE ESTHER BEECHER
Miss Beecher's Domestic Receipt-Book, 1846

nation with her antislavery novel *Uncle Tom's Cabin*, she went through great efforts to show the immorality of the southern table and the southern home. In the free state of Ohio, fugitive slave Eliza is taken in and protected by the good Quaker Rachel, who methodically sorts peaches in her spotless kitchen and presides over the cooking with motherly love. In a Mississippi kitchen, on the other hand, run by an unsupervised slave named Dinah, all is in chaos. Dinah may produce delectable southern fare, but she sits on the kitchen floor and smokes a pipe while dirty dishes pile up. She cannot find the onions or nutmeg because her cupboards are a disaster of old rags, old shoes, tobacco, onions, and yarn. She keeps the rolling pin under her bed and wraps meats in her mistress's best tablecloths.

There were plenty of American women who could not possibly achieve the sort of perfect home life called for by the Beecher sisters or Sarah Josepha Hale. The middle-class "cult of domesticity" was not within reach of slave women, factory girls, farmer's wives who still churned their own butter, the poor, and the growing population of immigrants living in city tenements. It quickly becomes obvious that during the nineteenth century, most American women hardly fit the middle-class Victorian ideals.

Yet, ultimately, these ideals would conquer America, not only in the nineteenth century but well beyond. Much like the Victorians, most contemporary Americans still idealize home as a safe haven in a heartless money-hungry world—under the primary care of an efficient woman (though she may work and her husband may help) with the smell of good food wafting from the oven. We yearn for home to be neat and well ordered, smoothing down life's chaos. Nutrition and fear of disease (as well as misguided dietary advice) remain perhaps the single-most influential force in American food, as newspaper cooking sections regularly link one scientific discovery after the next to what we eat. We learn to cook not from our mothers but from "experts" who host cooking shows and write cookbooks and articles. In the end, the virtuous culinary powerhouses shaped American homes and kitchens and gave us some of the dreams we hold most dear. We listened and learned the lessons well—even if we find it hard to live up to them.

FOOD IS POWER

Virtue may have been a nineteenth-century obsession, but few could agree on exactly what it was—not just in cooking but in the most fundamental aspects of life. The Civil War proved the failings of human virtue to be larger than life itself. It is beyond the scope of this book to discuss the extent of the human wreckage and the depth of suffering the war wrought on men and women of both sides. But it is important to note that as in all wars, women were called on to extend themselves beyond their traditional roles. This war—the bloodiest and most cataclysmic event in American history—would be no different.

Out of necessity, women volunteered as nurses, seamstresses, and cooks in hospitals and military camps, to feed soldiers and help the wounded. They endured hunger and privations and took jobs in munition factories. They carried out secret missions as spies. After the Confederacy surrendered and the fighting stopped, large numbers of American women wanted to continue their volunteer efforts, shifting themselves toward local community causes and charities.

As historian Nancy Cott has written, the creation of "separate spheres" that came with industrialism may have initially kept women out of commerce and jobs, but it backfired in an unexpected way. Women, left alone at home, turned to one another for support and friendship. These bonds of womanhood gave them strength to organize and extend their own influence into church groups,

Temperance Punch

To one gallon water add 4 cups sugar, squeeze and strain juice from one dozen lemons and one half dozen oranges, cut one pineapple into small dice, half fill bowl with cracked ice and pour juice and sugar over, adding pineapple. If fresh pineapple be used, it should be grated—Mrs. G. Berry

—*The W.C.T.U. Cook Book*
published by the Women's Christian
Temperance Union of Wenatchee, Washington

mutual aid organizations, charitable leagues, and women's clubs that ultimately gave American women a stepping stone into public life and careers.

To raise money for their many charitable works, American women often turned to the local charitable cookbook, a greatly underestimated force in American history.

To the best of our knowledge, the first charitable cookbooks were published during the Civil War to raise funds for wounded soldiers, orphans, and widows. From this beginning, they took off with amazing zeal. Charitable cookbooks (also called community cookbooks) helped build American libraries, hospitals, museums, settlement houses, historical societies, homes for the aged and orphans, educational associations, and schools across the country. They turned out to be a profitable financial vehicle for women who needed not just prayers or reformist goals, but cold hard cash to transform the world as they saw fit. "At a time when American women were without full political rights and representation, they found the community cookbook one very effective way to participate in public life of the nation," explains Jan Longone, cookbook expert and curator at the Clements Library in Michigan.

The scope, quirkiness, and simple beauty of these local creations are compelling. Go to your library, and you very well may find some that no expert knows about. What's most wonderful is that they befuddle the historian who wishes to generalize about American food, American women, or American life.

As might be expected, recipes range from treasured regional favorites to the

Members of Christian Commission, 1861–65. During the Civil War, many women threw themselves into charitable work. When the war ended, they shifted their efforts toward local charities and causes— a development that gave rise to a special American tradition: the charitable community cookbook. (Library of Congress.)

unabashedly wretched boiled celery on toast and endlessly overboiled vegetables. Charitable cookbooks give us the messy realities, not the ideals. We are as likely to find elaborate old English-style dishes such as larks roasted on a spit before the fire, or specialties of the Western frontier, like squirrel rolled in corn meal. In terms of politics, charitable cookbooks covered all possible ground, from liberal to conservative, domestic to political, religious to radical. Women's church organizations used their cookbooks to fund missionary efforts overseas, to pay for

Cooking for a Cause

When I wrote the following pages ... I did not think it would be of service to my fellow-creatures, for our suffering soldiers, the sick, the wounded, and the needy.

—MARIA J. MOSS
The Poetical Cookbook, 1864
published for Sanitary Fair, held in
Philadelphia to benefit Civil War victims

What is our work? ... We are working to combat a terrible calamity, or call it as some are pleased to, a disease. Whatever name it takes, whatever disguise it assumes, it is a terrible power in our land, this demon, Intemperance.

—THE LADIES OF THE M.W.C.T.U.
*The Massachusetts Woman's
Temperance Union Cuisine,* 1892

Give us a vote and we will cook
The better for a wide outlook.

—*Washington Women's Cook Book,* 1909
published by the Washington
Equal Suffrage Association

Bibles, bell towers, pews, kneelers, and, one can guess, many, many organs. The more radical female element published cookbooks for causes like workers' rights and suffrage.

By 1880, twenty-eight states had one or perhaps even a few charitable cook-books. By World War I, about three thousand had been published. Some were hand-printed little beauties of just a few pages. Others offered comprehensive cooking compendiums documenting high-brow French recipes, ethnic immi-

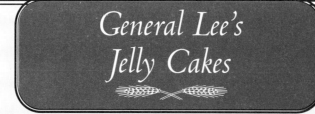

General Lee's Jelly Cakes

Ten eggs; one pound of sugar; half a pound of flour; rind of one lemon grated, and juice of half of one. Make a sponge cake and bake in jelly cake tins.

Then take the whites of two eggs, beaten to a stiff froth, add them to one pound of sugar, the grated rind and juice of one orange, and the juice of half a lemon. Spread this mixture on the cakes before they are perfectly cold, and place one layer on another.

—MRS. B. C. HOWARD
Fifty Years in a Maryland Kitchen, 1873

One of the most beloved cookbooks to document old southern foodways came out of the philanthropic tradition. Fifty Years in a Maryland Kitchen *was published in 1873 to raise money for "certain benevolent undertakings." The author, Mrs. B. C. Howard, a devoted philanthropist, had once raised $200,000 at a Confederate relief fair in Baltimore.*

grant recipes, or regional culinary culture. Cookbooks have been published by a huge number of groups, ranging from Dorcas Societies, United Daughters of Confederacy, Daughters of the American Revolution, and the YMCA to vegetarian groups, domestic science organizations, cemetery associations, and monument committees.

Because the Protestant Church had such an enormous social influence on American women in the nineteenth century, it's not surprising that the vast majority of early community cookbooks usually came from members of Methodist, Lutheran, Presbyterian, Episcopal, and Baptist churches. By the end of the century, Jewish and Catholic groups had their cookbooks too. And by the twentieth century, Asian-American Buddhists joined the tradition as well.

The earliest charitable cookbook known to have been authored by an African-American woman was the 1910 *Federation Cookbook: A Collection of Tested*

Recipes, Contributed by the Colored Women of the State of California. Though African-American women published fewer charitable cookbooks during the nineteenth century, it's important to note that according to one scholar's estimates, by 1850 there were at least two hundred African-American mutual aid organizations in the country's major cities, totaling 13,000 to 15,000 members. These societies embarked on a range of philanthropic and political activities: they built schools, libraries, orphan homes, public health clinics, hospitals, shelters, and churches. Many organized against slavery. Based on handbills and advertisements in African-American newspapers from the nineteenth century, we know, for example, that "The Ladies (of color)" in Frankfort, Kentucky, made "Ice Creams, Cakes, Lemonades, Jellies, Fruits, Nuts" for "benevolent purposes" in 1847. We know of an apple dumpling dinner given at the Bethel A.M.E. church in San Francisco in 1870 and a blazing pudding festival in 1879. Cooking was always a way for black American women to raise funds and gather community together.

We can't possibly know how much money charitable cookbooks have raised throughout history. In 1990, however, the Tabasco Company of Louisiana established a national award program to recognize this distinct cookbook genre. Winners of the Tabasco "Hall of Fame" award alone (charitable cookbooks selling

African-American women organized themselves into hundreds of benevolent organizations such as this one. These ladies were probably free black women living in Frankfort, Kentucky. (Clements Library, University of Michigan.)

FAIR.

The Ladies (of color) of the town of Frankfort propose giving a FAIR, at the house of Mrs. RILLA HARRIS, (*alias*, Simpson,) on Thursday evening next, for benevolent purposes, under the superintendence of Mrs. Rilla Harris.

All the delicacies of the season will be served up in the most palatable style----such as *Ice Creams, Cakes, Lemonades, Jellies, Fruits, Nuts, &c. &c.*

It is hoped, as the proceeds are to be applied to benevolent purposes, that the citizens generally will turn out and aid in the enterprise.

JULY 6, 1847.

more than 100,000 copies) have collectively raised more than $29 million—and, no, this is not a typo.

Because of the decidedly local nature of the best dishes (good cooking generally comes from locally grown ingredients), the women who compiled community cookbooks offered a great service by spreading, maintaining, and ultimately documenting the regional folk life and character of each state.

Scrapple means little in Maine or California. But in South-Central Pennsylvania, near Lancaster, it tells of the land itself, of stunningly green farmlands established on the wilderness by German immigrants, who put in place their orderly farming life, their love of meat, and ancient memories of pot puddings from Germany. In 1887, *The Parish Cookery Book of the Ladies Aid Society of St. Peter's Church* in Hazelton, Pennsylvania, helped record this history with a lovely "Deutsch" recipe provided by one Mrs. M. Bright.

In some cases, a charitable cookbook is the first published culinary work we have for a given state, as in the case of *The First Texas Cookbook* in 1883. I sadly report that the ladies of the Presbyterian Church of Houston did not include any recipes from the Mexicans or Indians who had lived there long before them. But they did include recipes using locally harvested figs, pecans, and peanuts that grew

Scrapple

Take one hogshead and the liver of one hog, boil the head until the meat drops from the bone, boil the liver one-half hour, chop both very fine, and return to the kettle, taking care to strain all the small bones from the liquid. Season highly with black or cayenne pepper, salt to taste, sweet marjoram, quarter pound of ground coriander seed. Boil about five minutes, then add three parts corn meal and one part buckwheat.

—MRS. M. BRIGHT
*The Parish Cookery Book of the Ladies Aid Society
of St. Peter's Church,* 1887

Still enjoyed today by many Pennsylvania Dutch.

Ladies of St. Thomas Church, Bath, New York, circa 1895, selling cakes and treats to raise funds. (Roughwood Collection.)

so well in the hot Texas sun. Under "Preparation of Figs for Market," readers are told that "Sheets are held under the trees, clear of the ground, and the fruit shaken into them." Whether or not this was practical, it is a lovely image just the same.

Perhaps as telling as the recipes and causes are the advertisements, which the women procured to finance printing and distribution costs. In this way, community cookbooks reveal the fabric of American life and its growing consumer culture. Ads for the newest ovens were popular, but there were also ones for corsets, Victorian furniture, groceries delivered by horse, and many health potions such as "Crosby's Vitalized Phos-phites (Composed of the Nerve-giving Principles of the Ox-Brain and the Embryo of the Wheat and Oat)."

Women had to go out and sell the advertising space, deal with the printers, distribute the books, and collect money. With these funds, they ran their volunteer organizations and projects like businesses, paving new roads for themselves. Earlier in the century, cookery had confined them to the kitchen. Now, it was possible for women to use cooking to meet their own ends—transforming the world as they saw fit. During the nineteenth century, women changed cookery, and in the process, cookery transformed women.

Chapter 5

A Woman's West

*I*f you were a Lakota Sioux woman living on the Northern Great Plains during the 1860s, nothing could have seemed so foreign to you as your first vision of a homesteader's wife standing enclosed in a fenced yard, feeding her hens. How strange the invader looked with her hair pulled in a tight bun, her puffy blouse chokingly high on her neck, and that starched white apron tied around her waist. How repellent her daily habit of pulling the dirty teats of cows for that repulsive substance called milk.

From the homesteader's perspective, the reverse view would be equally upsetting. The Yankee wife had heard that the Sioux women butchered buffalo. How horrified she would be to witness the common practice after the hunt, when the woman's hand reached into the creature's belly and pulled forth the intestines and liver, still warm, for her children and friends to eat raw.

Hundreds of miles south, similar encounters occurred. Presbyterian missionary women came to the "new country" of New Mexico to bring true Christianity and education to the housewives of these Spanish villages. Much to their disapproval, the Spanish women sat on the floor rather than on chairs like ladies. They prepared chile sauces that made the skin flush and heated the senses much more than could possibly be healthful or civilized.

Nothing makes the "other" suddenly seem more "other" than the sight of her

Hispanic girl in front of house with *ristras* (strings of dried chile peppers), New Mexico. (Prudence Clark Collection, Menaul Historical Library.)

putting something we believe repellent into her mouth. We have all felt this visceral revulsion at one time or other. And yet, our fear of alien food is somewhat baffling considering that as a species, human beings have evolved as opportunistic eaters, adapting our diets to wildly different environments and circumstances all the world over. Beyond the basic nutritional requirements, you'll never find scientific agreement on a single correct biological human diet designed by nature—on whether it should or shouldn't include roasted bugs, raw entrails, beans, rice, whale blubber, or cheese. So what is at the root of this readiness to quickly exert our own superiority over others, and why is it located within our stomachs?

In the 1840s the U.S. government and its citizens set out to claim the western part of the continent as its own. The movement west was not a cautious or incremental one but a feverish thing that swept deliriously across the landscape in a rush of dreams, hopes, backbreaking labors, gold fever, broken lives, disease, and destruction. Within less than fifty years, America extended its boundaries across twenty-five hundred miles west and southwest and dug its legacy into the very earth—in gold mines, transcontinental railroad tracks, the graves of Indians, and the wagon wheel trails that carried the aspirations of a quarter-million homesteaders mile after mile across the plains and cragged mountains to the fertile warm land near the Pacific Ocean.

Most American citizens considered the "frontier" to be a vacant, wild place where the savage should be civilized so that the United States could achieve its manifest destiny. In ancient forests, Americans saw timber. In mountains, they saw precious metals. Along pristine beaches of the Pacific, they saw the potential for great ports. On the Great Plains, they saw the nation's breadbasket, waiting to be tilled and made productive with seeds of wheat.

Of course, the West was not vacant at all. Hundreds of thousands of diverse Indians lived there with ancestral roots dating back millennia. Hispanics in California and New Mexico had farmed and ranched for generations. When the Americans came, the frontier became a landscape of human diversity.

In this meeting place, Western women made their lives—coexisting, clashing, and intermingling. To the already complex mix of Indians and Hispanics would come not only the bonnet-headed Anglo-Saxon farmwives but also Irish immigrant girls, former slaves, Eastern Europeans, and Asian picture brides. They were not all hard-suffering pioneer wives. Many worked as entrepreneurs, servants, cooks, ranchers, farmers, bakers, missionaries, and prostitutes—just to name a few of the many occupations. They lived not just on isolated farmhouses but in mining and logging camps, in polygamous Mormon communities, and in growing towns and cities.

After language, the greatest symbol of their differences was food. Because women controlled much of the food and cookery for their own groups, they became at times an especially potent symbol of the alien "other." Women could open the doors to new unions by inviting strangers to trade food or eat at their tables. On the other hand, they could choose to keep the lines drawn, stubbornly preparing their own traditional dishes, as if to say, "We eat this way because this is *who we are*, which is different from *who you are*." Or "We eat this way because *this is the food that comes from our land*." Or "We eat this way because *we are better than you*."

This drawing of lines and borders and fences around land and food tells an important part of the story of the American West. The fences around chickens and homesteads, the fences around ranchers' cattle lands, the borders around reservations, the fences around gold mines in the Indian land of the Black Hills, and the imaginary lines drawn in the desert above Mexico.

The claim to land was deeply bound up with the claim to food as well as the claim to religion. For native women, cooking was inextricably connected to a spiritual view of nature. For Hispanic women, cookery was crucial to the rituals and church celebrations of Catholic village life. For the American newcomers, properly prepared food was a reflection of civilization and true Christianity (i.e., Protestantism) in a savage wilderness. From these conflicts came many moral struggles concerning the appropriate way humans should get their food and prepare it—and from here deeper questions about what women should be and do.

When the U.S. government encouraged the mass extermination of millions of buffalo so the land could be used for American farms and cattle ranches, it was not merely greed at work but an unshakable cultural assumption that agriculture and husbandry were morally superior to the hunting-and-gathering lives of the natives who lived on the Plains. All good rural women were to be at home, baking light yeasty bread in European-style farmhouses, not following their men on the hunt and certainly not sleeping in tepees and hanging bison to dry in the sun.

As I have already described, the mid to late nineteenth century had bestowed the cult of true womanhood on American women—for better or worse. With no compunction, Americans imposed these ideals on Indian and Hispanic women who had already lived in the West for centuries. This made the collision of foods and women all the more intense and powerful in a vast landscape full of hunger and desire for the elusive thing called home.

It takes one brief visit to the borderlands to be reminded that the American Southwest once belonged to Mexico. This feeling comes on immediately as you drive through the bare, rugged mountains and see the treeless earth. You sense it in the dry air against your skin and your own sudden thirst for rain. The memory of Mexico is in the names of streets and cities and on the tongues of people who speak Spanish and love chile peppers, tortillas, *empanaditas, biscochitos,* tamales, and mole sauces made with ground chocolate and seeds. It is in the licorice scents of anise baked into yeasted breads.

Despite what immigration authorities may say, Mexicans are not really aliens in the United States. They were here first, and their northward trails across the borderlands are ancient ones that go back in prehistory to the paleoindians who

Taos, New Mexico, vicinity, 1939. A Spanish American tests the temperature of her earthen oven by measuring how long it takes to scorch a piece of wool. PHOTO BY RUSSELL LEE. *(Library of Congress.)*

"A Good Pinch of Anise Seed"

She mustn't dawdle on Christmas eve.

Doña Paula took out as much dough as both hands could hold, placing it in another pan while she said to herself, "This will be enough for molletes, the sweet rolls."

With a deft hand she kneaded the bread dough and soon was shaping it into beautiful loaves of bread. She patted them softly and laid them side by side in the pans. Then she covered them with a snow-white cloth.

"Leave the molletes to me," said Señá Martina. "I like to make sweet rolls."

Señá Martina had no patience with those who used measuring cups and spoons, worrying for fear they would put in an ounce too much of this or that. Her hands were so used to the amounts that without thinking she broke four eggs, beat them thoroughly and handed two handfuls of sugar and a good pinch of anise seed. She reached into the lard pail and took out a handful of fat for her mollete dough. She kneaded and kneaded until the dough was carefully mixed; then with a knife she cut a cross in the center of the dough, reciting Jesus y Crus, (Jesus and His Cross) for good luck in her baking.

—FABIOLA CABEZA DE BACA GILBERT
The Good Life, 1949

migrated down the western coast of North America to Central and South America and then back north again.

In the sixteenth century, the Spaniards followed similar trails. After conquering the Aztecs and creating a Spanish colony in Mexico, they crossed the desert and traveled north in search of more land and wealth. In 1598, fortune hunter Juan de Oñate and a band of Franciscan priests crossed a vast desert and traveled fifteen hundred miles north to found the town of Sante Fe. There, Oñate planted his Spanish flag in the dirt. Over the coming centuries, Spain continued to take northern territories, founding settlements in California, Texas, and many other outposts to the north.

New Mexico was the largest and the oldest of these colonies. Isolated from both Mexico and the eastern United States by deserts, mountains, and a great many miles, the region was left alone for more than two hundred years, with little outside influence. Here, a rural society flourished—a society of Catholic farmers and ranchers who developed close ties to the earth and to the Pueblo Indians, but kept their cultural memories of sixteenth-century Spain.

The Mexicans won independence, throwing off the rule of Spain in 1821, but their new sovereign nation would not be left in peace. In 1846, American troops instigated the Mexican-American War by invading Mexico City and plundering the countryside and cities along the way. There was no justification other than Manifest Destiny. The war ended with the humiliating Treaty of Guadalupe Hidalgo, in which Mexico had no choice but to give up California, New Mexico, Arizona, Texas, and parts of Nevada, Utah, and Colorado—some 1.2 million square miles of land, half of its national territory. Nearly eighty thousand Spanish-speaking people suddenly found themselves living north of this new border, an imaginary fence arbitrarily erected along the Rio Grande.

Doña Paula and Señá Martina are fictional characters. But in their cooking pots, they hold the keys to this past—a past that, by the 1940s, author Fabiola Cabeza de Baca Gilbert feared would vanish forever under the weight of modern American life. Using the cookbook as a form of protest, she wrote these women into being along with their folklore and recipes (notably in English). Though this scene takes place in the early twentieth century, there is little doubt that the cooks, Doña Paula and her servant Señá Martina, are women whose souls linger in the nineteenth century—daughters of Spanish and Indian legacy, a world of pueblos, outdoor ovens, sheep herders in mountain villages, and rancheros who could still remember buffalo hunts on the plains.

For the holiest night of the year, Doña Paula and Señá Martina baked the foods of this heritage. In addition to sweet breads called *molletes*, they rolled out *biscochitos* (sugar cookies) and *empanaditas* (pastries filled with savory meat and spices). Their tamales had been carefully assembled the day before and waited frozen on the back porch, ready for the oven. Meanwhile, a pot of posole, seasoned with chile peppers, bubbled on the stove. A bit later, the two women would take a break from their cooking, put on their shawls and clean the church for Midnight Mass.

Theirs was a communal village life where during the fall, villagers gathered in the evening to help one another string chiles for the winter. Where families bundled up together and headed for the hills to collect the annual harvest of wild pinyon nuts during the first snows. Where servant and mistress worked side by side to make sprouted-wheat pudding for Lent. Where the entire village came together for frequent Catholic festivals, celebrations of patron saints, religious holidays, and weekly mass. According to Fabiola, here were the secrets of the good life, long before the Anglos came—secrets held in the kitchens of old women like Doña Paula and Señá Martina.

Before we leave them, let's take a look at, or better yet, try out, their recipe for *molletes*, with the cross of their Catholic faith slashed into the dough.

Immediately after the Mexican-American War, only small numbers of people from the United States traveled to New Mexico, which was then considered an alien

Molletes
(Sweet Rolls for Catholic Christmas Eve)

2 yeast cakes [or 2 packets]	1 t salt
½ c luke warm water	1½ c milk
7 T fat (traditionally lard)*	2 beaten eggs
1 c sugar	2 t anise seed
6 to 8 c flour	

Soak yeast in lukewarm water. Place milk in pan on top of stove. Add fat, salt, and sugar and leave until fat is melted. Cool to lukewarm. Add yeast, mixing well. To this mixture add the beaten eggs and anise seed. Add flour, gradually, until a medium soft dough results. Knead lightly. Let rise until double in bulk. Shape into round rolls. Let rise for 1 hour. Bake in hot oven. Slice and butter to serve with chocolate, coffee, or tea.

—FABIOLA CABEZA DE BACA GILBERT
The Good Life, 1949

Since there are few Señá Martinas left among us who can make bread without measuring a thing, Fabiola provided precise directions so that Hispanic New Mexican foodways would live on. I have

sort of planet surrounded by pagan Indians and slightly less pagan Catholics.

Early on, New Mexican women shocked the Victorian sensibilities of Anglo newcomers. They sat on floors, smoked *cigarettas,* and even gambled. They let their babies run about naked and were astoundingly free with their own bodies, wearing only loose, low-cut blouses, short petticoats (which they'd readily hitch up to their knees in order to paddle across a creek), and *rabosas*—long fringed shawls of bright colors—which, as one observer explained, were used to conceal babies busy at "I shant say at what business."

New Mexican women did much of their work outdoors in groups. Excluding labor-intensive dishes for feasts and holidays, their diets for the most part were

---

adapted her recipe only slightly. In her original work, she first gives a recipe for plain rolls and then tells her readers how to turn them into sweet rolls. I have combined directions for simplification. The quantity here is enough to feed a small village at feast time, about thirty-six small rolls.

These are delicious and worth the effort. You can follow Fabiola's recipe, but if you are not famil-iar with the basic principles of bread making, kneading, or how yeasted dough should feel to the hand, consult a mentor or one of the many books available on the subject. After a few failures, I discovered some tricks that make all the difference.

- *Be sure to beat the eggs very well and vigorously mix them into the dough.*
- *When Fabiola says to add flour gradually, she really means it: first add 2 cups of the flour and beat very well for 3 to 5 minutes. Use your electric mixer. Add the rest of the flour a little at a time, using a spoon or your hands at the end.*
- *Knead the dough for 8 minutes, or until it is smooth and elastic. Place in a greased bowl and cover tightly with plastic wrap or a damp dish towel. Put in a warm (but not hot) place to rise.*
- *After it has doubled in bulk, punch it down and form your rolls. Be sure to cover them with wax paper for the second rise.*
- *These rolls go in a 350-degree oven for about 12 to 15 minutes, depending on their size.*

*A few words about lard. Authentic historic Mexican and southwestern cooking often relies on lard, which Americans have come to stigmatize. If you prefer, both of these recipies work perfectly well with shortening or butter, or a combination of both. If you're interested in authenticity, see the Resources for Historic Cooking section for a mail-order source for lard without preservatives.

Theresita Suaso returning from the river with a tub of laundry, wearing what Anglo Americans then considered a low-cut blouse and short skirt, 1853. WATERCOLOR BY ALEXANDER BARCLAY. *(Courtesy The Bancroft Library, University of California, Berkeley.)*

simple and nutritious: whole-grain breads, fruits, vegetables, and strips of sun-dried meat, dried chile peppers, and beans. They dressed up for special events called *fandangos* (dance parties) that were attended by all members of their villages.

Hispanic villagers appeared as poor peasants to many American outsiders. But as historian Janet LeCompte has noted, simple dress, simple diet, and simple homes left New Mexicans more time for rest, play, and participation in their communities. Because of geographic isolation, material goods were in extremely short supply, even for the fairly well-to-do. There were few linens to fuss over, no carpets or draperies to worry about, no furniture to polish, no flatware to clean each day, no tables to wipe off again and again. Most homes were two-room mud structures with little corner fireplaces for cooking. At midday, women even had time to take a siesta—unthinkable in the States.

Hispanic New Mexico was hardly a promised land for women's equal rights. The Catholic Church saw women as subordinate to men, and so had the Mexican and Spanish governments. But Hispanic women had a special and respected role in communal life and the public affairs of the church, and they also had more legal rights than American women. They were allowed to retain property they brought into a marriage. They could work in business under their own names as sole traders, and they inherited, by law, half of their husband's properties.

This lasted until the 1880s. When the railroads arrived, Americans came in great numbers in search of new lives and fortunes in homesteads, lumber mills, commercial agriculture, coal mines, and other businesses. These Anglos—as they came to be called—generally held the unwavering conviction that Americans possessed the correct social order, and quickly imposed their laws and social codes on the locals.

Pipian

Grind together a handful of roasted pumpkin seed nuts, handful of roasted white corn, and two red chiles from which seeds and veins have been scraped. Grind into fine powder, dissolve in cup of water and cook until it thickens. Fry quail or spring chicken and add to this gravy. Cover and simmer until meat is tender. Add salt.

—CLEOFAS M. JARAMILLO
The Genuine New Mexico Tasty Recipes, 1939

To balance out the European influence of the Christmas rolls, here's a dish that traveled north from Mexico, along the same routes as the Spanish colonists and Mexican migrants. Mole and pipian sauces go back to the Aztecs at least, deriving from the ancient Indian practices of binding together sauces with seeds and nuts. Today, pipian is eaten throughout much of the United States. Cleofas Jaramillo was, like Fabiola Cabeza de Baca Gilbert, a folklorist and great defender of traditional Hispanic life. However, unlike Fabiola's recipes, hers seem intentionally vague. She wants not only to pay homage—in English—to Hispanic foods of New Mexico but also to keep her methods secret. She was very critical of writers who wrote unauthentic Hispanic recipes for an English-speaking American audience.

Americans were especially bothered by the communal nature of Hispanic life, the villagers' habit of sharing unfenced lands for grazing and their custom of paying taxes with bushels of corn or livestock rather than cash. They were critical of women who pooled their labor to plaster their homes, bake bread, butcher animals, spin wool, and cook for public events. Their religion was troubling as well. Hispanics were under the influence of feudal "dons" and Catholicism's mystical *padres*, who were deeply distrusted by the staunchly Protestant American majority. In general, there was a sense that New Mexicans resisted the American ideal of progress.

When the U.S. government came, it confiscated unfenced lands from ranchers and farmers and declared them "public domain," making them available to

Frijoles (Beans)

2 cups frijoles (Mexican beans)   ⅓ pound salt pork

Pick beans carefully and soak overnight. Drain and cover with fresh cold water. Add salt pork, boil slowly until tender, 4 to 6 hours. If possible, soak at simmering temperature all day. As water boils away, add boiling water; never cold.

Frijoles may be served just as they come from the pot. If a larger quantity is cooked, they may be used the second day with chile.

This quantity will make ten servings.

—ERNA FERGUSSON
Mexican Cookbook, 1934

Use pinto beans. If you don't like salt pork, traditional methods also call for a little lard (fried in flour) or fried bacon, added to the pot at the end of cooking. I like using low-fat nitrite-free bacon at the end. I also add salt to the beans cooking in the pot.

the railroad and homesteaders. Within a few decades, 80 percent of Spanish land grants in New Mexico were taken over by the Anglo Americans. Hispanic men and women soon found themselves transformed from landowners into low-paid laborers, conveniently so for the many new American enterprises needing workers in agriculture, mining, and timber. New Mexican women lost many of the legal rights they had been guaranteed under Spanish civil law. Missionaries arrived shortly thereafter, hoping to civilize the natives beginning with home economics lessons in the kitchen. Local women selectively accepted wood-burning stoves and some American-style foods and manners.

And yet, despite 150 years of American influences, Hispanic women throughout the Southwest continue to cook foods that bridge past to present—frijoles, chiles, tortillas, anise-scented breads, tamales, and posoles—amidst a landscape that insists on a connection to Mexico.

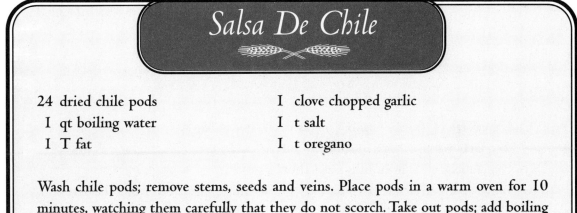

Salsa De Chile

24 dried chile pods
1 qt boiling water
1 T fat

1 clove chopped garlic
1 t salt
1 t oregano

Wash chile pods; remove stems, seeds and veins. Place pods in a warm oven for 10 minutes, watching them carefully that they do not scorch. Take out pods; add boiling water and let soak until peppers are soft. With hands work chile pods until pulp is separated from skins. Remove skins.

Place fat in skillet, fry chopped garlic; add chile pulp and seasonings. Cook for 5 minutes.

—FABIOLA CABEZA DE BACA GILBERT
The Good Life, 1949

Many hot sauces are now available in the market, but most of these are overpowered by tomato or vinegar. This has a wonderful smokey taste that is pure chile pepper. There are many varieties of dried New Mexico chiles, ranging from mild to killer hot. (See Resources for Historic Cooking section for mail-order information.) If you have sensitive skin, coat your hands in olive oil before peeling or wear gloves.

Adela Amador writes a food column in *New Mexico Magazine,* blending old Hispanic and Pueblo recipes with modern tastes. Somehow when Adela fuses ingredients, her foods remain honest. She has lived near the Sandia Mountains most of her life and vividly remembers the countrified ways of her girlhood, back when her father bartered with Pueblo Indians for corn and squash, when people sang Spanish songs on New Year's Eve, when long hours were spent roasting and peeling chiles, and when a young girl had to prove her worth by perfectly cleaning the honeycomb lining of the cow's stomach with a paring knife.

Adela Amador's Posole

(Serves 12)

½ package of frozen posole (comes in 32-ounce bag)
2 quarts water
2½ to 3 pounds pork, cut in bite-sized chunks
8 to 10 roasted, peeled (seeds removed) green chiles (probably from the freezer), chopped
1 medium onion, chopped
1 clove garlic, chopped
1 or 2 16-ounce cans stewed tomatoes (depending on how hot the chile is and how hot one likes it)

- Boil posole about 2 hours until it pops.
- Add pork, onion and garlic. Boil until meat is cooked, about 1 hour, on medium heat.
- Add chile and tomatoes, and season with salt to taste.

The tomatoes cut the "hotness" of the chile (acid neutralizes the base), and gives a tangy flavor. Chicken also makes good posole and is often used in place of pork.

—ADELA AMADOR
Southwest Flavor, 2000

Adela tells me that pork shoulder works best and canned or dried hominy is fine. (See Resources for Historic Cooking section in the back of the book for mail-order sources.)

This is her favorite recipe for *posole* (hominy) stew, and it is traditional for New Year's Eve. In the old days, Adela's family made their own posole. She remembers freezing her hands under the outdoor water pump to rinse away the slack lime. Today, she highly recommends using canned or frozen hominy.

After winning the Mexican-American War in 1846, the United States set its sights on taking the rest of the West, and this required moving natives out of the way. Though the government had been pushing Indians off their lands since colonial times, a major turning point came in the 1870s when it declared Indians "wards of the government." This was legal justification for ordering—with the threat of war and death—native people onto reservations, often in barren, remote places, away from the natural resources they had used for their traditional subsistence.

In return for the tribal lands, the government promised to provide Indians with rations of clothing, shelter, and food, reducing the most self-sufficient people of the continent to dependence.

Government food allotments featured wheat flour, lard, beef, coffee, and sugar and inflicted one of the most dramatic dietary shifts in history—with grave health consequences. After millennia of eating diets low in sugar, the rapid change to reservation diets and American processed foods created disproportionately high diabetes rates among Indians. As devastating as this change was, even worse was the fact that many of the rations never even got to the Indians because of corruption and mismanagement by Indian agents in charge of the reservations. "Our poor children are crying to us for food, and we are powerless to help the little ones," explained the Paiute Indian advocate Sarah Winnemucca Hopkins. When and if food arrived, it was often second rate, featuring rancid meat and dairy products, which so many had a hard time digesting. And so the Indians went through an excruciating period of severe hunger, misery, and malnourishment during the late nineteenth-century reservation era.

While some native leaders were willing to accommodate the Americans, others—including the Comanches and Navajo of the Southwest, the Cheyenne, Crows, the Mandans, the Assiniboines, Sioux, and Kiowa of the Plains, the Seminole of Florida, and the Nez Perce of present-day Idaho—resisted government appeals to give up their lands, usually with tragic consequences. When they faced U.S. military might, often there was no choice other than death.

The only time we put up tepees was the place where buffalo calves used to be found. We camped on the prairie by the river. The next day we digged camas [a root vegetable] and baked it in the ground. That is the old Indian way of cooking it. To be good, camas must remain in the earth overnight. It was still in the pits the next morning when the soldiers charged our camp. We were sleeping when they came. Many women who had camas were killed. Their camas was left where they had baked it.

—recollected in 1926 by Pe-nah-we-non-mi,
a Nez Perce woman
Nez Perce Women in Transition

Those who weren't killed fled U.S. troops, leaving their camas smoldering in underground ovens. The scene was prophetic of the tragedies that would come to the lives of Indians. In this case, it was Nez Perce tribal land that the government wanted—the land where women had dug camas and other roots since "time immemorial." The land of their subsistence—their food, clothing, and shelter—was located in the spectacular mountains, canyons, and alpine meadows of Idaho, Montana, and eastern Oregon.

To better understand the meaning of this scene, it helps to know more about the camas that these women were roasting beside their tents before they were killed. Camas root is a vegetable prized by Northwest Indians for its starchy bulb, which women have dug for generations using fire-hardened sticks. Camas bulbs grow in marshy meadows in elevations over three thousand feet. Lewis and Clark were astonished at the abundance of camas growing all over the Northwest and were deeply impressed by the skill and productivity of Nez Perce women in gathering and preparing them.

The Nez Perce were hunters and gatherers of the inland plateau country who traditionally lived on the seasonal rounds of salmon, wild game (mainly bear, elk, and deer), plus a variety of wild botanical treasures, including roots and berries. Women held a high status as providers of food, contributing 30 to 40 percent of the total Nez Perce diet in the form of gathered plants.

Dense, filling, and slowly digested, camas provided a valued source of complete protein and calcium. But what made them especially coveted was their sweetness. When roasted over long periods in underground pits, their starches converted to vanilla-scented sugars, creating a beloved treat sometimes called "Indian candy."

Annie Yellowbear, a Nez Perce, with camas roots, 1890.
(National Park Services, Nez Perce National Historic Park.)

But camas were about much more than good nutrition.

"Camas are a gift of the creator," explains Diane Mallickan, Nez Perce Indian and ranger with the Nez Perce National Historic Park. "You didn't just go out and dig. You had to be invited. You had to be trained. You had to be spiritually prepared. The gatherers had special personal relationships with the plants."

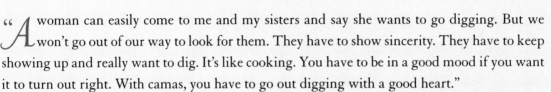

"A Connection between the Woman and the Root"

"A woman can easily come to me and my sisters and say she wants to go digging. But we won't go out of our way to look for them. They have to show sincerity. They have to keep showing up and really want to dig. It's like cooking. You have to be in a good mood if you want it to turn out right. With camas, you have to go out digging with a good heart."

Janet Black Eagle lives in a little town called Kooskia on the Nez Perce Indian Reservation in Idaho, which has a population of about three thousand. She, along with a small group of perhaps a couple hundred, still goes out and digs camas each summer. She learned from her mother's family, and her principal tool is a digging stick with a bone handle at one end and a sharp skinny metal spike at the other. She is a Presbyterian who mixes Christianity with native spiritual practices, and perhaps this is why she is willing to talk to me when other more traditional Nez Perce women wouldn't. After all the losses and the pain, why should they reveal sacred ways to me?

Janet sees things differently. When she and I spoke by telephone, it was December and snows covered the reservation, but she still had jars filled with camas, roasted and preserved from last summer. Her family always goes to a place called Mussel Shell. "Way up in the high country," she explained. "There's a stream that runs along side of it, and the meadow is all tall grass, bordered by old trees." The land is an open grazing area controlled by the U.S. Forest Service, which Janet says helps to keep cows from tromping over the camas fields.

After two weeks of digging, Janet's family brings the roots home, cleans them, roasts them in the family roasting pit for two days, and then stores them in quart-size jars. Last year, they accumulated twenty-four jars of camas during a period of about two weeks of digging.

In reverence to these plants, the Nez Perce held annual "first roots" religious ceremonies in summer and honored these roots during other religious occasions throughout the year. (For those who still practice the traditional Nez Perce religion, these ceremonies continue today.)

In the early nineteenth century, the Nez Perce had been on good terms with Americans and Europeans. This changed immediately when a band of miners found some gold on their tribal lands in 1860. Reneging on its 1855 promise to

Janet tells me she is very worried about the diabetes rate, which is quite high among her Nez Perce tribe. She believes women can play a crucial role in reversing this trend by leading their families back to the traditional ways of eating. This has been a mission for her. Some years ago, Janet worked for the Nez Perce Tribe on a nutrition project, teaching native women how to dig and cook camas. It was work she loved, but because she lived sixty-seven miles from the tribal headquarters, her job as a nutritionist conflicted with her responsibilities as a single parent, so she gave it up.

Today she works as a supervisor in a casino, hoping to avoid the graveyard shift because she heats her home with wood and needs to be home at night not just to watch her children but also to put logs on the fire so her place will stay warm. In her voice, there is an unmistakable twinge of weariness, the struggle between earning a living and raising kids in the modern world while still keeping connected to her traditional Nez Perce ways.

Despite these stresses, she remains a steadfast "plant person," someone who puts her faith in the nutritional, spiritual, and healing power of roots. "I've always loved the elders. When I was a kid, I wasn't always doing what the other kids were doing. I was spending time with the elders learning these things." She tells a story about a sister who wanted to get off drugs and alcohol. Janet gave her *cous*—another traditionally important root—to help quell the pain of withdrawal.

"The women are such a backbone. When a woman pulls that root out for the first time and sees the value of it and how it is a part of the culture and the tradition . . . there's just a connection between the woman and the root. Her ancestors before her probably pulled roots from the same spot. Our people lived on this, and now they can go back and live on it again."

protect Nez Perce lands, the federal government asked the tribal authorities to give up six million acres and move to a reservation one-tenth the size. When the Nez Perce nation resisted, many years of tensions and violent encounters followed. In 1877, U.S. troops attacked the Nez Perce and to their shock were beaten badly, losing one-third of their soldiers. Knowing that retaliation was sure to come, Nez Perce Chief Joseph then began an extraordinary military retreat, leading a loyalist band of 750 tribal members on a journey of eighteen hundred miles through canyons and mountains, all the while pursued by government troops. At the end of the three-month-long chase, the Nez Perce found themselves surrounded by U.S. troops. They were defeated while their camas were roasting, as described earlier.

After losing many lives, Chief Joseph finally surrendered with his much quoted speech: "I will fight no more forever." His band was then captured and sent to live in the alien climates of Kansas and Oklahoma, in malaria-ridden camps where great numbers died of disease.

The camas fields of the Nez Perce were then fenced by homesteaders, trod on by miners, destroyed by plows, and planted with wheat. Nez Perce women began cooking from government rations. Many gave up digging camas, losing their connection with the sacred roots.

From the U.S. point of view, the biggest problem with hunter-gatherers was that their wild foods required so much undisturbed land on which to flourish. The seasonal rounds of hunting and gathering sent dozens of nations far and wide over vast territories in the Great Basin deserts, the rocky mountain forests, the plains and prairies, the inland plateaus of the Northwest, and the edge of the Pacific Coast. To the Americans, it was simply unthinkable that such great swaths of nature would be left alone. They could not comprehend that the Indians had rights to these lands, some of which they used only for a few months each year during brief hunting or fishing seasons when certain animals or fish were migrating, or when certain plants or berries were ripe. And more to the point—how could a people claim to own soil that they hadn't tilled? Let's remember that Americans of the nineteenth century were deeply attached to the Jeffersonian idea that private landownership was essential to democracy. A nation of landowning yeomen offered a form of protection against tyranny and aristocracy. Private property—a concept that did not exist among Indians—was at the spiritual core of the growing American nation.

It became official federal policy to end the wild, roaming ways of hunting-and-gathering tribes. Not only did the U.S. government wish to settle the natives on reservations, but also it insisted on trying to change them. By the 1880s, the government moved an estimated 300,000 Indians (including Alaskans) onto U.S. reservations and subjected them to aggressive "civilization" efforts, a nineteenth-century term for total and complete erasure of native cultures. This project sought to transform hunters and gatherers into farmers and farmers' wives. It also required that natives convert to Protestant Christianity, American education, "citizen's dress," English language, and rationed American foods.

The government entrusted Protestant and Catholic missionaries with a large chunk of the "civilization" effort, chopping up the map and assigning tribes to various churches. Catholics got some. Presbyterians got some. Methodists got others. With amazing righteousness, they set about to radically alter centuries of traditions in which women had held significant roles of power complementary to that of men. They simply did not, could not, and would not comprehend that hard physical work out-of-doors could possibly be a source of respect and power

At a mission school dining table, Alaska, 1914. Note the sign on the wall says "Please do not speak Eskimo." (Courtesy Marquette University Archives.)

for women. And so came a concerted federal effort to recast Indian women into the American-style, middle-class housewife—morally elevated but dependent on a husband. Indian women were to be contained inside their homes, clad in calico, baking and cooking on wood-burning stoves, and organized by individual nuclear family rather than the tight bonds of clan.

Most irksome to the missionaries was the native inclination to the "wandering life." After all, imagine the freedom women had in going off with sisters and girl-friends to dig roots or gather berries for several weeks with no men around to supervise, or the all-woman camping excursions into mountains to collect pinyon nuts. These sorts of liberties were entirely foreign and inappropriate from the reformers' point of view. They saw little nutritional benefit in the plants gathered by women. And so in the name of God and Christian values, missionaries preached against the power of berries, roots, pine nuts, wild rice, and ramps, the wild onions of spring. They scorned hunting and fishing among men as a form of laziness—an idle sport.

Even the most pro-Indian activists who genuinely cared about the fate of the natives believed that these civilization programs expressed compassion. Most Americans were convinced that if Indians did not change and come into the modern age, they would inevitably become extinct.

No matter how assiduously the government distributed plows and seeds, many Indians continued to resist. Whenever possible, women who had always gathered roots and greens and berries preferred to continue to gather. Men who had always hunted continued to do so. For a long time the Plains Indians merely shifted their buffalo rituals to

At Rosebud about once a week the trader issues to the Indians their supply of beef. These animals are not butchered in the usual way, but hundreds of them are driven out of the corral on the hills, where the Indians await them and shoot them down. . . . With remarkable precision each Indian selects his victim and separates it from the throng. . . . There is a stirring abandon and daring in the way the men dash up and down the tumble of hills. Every few minutes comes a puff of smoke and a sharp crack of a rifle, then you wait and watch. Some heavy beast thunders on, staggers, stumbles, and his great bulk tumbles in a convulsive heap. After it is over come the squaws, like the stragglers on the field after a battle, knock those that are yet alive on the head with a tomahawk, and cut up the slain for their expectant families.

—HENRY PACKMAN PANCOAST
Impressions of the Sioux Tribes in 1882

the cattle when the rations still came in "on the hoof." The Sioux men persisted in "hunting," and the women did as they always had, following their men out to the "hunting grounds" to drag back the kill, butcher, and distribute meat to the clan. Working together in groups, they cut up beef and hung it to dry in the sun and wind, as was their custom with buffalo meat. They ate some of the organs raw immediately after the kill, and on these occasions a sense of celebration and joy pervaded the air. To government Indian agents, this was a scene of great distress.

"Issue day" on Rosebud Reservation, South Dakota, 1883. Forced onto reservations, Sioux women stand in line to receive U.S. beef and flour. (Courtesy Marquette University Archives.)

What role did the recipes of white women play in winning the West?

Between 1840 and 1870 at least a quarter million Americans migrated across the land from "the states" to the "new country," as it was called. And though the story has long been told as a man's dream of bravery and fortitude, it was very much a family endeavor.

"This Kind of Yeast Will Be Found Convenient"

Bread was a staple on the trail and at the homestead. While many women relied on quick breads leavened with eggs or chemical mixtures such as soda or saleratus, true yeast-risen bread was still the ideal.

Managing one's supply of yeast was not a simple job on the trail or anywhere else. Yeast is a living, single-cell organism that feeds on starch and in the process produces alcohol and carbon dioxide gas. The gas bubbles trapped in the elastic gluten of the dough expand with the heat of the oven, causing the bread to rise.

The dry active yeast we buy in packets today is dehydrated and dormant. When it is mixed with water, it comes to life again. Before commercial yeast, women made their own, but fresh yeast is perishable, destroyed by intense heat, and needs maintenance.

The Kentucky Housewife, published in 1839, gives recipes for several kinds of yeast: Common Hop Yeast, Malt Yeast, Potato Yeast, Rye Yeast, Milk Yeast, and Salt Rising Yeast. The paradox, as any first-timer quickly realizes, is that each of these recipes calls for one key ingredient: yeast. In other words, to make yeast you needed to already have some yeast. Go figure.

There were alternatives. Women knew that wild yeast spores are constantly floating in the air, and by simply leaving out flour, water, and salt, they could catch some and build up a new yeast starter batch. Wild things are not so easy to tame, however, and the results could vary greatly.

The U.S. government could take land away from Mexicans and Indians through wars, trade, and treaties, but there was simply no way the new territories would ever become part of the new nation unless women came to settle it. Only with a woman present on the overland wagon was there the promise of an American West. With a woman, there would be bacon frying and biscuits baking. There would be chickens in the backyard laying eggs, cows being milked, and a pot of coffee on the stove. There would be children growing strong from beans and bread. There is no greater proof of this fact than the Homestead Act, which the U.S. government passed in 1862 offering families free land if they were willing to put their blood, sweat, tears, and many years of their lives into the soil.

The following recipe will create a starter for the legendary sourdough breads of the West—perfect for the rough conditions of the trail or on the lonely, isolated homesteads of the Great Plains. Two cups of this foamy yeast can be substituted for a package of the chemical leavening.

Salt Rising, or Yeast

This kind of yeast will be found convenient when you get out of other kinds; it does not rise quite so soon as the hop yeast, yet it makes excellent bread. Make a quart of water lukewarm, store into it a table-spoonful of salt, and make it a tolerably thin batter with flour; mix it well, sprinkle on the top a handful of dry flour, and set it in a warm place to rise, but be sure you do not let it get hot, or it would spoil it. Turn it round occasionally, and in a few hours it will be light, and the top covered with bubbles; then make up your bread into rather a soft dough, adding as much lukewarm water as will be found necessary; grease and flour your ovens well, set them where they will keep a little warm till the bread rises and looks very light, and bake it as other light bread. The softer is the dough, the more light and spongy will the bread be.

—MRS. LETTICE BRYAN
The Kentucky Housewife, 1839

"I have realized this winter more than ever before that it is not good for man to be alone," wrote Uriah Oblinger in an 1873 letter to his wife, who was still back home in Indiana. Uriah had gone ahead to Nebraska to get his free land and build a sod house for his wife and baby. "You say I have had two men with me. Well that's true, but 20 men cannot fill the place of one woman. . . . I begin to want some bread that tastes like if a woman's fingers had been in it."

As they cooked beans and conjured up ways to bake pies on hot rocks, as they served biscuits to Gold Rush men and set up respectable hotels and farmhouse kitchens, women physically transported ideals and systems of the American home all the way to the Pacific.

The first overland families usually began along the Missouri River (at towns like Independence, Saint Joseph, and Council Bluffs) and ended in Oregon or California. Wagons had to be strong enough to endure twenty-four hundred miles of constant pounding including river crossings and mountain trails with

Pioneers of Hornsilver, Nevada, circa 1908. *(Nevada Historical Society.)*

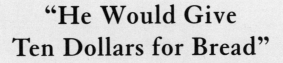

"He Would Give Ten Dollars for Bread"

Luzena Stanley Wilson had gold rush fever as much as any man. At age twenty-six, she and her husband had packed up their belongings and headed west with their two young sons, arriving in Sacramento amidst the peak of the California Gold Rush. After the trip, her clothes consisted of a skirt worn to rags, shirt sleeves in tatters, and broken shoes. But with youth on her side and the "power and will to work," she set out to make money cooking for miners who, in the rough and dangerous early years of mining camps, were bereft of homelike food and amenities and willing to pay a high price for a woman's cooking.

The night before I had cooked my supper on the camp fire, as usual, when a hungry miner, attracted by the unusual sight of a woman, said to me, "I'll give you five dollars, ma'am, for them biscuit." It sounded like a fortune to me, and I looked at him to see if he meant it. And as I hesitated at such, to me, a very remarkable proposition, he repeated his offer to purchase. He said he would give ten dollars for bread made by a woman, and laid the shining gold piece in my hand. . . . In my dreams that night I saw crowds of bearded miners striking gold from the earth with every blow of the pick, each one seeming to leave a share for me. . . .

As always occurs in the mind of a woman, I thought of taking boarders. There was already a thriving establishment of the kind just down the road, under the shelter of a canvas roof, as was set forth by its sign in lamp-black on a piece of cloth: "Wamac's Hotel. Meals $1.00."

I determined to set up a rival hotel. So I bought two boards from a precious pile belonging to a man who was building the second wooden house in town. With my own hands I chopped stakes, drove them into the ground, and set up my table. I bought provisions at a neighboring store, and when my husband came back at night he found, mid the weird light of the pine torches, twenty miners eating at my table. Each man as he rose put a dollar in my hand and said I might count him as a permanent customer. I called my hotel "El Dorado."

—LUZENA STANLEY WILSON

Luzena Stanley Wilson, Forty-Niner: Memories
Recalled for her daughter, Correnah Wilson Wright, 1937

Women wearing overalls, eating watermelon, circa 1890–1910. PHOTO BY HARRY BUCKWALTER. (Courtesy Colorado Historical Society.)

loads of up to twenty-five hundred pounds—all dependent on the breath and muscle of a mere four to six oxen, whose water and grass supply was a constant worry. Extended families and large networks of friends set off together in long processions of wagons, white canvas tops bright and shiny, billowing in the wind as high as their spirits.

Months later, only halfway to the promised land, overlanders usually found themselves alongside the muddy Platte River, beaten down by the relentless desertlike sun and wind of the American prairies and plains—sick, hungry, tired, often beset by tragedies. Children got crushed under wagon wheels or drowned in fast rivers. Mothers died in childbirth. Husbands were seized with cholera (an epidemic of the trail), dying within hours. Snake bites were fatal. And there was constant exposure to severe rain, wind, hail storms, hunger, and dysentery, as wagon wheels broke and poor maps sent the emigrants on trails that led nowhere. During the early years, families and friends set off together but frequently separated in bitter disagreements about the proper route, finding themselves alone in a vast terrifying wilderness and more hopelessly lost than before.

In Wyoming, the trail diverged into two paths—both less traveled. One path headed northward to the temperate and fertile valleys of Oregon. The other went south to the Eden of Sacramento, California—the dreamy climate of milk and honey. After inching painfully close to these promised lands there would be a final descent into hell. To get to California, the last leg featured a trek through fifty miles of scorching desert. En route to Oregon, there was an ascent up the steep ledges of the Blue Mountains—the wagons having to be hoisted up with ropes and pulleys. Oxen often broke down, leaving many emigrants to walk the last miserable miles, covered in dirt and dust, possessions lost or cast aside, shoes broken to nothing.

The migrants consulted various guides to tell them what foods to bring. The 1845 *Emigrants Guide to Oregon and California* suggested the bare survival fare of flour, bacon, coffee, sugar, and salt. Smart wives would also bring dehydrated vegetables (such as dried pumpkin) and dried fruits to prevent scurvy, perhaps even some cheese, rice, tea, dried beans, vinegar, and pickled vegetables. On the trail, they planned to gather raspberries and huckleberries (blueberries). Their husbands might fish and hunt, or more likely the women would trade with Indians who prized American calico shirts in exchange for fresh fish or meat.

Unlike the Hispanic and Indian women of the West, Euro-American women left voluminous written accounts of their experiences in diaries and letters. They were conscious of themselves as pioneers on a grand historic venture. In their writings, they recorded information they believed crucial for future emigrants and future generations.

Cooking must have loomed large in women's minds, for it frequently appeared in their journals. The biggest challenge was learning to use an open fire. "Rainy this morning; very disagreeable getting breakfast," Cecelia Adams com-

To Pickle Red Cabbage

Take a fine firm cabbage of a deep red or purple colour. Strip off the outer leaves, and cut out the stalk. Quarter the cabbage lengthways, and then slice it crossways. Lay it on a deep dish, sprinkle a handful of salt over it, cover it with another dish, and let it lie twenty-four hours. Then drain it in a cullender from the salt, and wipe it dry. Make a pickle of sufficient cider vinegar to cover the cabbage well, adding to it equal quantities of cloves and allspice, with some mace. The spices must be put in whole, with a little cochineal to give it good red colour. Boil the vinegar and spices hard for five minutes, and having put the cabbage into a stone jar, pour the vinegar over it boiling hot. Cover the jar with a cloth till it gets cold; and then put in a large cork, and tie a leather over it.

—ELIZA LESLIE

Miss Leslie's Directions for Cookery, 1851

Overland women often prepared pickled vegetables to take on the trail, believing, wrongly, that the vinegar would help prevent scurvy. This recipe comes from Miss Leslie's Directions for Cookery, *the best-selling cookbook of the nineteenth century. Note that in the style of the old English books, the recipe's title is "To Pickle Red Cabbage," suggesting an emphasis on action and doing rather than the creation of a product.*

plained in her diary. A few weeks later, she noted that she "could not raise enough fire to cook breakfast." On these wet dreary days, crackers and raw bacon would have to do.

There was firewood to think of too—impossibly scarce on the long stretch of the treeless plains. Women wrote loathingly of having to collect buffalo dung to use as fuel for their cooking fires. In time, they got used to it and were happy to find that burning dung made decent mosquito repellent as well.

On the sensual side was the daily struggle against the boring repetition of beans and bacon and bacon and beans. Many women worked hard to try to come up with interesting meals, finding ingenious ways to carry out all kinds of cooking processes, such as attaching cream to a wagon by day so the constant jostling

Dried Pumpkin

Cut a pumpkin in half lengthwise, take out the seeds, pare off the rind, and cut it in slices about an inch thick. String it on fine twine and hang it in a dry place.

In the winter stew and use it as green pumpkin. The cheese-shaped pumpkin is the best kind for drying.

—A Lady of Philadelphia
The National Cook Book, 1856

Recommended for the overland trail.

of the trail would churn butter by nighttime. They baked pies on hot rocks and breads in ovens they dug under the ground. Risking grizzly bear attack, they gathered berries so they could have pies and preserves. One Sunday in June, Cecelia Adams noted she had "cooked beans and meat, stewed apples and baked suckeyes [pancakes] . . . besides making Dutch cheese." Lucy Cooke described how she managed to roll out pie dough on the wagon seat in the midst of traveling. In 1853, Charlotte Stearns Pengra wrote: "hung out what things were wet in the waggon, made griddle cakes, stewed berries and made tea for supper. After that was over made two loaves of bread stewed a pan of apples prepared potatoes and meat for breakfast, and mended a pair of pants for Wm. pretty tired."

Historian John Faragher tells us that overland women generally began their day on the trail by getting up at four in the morning—an hour and a half before men—to start the fire, boil coffee, warm beans, fry bacon, and bake bread. After breakfast, they washed the tinware and stowed away their provisions. During a short noontime stop, women brought out a cold lunch prepared the night before, and after a quick bite, the journey resumed. Many hours later, after a long day of being jostled about the wagon or walking miles alongside to spare the oxen, it was time to make camp for the night. For men, this involved some rest, but for women, there were usually four or five hours of work to do—cook dinner, clean it up, prepare the next day's provisions, not to mention getting the children to bed. As Rebecca Ketchen summed it up in her journal, "to ride on horseback, rain or shine, tired or sick, or whatever might be the matter, then as soon as we get into camp, go to work!"

Husbands were usually swept up by the promise of the West, their desire for the adventure, the fresh start, the riches of gold, silver, and free land. Nothing could stop them once the fever took hold. Newlyweds and teenage girls described with delight the romance of dancing around campfires at night. But for women with children, it was a different story. After studying over a hundred overland diaries, historian Lillian Schlissel found most wives and mothers to be reluctant journeyers—particularly the many who were birthing and caring for little ones during their time on the trail. While men obsessed with navigations of the unknown road, mothers heard the cries of their children and recorded with precision the mishaps of the journey and the large numbers of graves they passed. They wrote with yearning for the stability of their homes back East, and the support of mothers and sisters and friends left behind. Pregnant women looked anxiously at the stark horizon by day, wondering when their "pains" would begin, if there would be water with which to wash or anyone to help them give birth

Ranch woman churning butter, circa 1890–1910.
PHOTO BY HARRY BUCKWALTER.
(Courtesy Colorado Historical Society.)

beneath a tree or in back of the wagon—or even worse, save an infant's life should things go wrong.

And yet they went on the journey—perhaps because they had to, perhaps because there was no other choice. But as Schlissel has noted, more than anything else they went with a passion to keep their families together—almost at any cost. And often their ideals of womanhood conflicted with the realities. To keep their families alive, they took on "men's work" of driving wagons and building homesteads if necessary. They bartered with Indians. Some learned to shoot a gun. But most overland women seemed to yearn for the gender roles they'd had back East, wary of change when so much already seemed at stake. They critically observed the savage ways of "squaws." Despite the wildness and opportunity of the new land in front of them, many held on for dear life to the old notions of a woman's proper place—a place that would be securely within four walls in the homes they were desperate to re-create should they ever survive the trail and get settled. Here was perhaps the greatest tool they had to keep their families together and alive, to hang onto whatever unity they could with the past. In this light, we can understand their careful devotion to the duties of cooking meals, of baking breads and pies in the most ridiculous of circumstances, their will to rise early and get coffee started, their steadfast determination to wear starched white aprons and dresses of "respectable" women, no matter how cruel the wilderness.

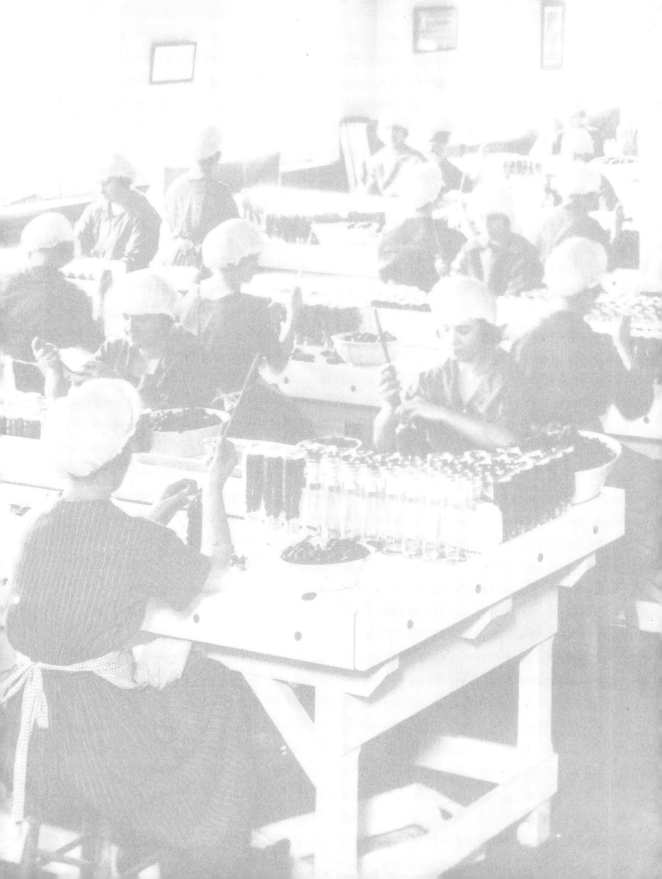

Chapter 6

She Fed the Industrial Giants

By 7:00 A.M., the mill women were hungry. They'd already been on the job for two hours, working at their spinning, carding, and weaving before the sun was up. Now, the breakfast bell rang in the courtyard, and the roar of power looms came to an abrupt stop. It was time to eat. Hundreds of feet rushed across the wood floors as the "girls," as they were called, raced to their nearby boardinghouses for the morning meal.

From all accounts, the food was quite hearty. A typical breakfast may have featured big plates of fried cod (a New England breakfast favorite), potato balls, pumpkin mush with molasses, fried hash, toast, and maybe even apple pie, along with coffee and brown sugar. On some days, there may have been flapjacks made with rye. But for the mill girls, the point here was *not* cooking. The point was having no kitchen and paying someone else to cook the meal with the wages that they had earned. When it was finished, someone else would clean the dishes. We can be sure that the women ate with speed. Within half an hour, the "ring-in" bell would clang again, sending them back to their jobs.

It was a new kind of eating, regulated by the call of bells. It was a new kind of living, too. These were Yankee girls, born and bred in the countryside and used to the rhythms of nature, not machines.

Between 1830 and 1860 thousands of young New England farm women

At first, mill jobs promised a way out of the kitchen. Two weavers, circa 1860s, holding shuttles, used to move thread across a power loom. *(American Textile History Museum, Lowell, Massachusetts.)*

eagerly flocked to these textile jobs in the mills of Lowell, Massachusetts, the place where American industrialism began in earnest, on the backs of women workers. To calm fears that the workplace would corrupt the fairer sex, the mill set up company-owned boardinghouses with strict rules for conduct and curfews. Church attendance was mandatory. Twenty-five to forty girls lived in each house, with meals served "family style" at regular hours.

Today, their labor conditions seem unfathomable. To keep thread moist, the windows in the mills were nailed shut (during an era notorious for tuberculosis), and the air was further polluted by flying lint and the fumes of lamps lit by whale oil. Historian Thomas Dublin tells us that during the mid-1830s, the mill women of Lowell worked seventy-three hours a week for a total of $3.25. After paying room and board of $1.25 per week, they were left with about $2.00, which compared favorably with the only other paid work available to women at the time: domestic service, teaching, and sewing.

The enthusiasm for mill jobs also gives us an idea as to just how exhausting farm life must have been. One weaver named Susan observed that mill workers' feet usually grew a size or two from standing so many hours a day, and that their right hands became bigger from operating machines. Still, she did not find the work terrible. "It is easy to do, and does not require very violent exertion, as much of our farm work does."

Young women came to the mills because they wanted to make money and buy some nice things. They wanted adventure and independence from their parents, as well as a chance to expand their minds. Unlike farmwork and domestic service jobs, a bell rang at the end of the day, and the women had their evenings free. In Lowell, a golden era of culture flourished as traveling lecturers visited, and the mill girls sought out classes, writing groups, social events, and friendships with one another.

It was a brief moment in time. Within a couple of decades, mill life changed dramatically. The push for profit and mass production intensified, and the feeling of optimism faded as work speedups and wage cutbacks brought deteriorating conditions in both the mills and the boardinghouses. By the Civil War, the original culture had faded, and country girls no longer came for jobs. Immigrants—more susceptible to exploitation—began to fill the mills.

Through most of the nineteenth century, there would be few good job opportunities for women. But the image of the first Lowell girls at their dining tables

Fried Codfish

Boil a piece of salt cod; take out all the bones, and mash with it equal quantities of mashed potatoes. Season it with pepper and salt to your taste; then add as much beaten egg as will form it into a paste. Make it out into thin cakes, flour them and fry them of a light brown.

—A Lady of Philadelphia
The National Cook Book, 1856

A classic New England breakfast food that fueled many a mill girl.

hinted at the future far far ahead, when young women could choose to live away from families, be unmarried, make money, and not be slaves to domesticity—a future when they could avoid cooking entirely.

FROM FARM TO CITY

Industrialism brought forth an immense new set of culinary conditions for women. One of the biggest of these was urbanization. By midcentury, the advent of steam power, along with other factors, made it possible for cities to grow explosively. The numbers speak for themselves. In 1790, less than a half million Americans lived in cities; by the century's end, there would be 30 million.

The ramifications on diet would be profound.

What if you lived in such a bereft airless tenement that you had no kitchen? What if you had a kitchen but needed to use it as a bedroom for your children? What if your only source of water came from a rain barrel on the roof, or a public pump many flights down?

How in the world do you cook? What in the world do you eat?

Cities were utterly overwhelmed by the immense number of human beings and unable to provide enough decent housing. No matter how many new tenements were built, basic living quarters and sanitation services for the "laboring classes" remained in desperately short supply and in horrendous condition

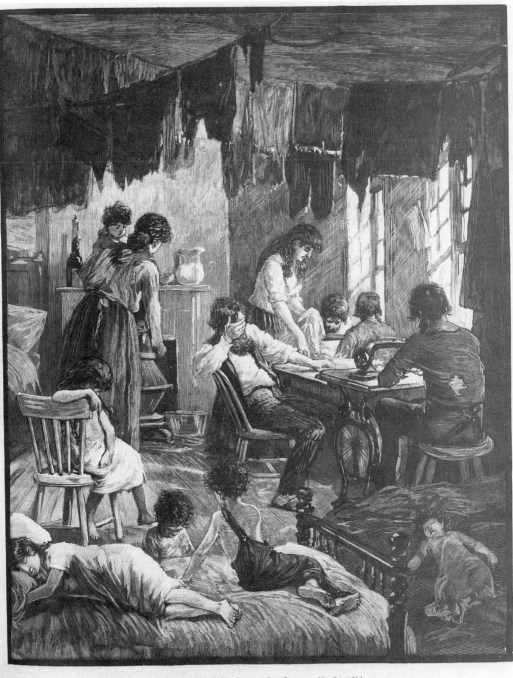

HOMES OF THE POOR.—DRAWN BY T. DE THULSTRUP.—[SEE PAGE 475.]

Not much cooking was possible in urban tenements like this one, where one room had to serve as kitchen, workplace, living room, and bedroom. *Homes of the Poor* BY T. DE THULSTRUP, *Harper's Weekly*, July 28, 1883.

throughout most of the century. In Philadelphia, working-class families often lived in one room with no garbage removal, no toilets, no fresh air, and no water. In New York, the poorest people rented damp, rat-infested cellars and attics. The poorest of the poor lay in the streets with garbage. There were no sewers in the slums of these years, and filthy water drained into yards and alleys, while the overflow from privies and cesspools mingled with the pump water used for cooking.

For millions of people, tenement kitchens had to serve as sleeping, living, washing, and bathing spaces. Thousands of women worked at their kitchen tables braiding straw hats, sewing shoes, or doing other kinds of "outwork" for a few dollars a week. Here, the ladylike ideals of Victorian domesticity were nearly useless, and the clean and tidy kitchens of *Godey's Lady's Book* but a dream.

Among the great deprivations was decent food.

With the growth of cities came the permanent severing of women and their food sources. Because good eating is inextricably connected to nature, the break from the land presented serious nutritional and cultural losses. The urban wealthy usually managed to get their hands on wholesome eggs, milk, meat, and vegetables imported from the countryside, but the working-class urban housewife usually found this to be a difficult task. For the poor, rural life had always had some advantages—the carrots and potatoes grown at the back door, the cool storage cellar in the basement, the cow whose milk went from pail to the child's cup, the rabbit shot in time for dinner, the fish caught before breakfast. For those who moved to cities, these provisions were gone.

Living in cities, women had to adapt and find new ways to eat and feed their families—whether this meant shrewd marketing, buying day-old bread, scavenging, trading, bargaining, stealing, rioting, or simply doing without. These private daily actions gave rise to industrialism as much as the transcontinental railroad and Andrew Carnegie's steel. Human beings were willing to live in new ways and eat in new ways, and this willingness provided the labor that transformed America from a rural nation to the largest industrial engine in the world.

As food manufacturing gradually moved away from the home to industry, various public scandals arose over adulterated foods. There were stories of fish poisoned by mill runoff, bread flour mixed with chalk, and pickles colored green with deadly copper. If you were poor then, as now, you were less likely to worry about such things and yet more likely to be affected by them. In New York City, poor women were most likely to buy the cheapest milk, drawn from city herds

Vegetable Soup

Pare two turnips, and cut into quarters; one onion into small pieces; one carrot, sliced; a sprig of parsley, chopped with a few tender leaves of celery; and one dessert-spoonful of rice. Put them into a stew kettle with three half pints of water, and season with salt to taste. Place it over a slow fire, and let it boil until reduced to half the quantity; then take it off and strain through a fine sieve, and serve hot with a hard biscuit or dry toast.

—HANNAH WIDDIFIELD
Widdifield's New Cook Book, 1856

Hannah Widdifield advertised her recipe book as "practical." This recipe is as practical as they come— the sort of soup women have always made when they are short on food and hunger is at the door.

that lived without ventilation or light, infected with disease, and fed on distillery swill. Swill milk was thin and blue, diluted with water and doctored with plaster of paris, magnesia, and chalk to make it look creamy and white. Despite thousands of infant deaths and excoriating news accounts from journalists, it took several decades for New York City government to overcome corruption and instigate reform.

The urban poor of midcentury were a diverse dietary lot who left behind few written records. There was little interest in recording exactly what "the other half" cooked, whether they were free blacks, Irish factory workers, or Welsh miners in the South. Still, we can conclude this much: For a woman living in a family of six, cramped into one or two tenement rooms with barely a kitchen to speak of, very little cooking was possible, or even advisable—save on Sundays, holidays, and special occasions. And so, though we love to look longingly backward to the days of better food gone by, the truth is that millions of urban Americans—because of space limitations, poverty, and sheer exhaustion—couldn't cook very much at all on a daily basis.

Just the same, the job wouldn't go away; children and husbands still needed to eat. Even the most modest diet required hours of effort each day to haul cooking water and fuel upstairs and to acquire the most basic foods. Enterprising women had to do their best to get the most efficient value for the dollar. While the popular literature of the day may have proclaimed that a woman's place was in the home, millions of urban women knew better. Eating often relied on what they could find in the streets.

Urban peddlers—or "hucksters," as they were called—set up stands in city markets and on street corners. Others traveled door to door, pushing carts on foot or via horse and wagon. They sold an amazing variety of foods: peanuts, popcorn, muffins, milk, soup, butter, cakes, bread, ice cream, lemonade, cider, root beer, mead, oysters, clams, hot sausages, hominy, fruits, and vegetables. Oyster vendors—notorious in the big eastern cities—sometimes traveled with carts that turned into on-the-spot cafes, complete with fold-out tables and cruets of vinegar. A customer could eat "al fresco" and then be on his or her way, the plate and utensils wiped out for the next victim. (In New York, oyster stands were shut down in the 1920s because of typhoid.)

"Rock-Fish! Buy Any Rock-Fish?"
Engraving in City Cries, by George S. Appleton, 1851.

Street hucksters sold their food for less money than the licensed, more respectable vendors who set up stalls in the city-run public markets. Perhaps the quality was not as good, but poor women understood that necessity demanded such choices. And while some purveyors of delicacies—such as the strawberry girls and baked-pear women—found their niche in the nicer neighborhoods, many peddlers found their best customers among the poor who had no kitchens and little time to cook.

The peddler's mode of advertising was an ancient genre, known as the "street cry," sometimes accompanied by the bleat of a handheld horn. Their calls created rhythms and poetry that filled nineteenth-century urban streets with energy and life.

In New York City, "Hot corn women" stood on many street corners, and some, such as Clio, daughter of a fugitive slave, became legendary. Her slow chant was so haunting that the famous songwriter Stephen

C. Foster allegedly tried to write a song based on her cry but gave up because he could not capture "the wild wooing tone in her voice" as she called out,

Hot corn! Hot corn!
'Ere's yer lily-white hot corn!

In Philadelphia, African-American women sold hot "pepper pot" soup in market stalls and on street corners. For a few pennies a bowl, you'd get a mixture of tripe, vegetables, and red pepper served from a steaming round kettle, to be

Street Food

In every meat-eating culture, women have found creative ways to use organ meats so that nothing would be wasted. This particular dish, Pepper Pot Soup, made a long and twisted journey across the world. African Americans brought it to the United States via the Caribbean. Philadelphia, which claimed a large population of Haitians and other Caribbean people, became famous for it. By the twentieth century, it would be appropriated by Campbell's Soup company and sold in cans.

Philadelphia
Pepper Pot Soup

Put two pounds of tripe and four calves' feet into the soup-pot, and cover them with water; add a red pepper, and boil closely until the calves' feet are boiled very tender; take out the meats, skim the liquid, stir it, cut the tripe into small pieces, and put it back into the liquid; if there is not enough liquid, add boiling water; add half a teaspoonful of sweet marjoram, sweet basil, and thyme, two sliced onions, sliced potatoes, salt, and dumplings made of butter and flour. Boil the whole until the vegetables are quite tender; serve hot.

—MRS. BLISS
The Practical Cook Book, Containing Upwards of One Thousand Receipts, 1850

eaten in open air, and at least for a while your stomach would be full. The pepper pot women called,

> *All hot! All hot!*
> *Makee back strong!*
> *Makee live long!*

The peddlers themselves were objects of love, hatred, and pity. Their foods were sometimes suspect for quality. But they were folk heros of sorts, often among the most down-and-out themselves—usually African American, immigrant, or poor—struggling to eke out a living from what they could.

If a woman couldn't afford to buy food, she might try her luck at scavenging. Historian Christine Stansell tells us that working-class women believed it perfectly reasonable to teach their children the survival skills suited to their station in life, and mothers instructed their boys and girls as young as six to go out to the wharves to collect some flour, coffee, sugar, and other sundry items that had "fallen off ships." The poorest women were known to arrive at the markets at the last hour, waiting for the prices of goods to go down minutes before closing. The most hopeless went through the garbage.

Most working mothers knew how to live in two worlds. They did what they had to do to hold their families and their lives together. Each day no doubt required decisions about which corners to cut. Amazingly even poor women took pride in cooking when they could. Weekly Sunday dinner offered this chance, standing apart from all other meals of the week. Even those with the barest shred of means or aspiration did their best to make sure that on the family's day together, there would be a real meal, the best they could muster.

In October, 1877, *Scribner's Monthly* described Catharine Market, the main food-shopping venue for the poor of the Lower East Side. Unlike the hustling bustling Washington Market, Catharine Street was a quiet and sleepy place during the week because few people had money to buy food. A *Daily Times* editorial referred to the "little heap of fish scales, eel heads, butchers' offal, and rotting vegetables known as Catharine Market." But on Saturday night, it noted, things were quite lively in preparation of the big meal.

> *Yet frugal as these people are, they choose one day in the hard-worked week for a feast, and on Saturday night go marketing in earnest. Then the business over-*

flows the building, and spreads up the street on both sides as far as Chatham square. Then the famished masses come out of their obscure homes and barter with shrill eagerness for the modest luxuries they have been greedily anticipating for a week past. As you enter Catharine street from the Bowery and look down toward the river, the sidewalks seem aflame from the spouting jets of tar-oil illuminating the long lines of costermonger's wagons that are drawn close to the curb-stone. The crowds are fairly wedged together, and a desperate struggle for room is waging all the while. The women who congregate here are often sharp, meager and scolding, plainly suffering from privations and excessive toil. But there are a few others whose good-humor and comely appearance are diffusive, and whose cheery laughter rings pleasantly in the Babel around. The great demand is for cheapness, and as the sidewalk vendors usually undersell the store-keepers and stand-holders, they attract most customers. Some of their carts are filled with poultry, not as wholesome-looking as it might be, and a stout fellow mounted on one of the wheels bellows to the people passing, "Here y'are now. Ten cents a pound, only ten cents a pound!" A slight, cadaverous, slatternly woman with a basket on one arm, and a small boy clinging to her skirts, pauses and thrusts a bony hand into the heap at the bottom of the cart. She brings out a flabby duck, and submits it to a severe examination. First she pinches it; then smells it, pinches it again, and throws it back into the cart, bringing out another and another until her exacting taste is satisfied. . . . Poor, overburdened soul! she has been cheated too often not to suspect such a vagabond as he, and she only follows the example of those around her, who finger the stock quite as warily.

The poor got poorer during the hard times of the Civil War and then again during the 1870s, when a major economic depression brought crippling unemployment, widespread hunger, and a succession of violent labor confrontations and a national railroad strike. Hunger intensified as mines, mills, and factories shut down and workers lost their jobs. Life in tenements and factory towns became all the more miserable.

To even begin to imagine such conditions, let us consider some basic statistics: Midcentury life expectancy was probably no better than around forty years for whites and worse for blacks; one in every ten or more infants died; diseases raced through cities and towns, and older children routinely died of tuberculosis, diphtheria, cholera, and various influenzas because water sources and sewage systems

ALL PERSONS [illegible]AUTIONED NOT TO PAY FOR THIS BOOK. THIS EDITION OF 50,000 COPIES IS PUBLISHED FOR FREE CIRCULATION ONLY.

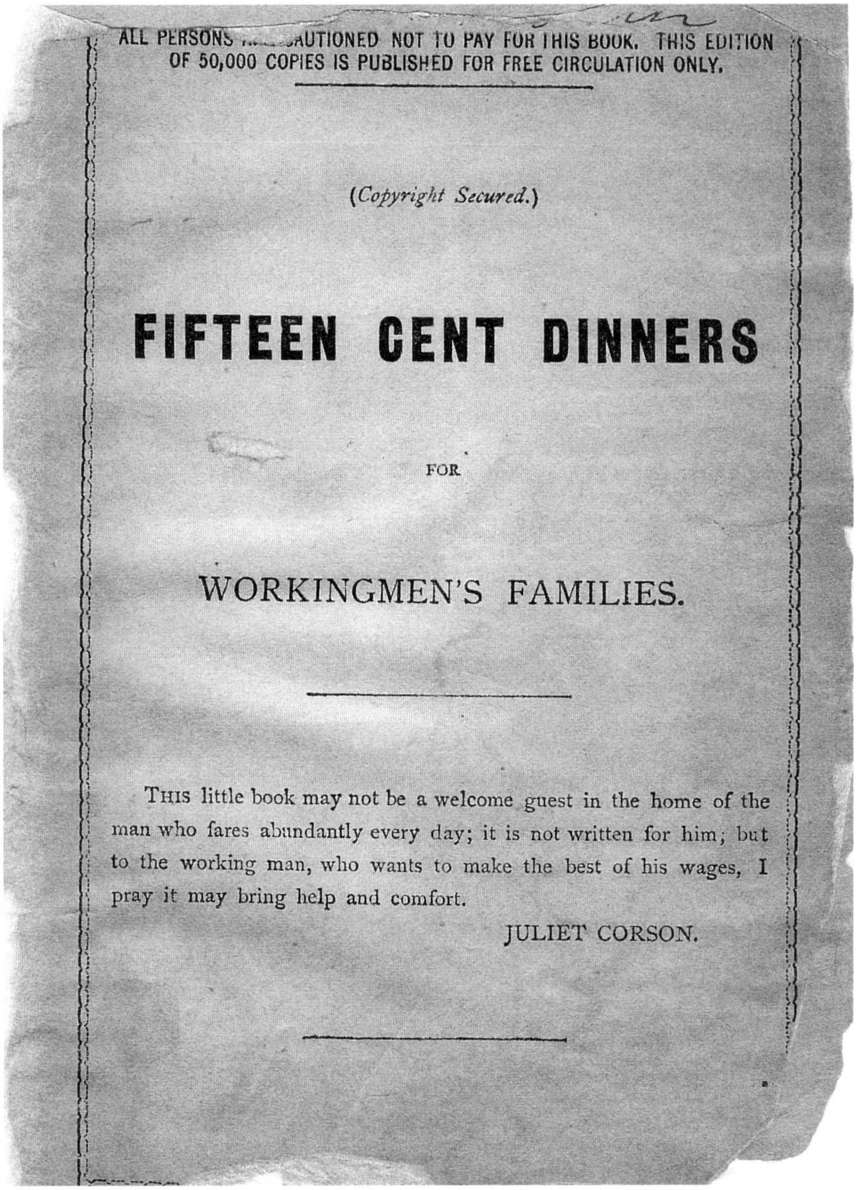

(*Copyright Secured.*)

FIFTEEN CENT DINNERS

FOR

WORKINGMEN'S FAMILIES.

THIS little book may not be a welcome guest in the home of the man who fares abundantly every day; it is not written for him; but to the working man, who wants to make the best of his wages, I pray it may bring help and comfort.

JULIET CORSON.

An interior page from *Fifteen Cent Dinners for Families of Six.* Juliet Corson wrote this cookbook to help the poor and hungry. "The cheapest kinds of food are sometimes the most wholesome and strengthening," she wrote. *(Courtesy The Lilly Library, Indiana University, Bloomington, Indiana.)*

were so bad. Before the 1880s, little was understood about bacteria and the spread of disease. During summer, dreaded as the dying season, the wealthy routinely escaped to the healthier air of the countryside, but for the poor and those of modest means, there was no escape. Harriet Beecher Stowe described an 1849 summer in Cincinnati when cholera was so bad that the city sent around a cart to carry away dead bodies. Her own baby, Samuel Charles, eighteen months old, was among those lost.

Considering just these few facts, it seems certain that any reasonable woman would have given her right arm to do anything she could to protect the health of her husband and children. Though she may have had little control over sewage, water, and housing conditions where she lived, the one thing she could control was food and cooking. Here, perhaps, she could make a difference to strengthen her children's and husband's bodies against the many risks they faced.

But how?

A modest woman named Juliet Corson believed she had the answer when she wrote a charitable little pamphlet called *Fifteen Cent Dinners for Families of Six* in 1877. Unable to find a willing publisher, she scraped together enough money to print fifty thousand copies. She then took out advertisements in newspapers offering it for free to "families of workingmen earning One Dollar and Fifty Cents, or less, per day."

It was hugely successful. One account has it that as many as two hundred people lined up at her door, asking for a copy. The *Baltimore Daily News* gave out one thousand copies; the *Philadelphia Record* printed it in its entirety. A small scandal

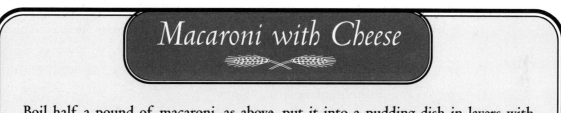

Macaroni with Cheese

Boil half a pound of macaroni, as above, put it into a pudding dish in layers with quarter of a pound of cheese, (cost four cents,) grated and mixed between the layers; season it with pepper and salt to taste; put a very little butter and some bread crumbs over it, and brown it in the oven. It will make just as hearty and strengthening a meal as meat, and will cost about twelve cents.

—JULIET CORSON
Fifteen Cent Dinners for Families of Six, 1877

Then, as today, macaroni was cheap food for the hungry. The small quantity is telling—8 ounces of pasta for a family of two adults and four children.

arose when some union leaders accused her of conspiring against the interests of workers because if women could cook so cheaply, companies would continue to keep wages down. (A ridiculous charge.)

Like many female reformers of the time, Juliet Corson believed with all her heart in the power of cooking. She promised her readers that properly cooked, good food would bring "good blood, sound bones, healthy brains, strong nerves, and firm flesh," and laid out a weekly menu plan totaling $2.63 for a family of six.

Corson seems to have spent a lot of time at the public food market in New York City, studying the shopping baskets of the women who came shabbily dressed. She assures us that her recipes are based on "the articles in common use among the working classes."

And so, what did the poor eat? If they ate according to Corson's book, they faced breakfasts of toast and broth, or rice with scalded milk, and midday dinners of baked beans or the occasional beef and potatoes. For suppers there might be bare-bones stews of broth and rice, or watery soups. For the cheapest meal possible, Corson suggested a one-pot meal of polenta—essentially cornmeal mush—to feed a whole family for a mere five cents. To her credit, Corson told her readers to use fresh herbs, but overall the diet is dreary and repetitive, with the same beef reappearing day after day, first as stew, then as broth for breakfast, then as soup with rice. Sunday's splurge—with a budget twice that of the other six days—featured special additions such as cocoa at breakfast (in a strange combination with fried lentils), a dinner of stew made of organ meat, along with a once weekly reward of a sweet dessert: pudding made with suet. The only other pleasures were a little extra bread, milk, and butter.

ANGEL FOOD CAKE FOR THE MASSES

For middle-class women, industrialism brought a different set of new conditions—most notably the innovations of commercial foods, kitchen tools, and appliances—and with these, new aspirations.

Almira MacDonald was one of many American women who did her baking without fail every Saturday. A mother of three children and the wife of a Rochester attorney, she led a respectable middle-class life. But it was hardly one of leisure.

Cooking meals each day, washing, sewing, mending clothes, cleaning house,

Would people gather round a cast-iron stove instead of the fire? Most Americans converted by the end of the Civil War. *(Library of Congress.)*

preserving foods, and making sick visits to the ill kept middle-class women working from sun up to sun down. For decades Almira did her baking each Saturday (in preparation for the Sabbath) and another time during the week, usually on Tuesday or Wednesday. A selective glimpse of her diary shows thirty years of baking—each and every week.

Saturday. April 19, 1856: baked as usual today.
Saturday, July 7, 1870: Baked this morning & C. Am feelng miserable.
Saturday, March 30, 1878: very ill . . . made lemon pies &c.
Saturday, August 29, 1885: baked bread, cake today.
Saturday, September 5, 1885: baked bread, cakes.

The most dramatic culinary development during this thirty-year span, of course, was the introduction of the cast-iron cookstove. This enormous beast of a machine ushered industrialism into the kitchen. Though it had been invented in the 1700s, it wasn't until the 1830s that mass production became possible, and over the next thirty-five years most American households gradually made this immense transition, saying good-bye to the hearth with its mess of trammels and lug poles and andirons. We can guess that a middle-class family such as Almira's had one sooner rather than later.

Women were enthusiastic to have cookstoves for many reasons. They required less fuel than fireplaces. They were cheaper to install. And they were more efficient for heating. A stove placed in the middle of the room sent its warmth in all directions. A hearth fireplace, on the other hand, would scorch you if you stood a couple of feet from the flames, while your apples a few feet away on the kitchen table might freeze on a particularly cold winter's day. As impressive as these benefits were, bread—when baked in an iron stove—would never taste as good as it did in a wood-burning brick oven. It never has and never will. By 1869, Catharine Beecher wrote, "We can not but regret, for the sake of bread, that our old steady brick ovens have been almost universally superseded by those of ranges and cooking-stoves, which are infinite in their caprices, and forbid all general rules." Nonetheless, when women could get rid of their old brick beehive ovens, they eagerly did so.

The nation was enamored of all things "scientific," and a patent frenzy brought one new product after the next, all advertised for labor-saving benefits. The wealthy began to get novel ice box refrigerators in the early to mid-1800s (now possible, thanks to the growing ice supply, harvested from frozen lakes and carried by trains), along with lightweight tin, foot-pedaled butter churns, apple parers, various food choppers, and the dazzling egg beater that would miraculously "aerify any number of eggs in just one minute." In her 1880 *Miss Parloa's New Cook Book and Marketing Guide*, culinary authority Maria Parloa recommended a minimum of 139 utensils in her list of necessary kitchen tools and stated that "the housekeeper will find that there is continually something new to be bought."

What did these new kitchen technologies do for women like Almira? The cast-iron stove did not make her bread taste better. And it did not remove the job of baking, as we see from her journal—the mixing of dough, the kneading, the leavening, the hours at the oven went on more or less according to the same routine for thirty years. Did the stove make her life any easier?

Probably not, writes historian Ruth Schwartz Cowan in her book *More Work for Mother.* According to Cowan, new inventions of the nineteenth century kept women's labor at about the same level or increased it, because higher standards were now within the grasp of the masses. During the eighteenth century, most Americans had no forks and ate with knives. Some did not even have tables. Now, mass production brought not only forks within reach of the middle class, but other new luxuries, too, such as linens, pretty candle sticks, and matching tableware. The result: middle-class women found themselves working harder to achieve homes and tables that imitated the styles of the well-to-do. And this took a good deal of work and attention.

How much bread can a woman bake? Advertisement for Sterling cast-iron cookstove. (Collection of the New-York Historical Society.)

Angel Cake

One cup of flour, measured after one sifting, and then mixed with one teaspoonful of cream of tartar and sifted four times. Beat the whites of eleven eggs, with a wire beater or perforated spoon, until stiff and flaky. Add one cup and a half of the fine granulated sugar, and beat again; add one teaspoonful of vanilla or almond, then mix in the flour quickly and lightly. Line the bottom and funnel of a cake pan with paper not greased, pour in the mixture, and bake about forty minutes. When done, loosen the cake around the edge, and turn out at once. Some persons have been more successful with this cake by mixing the sugar with the flour and cream of tartar, and adding all at once to the beaten egg.

—MRS. D. A. (MARY) LINCOLN
Mrs. Lincoln's Boston Cook Book, 1884

Being able to put out a good angel cake was not easy even with a dover egg beater, or with an electric mixer for that matter. It required then, as now, a fair amount of technical understanding. Here are some tips:

As Cowan points out, the arrival of the cookstove did not save women much work. In fact, it may have made cooking even harder because women used the new technology to do more than ever. The cookstove with its multiple burners allowed for simultaneous baking, boiling, and stewing of different dishes for one single meal. Many easier, wonderful, one-pot hearth meals of the rural folks were pushed aside for fussier dinners comprised of many separate offerings. The only person who saved labor was the husband, who no longer had to split so many logs.

Similarly, the advent of merchant-milled flour spared men some work. Husbands and sons no longer had to haul their grain to and from the local miller. But now that superfine white flour was readily available at reasonable cost, cookbook writers declared it a moral duty for women to bake their own light yeasted bread—previously the privilege of the rich and well-to-do. Home-baked bread became even more accessible once chemical yeast came to market in the late

- *Angel food cakes have no leavening but get their rise from egg whites beaten full of air, and to successfully achieve this you can't have a speck of fat or egg yolk in your mixing bowl or in your baking pan. Wash them well before starting.*
- *Since eggs come in different sizes, measure your egg whites so you're sure you have 1¾ cups (about 11 eggs, but it depends), and have them at room temperature. Beat them until smooth, wet, and shiny, and you can make trails and form peaks with your beaters.*
- *Add the sugar slowly—2 tablespoons at a time.*
- *I like both vanilla and almond extract—1 teaspoon of each.*
- *Use cake flour, not all-purpose flour.*
- *Most recipes say to fold your flour into the eggs. I find that it works well to sprinkle it on top of the egg whites ½ cup at a time, using an electric mixer on low speed.*
- *Use a 10-inch tube pan, with at least 3-inch-high sides, with a removable bottom so you don't need to mess with the parchment paper.*
- *Bake in preheated oven at 325 degrees for about 50 minutes, until golden and firm to touch*
- *Some suggest inverting the pan onto a narrow-necked bottle to prevent falling while the cake cools. After 90 minutes turn it right side up.*
- *As Mrs. Lincoln mentions, you've got to use a knife to loosen the cake from the sides and center of the pan. You may wish to add a glaze or serve with berries.*

1860s. Indeed, baking one's own white bread became an important status symbol for the well-bred middle-class wife.

More frequent cookie baking also became possible thanks to new technology. "Jumbles," as the English called them, are the predecessors of modern cookies and had been around in Europe for hundreds of years. Karen Hess notes in her *Martha Washington's Booke of Cookery* that Jumbles existed in Italy as the *cianbelline* and in France as *gimblettes*. The Dutch brought them to America under the name of *koeckjes*.

Most of these fancy little cakes were variations on what we now call a sugar cookie, in which the dough was rolled out and either cut or shaped in strands to form rings or other pretty designs. In any case, they took a lot of work, and women had usually made them for holidays, preferably with help from servants or family members. Now, with readily available merchant-milled flour, better

THE
DOVER EGG BEATER

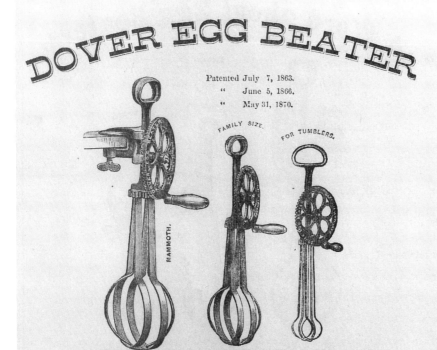

Patented July 7, 1863.

" June 5, 1866.

" May 31, 1870.

FAMILY SIZE.

FOR TUMBLERS.

MAMMOTH.

ABSOLUTE PERFECTION!

Beats the WHITES of Two Eggs IN TEN SECONDS,

The WHITES of Six Eggs IN TWENTY SECONDS,

And both so completely that the dish containing them may be inverted without a particle of the beaten mass falling.

Six eggs may be so thoroughly beaten as to FILL A QUART MEASURE.

Notice the revolving Flat Beaters are on TWO CENTERS; in turning, they *interlace each other* and draw the Egg to the center of the bowl, when by a

THOUSAND CROSS CURRENTS

THE EGGS ARE CUT AND AERATED IN A FEW SECONDS.

"Beats the WHITES of Two Eggs IN TEN SEC-ONDS, . . ." The original Dover Egg Beater, patented in 1870, was so popular that "dover" became the generic term for rotary egg beaters. *(Collection of the New-York Historical Society.)*

access to sugar, and the arrival of the cookstove, cookies became easier to make, and middle-class women applied themselves to the considerable effort of baking this luxury more regularly.

Similarly, when the mason jar was invented with its excellent air-defying seal, women were able to spend more time in their kitchens preserving vegetables and fruits from their home gardens. Though they embraced the mason jar for its benefit to their families' nutrition, the invention did not save much labor.

Ditto for the handheld egg beater, another miraculous labor-saving creation of the midcentury. This cute little appliance *did* relieve some of the enormous arm power formerly required to beat eggs light enough to make cake. But alas, as Cowan ruefully notes, more demanding cakes, such as Angel Cake, which required endless egg beating to get the egg whites to reach their heavenly peaks, soon came into vogue.

CAN YOU PUT IT IN A CAN?

The novel idea of producing food in large quantities had begun rather innocently with the invention of flour milling at the turn of the nineteenth century. By the 1860s, two dramatic developments sent mass food production through the roof: a rapidly growing population of Americans no longer had land on which to raise their own food, and the Civil War created an enormous demand for field rations. Entrepreneurs worked at a breakneck pace to provide large quantities of cheese, meats, milk, vegetables, and fruits for the soldiers at the front. After the war, new technologies such as canning were redirected toward the private family market.

There were great fortunes to be made in the food business, and not surprisingly, some of the most ambitious men of science and business turned their attention to the foods that had occupied women's attention since time immemorial. By the century's end, no common type of victual would remain untouched by the masculine hands of industry.

> What the mower, reaper, and thrashing machine have done for the farmer, the cheese factory has done for their wives and daughters.
>
> —*American Agriculturist,* 1878

The story of men and commercial food is an interesting one full of business heroes who have seen their names writ large in the history of the world, thanks

Food marketers used images of tradition to sell products that would end those traditions. *(Collection of the New-York Historical Society.)*

to their marvels of mass-produced foods. Let's take a moment to look at the most famous among them.

We would have to begin with the Frenchman Nicolas-François Appert. In 1804, Appert set up the world's first vacuum bottling cannery, where meat, fruit, and vegetables were corked in heated glass bottles and preserved—he hoped— for perpetuity. Entrepreneurs around the world copied and improved on Appert's ideas, which were still fraught with problems and the risk of dangerous bacteria.

By the 1860s, American canneries were churning out 30 million cans of safe, though dubious-tasting, meat, fish, fruit, and vegetables a year.

No catalog of early food entrepreneurs would be complete without Gail Borden. As the story goes, Borden first pinned his hopes on the invention of a rather bizarre new meat biscuit. It took $60,000 in capital and six years of experiments to extract the "nutritious properties of meat" and bake these into a cracker. The resulting product was intended for sea travelers, westward journeyers, explorers of the Arctic, and family use during warm weather. The only problem: it was fairly inedible if not repulsive. Never mind. Borden then moved on to something much bigger: the discovery that milk could be preserved in a vacuum pan. In 1858, he established the New York Condensed Milk Company, a hundred miles north of the city. New York was then in the midst of swill-milk scandals, and Borden's company offered a product of sanitary quality. The response was tremendous. A few years later, when the Civil War broke out, Borden's milk was once again ready to meet a huge market need, this time field rations. An immense packaged-milk business was born.

Another dizzying success story was that of Gustavus Franklin Swift, who began a gigantic meat industry by inventing refrigerated railroad cars. Before this, meat—that most beloved but perishable ingredient of the American diet—had always traveled to cities "on the hoof" to ensure freshness. City dwellers were accustomed to the sight of cows and pigs being marched through streets to the slaughterhouse. Now, with refrigerator cars, it became possible to breed cattle on the western prairies, slaughter them on assembly lines in Chicago, and then ship the "dressed" product to large markets of eastern butchers. Swift's example was quickly followed by meat entrepreneur Philip Danforth Armour, who also built a fortune in the slaughterhouses of the Midwest.

How very dramatic these developments were. Before industrialism, people of northern climates did not taste fresh meat during wintertime. Strawberries were a delicacy to be had only a few weeks each year. Fish came in summer. Milk perished quickly.

Now, the food magicians of industry would change all that. They'd figure out how to break the rules of God, nature, the seasons, and sometimes even common sense. They'd make cheese cure more quickly. They'd breed fruit without seeds. They'd freeze meat and ship it to the other side of the world.

They'd even design commercial substitutes for the most important female food product of all: breast milk. By the 1860s, doctors, scientists, and entrepreneurs promoted brand-named infant formulas and substitutes derived from canned condensed milks, despite repeated evidence that babies raised on commercial products had higher mortality rates than babies who were breast-fed. A label on Borden's condensed milk advised mothers to dilute the product with fourteen to sixteen parts of water for newborn babies and gradually increase the milk concentration so that by twelve months, babies were drinking it diluted with six or seven parts water. "Until that age no other food is required," noted the directions, putting babies at risk of malnutrition.

And so the industrial food men proceeded forth. Theirs was a sort of creativity that America cherishes—a creativity that could be applied in a profitable way toward making products available to the masses. Here was a prototype for the democratizing forces of industry—more stuff for more people but of lower quality. It was a trade-off Americans were willing to make for the sake of convenience and, for urban dwellers with no land, the sake of necessity. The industrial foodmakers would find a way to put even spaghetti in cans. And most amazingly, women would buy it and serve it.

It is fascinating to consider that men took over the foods and processes that women had originally invented for baking, butchering, dairying, and vegetable

Industrialism replaces mothers' milk. "Their lives were saved by Lactated Food." *(Collection of the New-York Historical Society.)*

gardening. Whereas women had previously carried out these jobs for the intimate uses of family, tribe, and kin, men did so for profit. And yet, it is widely believed that visionary men of science and business invented food preservation because they brought us the tin can and refrigerators. This is just not so.

Long before the advent of such things, women experimented with science to create far tastier preserved foods in the form of smoked fish, cured ham, pickled fruits, sun-dried berries, fruit preserves, butter, and cheese—all of which were non-patentable techniques designed and perfected by women to lengthen the eating season and promote good health. Women got little credit for their inventions and skills during these early years of industrialism. When they tried to get jobs in the food business, they were generally welcome to work only at the lowest ranks in canneries, bottling factories, and slaughterhouses. Employers considered unskilled repetitive production jobs to be appropriate for females, an extension of housework.

In general, the male emphasis on commercial food was mass scale and uniformity, made possible by machinery. One batch is exactly the same as the previous. This, of course, has continued today, so that in any supermarket we may marvel at how apples look indistinguishable and all chicken breasts appear the same size with the same pinkish hue. Orange juice from one manufacturer always tastes the same—even if the oranges have come from different continents. The captains of food industries have worked strenuously to achieve these standards.

Quite to the contrary, the female emphasis on cooking and food preservation has always been dominated by the personal and the local. A woman cooks based on the individual quirks of what's in her pantry or garden at a given moment, food is flavored according to her own taste, and dinners according to her own acumen or lack of skills in roasting, baking, and frying. Judgment, attention to detail, mood, and the number of children hanging on to one's legs all contribute to the unique results. In the old ways of cookery, it was hard to produce a dish the same way twice.

It was nature that made food quirky in this way, subject to many variables. The taste of tomatoes depends on the soil they are grown in, the weather, the sunlight. The quality of the pork depends on what the individual pig eats. The supply of milk from a cow—as old cookbooks explain matter of factly—depends on whether or not the cows have been treated kindly.

Nature also intended for foods to taste better when eaten fresh. Eliza Leslie, one of the best-selling cookbook writers of the early nineteenth century, wrote, "Every sort of culinary vegetable is infinitely best when fresh from the garden,

Condiments and Preserves
Once Made by Women

Tomato Catsup

Gather a peck of tomatos, pick out the stems, and wash them; put them on the fire without water, sprinkle on a few spoonsful of salt, let them boil steadily an hour, stirring them frequently; strain them through a colander, and then through a sieve; put the liquid on the fire with half a pint of chopped onions, half a quarter of an ounce of mace broke into small pieces; and if not sufficiently salted, add a little more—one tablespoonful of whole black pepper; boil all together until just enough to fill two bottles; cork it tight. Make it in August, in dry weather.

—MARY RANDOLPH
The Virginia Housewife, 1824

Tarragon Vinegar

Tarragon should be gathered on a dry day, just before the plant flowers. Pick the green leaves from the stalks, and dry them a little before the fire. Then put them into a wide-mouthed stone jar, and cover them with the best vinegar, filling up the jar. Let it steep fourteen days, and then strain it into wide-mouthed bottles, in each of which put a large quantity of fresh tarragon leaves, and let them remain in the vinegar.

—ELIZA LESLIE
Miss Leslie's Directions for Cookery, 1851

Cherry Chutney

Get your cherries and seed them; to one gallon half dozen silver skin onions choped fine; first put the onions to cook in half gallon of vinegar, 10 minutes, then add the

cherries, season with two ounces of ground cinnamon, one teaspoonful of cayenne pepper and one of black pepper, two tablespoonfuls of salt, then let it continue to cook with a slow fire, twelve hours, stir it occasionally and keep from burning.

—ABBY FISHER
*What Mrs. Fisher Knows
About Southern Cooking, 1881*

Women provided the unseen army of workers behind many big-name labels. Pickle Bottling Department of H. J. Heinz Co., Pittsburgh, Pennsylvania. *(Library of Congress.)*

and gathered as short a time as possible before it is cooked." Mary Randolph, author of *The Virginia Housewife*, agreed. About peas, she wrote, "To have them in perfection, they must be quite young, gathered early in the morning, kept in a cool place, and not shelled until they are to be dressed."

Men like Gail Borden and Gustavus Swift probably would have been perfectly content with canned peas. They were not interested in freshness, nature, or the messy personal processes that went on one batch at a time in the dairy barn behind the farmhouse. They did not care for individuality. And though all good cooks, chefs, and farmers know that large quantity is an enemy of quality, and only mediocre results can come from foods produced in batches of thousands, still, the industrial men designed ever bigger, more automated operations.

This is not to say that refrigerators aren't a great invention or that mason jars weren't useful, or that commercially canned goods should not exist. Canned foods certainly have the practical benefits of a long shelf life and long-distance travel. Some scholars of public health say that Americans became taller and healthier in the twentieth century in part because of improved nutrition in the form of year-round fruit, milk, vegetables, and meat (along with modern vaccinations and modern sanitation). But while the commercial food producers may have improved human health, ultimately they destroyed a lot of land, crop species, the environment, and lots of good food in the process. There is little doubt that they made food taste worse once they put it on conveyor belts.

The conflicts deepen when we consider that they succeeded because they served many women's desires. Women certainly bore responsibility for buying commercial food products. And buy them they did. By the early twentieth century, cookbook authors, cooking-school teachers, and home economists all championed commercial foods over fresh. (We will give them their due in a later chapter.)

AN UNMISTAKABLE YEARNING

> *Come butter come;*
> *Come butter come;*
> *Little Johnny's at the gate*
> *Waiting for his buttered cake.*
> *Come butter, come.*
> —An old churning song

During the years following the Civil War, commercial food production affected rural women as well. When historian Sally McMurry studied nineteenth-century cheesemaking in Upstate New York, she found that farm women were quite happy to relinquish the utterly exhausting job that made them "drudges of curd tubs and cheese presses." Immediately after the Civil War the number of cheesemaking factories rose from 250 to more than 900. The women in these regions seem to have had no regrets. One woman named Mrs. E. P. Allerton summed up the feelings of many farmwives in her 1875 essay "Dairy Factory System—A Blessing to the Farmer's Wife." She wrote, "In many farm houses, the dairy work loomed up every year, a mountain that took all summer to scale. But the mountain is removed; it has been handed over to the cheese factory, and let us be thankful time does not hang heavy on the hands of the farmer's wife now that it is gone. She does not need the dairy work for recreation."

Cheesemaking was grueling physical labor, requiring constant attention, skill, and much confinement to the dairying house during peak production times. To make good cheese, women had to manage the quality of the milk and curds, the temperature for "setting," the time for "cooking," and the correct amount of pressure. Each day, cheeses needed to be turned and rubbed. Equipment needed to be scrupulously clean.

In addition to their usual cheesemaking and farmwork, the intense pressures of the Civil War pushed women to their limits. Women ran farms while their husbands were away, and organized relief societies, supplying food and clothing to soldiers at the front. They made cheese for the war effort as well—quite a lot of it. A staggering 15 million pounds of New York State's wartime cheese production came not from factories but from home dairies run primarily by women.

It is not surprising that women jumped at the chance to be freed from some of their work after the war and wholeheartedly encouraged the cheese factory system. Interestingly, many women went to work in the factories, and in the initial phases over half the labor force was female. Unlike other food businesses, cheesemaking was somewhat exotic, requiring specialized skills, and women's knowledge was valued—at least at the beginning—until expertise was transferred from one sex to the other.

Once the factory system got under way, however, cheesemaking was quickly redefined as men's work, writes McMurry. It became an industry most admired when it was well organized and rational. Articles in the popular press derided the old-fashioned, "rude" cheesemaking of grandmothers and gave adulation to the new masculine methods of factory-run efficiency.

In fact, the basic essence of cheesemaking varied little, whether in factory or farm. When men took over the cheesemaking, they did it through organization and on a larger scale, *not* by applying any superior skill or knowledge of science. If anything, the factory product was inferior because milk from many farms and cows was mixed together and the cheesemaker had little control over quality and cleanliness.

Family farms sold their milk to the cheese factories. As a result of growing demand for cash, farmers soon found themselves shifting away from biologically sustaining methods. They began to buy feed for their cows and purchased fertilizer from sources off the farm (instead of relying on organic matter) and shifted toward more specialized and less environmental farming methods geared toward the cash market rather than family subsistence. The factory also brought some disintegration among families as young girls—no longer needed for the family economy—left home to get wage-paying jobs. Many farmwives (though certainly not all) even gave up milking and butter making too. "The dairy-maid going singing to the pasture with milkstool and pail is either a myth or a tradition in the dairy regions," reported *Harper's Weekly* in the 1870s. "The milking is done chiefly by men, and in surroundings which suggest no poetry."

But these changes were evidently worth it. Farm families had more cash on hand, and local newspapers, farm journals, and farmers proclaimed women's new freedom.

What did farm women do with the time they saved now that they weren't making cheese? Some women redirected their efforts toward the less taxing egg and poultry business. Others became more involved in local philanthropy and social groups. Many, however, simply wanted time to decorate and create more beautiful and comfortable homes. They wanted more culture, leisure, companionable marriages, and mental cultivation. As Mrs. Allerton wrote,

Hearty, honest work is a good thing for us all; but how much of it? that is the question. For my part, I think a little rest—a blessed little idleness now and then is good, for a change. I hate to hear it said of a woman that "she is always at work." If she can't help it, she is to be pitied, and if she can help it, she is to blame. . . . A wife should not forget that she has something else to keep clear of rubbish than the house she lives in. If there must be cobwebs anywhere, it is better they should lurk in dark corners of the room, than in her heart and brain. . . . If [the farmer] wants a companion, she must have a little leisure now and then in order to be companionable. . . . All work and no recreation of any kind,— what does that make of a woman?

Chapter 7

Give Her Your Hungry

You begin with stale bread. It is a stone now, but mix it with water and it comes back to life. Add capers, cured olives, some pecorino. Taste and add what you like—salt, pepper, maybe more cheese. Now take all this and stuff it into the peppers you've kept in brine since summer. Tuck in an anchovy if you like. Fry in olive oil, until brown.

Lou calls these "Christmas Peppers." They taste nothing like the comfortable Italian food many of us have come to know as pastas and lasagnes. These peppers are vinegary and pungent. At first bite, your eyes squint. They taste like a place very far away.

That place is Sant' Agata dei Goti, a mountain village north of Naples, circa 1910. This particular recipe descends from Maria Argento, who, in 1918 at age ten, left her village forever and came to a new life.

I never met Maria, now departed from this world. But I am in the kitchen of her son, Lou Palma, who is teaching me his mother's recipe at his six-burner, restaurant-size stove. In a world where recipes and people transport themselves like wind across the globe, there are some who remain rooted to tradition, acting as a culinary link to the past. These people are rare, and I've been lucky to meet some of them while doing this book—women like Alice Ross, who taught me how to cook over a hearth fire, or the Gullah sisters who shared their rice and

Trade card for Holmes and Coutts wafers, 1884.

crab recipes, or Janet Black Eagle, the Nez Perce woman who explained the importance of digging for camas root each year. Lou is one of these living links—what some anthropologists call a "hero of continuity," someone who still puts forth the effort to carry on the old ways despite the pressures of change.

I came to know Lou in an unlikely way. I had recently moved to town; I needed a handyman and someone gave me his name. "A retired gent," I was told. Lou showed up at my door with toolbox in hand, but within the hour he was talking about food, and his true identity immediately became clear—he was a culinary artist. "Cooking, that is my poetry," he said to me from atop a ladder while hanging a shelf. Later that day, a small dish of homemade gnocci, with a light marinara sauce and a pretty basil leaf on top, came to my doorstep. More tastings followed over the years.

Lou cooks the long, slow, old-fashioned way, like his mother—and then some. He makes sausage by hand. He catches his own fish and smokes them in a smoker he has built in the garage. He bakes breads. He makes twenty-five quarts of court bouillon at once and roasts peppers in vast quantity outside using a torch. He occasionally puts a whole pig on a spit. Friends bring him venison and turkey they have hunted. And each fall, he goes to the market and buys the right cheese peppers, which he puts in brine for several months in advance of Christmas Eve. "No dish is too much for me," he says.

The inspiration goes back to Maria. Memory of her food. Memory of her love. Memory of her village. The three mingle together inextricably as he makes esca-

Christmas Peppers

pickled cheese peppers, well rinsed of brine

stale Italian bread (good quality), broken up, soaked in water, and drained

cured black olives, pitted and chopped

capers

a few extra cheese peppers, chopped

fine pecorino cheese, grated

salt and pepper, to taste

olive oil (not virgin) for frying

Purchase your pickled cheese peppers, the type that are about 3 inches in diameter. (Or pickle them yourself.) Cut off the tops and hollow them out. Mix all ingredients and stuff the peppers. One fillet of anchovy may be tucked into each pepper. Bring olive oil (virgin oil not necessary) to frying temperature in a nonstick pan. Place peppers face down into oil and brown. Turn and cook on the bottom. Place on paper towel and refrigerate until needed. Serve at room temperature.

—MARIA ARGENTO
emigrated from Sant' Agata, Italy, 1918
recipe as told by her son, Lou

Lou gave me the above directions, but he is an instinctive cook and uses no measurements. Here are some quantities that worked well for me: 8 to 9 cheese peppers; enough stale bread to make 2 cups of wet filling; ¼ cup of olives; 2 tablespoons of capers; ¼ cup of pecorino cheese; 1 of your pickled cheese peppers minced; enough oil for the bottom of the pan. The beauty is that since there is no egg in this mixture, you can taste it and adjust according to your palate. It should taste nice and strong.

NOTE: Cheese peppers are available at holiday time from Italian specialty shops. Lou tells me they are named this way because they are shaped like a wheel of cheese.

role and beans like she did, pig skin like hers, Christmas Peppers, *minestra,* Easter Cake, and all variations of stews cooked with tomatoes.

"I could never displease my mother," says Lou. I marvel at the statement. Would my son ever say such a thing? And then I understand how love can live on—from past to present, from Sant' Agata to here, from the dead to the living—all through a simple reenactment of bread and peppers made for Christmas Eve.

In his sixties, Lou achieved the dream so many of us wish for. He returned to the lost homeland and reclaimed his ancestors. He takes out a photo album to show me the pictures.

Here he is sitting around a table with his Italian cousins and their children. They are eating, drinking, and smiling. Here he is with them outside, crushing grapes for wine, and at the family bread-baking oven. Here they are in the family fields, surrounded by fig trees and prickly pears. Sant' Agata is a small village built breathtakingly into the side of a mountain. In these shots it is spring, and all is emerald green, fertile, and abundant. Here is a life still lived close to the land, woven with traditions of cooking, baking, and preserving that have been perfected over generations through the bonds of family.

Why on earth did millions of people leave this verdant place to go and live in the concrete world of Brooklyn? Why did they leave such beauty and family and all these delicious ways of eating?

"It's very simple," Lou says to me. "They were starving."

Between 1880 and 1920, more than 23 million immigrants came to the United States. They came for many reasons: because they were politically persecuted, because they had lost family farms, because they had been pushed out of their artisan trades, and because they were poor. More often than not, they came because they were hungry.

Poverty had created starving times and famines since time immemorial. But at this unique moment in history, a torrent of economic change and population growth in Europe and Asia had collided, creating a different kind of suffering. A new, modern economy was just beginning to emerge across the globe—an economy based on money, technology, and large-scale production. These were all things that peasants and artisans did not have. Forced to live on smaller portions of bread and vegetables, scant bowls of rice or cornmeal, they eked out increas-

Woman placing seaweed, an important item in the Japanese diet, on a rack to dry. Japan, between 1890 and 1923. *(Library of Congress.)*

ingly meager lives. Finally, they could stand no more. America, it seemed, offered the only hope.

That hope centered on the chance to work hard and earn money. Unlike the first generations of European Americans who settled on family farms, this wave of immigrants came to get wage-paying jobs in manufacturing, transportation, mining, textile, and agricultural companies. Because of them, the American workforce nearly doubled between 1870 and 1910, and the American economy was transformed into an unstoppable machine.

Native-born Americans expressed curiosity, fear, suspicion, and at times hatred of these immigrants, who seemed terribly "foreign" in their habits, tastes, and religions. The nineteenth-century ruling classes of America were drawn mainly from northern European stock, especially German and British ancestry. Now, foreigners poured in from countries like Greece, Italy, Poland, Croatia, Romania, Russia, Ireland, China, Korea, Japan, and Mexico. They brought unusual ways of dress, eating, living, and religious worship. Many liked foods highly seasoned with exotic flavors, be it garlic, chile peppers, soy, or vinegar. They did not worship as Protestants but as Catholics, Jews, and Buddhists.

For immigrants who began with slim resources, the passage to America brought sadness and trauma. The reality of dehumanizing factory jobs, tenement life, endless work, poverty, racism, and the aching yearning for one's homeland could create unhealable wounds. It might take a generation or two—or even three—for a family to recover.

But immigration was a breathtaking act of human creativity as well. This wave of immigrants never saw pictures of America on television, never spoke on the phone to relatives, and usually could only afford one-way tickets. They ventured into a wholly unknown world, willing to re-create and reimagine themselves using only strength, resourcefulness, and hope.

TRACING A PATH OF HUNGER

How immigrant women re-created and reimagined their cooking and their lives in the United States depended on exactly where they came from, their social class, their religion, and the regions they settled in. It also greatly depended on the nature of the hunger that sent them.

The greatest tide of newcomers—approximately 4 million people—came from Italy. More than any other event, it had been the unification of Italy in 1860 that set them in motion. Old feudal systems collapsed, and so did the old ways of getting food. The poor lost their long-held privileges of hunting, fishing, and gathering on noble lands. A new system of sharecropping emerged in which peasants had to pay their landlords before they could eat. All this coincided with higher taxes from Rome and a population explosion, which meant even more people needed to live on shrinking resources.

In her book *Hungering for America*, historian Hasia Diner describes the desperation that sent Italians to America. By 1909, a government study reported that death from starvation was rare, but declared a "terrible permanent lack of food." "How can we survive?" Calabrian *contadino* Francesco Nitti testified before a parliamentary inquiry. "The better soils are far away. I'm old and it takes me four hours to get [to] a piece of land I work on." Maria Torno, a St. Louis resident, described her Lombardian childhood as *una vita di mesera*, a "life of misery." She lived on corn bread, vegetable soup, pasta, and cornmeal mush. A couple of times a year, perhaps, there was meat.

> *I* had no choice; we were so poor. If we had the money, I'm sure my mother would have kept me home. . . . We had no food to go with rice, not even soy sauce or black bean paste. Some of our neighbors even had to go begging or sell their daughters, times were so bad. . . . So my parents thought I would have a better chance on Gold Mountain [America].
>
> —LAW SHEE LOW, Chinese woman
> who immigrated in 1922
> as told to Judy Yung in *Unbound Feet*, 1995

The future did not promise hope, and Italian men felt compelled to try their luck in the United States. Many went ahead alone, intending to return home with a fortune or to send for their families later. Back in the village, Italian women and children waited month after month, year after year, worrying that they would lose their husbands forever. Once the decision was made to go, they packed up their belongings. When Italian wives arrived in the United States, they did so to reunite their families and reclaim their men.

Chinese wives and daughters also found themselves left behind, waiting while their laboring men went ahead to strike it rich. "Nice rice, vegetables, and wheat, all very cheap," said one 1870s handbill recruiting Chinese workers. "You cannot afford to wait. Don't heed wife's counsel or other threats of enemies. Be Chinamen, but go."

The pressures of international capitalism, wars, natural disasters, and corruption had brought desperation to China. During the 1870s, millions of Chinese were dying in famines, and the promises of "Gold Mountain" proved irresistible. Chinese wives seldom joined the migration. Confucian ideology had required women to remain inferior to men, confining them to the household to a greater degree than the cultures of Europe. The cost of passage also deterred women married to poor laborers, working for the lowest wages in America.

But anti-Asian hatred and laws posed the greatest barrier. Discrimination and violence followed the Chinese as they moved from the gold fields of California to work on the railroads and in agriculture. In 1882, the U.S. government passed the Chinese Exclusion Act, which halted the immigration of Chinese unless they were merchants or merchants' wives (or could provide false papers to pose as such). The explicit purpose was to keep Chinese women in short supply so that Chinese families would not permanently settle in the United States.

During the late nineteenth century, Japanese men also left their homelands, seeking work on plantations in Hawaii and in the agricultural fields of California. But they had slightly better luck at getting married. The early anti-Japanese laws allowed, at first, for immigrant laborers to send for wives. Relying on traditional matchmaking methods adapted to long-distance mail, Japanese men imported to Hawaii alone fourteen thousand Japanese women as picture brides between 1908 and 1924.

In contrast, millions of Irish women led the way to the United States not as wives but alone and single, eager for the chance to earn dollars. More than any other immigrant group, Irish women came to fill the ranks in the kitchens of America as cooks and domestic servants. They came because centuries of English colonization had left them, too, in the starving class.

Certain cultural values made it possible for Irish women to venture forth alone to the United States. Unlike Italian, Chinese, and Jewish women, who tended to marry young, Irish women delayed marriage and generally retained independence from men. Word about middle-class women in constant need of servants traveled back from American cities to remote Irish villages. They knew they could get off the boat and have a job practically the next day. Through domestic service, Irish women were known to save considerable sums and buy land and homes, or even return home to Ireland in style.

Beginning in the 1880s, more than 2 million Jews fled poverty, hunger, and persecution in the ghettos of eastern Europe. The majority came from western Russia and Poland, where they mainly worked as artisans and traders because they were not allowed to own land. While some prospered, many lived with scarcity, battling hunger. Then, at the end of the century, a series of Russian crop failures brought disastrous famine to Jews and gentiles alike. Simultaneously, competition from imported mass-produced goods pushed Jews out of their livelihoods. Amid these crises, Jews were scapegoated, threatened, and heavily taxed. Because they had never fully been accepted in Russia, Poland, and other eastern European countries, and because they were an international people with a long-standing history of transporting their culture wherever necessary, most did not look back. And so women came with their husbands or parents, or followed them soon after.

Cooking in Other People's Kitchens

When they arrived as domestic servants, in America, Irish women generally had to rely on their mistresses or other servants to teach them to cook according to middle-class American standards. Most came from bare huts on country lanes and had never laid eyes on a roasted goose or a plum pudding—never mind knowing how to cook such things. The Irish came to America from a culture that did not celebrate food. Back home, they had taken little satisfaction in developing a national cuisine around the potato, the staple food imposed on them by their British colonizers. It was a tuber that had brought famine and sorrow, and they tended to eat it simply boiled.

American women relentlessly complained about the poor cooking of their Irish servants, as well as their insolence, lack of skill, and habit of jumping from job to job. But there was a "servant crisis" in America—a household labor shortage—and Irish women took advantage of this situation, demanding high pay so they could send money home and better themselves. In the kitchens of American households, Irish women built a foundation for themselves to rise in American life.

Domestic staff of a single-family home in Black River Falls, Wisconsin, 1890. PHOTO BY CHARLES VAN SCHAICK. *(Wisconsin Historical Society.)*

Mexican women also tended to migrate with their families. Between 1910 and 1929, more than a million Mexicans crossed the northern border into the southwestern United States, hoping to escape poverty and the Mexican Revolution. Many of the women in this group came from farming backgrounds and were accustomed to agricultural work. The fields of California offered them a relatively nearby place where they could work alongside their husbands and children. But this migration trail differed from those forged across immense oceans. Once in the United States, many Mexicans continued to travel, following harvests, but home was never so far that it would not be possible, at times, to return to Mexico. As they struggled to feed themselves, Mexicans, more than any other group, would continue to provide cheap labor in the Eden of fruits and vegetables that would feed the nation.

FOOD AND WOMEN—THE LAST LINK TO HOME

"It was the taste of squab and saffron that stayed with me longest. I found the faintly bitter smoky intensity of saffron, made bolder with cinnamon and clove, intoxicating. Between bites of pickled onion I sucked off dark meat from diminutive bones, and probably stained my shirt. Afterwards . . . I laid my head on Delfina's broad lap and fell asleep as she smoothed my forehead, preparing me for dreaming."

In his memoir *Recipe of Memory,* Victor Valle recalled this childhood visit to his grandmother Delfina's house in Canta Ranas, Los Angeles—a barrio begun as a camp for citrus workers. After dispatching her sons and nephews to kill a dozen pigeons, Delfina simmered them in parsley, onion, and garlic. She cooked her rice in the broth of the squabs, adding freshly ground cloves, cinnamon, and saffron. She did all this according to one of the recipes she had carried with her from Guadalajara, Mexico, part of a written collection of more than 250 gathered from her own kitchen and that of her aunt and great aunt. Delfina knew that in the United States, her children and grandchildren might become lost to assimilation. By cooking dishes like Sopa de Camarón para Vigilia (Lenten Soup with

OPPOSITE: **Grinding corn for tortillas, circa 1920. Probably at El Sol Del Mayo, a tortilla factory in Los Angeles, owned by Mrs. Maria Queredo. (Los Angeles Public Library.)**

Shrimp Fritters), Torta de Garbanzo (Garbanzo Torte), and Consumé Violento (Violent Consommé), she worked hard to instill aromas and taste memories that would help sustain them the rest of their lives. Through cooking, she hoped to help her grandchildren remember, and remain proud of, who they were.

Delfina was not alone. No matter their ethnicity, immigrant wives, mothers, and grandmothers of nearly every nationality shared a common role in America. They were the "culture bearers," charged with preserving the ethnic, religious, and cultural memories of their families. This usually meant creating "proper" homes (according to each culture) and cooking beloved foods of memory. If immigration was indeed a trauma, then the experience lent food all the more meaning and comfort in a competitive new world. Food made survival possible. Food was about family and home. Food was a connection to lost ancestors. Food was about identity and strength. When they cooked, immigrant women found themselves pulled into a place of deep emotion. The sweatshops and slaughter-houses, the mining and railroad jobs, the canneries and fields of America might take all the labor of their bodies, but eating the foods of home was a way of keeping their souls.

These hungers became especially intense at holidays and during religious feasts, which demanded food of highest symbolic importance, sometimes involving labors that would go on for days. Decades later, children and grandchildren would never forget the dishes they tasted so long ago—whether matzo ball soup, moon cake, *mochi*, or Christmas Eve fish. On holidays, food seemed to contain the best life had to offer.

Some immigrants came from cultures that elevated food to a spiritual level above life itself, taken seriously by both men and women. When cooking or baking, many women understood their labors as part of sacred work. Add to this the memory of scarcity, and the ability to put together a decent meal on a holiday seemed to transcend the role of mere mortals. The Italian woman who could turn foraged greens into a delicious *minestra*, a Jewish woman who could produce a *challah* bread for Sabbath after weeklong hunger, a Chinese woman who could turn turnip root into festive cake for New Year's—all this seemed to mingle divinity and magic in homes where food was scant and the future uncertain.

This magical aspect of cooking couldn't have been further away from what was going on in middle-class America at the moment—an era of scientific cookery, labor-saving devices, and rational methods. The most cherished foods of immigrants, on the other hand, often took gargantuan amounts of time and effort for no good reason other than the irrational devotion to love, tradition, religion, home, and duty.

Perhaps most explicitly sacred of all was the cooking of eastern European Jewish immigrant women. For these immigrants, being Jewish meant eating specific foods in daily life and according to an annual calendar of holy days. Jewish women had to organize not just their souls but their daily labors around Jewish dietary laws known as *kashrut*. In the kosher kitchen, the observant wife kept meat and dairy foods separate, never served shellfish, and used only meat that had been butchered according to certain rules and had passed the inspection of a rabbi who declared them *kosher* (acceptable) or *treyf* (forbidden). Hours had to pass between eating dairy and meat products. These requirements sometimes made for oner-

A family gathered around the Sabbath or Passover table. Advertisement for Fischer Russian Caravan Tea, circa 1920. *(The Jewish Museum, New York, Art Resource, New York.)*

ous planning and labors, but the laws of *kashrut* also provided women with a special privilege. *Kashrut* had historically helped Jews ensure that their food achieved high standards of cleanliness and health, but the central reason for observing these rules was simply that God said so. When a Jewish woman cooked, she came into closer connection with God.

Italian and Mexican women were also accustomed to seeing their cooking as part of sacred and communal life. In the Catholicism of both Italy and Mexico, feasts and church celebrations bound families and communities together, giving shape and meaning to life. For these events, women regularly prepared foods to be placed on shrines and altars. In Sicily, for Saint Joseph's Day, women baked bread in the shape of Saint Joseph's beard. In Mexico, on Day of the Dead, there was a special sweet bread to give honor to the deceased.

Food and spirituality also mingled in Chinese cultures. Women strove to prepare dishes that balanced the Taoist notion of *yin* and *yang* energies and achieve the right harmony between grains and vegetables and meats, the right relationship between sweet, salty, spicy, and rich. Many Chinese believed that the kitchen god, Tsao Chun, watched over the domestic affairs of the family and acted as a moral guardian. For New Year's, women cleaned house and sent food as an offer-

Japanese immigrants pounding *mochi* (a sweet short-grained rice) for New Year's Day, 1920s. *(Gift of the Taketaro Azeka Family, Japanese American National Museum.)*

Ozōni (Mochi Soup)

This is a modern recipe for an old dish, brought to the United States from Japan as a sacred part of New Year's celebrations.

        5 cups dashi, simmering [dashi is a Japanese soup stock made with kelp—
           now available in packets]
        ½ teaspoon salt
        1 teaspoon shōyu
        1 carrot, thinly sliced
        8 napa leaves, cut into 2-inch lengths
    4 to 8 mochi [glutinous sweet rice cake, can now be purchased frozen and ready
           to use]

Bake mochi in 375-degree oven until it becomes a little soft, about five minutes. Place mochi in four bowls. Bring dashi to a boil. Add salt and shōyu to dashi. Cook carrot and napa in hot dashi for about five minutes. Pour over mochi in bowls. Serve immediately.

—National Japanese American Historical Society
The Rice Cooker's Companion, 2000

ing to Tsao Chun. They prepared special cakes for New Year's Day and went out to share gifts and food with neighbors. For the Chinese Moon Festival, women made moon cake. And on annual remembrance days for the dead, they prepared food for ritual offerings that would honor ancestors by "feeding" them, presenting their gifts to burial grounds or shrines.

In some cultures, the rituals of holidays were so large that they could not be borne by women alone. In Japan, New Year's festival was one of the most important holidays of the year and always demanded that families eat *mochi*, a sweet rice that required intensive pounding of grain in a large mortar and pestle—a job so physically demanding that men and women shared it together.

Almost all of the treasured foods brought by immigrants were rooted in

A Special Loaf for the Sabbath

*T*he baking of a special loaf of bread for Sabbath was an ancient tradition loaded with symbolism for Jews all over the world. In his *Eat and Be Satisfied*, John Cooper tells us that the name *challah* originated in South Germany during the Middle Ages, derived from a Hebrew word that means "portion." Before placing the loaves in the oven, the housewife broke off a portion of dough and tossed it in the fire, saying a prayer—a reminder of the Biblical commandment that a piece of dough should be torn off and offered to the rabbis.

In the Middle East, Jews baked round challahs. But in parts of Europe they braided their dough, a practice carried to the United States. In her 1871 *Jewish Cookery Book*, Esther Levy called this Sabbath bread a "twist," and noted, "It is usual on Friday for persons of our faith to use raisin wine to say the blessing of sanctification. It is placed on the table with the salt and twist."

---

slower-paced rural cultures. But life in the United States was based on commerce, technology, abundant resources, and jobs. Could men and women survive the transformation? Could their food survive fast-paced American life?

This remained to be seen. The United States would require endless flexibility and innovations in the roles of women, habits of eating, and treasured ways of life.

HEAVENLY ABUNDANCE

The overwhelming abundance of food in the United States shocked many immigrants. Not only did it come in large supply, but also it came cheaply—at least when compared with the high prices where they'd come from. American markets overflowed with vegetables, fruits, eggs, fish, milk, and—most coveted of all—meat. Restaurants and hot-dog stands seemed to dot every corner in New York. In California, fruits and vegetables sprouted to immense size in virgin soil never touched by a plow. Back home, harvests had come slowly from soil that had been

Twist Bread

Let the bread be made as directed for wheat bread; strew a little flour over the paste board; then take three good sized pieces of dough, and roll each piece under your hands, twelve inches long, making it smaller in circumference at the ends than in the middle; having rolled the pieces in this way, take a baking dish and lay one part on it, join one end of each of the other two to it, and braid them together the length of the rolls, then join the ends by pressing them together; dip a brush in milk, and pass it over the top of the loaf; after ten minutes or so set it in a quick oven, and bake for nearly an hour.

Wheat Bread

Three quarts of water, luke-warm, a spoonful of salt, half a pint of light yeast; stir in enough flour to make a thick batter, then let it stand to rise. After it is light enough add more flour to it and knead it well into loaves; then put it in pans greased with olive oil. When it rises sufficiently a second time, bake about three-quarters of an hour in a thoroughly heated oven.

—ESTHER LEVY
The Jewish Cookery Book, 1871

cultivated for two thousand years. Now Asians watched in awe as they plunked peach pits in the ground and saw fruit come forth within two years.

Word spread to villages back home that Americans ate cake for breakfast, huge quantities of soft white bread, and meat every day. The desire and expectation to eat abundantly came to express the very essence of America. Immigrants endured poverty. They pinched pennies and haggled. They transformed every scrap of organ meat or old bread. But despite all this, they ate better in the United States than they had ever eaten in their lives. They could enjoy meat a couple of

> *W*e got off the train, with the horse and buggy, and the snow was so deep my brother put me on his shoulders. And we went over to my father's brother to eat. Well, when I saw all that food, I almost went crazy. He had a fruit store. He had great, big pears. I picked one of those pears, and I started eating.
>
> —MARY NAZARO STRACCO
> emigrated from Italy 1921, age nine,
> interviewed by Ellis Island
> National Park Service, 1997

times a week, not a couple of times a year. They could savor the luxuries of eggs and milk and cheese regularly, not just on holidays.

In the United States, men became more deeply involved in cooking than they had been at home. Indeed, when you go searching for stories about immigrants and food, you'll often find recollections written by men. This was partly due to the fact that millions of men came to America by themselves as laborers, without women, and they missed the food of home. They quickly realized that they'd have to get into the kitchen and figure out how to do it themselves. This experience had long-lasting effects, making food all the more important.

In Chicago, Italian men formed cooperative clubs to manage marketing and cooking. The experience was revelatory. When Italian women finally arrived, they found their men somewhat transformed. Having done the job of cooking for themselves for a while, husbands now felt they understood a thing or two about matters of the kitchen.

Though Italian men happily relinquished the daily duties of the soup pot, they continued to peer over their wives' shoulders in the kitchen. In America, perhaps more than back home, they were exacting critics at the dinner table. Caring about food, knowing about food, being an authority on what was good and what wasn't—all this became a hallowed part of Italian-American manhood, a trait that has been passed on through generations, as many Italian Americans (including this one) will attest. In America, Italian men built wood-burning ovens in their backyards. They planted vegetable gardens and fig trees. They helped can tomatoes or cure salami. They made wine in the basement.

And while it may have seemed like a blessing, all this attention had its complications for their wives. Immigrant men developed higher ideals for what they would eat. Most of the Italians who came to the United States were *contadini*, peasants from the South. In villages, they had lived on polenta, bread, and vegetables, supplemented seasonally with fruits and nuts. Many could not even afford frequent macaroni. Women cooked simple meals—over an open fire, out-of-doors, relying on only a few pots and utensils. They baked bread in the community oven. Some villages had no stores. Josephine Nardone Scola, who immigrated from southern Italy in 1920 at age ten, recollected that they ate "vegetables and potatoes and stuff like that there, you know. And, it was nothing luxury like, like over here and so, so we got along."

But memory of Italian standards also influenced cooking in the United States. In the homeland, the beauty of bourgeois Italian cuisine had been well known to the *contadini* even though they couldn't afford it themselves. Peasants worked the fields of southern Italy processing crops they would never eat, preparing olive oil and wine they would never taste, making ricotta cheese that would go only to the wealthy.

Now, in the United States, they could finally have these foods. Despite low wages, Italian immigrants spent a high portion of their money on food—not only assimilating American items but also doing everything they could to get their hands on Italian imports. From modest budgets, they bought expensive imported olive oil, macaroni, and cheeses. And they ate meat whenever they could, perhaps as much as two or three times a week.

In an odd twist of history, these Italians could only eat Italian—and in some ways could only become Italian—when they left home and arrived in America. Only in America then could they finally enjoy the fruits of their heritage. And so, they re-created feasts and festivals—except now, in the New World, they could afford to go to the hilt. The result: a new cuisine was born—Italian-American cuisine—renowned for its abundance.

In the United States, Italians of many backgrounds came together to create fusions. In the old country, cooking varied distinctly according to region. Sausage, bread, and pizzas were different from town to town. But in America, Italians created "Italian sausage," "Italian bread," and simply pizza, and eventually, spaghetti and meatballs—a uniquely American adaptation. Here was a cuisine that combined memory of the old country with the lavish bounty of the new.

Could she bake a good Easter bread or panetone for holidays? Did she make her own ravioli? And by the 1950s, did she make a good sauce? Italian-American social life revolved around family dinners, communal feasts, and religious holiday

Shared meals gave families strength to withstand the hardships of immigrant life.
PHOTO BY LEWIS HINE. *(Milstein Division of United States History, Local History and Genealogy, The New York Public Library, Astor, Lenox and Tilden Foundations.)*

foods. In these settings, the Italian wife could take satisfaction in setting out the good food that made these events happen.

Chinese immigrant men also frequently found themselves in the kitchen. They too were forced—out of necessity and the shortage of wives—to cook for themselves. By 1900 in the United States, there was a ratio of about four Chinese women to every eighty-five men. In San Francisco's Chinatown, men were at the market stands, selling and buying the food; men were in the streets delivering cooked dinners.

Italian Easter Cake

1 package yeast	1 teaspoon salt
¼ cup warm water (100 to 115 degrees) for activating yeast	1 tablespoon rum lemon and orange rind
½ cup Crisco	1½ cups sugar
10 eggs, extra large	4½ cups flour

Mix yeast and warm water and set aside. Beat shortening and sugar. Beat in eggs. Add salt, rum, and rind. Add yeast and water mixture. Add flour one cup at a time, beating thoroughly after each addition.

Cover and put in a warm area and let rise for 24 hours. Transfer batter to a greased angel food tube pan and allow to rise for three to four more hours.

Put in preheated 350-degree oven and bake for 45 minutes. If you wish to add icing, use milk and confectioner sugar to create a paste and brush over cake when it is cool. Add sprinkles if desired.

—MARIA ARGENTO
emigrated from Italy, 1918
recipe as told by her son, Lou

All over eastern and southern Europe, women made very special breads for Easter. Like the Christmas Peppers mentioned earlier, this recipe also comes from Maria Argento's kitchen, but it joins an old recipe with the influence of American abundance, calling for a lavish 10 eggs. Also, this recipe calls for a uniquely American product: Crisco shortening, as well as optional sprinkles.

This is really a sweet bread. It requires little effort but much time, generating an atmosphere of drama and preparation in your kitchen during the days before the most important holiday of the Catholic Church. Tall and beautiful after more than 24 hours of rising, this cake tastes rich and almost custardlike because it has so many eggs.

Tips: When you scrape lemon and orange peel, don't go down to the white part of the rind. Two teaspoons work nicely. Use the biggest bowl you have to allow the dough to grow large. Remove from the oven when the top is light brown and a skewer comes out dry. Lou says 45 minutes, but mine finishes sooner. Begin checking at 35 to 40 minutes.

Those few women who did arrive lived deeply constrained lives in the shadow of a highly chauvinistic culture. According to the social expectations of San Francisco's conservative Chinatown, respectable Chinese women were not to be seen in public except on special occasions and holidays. Women of high social class had bound feet (a Chinese practice that dwarfed women's feet to about three or four inches in size), making it difficult and painful to get around.

Though thousands of Chinese men had to cook for themselves, they also cooked because they found it profitable. In the early California of the "frontier," females were in short supply for every ethnic group, and from all accounts, laborers, miners, and businessmen desperately sought something good to eat. Discriminated against in mining and agriculture, Chinese men found that they could survive by providing "women's work," opening laundries and restaurants that lured Americans and other western migrants with their flavorful dishes of rice and fresh vegetables stir-fried in oil. Chinese men excelled at cooking traditional dishes that relied on pickled ingredients, dried mushrooms, water chestnuts, and stir-fried bok choy. But they also adapted to American abundance, creating fusion dishes like Chop Suey, which included larger quantities of meat.

When Chinese wives finally arrived in the United States, they expected to take over the cooking, as it was considered a womanly virtue to excel in the domestic sphere. But some found themselves outclassed by men.

Gumgee Young waited for years to be approved as a merchant's wife so that she could leave her southern Chinese village and reunite with her husband in California. When she finally arrived in 1907, she found that she had no idea how to cook in an American kitchen. It was a man—her husband's partner—who gave her lessons. "She didn't like to listen to anybody. But it was a good experience. He was a fastidious and excellent cook. He taught her not only how to use an American wood-burning stove but to be precise in her cooking," recalls Gumgee's granddaughter Connie Young Yu, a California historian who, during a telephone interview, fondly remembered cooking at her grandmother's side. "My grandmother pickled everything. This was very important in Chinese culture. Food was so precious and scarce. She pickled garlic and peaches. Her bok choy and chicken were very fresh, but her pickled things would last for years. She would dry tangerine peels and add them to her braised duck. Nothing was wasted. Because they remembered being hungry, they could never take food for granted. Not even an orange peel."

By the 1920s, Chinese women had increased in numbers in the United States. But Chinese-American men remained involved in the cooking for a long time.

"My father used to take a fish and remove the meat, mix it up with goodies, put it back in the skin perfectly and serve it," recalled Fay Chew, whose father took over the family business, Three Star Restaurant, at 10 Mott Street in New York's Chinatown. Fay's mother cooked mostly because it was a job that had to be done. Her father, on the other hand, approached home cooking with zeal and inspiration. Because he had spent time as a cook in the U.S. Army, he excelled at old and new—from the American Thanksgiving turkey to a twelve-egg Chinese sponge cake, steamed in a large wok and decorated using a wooden stamp and red food coloring.

Fay tells me that many of her contemporaries growing up in Chinatown during the 1950s shared this experience: Fathers enjoyed cooking at home for their families.

Of course, some dishes—especially those that pertained to the rituals of birth and death—remained the exclusive province of women. Each year the women in Fay's family prepare food for their deceased ancestors, bringing poached chicken or other dishes to feed the cemetery, honoring those who have passed on. And when Fay gave birth to a daughter more than twenty years ago, her mother insisted on preparing a traditional postpartum soup according to Chinese tradition. It was made of pig's feet and knuckles boiled with "old ginger," red vinegar, and if the cook wished, boiled eggs and sugar. The nutrients in the bones and ginger were known to help the mother recover. "I didn't really like it," she confessed. "But I took some to appease my mother."

FINDING A PLACE IN THE FOOD CHAIN

Many women found it important to earn money—something that most of them had never done in their native countries. Although most married women preferred to stay home and raise children, sometimes their husbands' wages were insufficient and there was no choice. Young women and girls were also expected to quit school and get a job, if necessary, to contribute to the family's survival. Clerical and retail jobs were out of the question for those who did not speak English or have formal educations.

Immigrant women took jobs in canneries in Pittsburgh and California, in the stockyards of Chicago, in the chocolate factories of Pennsylvania, or peeling shrimp for California fishing companies. They took "outwork," shelling nuts at their kitchen tables so they could keep an eye on young children. Most of these jobs were mind numbing, repetitive, and low paying.

Women also got jobs in agriculture—particularly Japanese, Mexican, and some Italians who had come from cultures where it was customary for them to work family lands. Wage labor in American agribusiness was a very different story, however, as they quickly learned. Mexicans faced the constant uncertainty of seasonal layoffs, as they moved across the nation following planting seasons and harvests. Japanese families had to relocate every three years, leasing new farms, because American law forbade them from owning land.

If you were an immigrant and had just a few resources and some ingenuity, however, it was possible to avoid the fate of factory and field work. You could sell food yourself. You could cook for homesick, laboring men who had no wives. You could run a bakery from your house. You could grow vegetables and sell your produce on your front stoop or pushcart. From these beginnings, you might even grow an enterprise.

My mother, born and raised in Naka-gusuku, Okinawa, came to Hawai'i as a teenager to work the sugar cane fields of Hawai'i for 50 cents a day. However, she was able to save enough money from her meager earnings to send a small amount of money every year to relatives back home to buy land. I did not know this until she died. Going through her letters with a friend who could read Japanese, I discovered that my mother had, at one time, 18 parcels of land, one parcel for each year she worked in the cane fields.

—JULIA ESTRELLA
The Rice Cooker's Companion, 2000

In this way, historian Donna Gabaccia notes, many newcomers got their first foothold in the American economy. Immigrants first sold food in ethnic neighborhoods where their neighbors craved ingredients that American food companies did not offer. Decades later, perhaps powered by the influence of sons and daughters, they'd expand. Almost always, these businesses were family affairs. By involving sons, daughters, and brothers in nonstop round-the-clock labor, immigrants could beat the odds and achieve financial success. They could build a foundation for their families and pass on their livelihoods to the next generations.

Many of these businesses began mod-

Latino-owned grocery store, southern California, 1920s. Women were often essential partners in family-owned food businesses. *(Shades of L.A./Los Angeles Public Library.)*

estly—often from a wife's kitchen. At the turn of the century, hundreds of Italian women in New York City were selling Italian ices, manufacturing macaroni in their kitchens, and offering bread from their cellar bakeries. They hung up pasta to dry on tenement roofs. Italian women also worked with their husbands in "truck gardening" businesses that spread across the United States, selling fruits and vegetables at open-air markets and stands in Italian neighborhoods. Some of these businesses grew into import companies and dairy stores that imported specialty items like Italian cheeses and olive oils. Though Italians always put the man's name on the door, women behind the scenes were crucial to many of these businesses.

In 1914, Luigi Di Pasquale opened a neighborhood grocery store in Baltimore where Italians could buy things like *bacala* (dried codfish), snails, pasta, and *Romano* cheese. It was the kind of place that had no sign on the door, but chickens out front. He and his wife, Giovanna, lived upstairs, where they raised seven children. Luigi had worked for a while on a railroad job and hated it. When he started the grocery business, he found his passion and seemed to have unstoppable energy, working seven days a week. Though the business was ostensibly his, Giovanna was integral to its success. To expand profits, Luigi took merchandise out to country neighborhoods, selling from the back of his truck. He could only do this because Giovanna remained behind in charge of both the children and the store.

"She was a petite woman, but she would carry big pieces of meat from the refrigerator to the meat block," recalled her now eighty-year-old son during a recent phone interview. "She used to pickle pigs' feet and make codfish cakes to sell in the store." After her husband died in 1959, she still came into the store regularly. But by then, another generation was in charge, Luigi Jr. and his wife, Mary. "I had a wife who was just as good as my mother," recalls Luigi, who goes by the name of Louis. "She was with me in anything I started. She was sharp. Oh, she cooked. A very good cook."

Chinese women in San Francisco also worked in grocery stores, helping in the family business, though the first generation tended to stay behind the scenes and out of sight. After working on the railroads and saving money, Lee Wong Sang sent for his wife, and the family lived behind his general store. Although it was not considered appropriate for Mrs. Wong Lee to be seen in public, she was quite successful nonetheless at making, in the back of the store, sweet rice cakes that sold well for the Chinese New Year.

Immigrant food businesses provided more than just something to eat. At the *salumeria*, the bakery, the grocery store, neighbors could talk to one another in their native tongue. Restaurants and cafes, in particular, evolved into meeting places where neighbors (usually men) could gather and talk

In the Lower East Side of New York City, the Egyptian Rose, a Syrian restaurant opened by Rose Misrie in 1919, drew customers into a web of community. "The restaurant never had a menu," recalled Rose's eighty-seven-year-old daughter in a recent interview. "All of the customers would come into the kitchen and take off the covers of the pots on the stove and point, 'Rose, I want a bit of this and a little bit of that.'" The Egyptian Rose was a home away from home to Middle Eastern Jews, many of whom were men without their wives.

Italian market on Mulberry Street, New York, filled with crowds, food, and life, 1900–10.
(Library of Congress.)

While immigrants may have first marketed their wares within their communities, by the 1920s Americans began tentatively expanding their taste frontiers. Immigrant food businesses began to attract the native-born and those of other ethnicities who wanted more adventurous eating. Perhaps not coincidentally, at around the same time, the new immigration law of 1924 dramatically stemmed the tide of incoming foreigners to a mere trickle. It would remain this way for the next forty years.

CRISCO AND OTHER NEW IDENTITIES

While it was great to have everyone love your cooking, being a culture bearer came at a price. It could be quite confining.

Jade Snow's father thought it imperative that she learn how to cook rice properly by age six and eat traditional foods. But he did not think it imperative that she get an American education. One day, while Jade Snow was eating her hot breakfast of "fresh-cooked rice, oiled salt fish, sprinkled with peanut oil and shredded ginger root soup with mustard greens, and steamed preserved duck eggs with chopped pork," she began asking about schooling. Her mother described the many years of learning available, including college. But her father interrupted, "You are a girl, so you need not worry about that. It will not be necessary for you to go to college."

In America, a chasm lay between past and future: between cooking rice perfectly and going to school, between ritual Sabbath dinners and middle-class mobility, between the old mamma in the kitchen and the "New Woman" of the 1920s who motored about in cars.

Most immigrants loved America as a place for making money. But they did not always approve of American culture. By 1920, native-born American women had pushed the bonds of female social mores, slowly winning entry to a college education and careers and organizing themselves in community activism and philanthropy.

Generalizations nearly always fail, but it is fair to say that many immigrant men preferred their wives and daughters in "old world" roles, devoted to family. Some drew an invisible boundary at the kitchen door. They liked seeing their wives and daughters cook long and hard.

While the first generation of immigrant women may have happily kept faith to these ways, living out their arranged marriages and never learning to speak English, the next generation longed for more than just the America of abundant food. They wanted the America of leisure and education, if not for themselves then for their daughters.

Quick American cooking with packaged food products seemed to embody these choices. "My mother didn't cook all the things her mother did. She was in America and had to be American," recalled my father's cousin Adele Bachagaloupi, whose mother, Tessie, emmigrated as a young child from Genoa at the turn of the century. "You know, Italian cooking was a lot of work. Especially when you had little ones."

Younger, unmarried daughters sought American clothes and fashion, movies, and cars. Vicky Ruiz has written of Chicana teens during the 1920s who saved their earnings from work in canneries to bob their hair and dress as "flappers," against their parents' will.

For the second generation of women, education and philanthropic work pro-

vided stepping stones to American culture—
so did American recipes and table manners.
For some ethnic groups this came sooner
rather than later.

Jews in America tended to encourage
schooling for their daughters. Coming from
an international culture, they had always valued literacy because it ensured the continuity
of their religious beliefs around the globe.
Jewish women also had predecessors to help
them. A significant number of middle-class
German Jews had already immigrated in the
middle of the nineteenth century, successfully integrating into American life. These
more assimilated women set up charitable organizations and schools to educate
the newcomers and help them navigate their new country. By 1880, just about
every Jewish community in the United States claimed some sort of women's philanthropic group.

Look for cookbooks published in the United States by Italian or Chinese
women before 1920, and you'll encounter a great silence. Because of their high
level of education, Jewish women, on the other hand, published a fair number.
The most fascinating aspects of these cookbooks reveal the choices Jewish women
made and, at times, the conflicts that they felt as they negotiated the tension
between kosher laws and their upwardly mobile aspirations.

This balancing act begins in the 1871 *Jewish Cookery Book* by Esther Levy (an
immigrant most likely from England), who called for a kosher table while insist-
ing somewhat defensively that kosher could still be elegant. By contrast, a succession of Jewish cookbooks spoke to the new eastern European immigrant with a
folksier tone, rejecting kosher law but embracing "Jewish" traditions from all
over the world nonetheless. In 1889, "Aunt Babette's" popular cookbook rose to
prominence, featuring Passover specialties alongside the trendy American Charlotte Russe and the *treyf* Oysters on Shell. By 1923, *Fannie Fox's Cook Book*
appealed to a younger generation of Jewish women who were modern, educated,
and slim. She included gelatin salads in her Jewish repertoire and focused on
American time-saving techniques. For Jews who remained faithful to kosher

> To wash rice correctly is the first step in
> cooking rice correctly, and it is consid-
> ered one of the principal accomplishments or
> requirements of any Chinese female. When
> Jade Snow was six, Daddy had stood her on a
> stool at the kitchen sink in order to teach her
> himself this most important step, so that he
> could be personally satisfied that she had a sure
> foundation.
>
> —JADE SNOW WONG
> *Fifth Chinese Daughter,* 1950

practices, the Hebrew Publishing Company offered a number of Yiddish manuals emphasizing traditional observance.

As the twentieth century marched on, many Jewish women felt comfortable assimilating through the table, partaking in the fruits of American technology and convenience and all its symbols of progress. It was possible to do this, they proved, and still remain Jewish in identity, soul, and even according to religious law, if they wished.

One of the most famous American cookbooks of all time would emerge from

Americanization meant buying products. Because it was "neutral"—neither dairy nor meat—Crisco offered kosher women new options in baking and cooking. Published in 1935. *(Courtesy J. M. Smucker Company.)*

Cracker or Matzos Balls

This recipe comes from the best-selling fund-raising cookbook of all time, put together by German Jewish women to help immigrants learn American foods and preserve Jewish traditional dishes. Note that yesterday's marble-sized matzos have grown considerably over the decades, thanks to American abundance.

Butter size of walnut

I egg

Chopped parsley

Salt and cracker meal.

Stir the butter, add egg, then as much cracker meal as it absorbs. Moisten with a little soup, add parsley and salt. Roll into marbles and boil in the soup just before serving.

—*The "Settlement" Cook Book*, 1903

this legacy. When Mrs. Simon Kander and Mrs. Henry Schoenfeld originally compiled an array of German Jewish recipes, they intended to create a textbook for use at the Milwaukee Settlement House, which provided cooking classes to newly arrived Jewish immigrants. The resulting *Settlement" Cook Book* (subtitled *The Way to a Man's Heart*) captured the essence of Jewish assimilation. American Boston Brown Bread, Mint Julep, and Celery Salad recipes stand alongside Matzos Balls [*sic*], Pickled Herring, Kugel, and fourteen recipes for Kuchen. The original 1901 printing was revised and expanded through forty editions. It remains the best-selling charitable cookbook of all time.

For other immigrant women, assimilation would come along a different set of pathways and take many more decades. Chinese women saw the bonds of the past loosened with the 1911 Revolution, which ended the practice of footbinding and brought new ideas of women's roles. These ideas spread to Chinese communities in the United States, and women began appearing more frequently in public and organizing philanthropic groups and fund-raising events—classic features of American middle-class life. As the twentieth century moved on, they began to create community cookbooks—joining that great American women's tradition—raising money for causes they cared about.

By 1913, a San Francisco newspaper reported that two hundred local Chinese women were meeting regularly, offering evening classes—first in Chinese, then in English—to illiterate immigrants. Historian Judy Yung tells us that by the 1920s, Chinese-American women of the YWCA in San Francisco helped investigate and improve the working conditions of Chinese women in fruit factories. The YWCA was also succeeding in Americanizing second-generation daughters—especially in child care, offering extremely popular Well Baby Contests and translating the American book *Baby Diet* into Chinese. Meanwhile, Chinese-American women began showing up at men's banquets and marching in Chinatown parades. Change was coming.

Italian assimilation took more time. Though Italians worked hard and pros-

Well Baby Contest, 1928. The winner said she used a book called *Baby Diet* as her guide.
(Courtesy Chinese YWCA, San Francisco.)

Chinese Melon
Tung Kwa Tsun

1 melon
1 can of bamboo shoots
1 can of button mushrooms
  Meat of one small chicken
1 cup of lotus seed

Dice chicken, bamboo and mushrooms, scrape and wash melon, cut off the top and scoop seed out of melon. Put the melon in a large bowl and sprinkle with a little salt. Put chicken, mushrooms, bamboo and lotus seed in a bowl, add salt, mix thoroughly. Then put the mixture in the melon, and cover with the piece cut from the top of the melon, and steam for four or five hours. Add soy sauce just before serving. This will serve ten people. *Contributed by Thom Sui Seen.*

—FENN MO
Chinese Recipes, 1930

This banquet dish comes from one of the earliest Chinese community cookbooks published in America. The frontispiece reads "To Miss Donaldina Cameron and Her Chinese Daughters whose gracious hospitality has taught many friends to appreciate more than rare viands." Donaldina Cameron was a legendary social worker who worked at the Presbyterian Mission Home in San Francisco, rescuing Chinese women in trouble—prostitutes, abused wives, and women sold in slave trade to the United States. The book itself is a statement for the rights of woman and a testament to Chinese women organizing and asserting themselves in American life.

pered all across the United States, they seemed to resolutely delay becoming "Americanized." Fathers showed little interest in sending sons, much less daughters, to college. Italian-American women joined few philanthropic clubs.

For a culture that is renowned for hospitality and warmth, Italians, somewhat ironically, felt uncomfortable venturing from the circle of family, neighborhood,

1. IMPORTED MEATS, FISH AND VEGETABLES.

Chinese Name			English Equivalent	How Sold
白	菓	Bak Koh	White nuts	In Bulk
鮑	魚	Bau Yee	Abalone	In Cans
草	菇	Chau Goo	Dried long mushrooms	In Bulk
川	耳	Chin Ngee	Fungus or Truffles	In Bulk
竹	笋	Chuk Sun	Bamboo shoots	In Cans
冲	菜	Chung Choy	Preserved salted turnip	In Bulk
大 蝦	肉	Dai Ha Yuke	Dried shrimps, large	In Bulk
豆	豉	Dau See	Salted black soy beans	In Bulk
冬	菇	Doong Goo	Dried round mushrooms	In Bulk
髮	菜	Fat Choy	Hair-like sea weeds	In Bulk
腐	竹	Fu Chuk	Dried bean curd skin	In Package & Bulk
金	菜	Gum Choy	Lily flowers	In Bulk
蝦 米	仔	Ha Mai	Dried shrimps, small	In Bulk
生晒蠔	豉	Hau See, Sarng Sai	Dried fresh oysters	In Strings
熟㑐蠔	支	Hau See, Sook Sai	Dried cooked oysters	In Bulk
海	蜇	Hoy Jit	Sea vegetable	In Bulk
紅	棗	Hung Jo	Dried red dates	In Bulk
杏	仁	Hung Yun	Chinese almonds	In Bulk
燕	窩	Inn Wo	Bird's nest	In Boxes

Chinese-English glossary from *Chinese Home Cooking*, published in 1941 by Chinese-American women in Honolulu, to raise funds for the war effort in China. *(Courtesy YWCA, Honolulu.)*

and church. Of course, there are always exceptions, but perhaps until the 1960s, Italian men tended to stay in family businesses and work together in trades, while Italian women remained largely at home. For some, this was simply the right place to be. For others it was a choice made by fathers, and there was little to discuss.

Which brings me back to recipes like Christmas Peppers and Easter Bread and the bonds of family, food, and love that sometimes seem inseparable. Though many Americans shared traditional values, Italians seemed more single-minded about exalting family. They tended to emphasize work over education. Herein was the paradox. The bonds of love and labor that created their success in America also limited it. Family life held the center of gravity, and the dinner table pulled everyone together. For decades, Italians did not understand how they might compromise.

But eventually they did. Assimilation came, inevitably, with the passage of time, and today, the cuisine of Italian grandmothers is celebrated across the nation, while Italian-American women obtain careers and education. The memories of hunger eventually faded into the twilight, transformed and replaced by a new legacy of abundance and equality for men and women.

Crustelli, Italian cookies for Christmas, 1989, baked at the home of Carmy Destito, Walla Walla, Washington. PHOTO BY JENS LUND. *(Library of Congress.)*

Chapter 8

Technology's New Homemaker

*M*ore than 27 million people came to see it. They came by trains. They came by trolleys. They came by horse and by foot. They came by boat, across oceans. Never in the history of the United States had so many human beings gathered in a single place during such a short time.

That place was Chicago, and the event was the 1893 Columbian Exposition, a World's Fair of unprecedented proportions. Thirty-six nations participated, putting on more than five thousand exhibits. The nation's leading architects designed more than two hundred buildings and plazas, all painted white—including huge palaces designed to look like the temples of ancient Greece—and spread across 630 acres of woods, lagoons, and green acres.

At the "White City," as it was called, there were jugglers, bellydancers, and a magnificent ferris wheel. Visitors could take a gondola ride or gape at a fifteen-hundred-pound Venus de Milo made of chocolate. The Palace of Fine Arts displayed sculptures and paintings from around the world. Orchestras played symphonies. Intellectual congresses gathered the world's greatest thinkers to discuss religion, art, and every other conceivable topic.

But the main purpose of the fair was to promote commerce and invention.

"Entering the building the whirr of wheels and the roar of machinery assails

An electric kitchen, 1896—a futuristic vision. Note that each appliance on the stove top has a burner with its own electrical plug. (Library of Congress.)

our ears," wrote newspaper correspondent Marian Shaw as she observed displays of boilers, pumps, and automated factory machines. "We stand in awe before these mighty engines that seem endowed with life and intelligence."

Most visitors to the fair felt physically and mentally dwarfed by the futuristic inventions they beheld. They stared at the canons and telescopes, the steam engines and modern heating systems, unable to comprehend the mechanisms that made such things possible. Did it push? Did it pull? Who could guess? The Electricity Building brought the greatest wonder of all. Farmers who had never touched a mechanical lever cast their eyes on Thomas Alva Edison's Tower of Light, almost eight stories high, shining with incandescent light manipulated into kaleidoscopic designs.

The metaphors seemed clear that summer in Chicago. The darkness of human suffering would be chased away by the beautiful lights of science. Human beings were evolving into a higher race; they would live longer, labor less, be cleaner and better educated. Children would no longer face hunger and disease. Technology would bring utopia. It was only a matter of time.

THE EMANCIPATED WOMAN IS A HOUSEWIFE, TOO

In this dazzling modern fair of male-dominated science and invention, where would women find their place? This was the very question that obsessed some of the best female minds of the generation.

By the end of the nineteenth century, women had made some notable progress into professions, universities, and public life. It became clear that they deserved an active role of some kind at the World's Fair, and so the U.S. Congress appointed a "Board of Lady Managers" made up of 119 of the nation's leading women.

It was up to these women to plan some kind of women's angle for the fair. After much wrangling, they decided that the female gender needed to have its very own building. And so it was. By opening day, a gloriously designed Woman's Building stood grandly on the fairgrounds, filled to the rafters with paintings, sculptures, literature, books, inventions, and handicrafts—all produced by women. The purpose was to show the world just how far the female sex had come. Two women's congresses brought hundreds of speakers to discuss every important women's issue of the day.

Ladies of the respectable Victorian middle class dominated the events with issues like "the servant crisis," women's volunteer work, education, and child care. But the radicals arrived as well, including suffragists like Susan B. Anthony and Lucy Stone, who came to demand the vote. Dress reformers appealed for the end of long dangerous skirts. And African-American women stood up and called for the advancement of the black race. Even though they didn't all agree, the fair was a huge event in women's emergence into public life. For the first time in history, women of all kinds had a chance to gather together in large numbers, organize themselves, and talk about what mattered to them.

The World's Fair was also a huge event for food.

All the nation's greatest culinary women attended and gathered for the first time around a single mission—the improvement of the nation's cookery. This seemed to be one area of women's progress that everyone could agree on.

In this era of scientific breakthrough, a certain consensus had built that American women should not be left behind in slavelike drudgery. While the business world whizzed ahead with labor-saving machines, many housewives were still hauling water from public wells, still carrying wood to their stoves, and still boiling down sorghum in backbreaking quantity. It was time for this inequality to end, and the cooking experts came to the World's Fair to say so. They dispersed far and wide over the fair grounds, heralding a new message to millions of women about the possibilities of labor-saving science and efficiency in the kitchen. Unlike the culinary woman of the 1840s who apologized for working and making money, this generation boldly went forth.

In the Electricity Building, a rising culinary woman name Helen Louise Johnson demonstrated the amazing electric stoves and appliances in Edison's kitchen (not to become widely available for another thirty years). Juliet Corson, founder of the New York Cooking School, ran scientific cooking classes in the New York State Building, showing off new ideas of frugality and efficiency. In the Children's Building, Miss Emily Huntington explained how kindergarten girls could begin to learn cooking through play. At a women's congress, held in conjunction with the fair, Mary Lincoln, principal of the Boston Cooking School, gave a major address about the state of cooking in America.

Naturally, the Woman's Building put on a cooking show as well. A "model kitchen" appeared, raised up on a platform, emitting an unmistakable aura of "new and improved." Its "better kitchen table" featured a built-in slot for working utensils. New mechanical devices such as a bread kneader and dishwasher (both nonelectric) promised to relieve drudgery. "Invented by Women," signs proudly proclaimed. The very best cupboards and drainage systems were on display. A modern range, ice box, and gas stove stood in the rear. Manufacturers eagerly contributed their latest ironware, flour, spices, flour bins, and china. The housekeeping committee from the Board of Lady Managers supplied a fitting slogan: "The emancipated woman is a housewife too."

To bring some razzle dazzle, Bertha Honoré Palmer, head of the Board of Lady Managers, recruited the famous author and founder of the Philadelphia Cooking School, Sarah Tyson Rorer, to preside as grand dame of the model kitchen. Rorer was a celebrity cook whose spirited cooking shows drew crowds. That summer, more than 200,000 visitors stopped at her displays, listened, tasted, and happily took home samples and printed materials.

Successful though the model kitchen may have been, Bertha Palmer was disappointed. She had hoped to win another sort of celebrity cook. She'd wanted the much admired Ellen Swallow Richards to open a cafe in her Woman's Building.

Richards was a *femme célèbre* of women in science. The first woman ever to receive a degree from the Massachusetts Institute of Technology, she had made a name for herself as a founder of the Science Laboratory for Women at MIT, where she did pioneering research in ecology and advocated for desperately needed urban sanitation systems.

Richards had also won some acclaim for cofounding the Boston-based New England Kitchen, a "public kitchen" devoted to selling healthful, low-cost, "take-out" dinners to the laboring classes of Boston. Like many a rampant reformer of Victorian America, Richards believed that by teaching proper cooking, she could save the poor, the foreign born, and perhaps even the world.

Here was exactly the sort of impressive, yet not too radical woman whom Palmer was trying to cultivate.

To Palmer's chagrin, Richards said no thank you and instead went ahead and set up a cafe not in the Woman's Building but in a small freestanding clapboard house, closer to the serious display halls of "men." This strategic decision to relocate the ancient female art of cooking closer to the male realm of science was a significant gesture.

"Whatever the reason, we find ourselves now in a desperate case," Richards wrote. "The fact is that the

Ellen Swallow Richards, the first president of the American Home Economics Association, saw the kitchen without romance. *Chemistry of Cooking and Cleaning* was one of her best-known works. *(Special Collections, Vassar College Libraries).*

industrial world is ruled by science and that all things with which we surround ourselves are now manufactured upon scientific principles, and, alas! women are ignorant of those principles."

Richards was the leading intellectual of the new cooking movement that was rolling across the nation. This movement went by various names including "scientific housekeeping," "sanitary cooking," and "scientific cookery," but most often it was called "domestic science" or "home economics."

In the way of visionaries, Ellen Richards believed she could both see the future and shape it as she saw fit. Her mission was to facilitate women's education for the brave new technological world—to introduce a new science suited to the needs of housewives. In her view, it was time for the angelic Victorian housewife of old to transform into a turn-of-the-century technician—preferably a college-educated one—who would master the technicalities of sanitation, bacteriology, home engineering, and most of all, the chemistry of food and cooking.

"The woman who boils potatoes year after year, with no thought of how or why, is a drudge," observed Ellen Richards, "but the cook who can compute the calories of heat which a potato of given weight will yield, is no drudge."

HOME ECONOMICS TAKES ROOT

That summer in Chicago, the culinary leaders charted a beginning for the National Home Economics Association. Six years later, they would meet again for a conference in Lake Placid, where they would formally establish a new academic discipline called *home economics* (the term *euthenics* was a close runner-up). They established a scholarly journal (*The Journal of Home Economics*) and curriculum standards for elementary, secondary, and college education. In 1899, rechristened as the American Home Economics Association, this unique group of women would elect Ellen Richards as its first president and its most important leader.

Throughout the twentieth century, home economics would act as a huge force in American history—one so large and diffuse, so omnipresent and influential that historians have often overlooked it entirely. Home economics began on the community level with grassroots cooking clubs and schools around the nation. Ultimately, women used this foundation to create a new field of expertise for themselves, one that would open doors to jobs in universities, food businesses,

Immigrant girls at the Denison Settlement House learning how to cook with American-style efficiency. Boston, 1911. *(The Schlesinger Library Radcliffe Institute, Harvard University.)*

publishing, and government. Through home economics, ordinary women took a step into the public realm. They organized themselves to better their own lives and the lives of others. They improved public health, hygiene, and food standards for the nation. They lightened the burdens of rural women. They advocated for pure food and developed school lunch programs. They pioneered vitamin-fortified cereals and encouraged the inclusion of more fruits and vegetables in the American diet.

But home economics has an uneven legacy. It was used to eliminate the ethnic ways of immigrants and create a better servant class. It promoted convenience foods that would ultimately de-skill future generations of cooks. It would become a twentieth-century conspiracy to limit women's options. And home economics would create a bland American diet, featuring boring roasts, gelatin salads, and overboiled vegetables covered with white sauce; a national obsession with sterility; a passion for the science of nutrition; and an abiding trust in food factories as representing the "progress" of civilization.

In 1893, however, this was all in the future.

The home economics movement traces its roots to the ancient questions of whether or not women should be educated and if so, how much and in what subjects. Though home economics got an official beginning in 1893 at the Chicago World's Fair, its emergence had begun at least fifty years before with "domestic science." As mentioned earlier, Catharine Beecher had laid the groundwork during the 1840s when she called for women's education, an education that would include scientific cookery and professional housekeeping.

It wasn't until after the Civil War, however, that domestic science exploded.

Smothered Beef, or Pot Roast

Four to six pounds from the middle or face of the rump, the vein, or the round. Wipe with a clean wet cloth. Sear all over by placing in a hot frying-pan and turning till all the surface is browned. Put in a kettle with one cup of water, and place it where it will keep just below the boiling-point. Do not let the water boil entirely away, but add only enough to keep the meat from burning. Have the cover fitting closely to keep in the steam. Cook until very tender, but do not let it break. Serve hot or cold.

—MRS. D. A. (MARY) LINCOLN
Mrs. Lincoln's Cook Book, 1883

Mary Lincoln, the author of this recipe, was the first principal of the Boston Cooking School, one of the founding institutes for domestic science. Though many nineteenth-century cooking-school favorites do not stand the test of time, pot roast is an important exception. The goal here is take a cheap piece of meat and transform it into something wonderful using long, slow heat—classic women's home cooking.

Proud of their Civil War relief efforts, many American women wanted to do more good work. A new generation daringly applied to colleges. But could women possibly survive studying alongside men without collapsing? Many had their doubts, and domestic science offered the perfect solution. Women got their own sphere, and universities across the country set up classes and home economics departments for their new female students.

Some domestic science departments pushed a rigorous approach, featuring lab work in physics, chemistry, botany, physiology, bacteriology, and hygiene—all applied to the household. Others, particularly those in rural areas, reached out to farmers' wives, teaching the practical skills of cooking, dairying, preserving, and sewing that were crucial to their daily lives.

Tips: Pot roast has the major pitfall of often coming out dry and tough. There are two possible reasons for this. Either you have not cooked it long enough or, like many of us, you hesitate to buy fatty meat because it seems so unhealthy. For best results, push yourself to buy a piece of chuck in which you see lots of fat running through. This is what makes it taste as good as you remember it. Mary Lincoln's 6 pounder is a bit much. Most of us would prefer a piece between 3 and 4 pounds, which will still feed 6 to 8.

- *Be sure to pat your meat dry before browning it on all sides in oil. (I prefer olive oil, but don't let it smoke.)*
- *To add more flavor, consider the following: After browning, remove the meat from the pan and set aside. In the same pot, saute a chopped onion and a couple of carrots in oil. When these are tender, return your pot roast to the pot along with these vegetables. Add some thyme, 1 cup of water, 1½ cups of chicken and/or beef stock, and ½ cup of red wine. Your cooking liquid should come halfway up the sides of the roast.*
- *Put a tight lid on your pot roast and keep it at a simmer over medium heat—as Mary Lincoln says, just below a boil. This needs to cook long and slow to become tender. Another good way is to put the entire pot in a 300-degree oven. In any case, turn every half hour or so for 3 to 4 hours, until a knife slides easily in and out.*
- *When finished, remove pot roast and skim fat from your pot liquid. Add more red wine if you like. Boil it down until it tastes good. Season with salt or pepper. Carve meat and serve with sauce.*

In any case, the purpose of domestic science was to help women run better households. But there was another purpose as well: at this time in history, more women were wanting meaningful careers, and this transition to work outside the home seemed to be easier when women went into positions that did not veer too terribly far from their traditional roles as helpers, teachers, healers, and feeders of the nation.

Industrialism, westward expansion, mass immigration, and the Civil War had given rise to new forms of human suffering. But for the ambitious and altruistic, here were career opportunities. Emancipated slaves needed education, housing, and jobs. Poor immigrants lived in slums. Displaced Mexicans and Indians, so the thinking went, needed to be reeducated. Hearing their cries, huge numbers of women became teachers, missionaries, public health nurses, and social workers dedicated to uplifting the poor and needy. Like these other female careers, domestic science offered a new path to helping those less fortunate.

During the late 1870s, a collection of energetic and determined cooking teachers provided the greatest firepower for the domestic science movement by founding three highly influential schools: the New York Cooking School, the Philadelphia Cooking School, and the Boston Cooking School.

The leaders of these schools—women like Sarah Tyson Rorer, Maria Parloa, Fanny Farmer, Mary Lincoln, Emma Ewing, and Juliet Corson—became household names. They reached millions of American women through cookbooks, home economics texts, magazine articles, and editorial positions at hugely popular new women's magazines such as *Good Housekeeping* and *Ladies' Home Journal.* They traveled the lecture circuit, speaking at expositions, women's clubs, cooking clubs, philanthropic events, YMCAs, and business events. In those pre-television times, public cooking events were extraordinarily popular. When Juliet Corson arrived to do a cooking demonstration in Cleveland, for example, she found three thousand people and a small swarm of reporters awaiting her.

By the end of the century, universities and cooking schools were churning out thousands of women trained in domestic science. These eager young apprentices found themselves in high demand. A 1916 book, *Opportunities for Women in Domestic Science,* listed the possibilities: A woman trained in domestic science could manage institutional cafeterias in dormitories, hospitals, or insane asylums.

Fall Term, 1905

"Fall Term, 1905" is a college notebook kept by Bertha Rockstroh, a music major who took the first domestic science class ever offered at Wesleyan University in Ohio. "The Body as a Machine" is excerpted from her lecture notes. The Corn Custard comes from "lab."

Bertha was a daughter of German immigrants and a high school valedictorian. Like many women of her era, family duties came first. She dropped out of Wesleyan during her last year to work during a time of financial stress. Later she became a music teacher in California and raised two sons. Her granddaughter remembers her all-American meat-and-potatoes cooking and that she had a beautiful singing voice.

"The Body Is a Superior Machine"

Blood and muscle, bone and tendon, brain and nerve—all organs and tissues of the body are built from the nutrient ingredients of food. With every motion of the body, and with every exercise of feeling and thought as well, material is consumed and must be resupplied by food. In a sense the body is a superior machine. Like other machines it requires material to build up its several parts, to repair as they are worn out, and to serve as fuel. The steam engine gets its power from fuel, the body does the same.

Corn Custard

Cut corn from ears to make 1 c. Add 4 eggs beaten slightly with ½ tsp salt, a dash of cayenne pepper, a little grated onion and 1½ c of milk. Bake in buttered molds in hot water. Do not let the water boil surrounding them. When firm, turn from molds, serve with cream sauce.

Tips: Three eggs are plenty. Forget the cream sauce, but this dish has come back in style with recent additions of grated cheese and a bit more spice. A finely diced jalapeno pepper is nice. Use little molds if you like. But I prefer to bake at 375 degrees for 20 to 25 minutes in a buttered dish placed inside a pan of water. Take out when still a little loose in the center. Let sit for 10 minutes.

—BERTHA ROCKSTROH
"Fall Term, 1905," class notebook

She could open a tearoom, or by far the most common choice, she could become a teacher. Nationally, public schools were installing kitchen "laboratories," where millions of young girls got training early in life on the facts of nutrition, kitchen hygiene, and the correct preparation of roasts and puddings. Mary Lincoln's *The Boston School Kitchen Textbook* was one of the more sacred texts.

If all this wasn't remarkable enough, in 1914 the federal Smith Lever Act required that all the nation's "land grant" colleges (state agricultural schools) had to "extend" their agricultural and home economics knowledge to local communities. Now even the U.S. Department of Agriculture had a home economics department, hiring domestic scientists to write books and pamphlets and sending a small army of "extension agents" to rural communities to teach efficient methods of cooking and housekeeping.

WHERE PUDDING IS HEALTH FOOD

Fannie Merritt Farmer (1857–1915). She took a laboratory approach to cooking but enjoyed adding decorative frills to her presentation. She became a major American success story. *(The Schlesinger Library, Radcliffe Institute, Harvard University.)*

What were the goals of these early home economists?

Nutrition was their greatest passion. By the 1890s, scientific research had revealed the existence of calories, proteins, and fats—but alas, still not vitamins, which would not be discovered until the second decade of the twentieth century. And so the domestic scientists put their faith in meat and espoused its heavy consumption. They did not frown on sugar or cream. It wasn't until after World War I that the discovery of vitamins led home economists to revise their program to include more fruits and vegetables. Still, they remained devoted to meat and milk—a hallmark of the American diet to this day.

Home economists were not trying to create great cooks out of American women. They were public educators trying to bring the masses up to a certain minimum level of proficiency and nutrition. Reaching for broad appeal, they had to focus on a few key messages and in doing so succeeded in defining American middle-class food and American womanhood.

VEGETABLES.

Table showing Composition of Vegetables.

From Fannie
Farmer's *Boston
Cooking-School
Cook Book*, 1896.
According to these
calculations,
vegetables are
fairly useless.

Articles.	Proteid.	Fat.	Carbo-hydrates.	Mineral matter.	Water.
Artichokes	2.6	.2	16.7	1.	79.5
Asparagus	1.8	.2	3.3	1.	94.
Beans, Lima, green .	7.1	.7	22.	1.7	68.5
" green string .	2.2	.4	9.4	.7	87.3
Beets	1.6	.1	9.6	1.1	87.6
Brussels sprouts . .	4.7	1.1	4.3	1.7	88.2
Cabbage	2.1	.4	5.8	1.4	90.3
Carrots	1.1	.4	9.2	1.1	88.2
Cauliflower	1.6	.8	6.	.8	90.8
Celery	1.4	.1	3.	1.1	94.4
Corn, green, sweet .	2.8	1.1	14.1	.7	81.3
Cucumbers	.8	.2	2.5	.5	96.
Egg-plant	1.2	.3	5.1	.5	92.9
Kohl-rabi	2.	.1	5.5	1.3	91.1
Lettuce	1.3	.4	3.3	1.	94.
Okra	2.	.4	9.5	.7	87.4
Onions	4.4	.8	.5	1.2	93.5
Parsnips	1.7	.6	16.1	1.7	79.9
Peas, green	4.4	.5	16.1	.9	78.1
Potatoes, sweet . .	1.8	.7	27.1	1.1	69.3
" white . .	2.1	.1	18.	.9	78.9
Spinach	2.1	.5	3.1	1.9	92.4
Squash	1.6	.6	10.4	.9	86.5
Tomatoes	.8	.4	3.9	.5	94.4
Turnips	1.4	.2	8.7	.8	88.9

W. O. Atwater, Ph.D.

Efficiency was their hallmark. Home economists advocated for the redesign of American kitchens to be more like factory floors—saving steps, bending, and labor. Efficiency also meant dispensing with frills of taste. Fannie Farmer—perhaps America's most famous cook ever—embodied the new efficiency more than anyone. Her recipe for roast pork, for example, asks the cook to do nothing but salt, pepper, and flour the meat, then put it in the oven for three or four hours, regularly basting. Dinner could just as easily be some chunks of chicken put in a pan and covered with white sauce along with canned cream peas. Whereas cookbooks from just a couple of generations earlier offered a wide array of herbal vinegars, sauces made of chili peppers, wine, curry, and ginger, turn-of-the-

Following the Modern Recipe

With domestic science, recipes became written like laboratory formulas, giving exact fool-proof proportions, relying less on chance and instinct.

The Old-Fashioned Way
à la Hannah Glass, 1805

To Make Mutton or Veal Gravy

Cut and hack your veal well, set it on the fire with water, sweet herbs, mace, and pepper. Let it boil till it is as good as you would have it, then strain it off. Your fine cooks always, if they can, chop a partridge or two and put them into gravies.

The Modern Way
à la Fannie Farmer, 1896

Brown Sauce I

2 tablespoons butter	1 cup Brown Stock
½ slice onion	¼ teaspoon salt
2½ tablespoons flour	⅛ teaspoon of pepper

Cook onion in butter until slightly browned; remove onion and stir butter constantly until well browned; add flour mixed with seasonings, and brown the butter and flour; then add stock gradually.

century American cooking became bland. It also became sweeter, with extra sugar added to breads, desserts, and even salads.

And yet Fannie Farmer's *Boston Cooking-School Cook Book* and its revisions would sell upward of four million copies and remain in print for over a hundred years. She must have given women something that they desperately wanted, and

Many women saw a great future in table-side appliances that brought cooking out of the messy kitchen into the comfortable dining room. Advertisement for General Electric toaster, 1908. *(Library of Congress.)*

I suspect it was clearly written, simple recipes suited to busy lives, and uniform results they could count on.

Neat, clean, pretty to the eye—and above all not too spicy or offensive—these things both food and women were supposed to be. "Dainty" was a great accolade of this era—a high compliment paid to any dish. "Dainty Dishes for Dainty People," sang the tag line for Knox gelatin, with pictures of gelatin molds that shimmered like stained glass. What a perfect antidote to the heavy minced pies of the rural past and the image of the disorganized rural housewife with her arms up to the elbows in dough. Dainty was modern and clean.

What other lessons did these culinary ladies bequeath? Here was the era when ordinary women learned how to carve apples into baskets, make rosette potatoes, and put paper frills on the tips of their mutton chops. Fannie Farmer didn't want you to spend your time marinating your roast in wine or herbs, but she did favor croquettes (forerunner to the chicken nugget) and suggested you shape them in the form of ducks or use your lettuce leaves as nests. She liked to curl celery so as to make it look like foliage. Fannie Farmer and her colleagues helped transform food so it would no longer appear like food but like pretty sculptures, dioramas, and laboratory products that transcended any association with messy bodily needs such as eating.

WHITE SAUCE, WHITE NATION

One of the unabashed goals of domestic science was Americanization. The increasing ethnic diversity of the United States was worrisome to many Anglo-Saxon Americans who yearned for a more unified nation. How would Americans hold together if they didn't share the same culture and language, the same American ways? The Italian garlic, furry Bohemian mushrooms, Jewish gefilte fish, the unleavened bannocks of the Indians, Mexican chiles, Asian rice, the pork and cornbread of blacks—all these were reminders of unsettling differences. Some Americans even believed these more highly flavored "foreign" foods to be injurious to the system.

Cooking school teachers took it on themselves to teach frugal and plain New England cooking to the poor and foreign born. They wanted, in part, to help adhere the nation as a whole. A shared diet, a proper diet, was a way to bring peo-

Stewed Celery

Wash, scrape and cut celery in one-inch pieces; there should be two cups. Cook in boiling salted water until tender, drain and add one cup White Sauce.

—FANNIE MERRITT FARMER
Fannie Farmer's Book of Good Dinners, 1905

White Sauce

2 tablespoons butter	1 cup scalded milk
2½ tablespoons flour	⅛ teaspoon pepper
¼ teaspoon salt	

Put butter in sauce pan and stir until melted and bubbling, add the flour and seasonings and cook one minute. Pour on gradually, while stirring constantly, the hot milk. Beat until smooth and glossy, using a wire whisk.

—FANNIE MERRITT FARMER
Fannie Farmer's Book of Good Dinners, 1905

White sauce was a sort of holy grail to the domestic scientists. Known in France as béchamel, it has its worthy place in many dishes, but in the early twentieth century, our great culinary women took it to a sinful extreme, using it mercilessly to blanket vegetables, meats, and fish of all kinds. Some critics have blamed white sauce for encouraging a conservative American food style that favored bland and creamy—a preference that perhaps paved the way for commercial products like instant mashed potatoes, cream of mushroom soup, and American processed cheese.

ple together.

Former slaves were among the first recipients of this training. After the Civil War, the Freedmen's Bureau (a federal agency), the American Missionary Society, and various churches established schools and colleges throughout the South, designed to produce black teachers and leaders. Women at these schools almost always studied some form of domestic science, just as boys studied agriculture

One of the most famous of these schools was the Tuskegee Institute, founded by former slave Booker T. Washington, who became a national celebrity for educating blacks in practical skills. Domestic science held a revered role at his school, where students raised and cooked their own food.

Some critics, such as W. E. B. Du Bois, assailed Washington for teaching a vocational curriculum rather than a liberal academic education. Du Bois wanted blacks to agitate for power and claimed that the Tuskegee Institute was creating a better class of educated maids and field hands.

Despite these charges, many black educators insisted on keeping domestic science as part of the curriculum for girls. For one thing, tenant sharecroppers struggled with monotonous diets of pork, corn, and molasses, and they desperately needed nutritional information. But food also had a long history as a symbol of strength and common bonds among African Americans. Even aggressive advocates for full equality such as Mary McLeod Bethune believed that cooking was valuable for African-American women. Bethune's famous Bethune-Cookman College in Florida promoted both liberal education and domestic science. "Cease to be a drudge. Seek to be an artist" was the cooking motto hung on the wall of her domestic science classroom. In 1904, she herself had raised the five-dollar down payment for her first school by selling ice cream and sweet-potato pies—a testament to the power of cooking and baking. Bethune would become the most powerful black woman ever to work in federal government, serving the Roosevelt administration during the 1930s as an advisor to the president on minority affairs. She also founded the National Association of Colored Women's Clubs.

A far more bitter legacy is woven into the story of cooking classes forced on Indian girls. By the 1880s, even the most compassionate whites believed that if Indians did not accept modern ways, they would become extinct. The federal government established a series of Indian Schools that set out to strip young chil-

Learning to make cookies at Carlisle Indian School, circa 1901.
(*Cumberland County Historical Society, Carlisle, Pennsylvania.*)

dren of their cultures, religions, tribal educations, and loyalties. Historian Francis Paul Prucha estimates that by 1899, dozens of these schools were enrolling more than twenty-three thousand students a year.

Domestic science classes were essential to this mission. "Don't be discouraged girls," said Federal Indian Commissioner Jones in 1898, "much more depends upon you than upon the boys, and we look to you to carry home the refinement that shall really elevate your people."

In 1901, Estelle Reed, the federally appointed superintendent of Indian Schools, wrote that cooking was the "most important department" in these schools because it would help girls to "establish habits of neatness, promptness, and order" and to learn how to serve meals in a "dainty, appetizing way." For these classes, Indian girls were required to wear white aprons and tie their hair back in buns. Some schools required that they master table settings and proper table manners. Indian girls had to learn how to bake cookies and yeast bread. These were the luxuries of civilized societies, luxuries that promised the very refinement that Indians were deemed to be lacking.

Similarly, public school systems throughout the nation used home economics classes to change the dietary ways of immigrants. They fervently tried to get Italians off of olive oil and onto cream and butter. Domestic science classes taught Irish, Slavic, Italian, Greek, Armenian, Jewish, Czech, and Polish girls how to make pea soup, Boston brown bread, corn bread, and apple pudding.

Those the public schools didn't reach, the charities did. At the turn of the twentieth century, more than two hundred settlement houses across the nation were offering some kind of cooking classes to immigrants to help them adjust to the foods and expectations of American life.

The women who taught these classes were often sincere and idealistic, certain that they were on a mission of mercy. They wanted to improve hygiene and nutrition among those who did not know that germs transmitted disease, or that it was essential to wash the baby's bottle before filling it with milk.

> *I*t is not expected that the average Mexican girl in our elementary school can comprehend chemical terms as applied to Household Science, but we can teach her a general knowledge of foods for regulating, building, and furnishing energy to the body, also the methods of preparing cooking, and serving them.
>
> —PEAL IDELIA ELLIS
> *Americanization through Homemaking*, 1929
> Covina School System, California

> *T*o wash currants is one thing, to buy them beautifully clean, in a neat compact package, is quite another and more acceptable method.
>
> —*Table Talk* magazine, January 1893

Racial uplift through cooking. The Bethune-Cookman College in Daytona Beach, Florida, 1943.

PHOTO BY GORDON PARKS. *(Library of Congress.)*

"Made Dandy Cake . . ."

Technology came more slowly to rural areas, most of which were not electrified until the 1930s. This daybook for 1913 was kept by an unmarried thirty-nine-year-old woman who lived in rural Ohio, probably with her parents. She never wrote down her name but made an entry for each of 365 days. She describes her chicken raising, her baking, and preserving. She has faithful evening visits from a male caller named "Orville," who usually came at 7:30.

A remarkable number of her interactions with neighbors pertain to food preservation and labor sharing. Technology would change this life, and it was on the horizon.

Below are selected excerpts showing her mention of food throughout the year.

Jan 14	Am helping Mrs. Smith butcher. Home 5:15. Effie Crawford visited me in PM. An awful pretty day.
February 21	Partly cloudy and very warm. Cleaned up the house a little and made a cake and also a square for comforter. Made hickory nut cake.
April 18	Sold 60 dozen eggs at 15 cents each. Made pies for Mrs. Shinkle.
May 17	Made dandy cake—coconut.
June 27	Very hot. Canned 6 qts of cherries. Sold Mr. Rhodes 42 doz. eggs at 17 cents. All took a nap in P.M. and then took my first Kodak pictures.
December 11	A fine day . . . Made my fruit cake for Xmas. Cleaned upstairs this P.M. Was talking to Jessie.

Despite their sincerity, they often did not win the hearts and stomachs of their victims, at least not among the first generations. Generally, immigrants were deeply attached to their own ways of eating—not just out of habit but for reasons of religion and deeply cherished ideas about cultural identity.

HANDMAIDENS OF INDUSTRY?

The scientific cooks wanted to see women lighten their burdens, and they wanted to create a national palate. All this fit very nicely with the goals of companies interested in selling products.

The famous culinary women endorsed commercial foods and appliances quite freely, allowing their names to be used in advertising. They also put their names on "advertising cookbooks," which ran the gamut from small pamphlets to lengthy works featuring recipes, social advice, and women's etiquette. Food and appliance manufacturers churned out millions of these little books to teach American housewives how to use the newest technological marvels and to win them as consumers.

In this way, home economists—both famous and anonymous—acted as mediators between American women and companies. Virtually every major food and appliance company set up a test kitchen and hired home economists to develop recipes and products and to correspond with consumers.

American women wanted this information. In 1933, when the Bisquick Company announced its first cookbook, more than 700,000 requests came flooding in. New products and appliances were confusing, and women were eager to learn the new tools of their trade. An electric refrigerator booklet carefully explains where various foods should be kept within the refrigerator and the proper way of making ice cubes. A Crisco cookbook details the differences between shortening, lard, and butter. Gelatin companies published booklets that showed how to adhere all sorts of meats, fish, vegetables, and fruits into "salads" you could slice.

Because they were so cheaply made and so widely distributed, advertising cookbooks created a foundation of American cooking and etiquette that lasted for much of the twentieth century. Many of the new recipes played on a sense of novelty. You could use Post Grape Nuts cereal to make meat loaf or build a gelatin ring around canned asparagus. Hilarious as some of these ideas may seem, they had their place. Ingenuity was a hallmark of American life, and American women had always been flexible in their cooking, always willing to borrow and try new things. This culinary flexibility helped fuel the American food business. It also relieved the daily monotony of predictable dishes for those who had to cook each and every day.

Confectionery
factories preferred
women workers.
PHOTO BY LEWIS
HINE. *(Courtesy
George Eastman
House.)*

Not everyone was willing to lie down and take whatever the commercial food-makers passed off without asking questions. The new technological revolution motivated women to get involved in the politics of food—as consumers, activists, and workers.

In 1905, Upton Sinclair published his scathing critique of the meatpacking

Latino and Anglo women at work in a tuna-canning factory, 1920.
(Shades of L.A./Los Angeles Public Library.)

industry, detailing practices that mangled workers and passed off sausage containing rat meat and tripe disguised as ham. The next year, Congress passed the Pure Food Act, after a thirteen-year campaign led by Harvey Wiley, a government scientist. Pure food was a female issue. National women's organizations and local women's clubs had helped work for its passage, and women's magazines took a leading advocacy role. Wiley would later credit women of the nation for turning public opinion in favor of the pure food bill.

This consumer watchdog activism continued. In 1915, local chapters of the National Housewives League organized themselves to seek out and rectify unsanitary conditions of grocers and foodmakers. That same year in a *Ladies' Home Journal* article, Mrs. Julian Heath, president of the NHL, wrote, "We women must realize that we are occupying a new economic position; the responsibility is great."

In 1928, a like-minded organization, the National Consumers League (later renamed the Consumers Union) investigated labor abuses in the candy industry, where the majority of the workforce was female and, not uncoincidentally, dangerous, unsanitary conditions, long hours, and low pay prevailed. When the League published a hair-raising report called *Behind the Scenes in Chocolate Factories,* consumers were horrified. Afraid of losing sales, candy companies immediately responded. They promised to make factories cleaner and, more reluctantly, to bring minimum wage up to $14 per week. The League then produced a candy "white list" that told consumers which brands had complied with these demands.

It was, of course, a myth that commercial foods were produced by machines and not by women. When technology sent food production out of the home to the factory, women workers went with it, working in bakeries, canneries, confectioneries, milk and butter companies, meatpacking houses, grain mills, and other food factories. During these early years, men got men's jobs and women got women's jobs, which were always worse.

Canneries and confectioneries, for example, preferred low-wage female workers. Both offered seasonal work, requiring long hours during busy times and then laying off workers during slow times. This practice, the companies believed, could be better borne by young women who didn't have to support families. By 1930, 44 percent of all canning and preserving workers and 58 percent of all con-

Applying scientific management to housework. A man uses a stopwatch to evaluate the time efficiency of a woman beating eggs, 1912–14. Conducted at the Applecroft Home Experiment Station, founded by home economist Christine Frederick to study labor-saving food preparation and household products. (*The Schlesinger Library, Radcliffe Institute, Harvard University.*)

"Why the American Family Is Eating Less Each Year"

We do eat less, and here are some of the explanations for the why of it:

1. Fewer persons (in ratio to the population) are doing heavy manual, muscular or outdoor work.
2. Fewer persons are affected by climate and cold, now better controlled by modern heating methods in home, office and industrial plants.
3. Less leisure and time is allotted to eating, owing to complications of commuting, transportation, etc.; general "speeding up" affects eating as well as other habits.
4. Eating as an amusement and pleasure is largely superseded by other amusements, automobiling, movies, travel, etc.
5. There is today wider acceptance of educational direction on matters of dietetic, health and nutritive food values.
6. There is market fashion trend for the slender figure and accompanying slenderizing, reducing, etc., particularly by women.
7. The "servant problem" lessens possibility of elaborate home entertaining and complicated cooking.
8. Women, when themselves doing housework, cook less and spend less time in the kitchen because of a desire for more leisure; what they do cook is simpler and prepared in a shorter period.
9. Present kitchen and storage space is limited and confined and not conducive to elaborate meal preparation.
10. Cooking is no longer a means of "showing off" or emulation by "conspicuous consumption."
11. More women in industry, professional and business fields lessens the amount of former "free help" in the home devoting itself to cooking and household duties.

—CHRISTINE FREDERICK
Selling Mrs. Consumer, 1928

fectionery workers were female—including many immigrants. By the 1930s, growing numbers of women workers began to organize themselves into unions, striking to win better working conditions and pay.

MRS. CONSUMER

It seemed like the unthinkable was finally coming true: housework was becoming less physically demanding. The beautiful lights that Edison had revealed back at the 1893 World's Fair were now shining on the female domain. By 1925, more than half of American homes had access to electricity, and sales of household appliances tripled. Expanded credit and "buying on time" made it possible for even working-class families and farmers to drive cars and get hold of radios, even if they had to be powered by a windmill.

During the 1920s, consumer goods became the most exciting and prolific part of the American economy. Better transportation, electric power, and work "speedups" had enabled factories to churn out and distribute millions of refrigerators, toasters, radios, and vacuums at relatively low prices, giving birth to the "mass market." The result for women's lives and cooking was nothing short of a revolution. And the alliance forged between domestic scientists and businesses began to tilt in favor of the corporations.

Convenience foods gained immense distribution and popularity. Sliced bread, canned coconut, jarred peanut butter, a wide variety of cold breakfast cereals, baby food, cheeses, cakes, and cookies became part of a national American food culture. White Castle hamburger joints and cafeteria chains opened to rave reviews. Famous candy bars like Baby Ruth and Mounds were born, bringing the sweet taste of chocolate to everyday life.

The modern middle-class housewife was not going to be a chemist or a bacteriologist after all, as the early domestic scientists had hoped. Rather, she was going to be Consumer in Chief of the household. And though the visionaries at the 1893 World's Fair knew that food would increasingly be taken over by companies, they expected that women would still retain a significant managerial and scientific role over food in their own home. What they failed to foresee was that technology would not only bring electric stoves and prepared foods but also automobiles, and

Searching for Betty Crocker

Though General Mills says that Betty Crocker was never a "real person," a succession of professional home economists in corporate test kitchens have used her name, spoken with her voice, written her recipes, and done all the other behind-the-scene jobs required to fill her shoes.

Janette Kelley was one of the first women behind Betty. It was Kelley, a home economist at the Washburn Crosby Company, who answered fan mail and tried to figure out why homemakers' cakes sank or why their breads didn't rise. A male executive had always signed the let-

Betty Crocker's many faces since her first official image in 1936. (Courtesy Betty Crocker Kitchens/General Mills Archives.)

ters until someone realized that a woman's touch might be more effective. In 1921, the company invented the character Betty Crocker to help women with their cooking troubles.

In 1928, the Washburn Crosby Company and several other milling companies merged to form General Mills. Janette Kelley left, and home economist Marjorie Child Husted became the director of the company's Home Service Department, overseeing a staff of five, a position she held for twenty years. Husted's was one of the first voices to introduce the *Betty Crocker Cooking School of the Air* radio show in Minneapolis. When it expanded to thirteen regional stations, each station had its own "Betty Crocker voice," which read the scripts prepared by Husted's department. A popular television show followed led by a couple of hired "Bettys."

By the 1940s, *Fortune* magazine reported that Betty Crocker was the second-best-known woman in America, following First Lady Eleanor Roosevelt. Since the 1950s, Betty Crocker has authored some of the best-selling American cookbooks of all time. Betty was the ultimate home economist who shared her technical knowledge with American homemakers and helped women "speed up their cooking by using convenience foods," as noted in the 1960 edition of her *Good and Easy Cookbook*.

Betty got her first "official" image in 1936 as a serious-looking matron with salt-and-pepper hair. Her first update came in 1955. She became more youthful and prettier in the 1960s and then got an unintimidating "career woman" look in the 1980s. In 1996, she became an olive-skinned composite of seventy-five computer images of diverse women of different backgrounds. Her blue eyes turned brown, and she expanded into Latin America. In 2000, she sponsored a national soul-food contest.

Explaining why her looks have changed seven times over eight decades, General Mills says, "Through it all, the goal has been to present an image of Betty Crocker to which modern women can relate, an image that recalls the promise of thoroughly tested products and up-to-date recipes."

Food advertising used images of black women who were happy to serve. Aunt Jemima presents pancakes to Confederate soldiers. Advertisement in *Saturday Evening Post,* November 20, 1920.

that many women would prefer to get in those cars and leave the house. Rather than calculate the calories of a potato or study the household plumbing, they would prefer to go to a movie playing downtown. In fact, technology would get so good that cooking would require less and less scientific skill and training—but increasing intelligence in understanding what products and appliances to buy.

A new economic reality emerged: women—who not so long ago were sup-

Aunt Jemima:
"Warmth, Nourishment and Trust"

Aunt Jemima was born in fits and starts. In 1889, a writer named Chris Rutt and his friend Charles Underwood decided to market the new "self rising flour" in the form of instant pancake mix. According to historian M. M. Manring, Rutt got the idea for the product's name after he saw a blackface minstrel perform a number about a mythical slave named "Aunt Jemima." But without money, expertise, and distribution channels, his pancakes failed. He and his partner sold the company to the R.T. Davis Milling Company.

Under Davis, the product had its world debut at the 1893 World's Fair, where a former slave named Nancy Green was hired to play the role of Aunt Jemima, an old mammy cook of the southern plantation. Set up in a booth designed in the shape of a giant flour barrel, Nancy Green cooked, sang songs, told stories about the Old South, and offered samples to visitors. She was an immense success.

After World War I, the Quaker Company bought the brand, then hired the J. Walter Thompson advertising agency, whose legendary adman James Webb transformed Aunt Jemima. In various ads, illustrated by American artist N. C. Wyeth, her story went like this: Aunt Jemima had been a loyal and loving slave to Colonel Higbee and looked fondly on her antebellum days. During the Civil War, she saved the lives of Confederate soldiers by feeding them pancakes. After slavery, she reluctantly sold her secret recipe to a Northern milling company so that thousands of people could enjoy her pancakes.

In keeping with the mammy stereotype images, Aunt Jemima was happy to serve whites and continued to do so for many decades on the pages of women's magazines, where she warmly invited women to buy her pancakes and enjoy the old southern tradition of black labor in the service of white leisure. Blacks began protesting the image in the 1920s. But it was not until the 1960s that Quaker finally changed Aunt Jemima and replaced her bandanna with a headband. During the 1980s, the company altered her once again, this time finally erasing all traces—at least visually—of slavery. Aunt Jemima looked older, lost her headgear, put on jewelry, and appeared thinner. But, as writer and critic Alice Walker has noted, Aunt Jemima was still a slave because her image was too firmly rooted in the American unconscious as one.

Today, the company's Web site notes, "Aunt Jemima products continue to stand for warmth, nourishment and trust—qualities you'll find in loving moms from diverse backgrounds who care for and want the very best for their families."

"Fortunately, Those Days Are Past . . ."

Fortunately, those days are past when the homemaker must sacrifice all outside interests for the sake of her home.

First came the electric iron—the steps it saved from the stove to the ironing board and back again amounted to several miles a year. Next, the washing machine, to save backs from aching and knuckles from cracking—and again a saving of time. And then the vacuum cleaner—what a relief from the tiresome dirty task of sweeping! Each new electric appliance contributes its share to the lightening of household tasks.

And now the electric refrigerator. Not only can it save the housewife time and energy, but it can actually work for her. With a little planning on her part it can take an active part in the preparation and serving of her meals.

—*The "Silent Hostess" Treasure Book*, 1930
published by General Electric Company

posed to be kept safe in their homes, apart from the harsh world of commerce—were now central to the survival of the American economy because of their purchasing power. In 1929, home economist Christine Frederick documented "the breath-taking speed" with which Mrs. Consumer spends money in America, "a total of $52,000,000,000 annually."

Frederick was not the first to see women as a burgeoning economic force. But she was perhaps the first to lay it all out in full detail for the benefit of advertisers. Her 1929 manifesto *Selling Mrs. Consumer* brilliantly detailed social trends and psychological perspectives among American middle-class women purchasers. Those wants and needs, she explained, could be turned into dollars by marketers who made the effort to understand women's "buying psychology."

Refrigerators would bring golden hours of leisure time to spend with children. Boxed cereal would bring happiness. Gelatin would inspire creativity and self-expression. Food and appliance advertisers had always claimed that their products offered efficiency, scientific methods, and better health—the credo of home economists. But by the 1920s, advertisers became more sophisticated. They also sold food in terms of beauty, guilt, and boundless longings for perfection.

Did the new food products actually save a lot of physical labor?

Yes and no. In her article "Time Spent in Housework," Joann Vanek noted that unemployed women in 1926 spent close to twenty-three hours a week on cooking and food cleanup, while by 1968 this amount had declined to a little less than twenty hours. And so, it's true—new food products did save time. The confusing thing, however, was that the total time devoted to housework increased during these years, from fifty-two hours a week to fifty-five. At least four extra hours were spent shopping and performing "managerial" tasks. More time also went to care of the home. And so, though women cooked less, they spent more time buying food and doing other kinds of house-related jobs. (Working women spent about twenty-six hours on housework, during nights and weekends.)

Why didn't technology set them free? For one thing, more middle-class women were doing their own housework now, without servants or household help. They also had to spend more time shopping and driving in cars to buy food and run errands.

But, also, thanks to technology, middle-class women had higher goals. They wanted sparkling kitchens, clean sheets, ironed clothing, white dresses, nurtured babies, educated children, and dainty dishes. These high standards of home life—once enjoyed exclusively by the rich—were put within reach by technology and the willingness of the American woman. Cooking did take less time. But it seemed to require more thought, more information, more worry about nutrition and diets—and much more fussing about what children wanted or didn't want to eat.

EVEN youngsters recognize the difference! *They* know when it's Beech-Nut. And how they do flock around when it's time for a snack of pure *Beech-Nut* Peanut Butter! You don't need to coax, for Beech-Nut (real flavor of fresh, roasted peanuts) *builds* appetites. Just spread one slice of bread with Beech-Nut and the other with good dairy butter, and there's a sandwich fit for a king—or better still, fit for a growing American boy or girl. A handy, nourishing food for dozens of household uses for every member of the family. Sealed in vacuum jars. Sold everywhere. Beech-Nut Packing Co., Canajoharie, N.Y.

Beech-Nut
*"Foods and Confections
of Finest Flavor"*

Beech-Nut Bacon
Beech-Nut Peanut Butter
Beech-Nut Coffee
Beech-Nut Macaroni, Spaghetti
   Vermicelli
Beech-Nut Macaroni Elbows
Beech-Nut Macaroni Rings
Beech-Nut Pork and Beans
Beech-Nut Prepared Spaghetti
Beech-Nut Catsup, Chili Sauce
Beech-Nut Prepared Mustard
Beech-Nut Jams and Jellies
Beech-Nut Marmalades
Beech-Nut Preserves

Beech-Nut Confections

Beech-Nut Mints
Beech-Nut Fruit Drops
Beech-Nut Candy Drops
Beech-Nut Chewing Gum

Beech-Nut
Peanut Butter

BEECH-NUT QUALITY · · · AT EVERYDAY PRICES

ABOVE: The refrigerator promises comfort, convenience, and, above all, leisure. *Ladies' Home Journal*, August 1927. (2001 General Motors Corporation. Used with permission of GM Media Archives and courtesy Electrolux Home Products.)

OPPOSITE: There for the kids. Advertisement, *Ladies' Home Journal*, November 1927. (Courtesy Beech-Nut Nutrition Corporation.)

In four-color illustrations, the new ideals came to life on the pages of women's magazines. The rise of modern advertising gave both women and men more to strive for. Advertisers created longings by showing women visual images of perfection they'd never seen in the real world around them. The packaging for Sunshine biscuits, Jell-O brand gelatin, Campbell's soup, and SunMaid raisins radiated with symbols of energy and emotion in the hands of 1920s-style women with slender elegant bodies and bobbed hair. Here were pictures of the good life. Who didn't want that?

Food companies understood that if their products took away all labor and work, women would no longer care about cooking at all. And so, countless advertising campaigns reminded women of their emotional connections to food, even

Honeymoon Special

INGREDIENTS: **Three thin slices of Wonder Bread cut in heart shape. One heart-shaped piece of green pepper about ¾ inch across. Arrow 1¼-inch long, cut from pimento. Cream cheese. Egg yolk mixed with mayonnaise. Sardine or anchovy paste.**

Heart-shaped sandwich from *Wonder Sandwich Suggestions,* 1930. *(Courtesy Wonder Bread/Interstate Brands Companies.)*

DIRECTIONS: **Spread bread with creamed butter. Between first and second slices spread fish paste. Between second and third slices spread egg-yolk mixture. On center top, place small decorative pepper heart with pimento arrow thrust through it. Edge top with a frill of cream cheese. Sprinkle with paprika.**

NOTE: **Minced ham or Chicken may be used instead of fish paste.**

—ALICE ADAMS PROCTOR
Wonder Sandwich Suggestions, 1930

if the products came in boxes and tins. Manufacturers encouraged women to express their love and creativity with food by making time-consuming dishes using their products. In a strange paradox of modern life, the new world of commercial foods promised freedom and then reminded women that they were not so free.

Recipes for Tough Times

The year was 1917, and on the grim tenement streets of Brownsville, Brooklyn, the air was charged as local women walked along the rows of pushcarts, angrily looking at the high prices of food. Onions: 18 cents a pound—up from 10 cents just a week ago. Potatoes: 7 cents—double what they used to be.

"Here. I'll give you all the money I have," said a woman whom the *New York Times* would later identify merely as "the troublemaker" of the open-air market. Now, beneath these cold February skies, she stared defiantly at the pushcart vendor. "I'll give you all I have, but I've got to have the onions."

When the grocer shook his head no, the woman leaned her body against his wooden cart and thrust it over, sending onions and potatoes tumbling down onto the muddy street. Soon, hundreds of women joined in, and pushcart after pushcart went down, as the shoppers stomped on food, attacked grocers, and shouted furious insults. By the time police arrived, the market was in chaos. Only after a two-hour fight did they succeed in controlling the mob.

The calm did not last long. Later that day, another riot broke out in a different neighborhood of Brooklyn. This time, a group of women carried torches made of newspaper and set pushcarts aflame. By the end of the day, police had

Woman being led away by New York City police, following a food riot on the Lower East Side. February 1917. *(National Archives.)*

gone toe to toe with three thousand female protestors—all of them clamoring for food and demanding justice over unfair prices.

What sent ordinary housewives into such a fit of violence? Though the United States had not yet joined the Great War, long years of fighting abroad had caused desperate food shortages worldwide. With slender resources to begin with, these women had already cut back as much as they could. They had bought cheaper meats or no meat at all. They had given up fish, milk, and eggs for all but the youngest children. They had taken in extra sewing to be done late at night, or sent children to do factory work—just to pay the food bill. But now, over the last eight months, food prices had soared once again. They feared for their very survival, and the hunger of children was their rallying cry.

Over the coming days, thousands of protesters gathered in meeting halls and public squares, making wild and passionate scenes. One after another, mothers fought their way through crowds to give tearful speeches, displaying their thin children. Lives of relentless work, meager wages, and squalid apartments—all this could be endured, but to watch hungry babies become thin and sickly, from here came madness and fury.

Ida Harris, local mother and watchmaker's wife, took charge and led several hundred Jewish women of the Lower East Side on a march to the office of John Mitchel, New York City mayor. Parading through the streets, many of her followers held wailing babies as they cried, begged, and chanted in both Yiddish and English, "Feed our children! Give us food!" As the women got closer to City Hall, policemen closed its big iron gates, and a crowd of men—police, office workers, and politicians—gathered in front as though protecting a fortress from siege.

Look at old photographs of these women, and you see work-worn faces and beseeching eyes—like some collective mother guilt—gathered on the steps of City Hall. Clad in drab dark coats with shawls over their heads, they seem to be throwing themselves at the foot of power, begging for mercy. Behind them across the street, hundreds of passersby—nearly all men wearing top hats—have stopped to watch in awe.

What politician would be so coldhearted as to turn them away?

It was one thing to snub women protesting for the vote (a growing annoyance in American life). But protesting for food, well, that was another matter. Was it not, after all, a woman's inalienable right to feed her babies? Was it not her true role—one of the very reasons she was put here on this earth? Many believed it was. "When women and children cry for bread you cannot designate it as a riot," said one congressman. "It is an outcry to heaven for relief."

Ida charged her way to the front of the crowds. "We do not want to make trouble," she cried. "We are good Americans, and we simply want the Mayor to make the prices go down. We are just mothers, and we want food for our children. Won't you give us food?"

With her dramatic appeal, Ida Harris managed to get herself heard by Mayor Mitchel, who promptly made a public promise to help. Meanwhile, the women launched an ironclad boycott of onions and potatoes. Within days, these items disappeared from the marketplace because no one would buy them. Alas, it was but a momentary success. By week's end, when the women arrived at their butchers to buy poultry for the Sabbath, they found outrageous prices: 30 cents a pound— from only 20 or 22 cents the previous week.

A wild outburst followed, as Jewish women around the city declared that no poultry should be bought. They patrolled the marketplace in search of shoppers breaking ranks, and anyone found holding a chicken soon found it torn from her hands. The situation reached a surreal crescendo when an angry mob of women seized a crate of chickens from poultry vendors and tore them to shreds. Marching through the freezing streets, they waved dismembered parts of chickens over their heads and chanted for fair prices. The result: poultry prices went down.

Food riots—led almost entirely by women—spread throughout the Northeast, making headlines in almost every major city. In Philadelphia, women declared that they would "live on bread and water rather than pay the prices demanded." In Boston, eight hundred women in the West End invaded grocery stores, seizing food and wreaking havoc.

During February of 1917, all the major newspapers pushed aside front-page stories of military actions overseas. Now women were in the headlines, and politicians, from City Hall to the White House, were scrambling for solutions. President Wilson began a $400,000 inquiry into the food crisis. Mayors in major northeastern cities, including New York, enacted legislation to allow them to purchase beans, smelts, grains, and other foods, which grocers were forced to sell at low prices.

Chicken for the Sabbath

Amastich

Cook one pound of rice in a quart of stock for half an hour, stirring frequently. Then add a chicken stuffed and trussed as for roasting; cover closely and cook thoroughly. After removing chicken, pass the liquor through a strainer, add the juice of a lemon and the beaten yolk of an egg, and pour over the bird.

—FLORENCE KREISLER GREENBAUM
The International Jewish Cook Book, 1918

This recipe for good old chicken and rice is a timeless comfort food, although nowadays it's best to skip the raw egg. A million variations exist. Here's a good one that makes a quick homey dinner.

2- to 3-pound chicken	3 cups chicken stock
2 tablespoons olive oil	1 fresh lemon
1 cup onion	salt and pepper
1½ cups rice	spices you like—turmeric, ginger,
2 cloves garlic, minced	garlic, or saffron

- *Cut a 2- to 3-pound chicken into serving-size pieces. If you wish, cut away skin because this dish stays very moist without it.*
- *Put olive oil in skillet on medium-high heat and add 1 cup of chopped onion. When onions are translucent, add 1½ cups of rice and stir well until all grains are covered with oil. Add garlic and whatever spices you wish.*
- *Add chicken, salt and pepper, and 3 cups of chicken stock (in a pinch, boiling water will do). Turn heat to medium-low and cover. Cook 20 to 30 minutes, until all water is absorbed and chicken is thoroughly cooked. Add fresh lemon or lime juice to taste.*

Chopped fresh cilantro at the end adds a nice flavor.

Women's food riots had been effective before the war. But when the United States finally entered the conflict in April of 1917, popular support for protests came to a halt. All dissent—many people believed—should be laid aside for the larger good of the nation. Now American men would be fighting too, and the best food supplies would go to the military. On market shelves, the very staples of American life—meat, eggs, butter, sugar, and wheat—became increasingly scarce.

> *The war must be won in the kitchens and on the dining tables of America as well as in the trenches.*
>
> —CARL VROOMAN, Assistant Secretary of Agriculture, 1917
> *Good Housekeeping*

Suddenly, the housewife was a major player in the drama of war, a fact that brought her into unimagined prominence. U.S. officials cast fresh eyes on her image as she stood apron-clad in her kitchen, holding the key to the domestic cupboard. Certainly the recent riots had demonstrated her power. If food was a determining factor in the outcome of the war—and it was—then government would desperately need her help. How women ran their kitchens was no longer their own private business.

The first step was to set up a "food dictator." President Wilson appointed Herbert C. Hoover as head of the newly formed U.S. Food Administration, a wartime body in charge of the food emergency. Hoover set up a hierarchy—mostly captains of industry and agriculture—to serve as volunteer managers in his conservation campaign.

American women were to be the foot soldiers, and they were indeed ready. The home economics movement had prepared them perfectly. Cooking clubs were already set up in cities and rural areas across the nation. Teachers were well trained. A network of food information and cooking advice was already in place—in the form of cooking schools, YMCA lectures, advertisers' recipe pamphlets, and cooking columns of women's magazines. Here was a nation of women who had become accustomed to being told how and what to cook by authorities, and who were ever ready to try new things.

Hoover saw in American women an infinite loyalty and willingness to help their country. This was something he intended to make the very most of. Instead of mandatory rations, he designed a brilliant strategy of volunteerism based on psychology, propaganda, and grassroots organizing. In a massive nationwide campaign, Hoover urged, begged, and shamed American women into voluntarily conserving food. "Food will win the war," he proclaimed. His sacred mantra was repeated over and over again on billboards, posters, and pamphlets, and disseminated by state and local governments, libraries, schools, colleges, businesses, women's clubs of every stripe, and even chain stores. A master of the media, Hoover also got newspapers and magazines to scold women on a daily basis to save more food for the sake of liberty and democracy.

Female guilt had a major role: the campaign routinely pointed to the heroic, starving women of England and France. Wouldn't American women conserve for the sake of their starving sisters across the Atlantic?

Every morsel needed to be saved. No scraps of bread, no bits of cheese, no tops of celery stalks, not even the outside lettuce leaves or the smallest scrap of meat should be thrown away. Wartime recipes showered down from on high, giving women instructions to make sour cream out of soured milk, casseroles out of leftovers, and one-pot stews of beans and fish.

Most American women responded to the call of kitchen duty. As requested, they enthusiastically planted "liberty gardens" in their backyards. They canned vegetables. They baked their own "war breads." They carried out "meatless and wheatless days" when asked.

Hoover's female army even had its own uniform. "Pretty, practical, and patriotic,"

> ## "To the Food Administrator, Washington, D.C."
>
> I am glad to join you in the service of food conservation for our nation, and I hereby accept membership in the United States Food Administration, pledging myself to carry out the directions and advice of the Food Administration in the conduct of my household in so far as my circumstances permit.
>
> —Mail-in pledge card
> *Good Housekeeping*, 1917

the official food conservation uniform gave housewives a ready-to-serve look—a cross between a maid and a nurse on her way to the battlefield.

Do You Know Corn Meal?
Its Use Means Service to Your
Country, Nourishing Food for You

The U.S. Food Administration published wartime pamphlets to help American women conserve food. This tasteless recipe for Corn Dodger was one of endless suggestions for alternatives to wheat suggested by the federal government. I heartily discourage it.

Corn Dodger

2 cups corn meal

1 teaspoon salt

2 teaspoons fat

1¾ cups boiling water

Pour the boiling water over the other materials. Beat well. When cool, form into thin cakes and bake 30 minutes in a hot oven. Makes 14 biscuits. These crisp little biscuits are good with butter or gravy. Eat them with your meat and vegetables.

—U.S. Department of Agriculture, U.S. Food Administration, 1917

Naturally, there were a few stumbling points. Canvassers were not always welcomed when they came knocking. Accounts of sugar and flour hoarders came to light. Hysteria sometimes took over, as "vigilance committees" went on witch hunts for kitchen criminals, searching homes for hoarded sugar and rampaging through people's garbage cans for proof of waste.

Food companies didn't miss the opportunity afforded by the patriotic fervor. Just about every possible food product was relentlessly advertised in connection to the war effort. Advertisements for "economical" pancake mixes, war bread flours, and cookware crammed the pages of women's magazines. Accompanying

Women wearing official food conservation uniforms ride the "War Bread Wagon," World War I. *(National Archives.)*

these ads were images of obedient women in conservation gear, or a reprimanding Uncle Sam waving his finger and ordering, "Madam, Save More Food."

American women did not have a constitutional right to vote, yet the food conservation campaign appealed to their love of democracy. With the housewife's help, liberty and freedom would prevail. Each extra bit of food conserved meant more for American soldiers and the Allies. All this was a woman's job—essential, morally right, and heroically grounded in the kitchen.

Be Patriotic
sign your country's
pledge to save the food

U.S. FOOD ADMINISTRATION

It was a voluntary campaign to save food, but who could say no? ILLUSTRATION BY PAUL STAHR FOR U.S. FOOD ADMINISTRATION, 1917 OR 1918. *(Library of Congress.)*

To can beans for democracy or to go on a hunger strike? This was no small decision for women in search of the vote. Why should they support a war against tyranny abroad when there still was tyranny at home? Suffragists were deeply divided on how to respond to the war.

The more radical among them had been picketing the White House since early in 1917. At first, they were amicably tolerated by President Wilson, who on one particularly cold day even invited them inside to warm themselves. But by the time spring rolled around, picketers were being arrested, thrown into jail, and sent to workhouses. Alice Paul launched her famous hunger strike and endured forced feedings with a tube pushed down her throat. Here was the live-free-or-die approach of her National Women's Party.

On the other hand, there was the far larger National American Women's Suffrage Association. Shying away from confrontation, these more conservative women rallied behind the war machine with the traditional female repertoire of home-front activities—including group canning and war bread baking.

Their loyal cookery was a calculated strategy in which they promised not to rock the boat. "Yes," they seemed to say, "we'll do your cooking. Yes, we'll still be women in all our cherished feminine ways—the aromas of fresh-baked bread rising from our kitchens." But in exchange for this loyalty, they expected to be rewarded after the war. Both camps of suffragists—the radical hunger strikers and the bread-baking appeasers—would later claim responsibility for the victory of suffrage in 1920.

CANTEENERS ABROAD

"We ought to have something more than just chocolate to sell the soldiers," said one girl. She was a Salvation Army volunteer who had gone overseas to help serve the soldiers. Standing about a muddy camp in France, the other women agreed with her. Not far away was a cluster of soldiers looking especially grim, trying to find comfort in some scratchy records on the Victrola.

The original plan had been pies, as apple orchards were all around, but lard

Salvation Army canteeners, wearing military helmets and gas masks, make pies for soldiers, overseas, 1918. *(National Archives.)*

for the crust would be impossible to come by, and they still didn't have stoves or ovens. With only flour, fat, and sugar, one girl suggested doughnuts, and they gave it a try, patting dough out in the rain, using an empty grape-juice bottle as a rolling pin.

Several hundred soldiers followed the sugary smell and stood patiently for over an hour waiting in the cold drizzle. More than twenty batches later, the "lassies" (as they were affectionately known) had made 150 doughnuts. The next day, they made twice as many—this time improving their method, using can lids and the tube of a coffee percolator to stamp out circles and holes in the dough. Such was the birth of the legendary Salvation Army doughnut—beloved by American soldiers in Europe. Soon the lassies would be making thousands a day.

Lassies also helped lead religious meetings that were sometimes so well attended that they had to be held out-of-doors. It was not unusual to see a thousand men standing around two or three Salvation Army lassies out in the twilight by the woods, singing gospel hymns and favorite songs. Inevitably, someone would call out for "Tell Mother I'll Be There."

"That Is a Day's Work"

We open the hut at 7; it is cleaned by some of the boys; then at 8 we commence to serve cocoa and coffee and make all kinds of eats until it is all you see. Well, can you think of two women cooking in one day 2,500 doughnuts, 8 dozen cup cakes, 50 pies, 800 pancakes and 225 gallons of cocoa, and one other girl serving it? That is a day's work in my last hut. Then [religious] meeting at night, and it lasts two hours.

—Salvation "lassie" describing her work cooking for soldiers
The War Romance of the Salvation Army, 1919

If you were willing to cook and care for soldiers, here was a chance to step into one of the most dramatic events in history. Some twenty-five thousand American women boarded ships for Europe to volunteer for the American cause during World War I. They worked as nurses, typists, telephone operators, ambulance drivers, clerks, entertainers, and canteen workers serving soldiers food. Mainly in France, but also in England, Serbia, and other war-torn countries, they served under the American Red Cross, the YMCA, the YWCA, the Knights of Columbus, and the most beloved, though much smaller, Salvation Army.

"Canteeners" ladled out soup to refugees and served food, coffee, doughnuts, and hot chocolate to long lines of soldiers. They baked thousands of pies and treats. They were a new breed of women who followed men into overseas battle. Some of the huts they worked in were far back from the fighting, newly built, and well equipped. Here canteeners might offer full meals of soup, meat, salads, and vegetables—all for just a few francs. In other assignments, women found themselves toting gas masks while serving hot drinks in rubble-strewn wreckage, using a broken-down wall as a counter. A canteen might be in a make-shift tent in the woods, a barn with the roof shot off, or a truck that rolled through war zones, equipped with a portable stove. Sometimes the women had to make their own fireplaces out of stone and sewer pipes. Amid these circumstances, canteeners slept on floors with no blankets, on haystacks, in unheated rooms—even in dugouts abandoned by Germans. They went without baths, heat, and lights.

Women were supposed to be far back from the conflict, but many broke the rules and followed troops into danger—sometimes at the request of a commanding chief who wanted them along for morale. One YMCA woman recalled, "We used to feed the men coming back from the front. The relief would come up at 10:30 when it became dark and the men coming from the trenches would be served hot chocolate from 2 til 3:30 in the morning. We would get to bed about 4 o'clock and had to be up at 8."

One Mrs. Fitzgerald, known as "Ma," was a white-haired woman of mature age who had run a successful canteen in France for soldiers of the 89th Division from Kansas and Missouri. After her boys went into combat, she spent five days following after them, carrying cigarettes, tins of hot cocoa, dried milk, sugar, and

Mrs. Hammond, American Red Cross volunteer, serves water to badly wounded soldier on a train platform in France, 1918. *(National Archives.)*

a portable stove, hitching rides along the way. When she finally arrived in the shelled town where they had landed, she immediately set up a little canteen in a fragment of a bombed building.

Despite these legends of heroics, the vast majority of canteeners had far more ordinary experiences. They worked long days performing repetitive work, pouring coffee, washing dishes, and peeling potatoes. Yet their work was extremely important. Through food, they offered comfort and humanity to men who faced existential fear and the constant threat of imminent death. The soldiers were enormously grateful, and women described an immense sense of meaning gained from doing the most mundane jobs in the most extraordinary circumstances. "I could not drop this work now and feel right about it, especially as I have no excuse so far as health is concerned," wrote one canteener. "I *love* my job. . . . While there is a bit for me to do, I *have* to stay with it."

Unfortunately, canteens were far from perfect refuges. African-American soldiers were not allowed into most of them, and only a handful of African-American women were allowed to serve as volunteers. Addie Hunton and Kathryn M. Johnson, two former teachers in their early fifties who were deeply devoted to improving the condition of the black race, were among the minority. In their book *Two Colored Women with the American Expeditionary Forces,* Hunton and Johnson described themselves stepping on the gang plank to set sail for Europe. "We were crusaders on a quest for Democracy! How and where would that precious thing be found?"

Once in France, however, they saw that black soldiers lived in inferior barracks, got assigned the worst jobs, and endured constant indignities, writing that their service was "more or less clouded at all times by that biting and stinging thing which is ever shadowing us in our own country." They recalled one soldier who had been up at the front marching for two days and had arrived at a YMCA hut muddy to the waist, cold, and starving, only to be turned away when he tried to buy a package of cakes.

When Hunton and Johnson first arrived, they were not allowed to serve "colored" men, but they would not accept no for an answer and eventually won support to start canteens for black soldiers. At a furious pace they worked serving food, lending library books, helping men write letters, providing tutoring, shopping, and offering a social hour with homesick men who needed to talk. Despite the racism, they write with love of their work as "the greatest opportunity for

African-American troops receive food from YWCA volunteers, 1917. (Photographs and Prints Division, Schomburg Center for Research in Black Culture, The New York Public Library, Astor, Lenox and Tilden Foundations.)

service that we have ever known; service that was constructive and prolific, with wonderful satisfying results."

At the end of World War I, American women seemed greatly changed.

"Food will win the war." Hoover's slogan had a ricochet effect. For if food had in fact won the war, then didn't women deserve a seat at the dinner table?

Hadn't women grown liberty gardens in the soil of their own backyards? Hadn't they baked war breads in their own ovens and toiled in the cornfields? Hadn't they hauled hot cocoa all over Europe, risking their lives? After all this, weren't they qualified to vote? In this way, food—in its endless connection to women's lives—pushed forward the cause of suffrage. In 1919, Congress passed an amendment to give women the constitutional right to vote in all elections. In 1920, it was ratified, and a seventy-year battle was won.

RECIPES FOR DEPRESSION

After the wildly expansive years of the 1920s, the economy screeched to a halt in 1929 with the stock market crash. Legend and history books have long told us

Poor Man's Cake

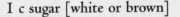

1 c sugar [white or brown]	2 c water
2 c raisins	2 t cinnamon
1 t cloves	1 t nutmeg
½ c lard	pinch of salt

Boil all ingredients 3 minutes. Cool. Add 2 teaspoons baking powder, 1 t soda, 3 cups flour. Mix and bake in medium oven about 45 minutes.

—recalled by BLANCHE EDDY
in *Making Do: How Women Survived the '30s,* 1976

In its humbleness and simplicity, this raisin spice cake somehow tastes like the depression, and yet it is surprisingly good, even though it has no butter, eggs, or milk. It's also easy and quick to make.

Use a bundt pan and a 350-degree oven. Instead of lard, you can use shortening. Canola oil works too, if you don't mind a slightly dense cake. Unless you're a die-hard raisin lover, 1 to 1½ cups should do.

about this Great Depression in terms of men: men who resorted to selling apples on the street, men who stood on bread lines in shame, men who jumped from their office windows when the stock market crashed. Where, behind these famous images, are the stories of their wives, daughters, mothers, sisters—most of whom experienced the depression in a far less visible or public way?

According to a 1936 Gallup poll, 82 percent of Americans believed that a woman's place was in the home. With so little work out there, the real breadwinners should get priority—so the thinking went. Women were fired from their jobs, and in some places it was even illegal for them to work. Faced with financial hardship, many women turned inward, back toward their homes and their kitchens.

On the heels of the Progressive Era, 1920s flapper culture, suffrage, and new technologies designed to free women from drudgery in their kitchens, the depression brought a major shift in tone. The strong gust of feminism and career advancement of the early century seemed to go underground and quiet. During the depression, women were busy with other things—namely, survival.

Though people experienced the depression in a wide range of extremes, nearly all American women of every race and class shared a common experience: feeding their families on less money. For most women, this meant more thoughtfulness in the kitchen, more ingenuity, and more work. Through careful menu planning and age-old tricks of thrift, women strove to make up for the buying power that their households had lost.

One way of doing this was to turn the clock back on technology. For many

Migrant packinghouse worker from Tennessee in Belle Glade, Florida, with four of her own children and two relatives, 1939. PHOTO BY MARION POST WOLCOTT. *(Library of Congress.)*

years it had been a simple matter to go to the store and buy canned soups, cereals, and "ready-made" foods like bread. But now many women had no choice but to grow and preserve their own fruits and vegetables, to bake their own breads, and to find countless other ways to scrimp and use leftovers to greatest possible advantage. More like their grandmothers than their mothers, they added to the family purse through foods they manufactured with their own hands.

Nellie Yost of Nebraska was one of the millions who strived to save a dollar every which way. During a 1980s interview for the *Voices of American Homemakers* project, she remembered how she eagerly learned how to make dry cereal at a home economics meeting. It saved only a few cents, but in Nellie's mind it was obviously worth an hour or two of work.

Dry cereals were very inexpensive at that time, but in the depth of the Depression, you just couldn't afford anything, there was so little money to go around.

So this lesson showed us how to mix grains together—rye, wheat, and graham flours—and make a thin dough that we rolled out like pie crust. Rolled as thin as possible and then baked it in the oven. Then, when it was baked hard—very hard—you broke it up with a hammer. You could crumble it or roll it as fine as you wanted to, like Grape Nuts, say. You'd use a rolling pin to crumble it that fine.

It made a good substitute dry cereal. We made quite a lot of it and it was quite a little cheaper than buying the manufactured cereals.

Food was a major preoccupation for women during the depression, and cheap nutritious recipes were an obsession. Again, the cooking networks set up by the domestic scientists and reinforced during World War I continued to be important. Radio homemakers, culinary writers, woman's columnists, and food manufacturers all offered American women ideas for dishes that used fillers like bread crumbs, crackers, and cereals. The U.S. Department of Agriculture created a radio persona known as Aunt Sammy (none other than Uncle Sam's wife) who broadcast a cooking show. In an era when Americans were spellbound by radio, women tuned in faithfully. They put down their housework and fetched a pen to write down recipes.

According to Mary Grace McKenna Monahan of Nebraska, "Those days you did everything to save a penny. Pennies mattered because they were worth some-

Joy

Joy began as a remedy for loneliness. At fifty-three years old, Irma Louise Rombauer lost her husband, and her two grown children, Marion and Edgar, suggested she write a cookbook to keep herself busy. Marion helped out, testing recipes and providing illustrations, and in 1931, it was complete. Irma self-published her compilation of five hundred recipes and called it *Joy of Cooking*. A first run of three thousand copies sold well.

But *Joy of Cooking* is a story of continual evolution. In 1936, Bobbs-Merrill offered to publish the book, and Irma refined and retested the recipes, making them ready for national publication—at 345 pages. Sales were steady. In 1943, she expanded the work to 628 pages, including hostessing tips, charts, and tables, and this time, the nation caught on. *Joy* was declared indispensable, and Irma Rombauer officially replaced Fannie Farmer as America's most beloved cook. In 1952, Marion officially became a coauthor.

What was the secret? The Rombauers offered the ultimate compendium of reliable household information. But *Joy* offered something else: a warmer, more human tone that seemed appealing after the laboratory approach of home economists and was especially welcome during the depression and the war. *Joy* came from a family perspective—not a cooking school or settlement house. It was personal. And it was a bit more relaxed, including even a few ethnic dishes, expanding (just a little) the American palate. Many revisions and expansions followed, including the most recent in 1997. Today *Joy* has sold more than 15 million copies, making it the most popular American cookbook of the twentieth century.

thing. My next door neighbor and I used to shop together. You could get two pounds of hamburger for a quarter, so we'd buy two pounds and split it—then one week she'd pay the extra penny and the next week I'd pay."

If the depression was hard for white women, it was treacherous for blacks. Already on the very bottom rung of the economic ladder, African-American women were pushed further by dried-up jobs and pitiful wages: 23 cents compared to 61 cents earned by white women to every dollar earned by white men.

It was always easier to feed your family if you lived in the country. At least there a woman could hunt for nuts, berries, and edible plants. She could cast her line into the local lake for bass or catfish to fry for the evening meal, and perhaps even take a moment to enjoy the peace of the water. She could grow potatoes and carrots outside her back door and take joy at the sight of green sprouts pushing through the soil.

But if she were a black woman living in the city, working for a living, chances were she had a job as a domestic servant or perhaps at a factory, making far less than a living wage. To feed her family, she needed to have her wits about her. In Washington, D.C., one social worker recorded with awe how "Auntie Jane," a forty-year-old black woman, gathered together her neighborhood friends and, with "the vigor of a hunter or a fisher," led them into partly demolished buildings one freezing winter day. There amid rubble, they yanked wooden beams from the walls and tore planks up from the floors. This would be kindling for their wood-burning cook stoves.

Jorena Pettway sorts peas inside her smokehouse. She still has many fruits and vegetables, which she canned the previous year. Gee's Bend, Alabama, 1939. PHOTO BY MARION POST WOLCOTT. *(Library of Congress.)*

The bond among sisters, grandmothers, daughters, and friends could make all the difference. Sharing was a measure of grace in the face of poverty. In the tradition of African-American church socials, black women volunteered, cooking in church kitchens for a weekly congregational meal with neighbors and friends. Here, cooking was a labor of love for the higher good. Their biscuits, beans, cornbread, and fried chicken not only tasted delicious but also provided a spiritual offering.

Of course women were not the universal feeders and healers of Americans during the depression. The truth is that many were out on their own, alone and hungry themselves. In fact, the marriage rate dropped by 22 percent because people thought they couldn't afford to get married. A few—mostly the young and unattached—took to the road, riding box cars, leading hobo lives far away from the kitchen drudgery of their mothers. Other women turned to prostitution in order to get by. Still others found themselves alone and wandering hopelessly about cities, with no place to turn after they were fired from their jobs or abandoned by husbands or family.

"Women are hungry," insisted Meridel Le Sueur, a midwestern journalist who, in her 1932 essay "Women on the Breadlines," documented the lives of this silent population of single, unemployed women, who lived quietly on the fringe of society, lying low, trying to survive.

> *I*t's one of the great mysteries of the city where women go when they are out of work and hungry. . . . I've lived in cities for many months broke, without help, too timid to get in bread lines. I've known many women to live like this until they simply faint on the street from privation, without saying a word to anyone. A woman will shut herself up in a room until it is taken away from her, and eat a cracker a day and be as quiet as a mouse so there are no social statistics concerning her.
>
> —MERIDEL LE SUEUR
> *"Women on the Breadlines,"* 1932

STRENGTH IN NUMBERS

Food had always been a mainstay in rural homemakers' extension clubs. But during the depression, it was all the more important. Once or twice a month, among a circle of friends (and often over a potluck luncheon), women would come together to learn how to make cottage cheese, how to care for chickens, how to gather vegetable seeds, or how to cut up a pig and cure the meat. It was no wonder women flocked to the meetings. Many farms were without electricity and nearly self-sufficient for food. Farmwives cooked large meals several times a day, including home-baked breads and desserts. They chopped wood for their stoves, raised chickens, and milked cows. Many had no sinks and hauled every drop of water they needed into their kitchens. Without refrigerators, they cooled their food in springhouses or cold cellars, using ice they had stored from winter. These women were eager for any chance to learn practical skills that would help them with their lives.

And there was the loneliness of farm life, too. Set off alone in a house amid empty fields, with long days of chores, it's no wonder women readily got on their horses or walked long miles for the chance to be with other women. These gatherings created threads of friendship and food that wove through decades of their lives. Many women in homemaker clubs knew one another from the time they were young brides until death.

> *I*n berry season I would take boxes or a pail and I'd go out and gather wild berries and bring them in. I would go out every morning and I'd get elderberries and blackberries, or whatever we had. I made so much jellies.
>
> I learned to make jelly in Home Extension. You know, really, you get so much out of Home Extension that you can't start to tell all the things.
>
> —MABEL HUGHES, Florida
> *Voices of American Homemakers*

THAT LIFE MUST GO ON

First Lady Eleanor Roosevelt believed in a woman's right to work outside of the home. But she also believed that women could help save their families and their country from the depression by providing emotional strength, organization, and nutritious, tasty food for their loved ones. As first lady, she used her high pulpit to give women cookery advice, sample menus, and pointers on balanced, inexpensive meals. "Too much emphasis," wrote Eleanor Roosevelt, "cannot be laid on the importance of the preparation of food and the choice of food where the family health is concerned."

> The women know that life must go on and that the needs of life must be met and it is their courage and their determination which, time and again, have pulled us through worse crises than the present one. The present crisis is different from all the others but it is, after all, a kind of warfare against an intangible enemy of want and depression rather than a physical foe. And I hold it equally true that in this present crisis it is going to be the women who will tip the scales and bring us safely out of it.
>
> —ELEANOR ROOSEVELT
> *It's Up to the Women*, 1933

Women surely suffered from overwork and constant worry during the depression. Many lived bleak lives of want. And it is true that they were pushed out of jobs in favor of men. But to sum up their lives during the 1930s as pure drudgery and powerlessness would be terribly wrong.

When men lost jobs during the depression, they sometimes found themselves unable to fulfill their societal roles as providers. But for most women, the depression reinforced ancient lessons. Transforming leftovers into soup, making bread crumbs from stale bread, recycling corn seeds into new plants—these womanly skills of thrift had been stressed for centuries. In these hard times most women had concrete skills and comforts they knew how to offer.

"Every True Baking Artist Could Reveal Her Prize"

The summer picnic gave ladies a chance to show off their baking hands. On the barbecue pit, chickens and spareribs sputtered in their own fat and a sauce whose recipe was guarded in the family like a scandalous affair. However in the ecumenical light of the summer picnic every true baking artist could reveal her prize to the delight and criticism of the town. Orange sponge cakes and dark brown mounds dripping Hershey's chocolate stood layer to layer with ice white coconuts and light brown caramels. Pound cakes sagged with their buttery weight and small children could no more resist licking the icings than their mothers could avoid slapping the sticky fingers.

—MAYA ANGELOU

description of a depression-era annual fish fry, *I Know Why the Caged Bird Sings*, 1969

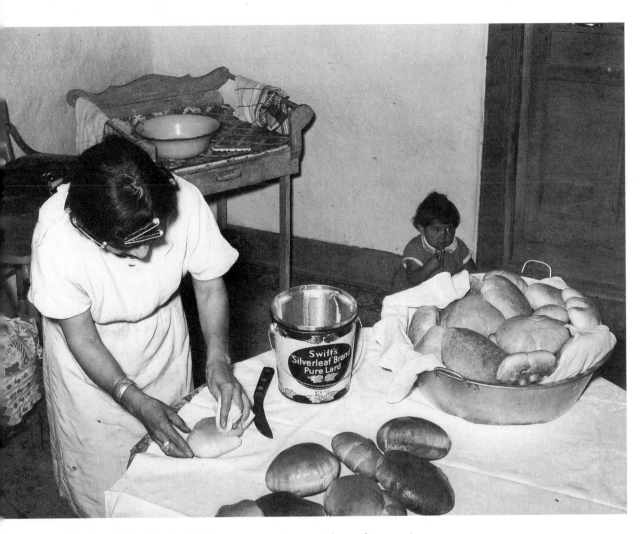

Making bread, New Mexico, 1939. PHOTO BY RUSSELL LEE. *(Library of Congress.)*

In oral histories and memoirs, many women express undeniable pride in their creativity and ingenuity in coping with tough times. When the bank account is low and there is a wonderful pot of soup made out of bones, vegetable scraps, and herbs, how do we measure this value? When the boredoms and sorrows of being human weigh us down to despair, how do we measure the value of food, in its comfort and simple physical pleasure? During the Great Depression, women used cooking to create economic value. They also made daily life better, more gracious and humane.

We look into the tidy diorama that popular culture has given us of the World War II home front: an overalled Rosie the Riveter with her hair in a bandanna, a woman's hand holding ration coupons and war bonds, a hoe for the "victory garden" out back. America pulling together. It seems almost quaint.

Perhaps it is impossible to imagine the deprivations of war unless one has lived them—the constant state of emergency, blackout drills, fear for one's children, shortages of clothing, shoes, gasoline, bicycles, heating oil. In this long war, deprivation was a state of mind constantly reflected in the stomach—yearnings for a steak, or a piece of fish, or even a banana, which was impossible to find.

As in the last war, the very best of everything went to fuel the enormous military effort. This time, food conservation was not voluntary. To prevent chaos in the consumer market, a legendary system of rations and price controls began in 1942—with its blue and red tokens, its flimsy coupons to be torn out of ration books, and endless lines at the grocer. Each month, every American got two ration books: forty-eight blue coupons (for canned goods) and sixty-four red coupons (for meat, fish, and dairy).

To buy for her family, a woman needed to be a tactical master, calculating hundreds of red and blue points each month. With constant shortages, shopping became a competitive sport: to get what they wanted, women had to go to the store early in the day, early in the week, and early during the ration period. "One week there is no hamburger, the next week no tomatoes," wrote one woman. "You scurry around, wasting time and rationed shoe leather." For those who worked all day and raced to the store by closing hour to find nothing left, it was tough luck.

The extra labor was considerable. Women dusted off their mothers' and grandmothers' conservation recipes from the last world war. They hauled their empty cans to the recycling depot to be used for munitions. They collected their extra kitchen fats (valuable for glycerine, which could be turned into gunpowder) and carried them back to the butcher. They learned new ration-smart recipes and grew vegetables in victory gardens on any spare soil they had.

Beyond the public face of loyalty were the private emotions surrounding food and loneliness for women separated from their husbands, sons, and friends. What

Canning beans and greens raised in a victory garden, Jeffersontown, Kentucky, 1943.
Women paid five cents for a can and use of a pressure cooker at a government-run canning center.
PHOTO BY HOWARD R. HOLLEM. *(Library of Congress.)*

a sickening feeling it must have been to walk to the post office with a tin of home-made cookies for a husband, brother, or son, wondering if you'd ever see him again. For others, cooking for one was simply not worth it. "I don't want to bother about brewing coffee just for myself," wrote Sonokou Iwata to her husband who had been taken away to a Japanese internment camp.

Present on everyone's mind was the possibility that Germany or Japan would bomb the United States. Millions listened with terror to reports of British families bombed in their streets and homes. Accordingly, American women stocked

The Blackout Cupboard

"Blackouts happen at night, of course, and so, usually does dinner. For that reason, it is wise, if possible, to have the kitchen one of the rooms most adequately equipped to operate normally under the various restrictions of your neighborhood and your own common sense, when the siren sounds. . . ."

"In the old days, before Stuka and blitz became a part of even childish chitchat, every practical guide to cookery urged you to keep a well-filled emergency shelf in your kitchen or pantry. Emergency is another word that has changed its inner shape; when Marion Harland and Fanny Farmer used it they meant unexpected guests. You may, too, in an ironical way, but you hope to God they are the kind who will never come."

So wrote the great M. F. K. Fisher in her wartime book How to Cook a Wolf. *Fisher told women that despite rations and short budgets, they could still live and eat with grace and gusto. One of her recommendations was this frittata. "With a glass of wine and some honest to God bread it is a meal. In the end you know that Fate cannot harm you, for you have dined."*

In a later revision—once rations had ceased—Fisher suggested adding a scant cup of good dry Parmesan cheese to the eggs when mixing them, and even rich cream, too. Here is her basic wartime recipe. You can't go wrong. And to make things easier, we now have the benefit of no-stick pans—a great breakthrough for frittata making.

their own cupboards with "emergency rations" in preparation for some ugly disaster. Some even signed up for nutrition and canteen courses, such as those given by the Red Cross, which prepared them to make huge quantities of soups and sandwiches for crowds of survivors should that day of catastrophe come.

THE MYTH OF ROSIE

So immense was this global conflict that the United States simply could not afford the luxury of keeping the traditional social order. Women had to be "called out of

Frittata of Zucchini
(For example)

3 tablespoons olive oil
   (or some reputable substitute)
1 onion or three green onions
1 clove garlic
5 small zucchini
9 eggs

1 large fresh tomato or 1 cup solid-packed canned tomatoes
salt and pepper
1 teaspoon herbs . . . parsley, sweet marjoram, or thyme

Heat oil in skillet and cook minced onion and garlic slowly in it 10 minutes. Add zucchini cut into thin slices. Add peeled and cut-up tomato, seasoning, and herbs. Cover, and cook until the vegetable is tender. Take from stove and cool.

Beat eggs lightly, season, and mix with cooled vegetables. Pour back into skillet, cover tightly and cook over a slow fire until the edges of the frittata pull away from the pan. If the middle puffs up, prick it with a long sharp knife.

When it is solid, brown lightly under a slow broiler flame in a preheated oven, cut in slices like a pie, and serve at once.

—M. F. K. FISHER
How to Cook a Wolf, 1942

the kitchen onto the assembly line." Government and business begged women to stand behind their country and take a job. Now women were suddenly encouraged to put on overalls and do "men's work" as welders, riveters, ship builders, auto workers—just about anything men could do. The result: between 1940 and 1945, the number of women workers surged from 12 million to 18 million.

"Rosie the Riveter" was one of the greatest propaganda creations of all time. According to popular culture, she was a middle-class housewife who didn't really want to work but selflessly cast aside her apron out of patriotism. Government recruiting ads portrayed women war workers as lipsticked beauties, strong and fearless, but undeniably feminine. Rosie reassured the public. Women were still women. They would return to their kitchens when the war was done.

It was true that as many as five million "new" female workers were in the workforce. But contrary to the beloved myth, most Rosies were working-class women who had taken home paychecks at some previous time in their lives. For many, the war was a chance to get out of menial "women's" wage labor and make good money for the first time in their lives. Sure they may have been patriotic. But they took war jobs because they needed money, particularly after the hard years of the depression. As one woman worker put it, "I got a job because I had to eat."

Just the same, what a dramatic new vision it was. Instead of working as domestic servants, typists, or department store clerks, women were building bombers and ships. They were making better money than they ever had.

But a sticky question arose during these years—one that to this day has not been fully answered: If Rosie was now out of the house working, who would do the cooking?

"If you've followed recipes exactly in making cakes, you can learn to load shell," went one piece of government propaganda. The irony is that for most working women with husbands, children, or families, the war meant having to load shell *and* make cake (not to mention cook the dinner, pack the lunch, prepare breakfast, grocery shop, and clean the dishes). According to food writer Gerry Schremp, it took about four to five hours a day to cook "three square meals" in the typical 1940s kitchen that had no dishwasher and perhaps no modern refrigerator. One out of every three American women still had to gather kindling for a wood stove. Without a supermarket, shopping required trips to the grocer, fish monger, and butcher, most of whom shut their stores by six in the evening—a big challenge for war workers. "Convenience" foods merely meant cake mixes, boxed gelatin, or canned vegetables and soups (which you'd be lucky to find because metals were needed for munitions).

In light of Rosie's busy day, husbands may have helped a bit more with the cooking or dishwashing, but the women's movement had not yet arrived. Woman's work was still woman's work, her domain and her ultimate responsi-

Duty called her to the garden. Men and women tended millions of "victory gardens." (Library of Congress.)

bility in most households. Cooking was something Rosie the Riveter simply had to squeeze in, somehow, when she could.

APPLE CRISP PRONTO AND OTHER SOLUTIONS FOR THE DOUBLE-DUTY WOMAN

In its great wisdom, the Women's Bureau at the Department of Labor wanted to help lighten the cooking load of working women. Somehow, the Bureau persuaded a number of factories to set up canteens where women workers could buy precooked meals at a reasonable price to take home to their families. Upon arriving on the job, women brought their young children and a few clean bowls to work-site day care centers. At the end of the day, they picked up their precious ones and containers now filled with dinner. These sorts of solutions were hardly widespread, but miraculously, they did happen in a few special places—Henry Kaiser's West Coast shipyards and a good number of day care centers in Baltimore County. Some other factories tried to help women workers solve the vexing problem of food shopping. In New York and New Jersey, food grocers took orders from women every morning at the plant. At day's end, they received their groceries, delivered to the factory.

But much to the Bureau's disappointment, these innovations for women workers never became widespread in America. The issue of women's "dual burden" of housework and war work simply did not capture the hearts of many executives in industry. Perhaps they thought it wasn't worth the investment. After all, when the war was over, they expected that women would leave the workforce or be fired, and everything would go back to the way it was.

Popular culture also tread carefully on the issue of working women and their home duties. If Rosie the Riveter was looking for any solutions to her cooking

> Cleveland, Oct. 21, 1945
>
> Darling,
> At last a bunch of your letters came through. . . .
>
> Sweetie, I want to make sure I make myself clear about how I've changed. I want you to know now that you are not married to a girl that's interested solely in a home—I shall definitely have to work all my life—I get emotional satisfaction out of working; and I don't doubt that many a night you will cook the supper while I'm at a meeting. . . . Do you think you'll be able to bear living with me? . . .
> I love you,
>
> EDITH
> —in *Since You Went Away*, 1978

Women welders on their way to the job, circa 1943. PHOTO BY ALFRED T. PALMER. (Library of Congress.)

problems, she was not likely to find them in the pages of women's magazines. Besides quick ration-saving recipes, magazines rarely broached the subject of men helping out with the cooking or any other housework.

Instead, the women's press fell back on the same tired old themes of home economics—mainly, better efficiency. *Good Housekeeping* magazine advised, "The busier the homemaker, the more important that she use system in running her home." Among the suggestions: Scrape, stack, and rinse dishes more systematically to save time in dishwashing. Set the breakfast table at night. Cook double batches of food in advance. Plan meals carefully. Bake cookies and breads on the weekends. And the very best—use a tray to carry food to the table so as to save steps and increase speed.

If you were a "double-duty woman" who needed to save precious time, *Woman's Home Companion* recommended quick meals like Pork Chops Creole, South County Frankfurters, Corned Beef Platter, and—in a pinch—canned luncheon meats over spaghetti. Preparation times ranged from thirty minutes to one hour. But homemade desserts—expected even of Rosie—tacked on extra

Apple Crisp Pronto

Pare, quarter and core 1½ pounds apples. Put in saucepan with small amount of water; cook covered until soft. Sweeten to taste. Return to heat and cook long enough to dissolve the sugar. Lemon juice, nutmeg or cinnamon may be added. While apples are cooking, spread 2 slices of enriched or whole-wheat bread on both sides with fortified margarine, then with honey; dip in sugar. Place in hot ungreased skillet over medium heat and brown on both sides. Cool, cut into small cubes. Serve hot applesauce topped with toasted cubes in individual dessert dishes.

—*Woman's Home Companion*, September 1943

cooking time. Among the suggestions: Apple Crisp Pronto. Coming home from work in her sweaty overalls, Rosie the Riveter had to immediately begin simmering pork chops and peeling apples for dessert. Somehow she'd have to provide everything she had always provided before—only now, more quickly.

Within nine months after victory, four million women were out of work. It was largely assumed that they would happily return home to their kitchens—or to the low-status, low-paying jobs they'd had before the war. But according to a survey by the Women's Bureau, approximately 75 percent of women war workers wanted to continue working when the war was done. Some polls showed that half of the women who had previously been homemakers wanted to continue working. Despite these wishes, women were laid off in favor of returning soldiers, and to this day they have never regained a major presence in heavy industrial jobs.

"I happen to be a widow with a mother and son to support. . . . I would like to know why, after serving a company in good faith for almost three and a half years, it is now impossible to obtain employment with them," wrote Juliet Gattuso Ottilie to President Truman. "I am a lathe hand and was classified as skilled labor, but simply because I happen to be a woman I am not wanted."

At the heart of America was great worry about sex roles. Women had taken men's jobs. They also had taken over the checkbook and mowed the lawn. What would all this mean when the war was over? How would women relate to men?

"In wartime, men and women get out of step and begin to wonder about each other," wrote the anthropologist Margaret Mead in an article called "Women in the War." " 'What will he be like after all those years in the Army?' 'What will she be like after all those years alone at home?' . . . 'Will she have learned to be so independent that she won't want to give up her job to make a home for me?' "

Perhaps this is why the government and business clung to the notion that after the war, everything would return to normal. If they made it too easy for women to work *and* get their cooking done, perhaps they'd never quit their jobs. And if women wouldn't go home after the war and make dinner, how would the nation ever be right again?

After the stress and disruption of two world wars and a depression, Americans yearned for normalcy and the conventional order—so the traditional interpretation goes. After the war, kitchens would be designed as large living spaces where women could not only cook but also visit with friends, do laundry, and perform other household chores—in short, space where women could spend most of their time. Tailored and practical "uniform" fashions inspired by Rosie the Riveter were replaced by flouncy skirts and tight-fitting sweaters. Women would bear children at an unprecedented rate.

But popular culture tells only one part of the story—and often reveals more what people yearn for than what really is. Though the proportion of women workers plunged immediately after the war, it never fell back as low as prewar levels. And by the end of the 1940s, the number of women workers would once again begin to climb. Laid off from their higher-paying "men's work," women took pink-collar jobs as typists, office workers, and retail clerks. Though they lost wages and job stature, they did continue to work. By 1960, more women were working for wages than ever before in history.

Women's desire—or need—to work, along with a stunning postwar rise in consumer goods and fast foods, would transform cookery over the coming decades. Marketers were more than ready to offer defrosting refrigerators, frozen dinners, Tupperware, electric percolators, dishwashers, and new grease-cutting cleansers that made cooking and cleaning up easier.

Historians continue to debate whether or not World War II had any lasting impact on women's roles. Regardless of their conclusions, the image of the working woman in overalls by day and baking Apple Crisp Pronto by night was an indisputable foreboding of the future. The seeds of conflict had been planted.

Chapter 10

Apron Strings: Did She Cut Them?

"Can I touch it?" my six-year-old son asks, after I take it out of the box.

He tentatively puts his index finger on the icy plastic package, then grabs the whole thing with one hand and throws it on the kitchen counter to see what happens. It makes a loud thud, something like a brick. This strikes him as hilarious. He does it again.

I put the brick in the microwave, along with one for his brother. This is their dinner—lasagne, in single-serving portions, ready in just a few minutes.

While the microwave hums and the timer counts down, I glance at the package and put a check mark on some invisible ledger in my mind. Good—organic. This is not *really* a TV dinner. A personal note declares the product's good intentions from the company's founders, along with a picture of an old-fashioned farm woman feeding a child.

In five minutes, the microwave beeper goes off. I remove the cartons, which now contain boiling hot noodles, cheese, and sauce. I mull over whether to serve them on the cardboard or on plates. Okay, on plates. I cut the lasagnes into bite-size pieces. From a bag of presorted and trimmed lettuce, I make a salad for the big boy, and I cut up fruit for the little one.

They love the lasagne. Another check mark in the plus column.

Within an hour, both children have finished, and all signs of cooking, eating,

"Modern Diner, Pawtucket, Rhode Island." *From Diners: People and Places, 1990.* PHOTO BY GERD KITTEL.

and cleaning up have been erased before Dad gets home from a long commute. All hands and faces washed. All smudges wiped from the floor. A final check mark. No dishes.

Frozen lasagne gives a woman some options, and that is what my generation is all about. Thanks to frozen lasagne, I have time to give my young children undivided attention after not seeing them all day. Frozen lasagne also allows me to do other things I feel I must do—have a career, exercise, do my laundry, go out, or simply be with my husband after a long day of work, instead of cleaning dishes until nine o'clock at night.

Ah but the fat content. Lasagne is loaded with cheese. A check mark goes into the bad column. Another check mark goes in the inauthenticity column. I remember the Italian-American lasagnes of my childhood, enjoyed two or three special times a year with many relatives for celebrations—now deceremonialized and isolated, frozen in a solitary block, wrapped in single-serving plastic.

What kind of life is that?

Like many American women living at the beginning of the twenty-first century, I can hear an array of voices speak to me about food. Voices that tell me not to cook so I can have freedom. Voices that tell me I should cook so I can be a better mother. Voices that tell me to eat because it is sensual. Voices that tell me not to eat because I will get fat. Voices that tell me to measure vitamins and calories and to avoid pesticides. Voices that tell me to think about the lives of people who pick and package my food. Voices that tell me to cook because it will please my man. Voices that call out from my own distant ethnic heritage one hundred years after immigration. Voices that lure me to dreams of leisurely taken meals in beautiful restaurants. And a voice somewhere amidst all these telling me to create some-

Frozen has become a fast-growing "natural" category. (Courtesy Amy's Kitchen.)

thing beautiful on the table for the people I care about so I can help us enjoy life and one another just a little bit more during our brief time here on earth.

Where do these voices come from? And how did so many conflicts get to be wrapped up in a simple dinner?

Every generation in history has struggled in its own way over how to eat and how to live, as we have seen. Some themes of hunger and poverty, war and migration are eternally interwoven with food. But during this current era in the United States, we face some unprecedented conditions: an abundant (some say overabundant) commercial food supply, advanced technology, and new ideas of personal freedom that have radically transformed what people eat and how women believe they should lead their lives.

For one thing, it is no longer necessary for a woman to cook. Because of convenience products, fast-food restaurants, and take-out options, a woman can live her whole life quite happily and productively without ever knowing much more than how to boil pasta, follow directions on a box, and order something good off a menu. And while wealthy women have always enjoyed a certain freedom from the backbreaking labors of the kitchen, now the masses of Americans are also freed. For untold multitudes it has been quite liberating.

But many of us feel a strange sense of change, nonetheless. In 1900, most meals were still cooked and eaten at home. Most women were at home to do the cooking. And most food came from local sources and small family farms. By the year 2000, almost half of American meals were eaten outside the home. More than 60 percent of women participated in the labor force. Within a mere one hundred years, our perception of life and food and women's roles have been radically altered. For many, the change has occurred within a single generation.

How do we make sense of it all?

Mass media has given us unrelenting repetition of our own recent history. We all have seen the images flicker in decade-by-decade succession on our television screens, from the 1950s housewife, to Civil Rights activists, to Reaganism, to Yuppies, to the presidency of the second George Bush. Our own recent history—an extraordinarily eventful one—is on the verge of being swept away from us by sheer numbing repetition. This overexposure severs us not only from the events and decisions that have shaped our lives but also from one another. This is a grave loss. It is the wide lens of history that gives us a chance to understand where—

despite the immense diversity in this nation—we might overlap with one another and share a common set of concerns.

One of these concerns is food.

Today, food has become an intensely political issue. The corporatization of the food and farming businesses has brought high tolls: environmental damage from fertilizer runoff, loss of regional cooking traditions, and higher health risks due to pesticides and herbicides. Most of our food supply is in the hands of large private enterprises whose mission is to make profits—*not* (despite all the packaging claims) to make Americans healthy or to safeguard the environment.

Americans suffer from epidemic levels of obesity and heart disease, not to mention cultural alienation that comes from eating out of plastic in front of computers or while driving in the car. Children are the targets of round-the-clock advertising for junk food. The ideals of thinness and beauty have brought women into combative relationships with food. During the year 2000, a national pollster found that 30 percent of all American women and 20 percent of men were on a diet.

Meanwhile, we seem to yearn for home cooking and the nourishment that comes from meals eaten at a slower pace. But many of those now attempting to take up cooking once again find that they do not know how because they themselves were raised on convenience foods, or they simply do not have the time.

GELATIN LONGINGS

Many of our present food conflicts, emotional and otherwise, took root during the post–World War II era of the 1950s and 1960s, when government and businesses put overwhelming pressure on women to quit their wartime work and return home to raise families. It was a woman's job to heal the emotional wounds and bring forth the next generation.

Unlike the previous "cult of domesticity" invented a hundred years earlier, this one did not ask women to adopt serious cooking into their sacred duties but instead embraced the

> Some women, it is said, like to cook. This book is not for them. . . . This book is for those of us who want to fold our big dishwater hands around a dry Martini instead of a wet flounder, come the end of a long day.
>
> —PEG BRACKEN
> *The I Hate to Cook Book,* 1960

Tupperware was invented in the 1940s, but it didn't take off until Brownie Wise joined the company and invented the Tupperware party—a major marketing innovation that brought hands-on demonstrations and sales directly into women's homes. Here, Brownie Wise tosses a liquid-filled plastic ball across a crowded Tupperware party, 1952. Two years later, she was the first female chief executive to get on the cover of *Business Week.* PHOTO BY JOE STEINMETZ. (*Brownie Wise Collection, Archives Center, National Museum of American History, Smithsonian Institution.*)

frozen, the canned, and the boxed. If it came from a factory, it was better than fresh. The technological revolution—held in abeyance since the stock market crash of 1929—now resumed in unstoppable force. American genius came in the form of Reddi-wip, Cheez Whiz, Sara Lee cheesecake, Frosted Flakes, and the Swanson TV dinner. It became possible to boil your food in a plastic bag and sweeten your coffee with a chemical substitute.

Women—who had carried out extreme austerities during the depression and war years—would now preside over a national spending spree. "An American

Blueberry Cream Salad

1   3 oz package lemon gelatin
1   cup boiling water
1   1 lb can blueberry pie filling
2   tablespoons lemon juice
½   cup sour cream
1   tablespoon sugar

Dissolve gelatin in boiling water and set aside to cool. Stir in pie filling and lemon juice. Chill until partially set.

Spoon half gelatin mixture into mold. Chill until set, keeping remaining gelatin at room temperature.

Combine sour cream and sugar. Spread evenly over gelatin in mold. Top with remaining gelatin.

Chill four to five hours or overnight until firm.

—MARCIA SCHENONE, circa 1970s

Back during the seventies, we called it "mold" without even a smirk. Sometimes it was a dessert and sometimes a side dish, sometimes a "salad." You never could tell.

When I once asked my mother if she ever wondered what gelatin was made of, she replied without hesitation, "No, I never thought about it."

"But how could this be?" I asked.

"Trust," she replied. "Trust in America. If it was made in this country, then it had to be good." This recipe comes from that place of trust.

Way of Life" emerged, featuring a certain entitlement to higher standards in leisure, cleanliness, and convenience, orchestrated by the stay-at-home, middle-class mom for whom no small detail of family perfection was too small.

Home cooking trends exalted gargantuan steaks and hamburgers, as well as a cuisine of ornament, or, as philosopher Roland Barthes has called it, a cuisine of disguise. Here was the era of frozen vegetables and meats covered with cream of mushroom soup. Eggs blanketed in hollandaise. Chicken in pufflets. Pigs in blankets. Hot dogs coated with cornmeal and baked on a stick.

Perhaps no other food has come to embody postwar conservatism and suburban womanhood as JELL-O brand gelatin, which peaked in sales during the early 1960s. Pastel colored with fruity perfumes, gelatin was a pretty, shimmery thing, a decorative object as much as a food. Pliable in spirit and texture, it could form itself to the trends of any generation—not unlike the stereotypes of women. During the 1920s, it had been dainty. During the 1930s, economical. During the 1940s, quick. Now, during the 1950s, JELL-O was light-hearted and comforting, perfect for a generation struggling with the memories of war, fear of communism, and worry that an atom bomb might fall.

Feminists have damned the product for trivializing women's work and women's lives, and for de-skilling a whole generation of cooks. But many Americans recall the JELL-O brand gelatin with some nostalgia, as an icon of innocence, way back when mom had time to mold sweet and silly creations for our pleasure. What was so bad about that?

PROTEST AND FOOD

The first major challenge to the old food hierarchies came on February 1, 1960, when four African-American college freshmen walked into Woolworth's in downtown Greensboro, North Carolina, took a seat at the "whites-only" lunch counter, and demanded peacefully to be served. When refused, they remained seated, waiting all day.

There had been other protests against segregation, and other "sit-ins" that got little attention, but this one was different. As historian Taylor Branch has noted, these young men had not planned to start a revolt. They had no set agenda or goals but went forth spontaneously on an impulse, culminating in "Okay, we might as well go now." To their shock, the Woolworth's management threatened to have them arrested, but floundered, unsure about what actually to do.

That night, the campuses buzzed with the news, and the next day the four boys returned with nineteen more students. The day after that, more than eighty students arrived. By the end of the year seventy thousand people participated in peaceful lunch counter sit-ins throughout the South, protesting segregation

Lunch counter sit-in at a
Nashville store, 1960.
(Library of Congress.)

and racial discrimination that had denied them access to food, education, and public places.

The urgency was suddenly clear. Until African Americans had the right to eat at the same table with whites, the sins of slavery could never be forgotten, the memories of hunger would never abate, and the fight for civil rights and economic empowerment could not begin.

By the end of 1960, Woolworth's opened its lunch counter to blacks, and the Civil Rights movement gained the momentum it needed. There would be no turning back. Blacks marched on Washington. They organized freedom rides on buses. They went to jail if necessary. Some were murdered. But they would not give up.

Protest brought new civil rights laws, but all too often discrimination continued. By the mid-1960s, a new militant movement called "Black Power" replaced dreams of integration with calls for separatism, black economic power, and self-defense with guns if necessary. Malcolm X, the most vocal leader for Black Power, distrusted any racial progress offered by whites. He declared that the worst crime of the white man was "to teach us to hate ourselves."

Black Power celebrated African roots, history, and contributions to American music, literature, and food. Now, in African-American neighborhoods, restau-

"I Don't Have Culinary Limitations Because I'm 'Black.'"

The question I was most often asked was why didn't I consider myself a "soul food" writer. Over and over I would try to explain my philosophy on the universal aspects of black-eyed peas, watermelon, and other so-called soul foods on TV, radio, and in lectures. It seemed to me while certain foods have been labeled "soul food" and associated with African Americans, African Americans could be associated with all foods.

I would explain that my kitchen was the world. Indeed, I experimented with all the cuisines of the world. Each month I chose a country, and for every meal that month I would prepare only dishes from that country.

My feeling was/is any Veau à la Flamande or Blinchishe's Tvorogom I prepared was as "soulful" as a pair of candied yams. I don't have culinary limitations because I'm "black." On the other hand, I choose to write about "African-American" cookery because I'm "black" and know the wonderful, fascinating culinary history there is. And because the African-American cook has been so underappreciated.

—VERTAMAE SMART-GROSVENOR
Vibration Cooking; or, The Travel Notes of a Geechee Girl, 1992 edition

rants advertised "soul food." Inside, you'd usually find fried fish, collard greens, cornbread, and other items served up for a modest cost. Soul food was solidarity. Soul food was pride. And soul food was protest.

African-American women were as likely as men to run soul food restaurants—and in highly visible fashion, too. Unlike Greek and Italian immigrant women a generation before who toiled in family-owned businesses without public credit, many black women put their names in capital letters on the doors. In Chicago, there was Edna's and Gladys's. In Charleston, there was Alice's. In New York, there was Sylvia's. Through their soul kitchens, as historian Tracey Poe has noted, these women provided a meeting space for civil rights activism, politics, and networking. They gained some influence, money, and social capital in their communities.

"My business gave me pride and independence," says Helen Anglin, the fifty-three-year owner of Soul Queen in Chicago. Photos of Jesse Jackson, Harold Washington, and other famous politicians cover her walls. "My restaurant was used as a meeting place. The food was nominally priced. . . . You could get a $3.95 meal," recalls Anglin, who describes herself as "a lover of humankind" willing to help "worthy projects" or "spend some time motivating."

Soul food rallied some African Americans, but it did not appeal to all. Before the 1960s, black Americans had never raised any banners over their diverse culinary habits, nor had they labeled what they ate with any single term. Now this label brought up thorny debate. Writer Amiri Baraka proclaimed soul food as a source of strength. Activist Eldridge Cleaver argued that soul food was a product of the black bourgeoisie who could afford steaks but wanted to go slumming. Elijah Mohammed, leader of the Nation of Islam, condemned soul food as an unhealthful "slave diet," a remnant of white racial genocide.

Edna Lewis, the dean of southern cooking, emphasizes freshness and eating with the seasons, avoiding the label "soul food." From In Pursuit of Flavor, University of Virginia Press.

While some people argued over whether soul food was good or bad for African-American progress and health, others wanted to know exactly what it was. Was it hoe cake, collards, and chitterlings, born from the supposed diet of plantation slaves? Or did soul food also embrace fried chicken, candied yams, buttermilk biscuits, pancakes, gumbo, and sweet-potato pies, which white southerners also claimed as their own? Could Chicken Yassa, transported to the United States from Senegal, be soul food, too? What of codfish and ackee remembered from Jamaica, or manioc dishes transported from immigrants living in Brazil?

Implicit in the idea of soul food is the mythology of a homogeneous blackness that has never existed and never will exist in the United States. African-American women are bound together by shared culinary history for sure. But they also represent a diversity that many Americans have had trouble understanding. As historian Deborah Gray White has written, black women have long been stuck between two stereotypes: the mammy and the sexually loose Jezebel. Soul food, created and produced primarily by black women, has run into similar stereotyping. At times, it is romanticized as the nurturing food from mothers and a lost connection to the rural South. Other times, soul food is demeaned because it embraces frying, fatback, and chitterlings.

Soul food continues to win supporters and critics. Soul cookbooks and restaurants continue to thrive, while some of the nation's most prominent black female chefs, such as Edna Lewis, avoid the term, embracing southern and black traditions, drawing on a large culinary world.

THE KITCHEN AS A PRISON

Beginning in the 1960s and 1970s, every precious tenet of American culture came under question, including that most sacred and ancient ritual of human civilization—whether or not a woman should cook for her husband and her children.

If books can change the world, then Betty Friedan's 1963 *Feminine Mystique* was one of them. Full of passion and fury, Friedan declared that the kitchen had become a prison and American women were suffering from a "problem that had no name." Technology and public education, she claimed, had replaced much of women's meaningful domestic work. In her bleak picture of suburban America, women were lonely, depressed, and unfulfilled, taking Valium to stave off the pain. Meanwhile, women's magazines—and the advertisers who funded them—

"How can I worry about the damned dishes when there are children dying in Vietnam."
From *Suburbia, 1972.* PHOTO BY BILL OWENS.

encouraged female readers to find childlike happiness in wearing pretty clothes, polishing their kitchen floors to a high shine, and baking bread.

Friedan did not speak to working-class or poor women who'd never had the luxury of quitting their jobs to stay home. She wrote from her own experience as a white middle-class housewife who felt trapped. Her message struck a deep chord, helping ignite the modern women's movement.

The kitchen with its pots, pans, heat, and dirty dishes came to symbolize women's oppression. Feminists described it as a place of shackles and drudgery that numbed women's minds. There was a world out there. Education to be had. Fulfilling careers. Novels to be written. Money to be made. Women had to be liberated, and as many feminists saw it, this meant they had to get out of the house.

Beginning in 1965, American consumers showed their support of farm laborers by refusing to purchase table grapes. It was one of the most successful boycotts in American history. By 1970, several large grape growers signed United Farm Worker contracts offering better pay and working conditions. *(Library of Congress.)*

They had to let someone else make dinner. Since 1900, the number of women going out to work had been increasing, but by the 1970s it reached a new critical mass.

Though most American women didn't like to call themselves "feminists," the movement itself was hugely successful. By the century's end, what was once considered a radical feminist agenda simply became normal life. It was largely accepted that women should have higher education and careers outside the home if they wanted, that they could delay marriage, earn money, become professionals, play sports, start businesses, or run for political office.

Blame or credit the women's movement as you choose, there is little doubt that it helped to send millions of women out of the house and the kitchen. Cooking, as a direct result, became less central to most women's lives.

KITCHEN GODDESSES: THE NEW GENERATION

After the 1970s, a woman didn't have to be a home economist anymore if she wanted a career in food. She could be a chef, a restaurant owner, a baker, an environmental activist, a nutritionist, a doctor, an artist, a foreign traveler, a food importer, an academic, and even a media mogul. The options for women's lives and for food became staggering, even overwhelming.

Now that cooking wasn't so much a day-to-day necessity, a new generation of energetic women transformed it into an outlet for creativity, rebellion, health concerns, internationalism, and spirituality. A new generation of kitchen goddesses rose to prominence.

Naturally, the first one to harness the power of television would win the prize. Her name was Julia Child, author of the landmark *Mastering the Art of French Cooking*, published in 1961. With her public television series *The French Chef,* which began the following year, she would become an American icon and the most publicly celebrated cook of the twentieth century.

Unlike previous culinary women, Julia Child did not fret over vitamins or nutrition or how women could use food to improve the world. She was not particularly interested in housewives or budgets, and certainly not in getting dinner on the table quickly. Child insisted that good cooking required a knowledge of technique, fresh ingredients, time, money, and love. For many Americans, this was a startling vision.

But even more startling was Julia herself—standing at six feet two inches, exuding remarkable confidence to the camera. She flourished knives, made jokes about naked chickens, and turned her own klutziness into comedy. When she accidentally flipped a potato pancake on top of the stove instead of into the pan—with a million viewers watching—she quickly noted, "But you can always pick it up. You are alone in the kitchen, whoooo is going to see?" When she dropped flour, she wryly noted, "I have a self-cleaning floor."

Vowing to take the "la-de-da" out of French cuisine for ordinary Americans, she demystified fancy dishes like beef bourguignon, coq au vin, souffles, and crepes, giving step-by-step instructions that anyone (with some time on his or her hands) could follow. Tired of processed foods, Americans were becoming better educated and better traveled. Many food critics said Child led the beginning of an international food movement that encouraged Americans to open their minds first to French food and then to Chinese, Italian, Mexican, Middle Eastern, and Indian food, a trend that hasn't abated yet.

For certain she broke new ground for women. Julia was childless, wealthy, and caught up in a passion. She exuded authority, showing that cooking could be a source of power rather than subjugation—a serious endeavor for women or men. She also did the most unfeminine thing of celebrating appetites and sensuality in food at a time when women were just beginning to explore their own hungers and needs, ready to open themselves up to more adventure and sexual freedom.

"I was always hungry," she confessed of her youth. "I had an appetite like a wolf."

BACK TO THE KITCHEN GARDEN

Women's liberation may have given women a path out of the home kitchen, but another movement offered a path directly back and included the kitchen garden.

Inklings of the modern American health food movement began during the 1950s, but these were mere rumblings beneath the broad surface of a meat-and-mashed-potatoes landscape. By the 1970s change began to take hold. Unlike history's many previous health food movements, this one would get its most significant leadership from women.

In 1962, a scientist and writer named Rachel Carson led the way when she published *Silent Spring*. Meticulously documenting case after case, Carson showed how government, agribusiness, and chemical corporations were poisoning rivers, oceans, air, animals, birds, and people in a ludicrously misguided effort to kill bugs and weeds. Carson wrote of blueberries drenched with arsenic, vegetables coated with insecticides, and meat polluted by DDT, which was killing birds and doing who knew what to humans.

The modern environmental movement was born.

Beginning with *Silent Spring*, many Americans would never feel entirely safe about their food again. After more than a hundred years of unabated growth, the

> *I* contend, furthermore, that we have allowed these chemicals to be used with little or no advance investigation of their effect on soil, water, wildlife, and man himself. Future generations are unlikely to condone our lack of prudent concern for the integrity of the natural world that supports all life.
>
> —RACHEL CARSON
> *Silent Spring,* 1962

power of industry and laboratory science to perfect human life now seemed suspect. For those with the luxury or inclination, a new way of eating was born, proclaiming "You are what you eat" as its motto. The trust with which women so easily purchased commercial food in plastic bags and trays began to wither.

A group of young energized women began to draw the connection between individual eating choices and the larger world.

"The act of putting into your mouth what the earth has grown is perhaps your most direct interaction with the earth," wrote Frances Moore Lappé in her *Diet for a Small Planet*, published in 1971. Lappé was something of a throwback to the nineteenth-century culinary women devoted to helping the hungry and poor. But where those early reformers struck a resolutely pro-American note, Lappé took a different approach. She attacked the nation's beef-loving culture as the root of social injustice. A vegetarian diet, she argued, would supply sufficient protein to humans and it would be more ethical. Millions of people around the world were going hungry each day *not* because there wasn't enough arable land on earth but because most of it was being used to feed cows. Americans—with their vast agricultural resources—were giving about three-fourths of their grain to livestock. According to Lappé, it took twenty-one pounds of grain to produce every one pound of meat for human consumption. *Diet for a Small Planet* sold more than three million copies and helped inspire the largest vegetarian movement the nation has ever seen.

Many of the young and socially committed saw vegetarianism in terms of not only politics and ethics but also culinary and spiritual beauty. Cooking from the garden brought forth more beautiful foods in a world becoming overrun by plastic.

In 1977 the hugely influential *Moosewood Cookbook* came forth from Mollie Katzen, one of the original seven members of a cooperative vegetarian restaurant in Ithaca, New York. Perhaps more than any other book, *Moosewood* helped bring vegetarianism to mainstream acceptability. Katzen was neither a food activist nor a trained chef, but an aspiring artist who loved to cook. Her book—hand lettered and decorated with her illustrations of fruits—looked more like a private journal than a cookbook. It also seemed to possess a certain creative joy, without imposing moral guilt. Sidenotes encouraged the cook to have fun and improvise. It was a revelation. And it became one of the best-selling cookbooks of all time.

The new vegetarian cuisine was liberating. The first sight of raw mushrooms and peppers in the midst of dark leafy salads seemed thrilling after the iceberg salads of childhood. A dish like Gypsy Soup offered not only a chance to rebel against the corporate powers that built weapons, pesticides, and commercial foods but also a chance to challenge mother's bland dishes and the narrow gender roles prescribed by Betty Crocker. The main ingredients—brightly colored sweet potatoes and wholesome garbanzo beans—seemed to stir ancient memories of Mother Earth. The "gypsy" could be found in the scent of garlic and onion and turmeric, promising an adventurous culinary and spiritual journey far away from those commercialized kitchens of the 1950s.

"Now they kind of make fun of the 1960s and 1970s," says Katzen. "At the time this was not a joke. It was not a silly little thing where we put flowers in our hair and wore bell bottoms. There was a general sense of the preciousness of life and our personal choices. We weren't being grandiose. Our friends were really being shipped off to Vietnam. It really did touch home. We were seeking to live on this earth in a way that was a higher version of the human spirit. This did inform where a lot of us were coming from, it was very real."

OPPOSITE: From Mollie Katzen's 1977 *Moosewood Cookbook*.
Recipes like Gypsy Soup seemed to promise adventure.

Gypsy Soup

About 45 minutes
to prepare

NOTE: Chick peas need
to be cooked in ad-
vance. (canned = OK)

... a delicately spiced
Spanish-style
vegetable soup...

Yield: 4 to 5 servings

The vegetables in this soup can be varied. Any orange
vegetable can be combined with any green. For example,
peas or green beans could replace— or augment— the peppers.
Carrots, pumpkin, or squash could fill in for the sweet
potatoes. Innovate!

✤ ☾ ✿ ❨ ❀ ✤ ❨ ❀ ❩ ✿ ❨ ❀ ❩ ✿ ❨ ❀ ❩ ✿ ❨ ❀ ❩ ✿ ❨ ❀ ❩ ✿ ❨ ❀ ❩

2 medium-sized ripe tomatoes
2 Tbs. olive oil
2 cups chopped onion
3 medium cloves garlic, crushed
1 stalk celery, minced
2 cups peeled, diced sweet potato
1 tsp. salt
2 tsp. mild paprika

1 tsp. turmeric
1 tsp. basil
a dash of cinnamon
a dash of cayenne
1 bay leaf
3 cups water
1 medium bell pepper, diced
1½ cups cooked chick peas

1) Heat a medium-sized saucepanful of water to boiling. Core the
tomatoes, and plunge them into the boiling water for a slow count
of 10. Remove the tomatoes, and peel them over a sink. Cut them
open; squeeze out and discard the seeds. Chop the remaining
pulp and set aside.

2) Heat the olive oil in a kettle or Dutch oven. Add onion, garlic,
celery, and sweet potato, and sauté over medium heat for about
5 minutes. Add salt, and sauté 5 minutes more. Add seasonings
and water, cover, and simmer about 15 minutes.

3) Add tomato pulp, bell pepper, and chick peas. Cover and simmer for
about 10 more minutes, or until all the vegetables are as tender
as you like them. Taste to adjust seasonings, and serve.

❨ ❀ ❩ ✿ ❨ ❀ ❩ ✿ ❨ ❀ ❩ ✿ ❨ ❀ ❩ ✿ ❨ ❀ ❩ ✿ ❨ ❀ ❩ ✿ ❨ ❀ ❩ ✿

By the 1980s, many culinary women had reached mainstream America, while others struggled to break into the upper echelons of international chefdom. Though women quickly advanced as pastry chefs, they were still routinely shut out of executive positions in high-quality restaurants.

In 1971, a woman named Alice Waters began to change that when, still in her twenties, she and a small band of friends founded a neighborhood bistro called Chez Panisse in a remodeled house set in the hills of Berkeley, California. At first, Waters envisioned a place where she could cook for her friends, a collection of politically active artists and radicals. The food she envisioned had been inspired

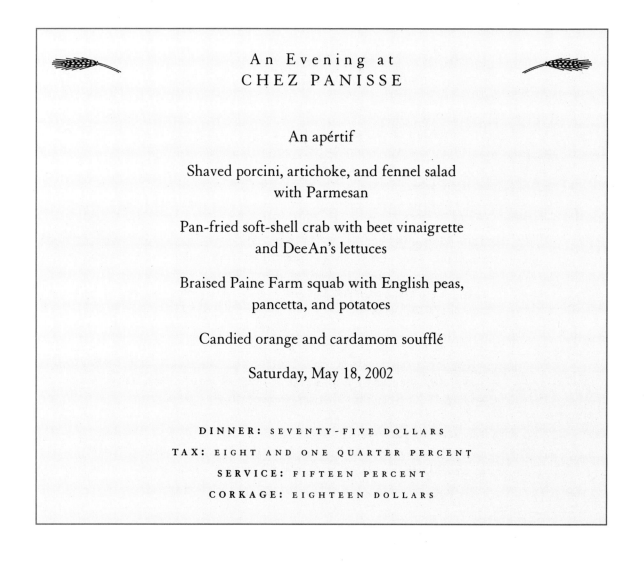

An Evening at
CHEZ PANISSE

An apértif

Shaved porcini, artichoke, and fennel salad
with Parmesan

Pan-fried soft-shell crab with beet vinaigrette
and DeeAn's lettuces

Braised Paine Farm squab with English peas,
pancetta, and potatoes

Candied orange and cardamom soufflé

Saturday, May 18, 2002

DINNER: SEVENTY-FIVE DOLLARS
TAX: EIGHT AND ONE QUARTER PERCENT
SERVICE: FIFTEEN PERCENT
CORKAGE: EIGHTEEN DOLLARS

Alice Waters, one of America's most highly regarded chefs, broke through the glass ceiling. At her renowned Chez Panisse restaurant in Berkeley, California.
PHOTO BY
FRANKLIN AVERY.

by a life-changing journey to Europe, where she'd fallen in love with French country cooking and local ingredients of perfect quality.

Financed by investments from family and friends, Chez Panisse promptly found itself $40,000 in debt. But in time it turned around and became a stunning success. Waters's cuisine was startling, bringing together unexpected combinations of the freshest possible foods. She nurtured relationships with local organic farmers, fishermen, bakers, and cheesemakers, and she began gathering international attention as the "mother of California Cuisine," a profoundly influential new culinary movement that emphasized ethereal beauty based on simple preparations.

All this was a huge accomplishment. But it was even more so considering the discrimination against women chefs. In Europe and America, the kitchens of top restaurants had been entirely male-dominated, according to the hierarchical and militaristic tradition of the French. In New York, this continues to be so. As Marion Burros reported in the *New York Times* in February 1999, only 14 out of 184 top New York restaurants had female chefs.

Alice Waters showed a different way, a West Coast way, where women could rise to the top not only through nonstop work but also through creativity and innovation, inspiring female chefs across the nation and helping to lead California to the vanguard of American gastronomy.

"Wouldn't It Be Great If People Would Make Cheeses like This in the U.S.?"

For most of the twentieth century, men had dominated the cheese business with large commodity-type wheels made in giant blocks of mediocre quality and sold at low cost. By the 1980s, American women led a stunning revival of handmade goat and sheep cheeses at small farms across the country. In this 2001 interview, Judy Shad of Indiana told me the story of how she became a pioneer in the new American cheese business.

In the late 1960s, there was the whole "back-to-the-land" thing, and it hit the Midwest a little later. We purchased a farm in 1976 here in Southern Indiana and left our suburban home. We came out here and built a log house. There was an old barn on the land, and we thought that meant we had to have something to milk. An animal that was very manageable for city people was a goat of course.

A cow is big, about 1200 to 1600 pounds. But a goat is about 200 pounds—sort of like a cow for suburban people. Goats have wonderful personality. They're interesting, smarter than cows and sheep. They're very affectionate, too. They want to sit in your lap and bond like a dog does. We had cows. We had sheep. But it was goats we really loved.

When I started to make cheese in 1982, I did it in my own kitchen. I didn't get into it commercially until 1989. There was a very small network of women cheesemakers at that time. In the late 1980s, I met Ann Topham from Phantom Farm in Wisconsin and Mary Doerr who had a farm called Dancing Wind. There was Jennifer Bice of Redwood Hill, and Mary Keehn, who had Cyprus Grove Chevre. We were all friends. We did the same thing—either raised goats or made cheese.

Today, Waters is one of the world's reigning chefs. She has also gone on to become a tireless advocate for organic farming and sustainable agriculture in the United States. On a more local level, she founded "the edible schoolyard" at a Berkeley public school, which teaches young children to grow, raise, and appreciate eating organic vegetables. Waters currently promotes this program as a model to be replicated across the nation.

I think we repeated the early history of women's cheesemaking. . . . We had to recover lost knowledge and we had to talk to each other. There was no place in the United States to go and learn. You had to figure it out by trial and error. We just threw out tons of cheese.

Goat cheese is an ideal product for women. First of all, the animal is easy to handle. Second of all, it doesn't take complicated expensive equipment. You make it in small quantities, doable in your own kitchen. It's the simplest form of cheese, too. It takes a small amount of bacterial culture to make the milk separate into curds and whey. When it reaches a certain acidity level, the milk begins to coagulate and thicken automatically. You add rennet. It's very soft and delicate. In the morning, you come in and it's white as snow and on top is a liquid layer of whey, and you have to ladle it very carefully into layers and molds. It's full of moisture. This is a very different process than what men do in factories.

It's hard though. To run a cheese business takes a level of commitment that most people don't have. It's hard to manage animals, produce cheese, and market it too. We have 300 animals. I spend a lot of time scrubbing down equipment.

You'd think my greatest moment might have been when we won the best of show at the American Cheese Society in 1995. That was great.

But some of my best moments have been the private ones—when I knew I was doing the right thing. Like in 1994, the first year we previewed these little ripened *chevres* at the fancy food show in New York. People tasted our cheeses and assumed they were from France. They said, "Wouldn't it be great if people would make cheeses like this in the U.S.?" and I would say. "Guess what? These are made in southern Indiana."

FROM THE BAKERY TO THE TAQUERÍA

The renaissance of American food was not just a top-down phenomenon created by celebrity cookbook authors and chefs. Between the 1970s and 1990s American women all across the nation opened hundreds of thousands of local restaurants, bakeries, and small food businesses where they could not only express themselves

On the Rise, a cooperative whole-grain bakery, in Syracuse, New York. PHOTO BY JAN PHILLIPS.

but also earn a living. Many of these businesses have focused on the fresh, the local, the natural, and the ethnic. Women have been especially successful as bakers, reviving the old craft of brick-oven baking, and as artisanal cheesemakers, with an emphasis on goat's and sheep's milk cheeses.

Women have also taken a special role in bringing a new internationalism to American eating and consciousness. Since immigration quotas began to relax in 1965, more than 20 million foreign-born people have arrived in the United States, the majority coming from Asia and Latin America. As during the first huge wave of immigration at the turn of the last century, these immigrants came seeking economic opportunity and political freedom. They arrived hungry for their own foods, and many set up family-run grocery stores, import businesses, and restaurants so they could survive economically while re-creating their beloved recipes

Mirna Pineda sells Guatemalan food at the California Marathon, 1991. (Shades of L.A./Los Angeles Public Library.)

from home. An increasingly open society greeted them eagerly, interested in trying "authentic" and exotic foods, usually tempered for the American palate.

Perhaps it was adventure. Perhaps it was the increasingly educated urbane sensibility of the 1980s. But I think that Americans suspected (whether true or untrue) that immigrants still possessed something that they had lost—a connec-

Shrimp Stew
(Camarones a La Criolla)

1 tablespoon annatto oil combined with 2 tablespoons olive oil

¼ cup basic *recaíto*

3 bay leaves

½ cup *alcaparrado* or pitted manzanilla olives

3 ounces smoked ham, cut into small dice

1 cup tomato sauce

1 16-ounce can whole tomatoes, drained and roughly chopped

2 pounds medium shrimp, peeled and cleaned

2 teaspoons salt

2 teaspoons black pepper

Heat the oil in a soup pot. Add the *recaíto*, bay leaves, *alcaparrado*, and ham. Saute over medium-high heat for 3 minutes. Add the tomato sauce and canned tomatoes. Bring the mixture to a boil, reduce the heat to medium, and add the shrimp. Cook until the shrimp turn pink, about 5 minutes. Stir in salt and pepper and cook 2 minutes more.

   Serves 6 to 8

—Adapted from YVONNE ORTIZ
A Taste of Puerto Rico, 1994

Annatto Oil

Annatto is a replacement for saffron. Its chief job is to provide a bright yellow color. To make annatto oil, heat two cups of olive oil in a small saucepan. Add ½ cup annatto seeds (available at all bodegas and many supermarkets) and cook about 5 minutes over low heat. When the oil is a rich orange color, remove, let cool, and strain.

Recaíto

When heated, this becomes *sofrito*—the essential flavor base for many Caribbean dishes.

½ medium yellow onion, diced
1 Italian frying pepper, seeded and diced
2 garlic cloves, peeled
3 sweet chile peppers, seeded [These are small. Use your judgment.]
3 *recao* leaves (if *recao* leaves are unavailable, triple the amount of cilantro)
1 sprig cilantro

Combine all of the ingredients in a blender or food processor. If using a blender, add some water or oil if needed.

Makes ½ cup.

—YVONNE ORTIZ
A Taste of Puerto Rico, 1994

In 2000, more than 32 million Latinos were living in the United States, representing 12 percent of the total U.S. population and coming from Mexico, Central and Latin America, Cuba, and Puerto Rico. In many bodegas and other grocery stores around the nation, you can now find rice, black beans, and mixes for sofrito. In southern Florida, around Miami, open-air food stands re-create those of the Caribbean, where women come to shop daily for tropical fruits and vegetables like guayabana, yucca, and plantains. In some neighborhoods of New York City, street vendors sell snowcones in the style of Latin America, with tropical flavors like coconut and tamarind.

My friend Vivian, whose parents emigrated from Puerto Rico, tells me her mother's cooking is like a tropical breeze but difficult to re-create. Unlike Asian immigrants who have been so successful in restaurants all over the nation, Puerto Rican cooking tends to be practiced inside the home, passed on from mother to daughter.

This recipe for shrimp stew is excellent. Serve it over white rice with beans on the side. First make the recaíto and the annatto oil. If you are pressed for time, use plain olive oil instead of annatto.

tion to food that had not been corrupted by convenience products, a connection that still expressed local culture and intense flavors.

During the 1980s and 1990s, immigrants responded profitably to these yearnings by working long hours and long years to build restaurants, bakeries, and grocery stores. A new legacy of international foodism spread across the nation in the form of fresh new culinary ideas from sushi and Pad Thai to tortillas and Babaganouj.

During the recent big wave of immigration, women from Southeast Asia have been especially influential as restauranteurs. For every Vietnamese restaurant in America you'll find a story of loss and tragedy from war a quarter century earlier, transformed into a new life. One of these stories belongs to Cam Jeffries.

"We had two chauffeurs. We always had three servants. One to cook, one to take care of the babies, and one to do the cleaning. We had two big houses in Saigon," she recalls of her youth.

Born to a wealthy Vietnamese family in 1955, Cam grew up in luxury with her grandmother, parents, and eleven sisters and brothers. When the communists took over, they lost their land and money, and she took a succession of jobs to contribute to the family's survival. In one of these jobs, Cam was a bus girl at the American Embassy restaurant that served diplomats. That's where she was in 1975, the day that Saigon fell. After being trapped in the embassy for a day, American helicopters came and lifted her and many others out. "When I looked down, it looked like the whole world on fire. I was sure my family was dead."

Relocated to the United States, she married an American military man and spent two decades devoted to her husband and children. To help put them through college, she worked from ten in the morning until ten at night, at three different Vietnamese restaurants. Then she opened a place of her own with the labor and financial help of her husband and children.

I met Cam during the summer of 2001. Her restaurant Saigon Village was so overwhelmed by customers that Cam was racing about to serve them. It was a notable hubbub on Chincoteague, a quiet Virginia fishing island renowned for plain food. Here, the locals like their shrimp steamed and their flounder fried. Tartar sauce is about as wild as it gets. Now the scent of lemon grass and ginger was bringing people in off Main Street, and within a year of opening, Cam won a regular clientele of locals, as well as a large following of tourists from Washington, D.C. She was working six days a week, spending her seventh day driving to distant cities where she could buy the essentials for Vietnamese cooking—fresh vegetables, cilantro, rice noodles, rice paper, stir-fry sauce, and seasoning.

It is no surprise when she tells me that in Vietnamese culture, women are very strong. "They run 95 percent of the restaurants. They run the household. They're in charge of the money. The man is the provider, but the woman makes all the decisions about the children."

Today, among the younger, more recent generation of immigrants, Asians in the United States have been just as likely to go to elite culinary schools and approach food as a form of art and personal expression. Many come from higher educational levels than immigrants of the past. In big-city restaurants, they have been eager to create fusions and adaptations that comment on their global experiences and ideas.

New York's Cendrillon is one such restaurant. Proprietor Amy Besa and her husband, chef Romy Dorotan, approach each dish like a work of art. "We think about each dish. We talk about each dish. It's very intellectual," explains Amy, who says she has become more aware of her Southeast Asian identity since she has come to the United States from her native Philippines.

Cendrillon is a beautiful and calm place, where the smells of ginger entice you when you come in the door. Here, the national dish of chicken adobo is done to perfection with salt, chiles, and vinegar, served over coconut-flavored rice. The traditional Philippine dish of *lumpia* is newly interpreted with a wrapper made from purple yams, served with two unconventional sauces, one tamarind, the other peanut—challenging yet remaining honest to Southeast Asian tradition.

"This whole restaurant is a work of love," says Amy, who admits that she would have probably been put in jail if she'd stayed in the Philippines under Marcos because of her activism as a university student during the 1970s. "We come from a place where we don't take anything for granted. Here you have electricity, running water, and flush toilets. We don't have these things throughout the Philippines."

Amy and Romy someday hope to set up a foundation in the United States to promote greater understanding of Southeast Asian cuisine, its culture and its people, and the importance of traditional food and farming practices now under constant threat from globalization. "I want to take the good values of my culture and the good values of the American culture and make synergy."

By the last decade of the twentieth century, the food critics were congratulatory. American food had gotten better and better. American supermarkets were filled with interesting fresh fruits and vegetables. You could get balsamic vinegar, chile peppers, leeks, escarole, couscous, mangos, and kiwis. Sales of organic produce were skyrocketing, as wealthier and more educated Americans sought higher levels of gastronomy and refuge from the threat of pesticides and chemicals. Crusty artisan breads were popping out of bakery ovens everywhere. American cheese-makers began putting out lovely little goat cheeses to rival those of France. And in medium-sized American towns, you might find a Thai, Indian, or Japanese eatery on Main Street.

American women were learning how to entertain at a higher level, too, thanks in no small part to Martha Stewart, the Connecticut caterer turned media scion. Women whose mothers served pot roast and gelatin salads discovered, under Martha's tutelage, how to throw parties featuring Paté on Apple Slices or Blini with Red Caviar.

Finally, it seemed that Americans cared about eating well. For aging baby boomers, including a growing number of men, home cooking became a satisfying hobby for leisure time and a creative pursuit. Thousands of cookbooks were published, and a torrent of new cooking experts revealed the secrets to making everything ethnic from Thai Peanut Sauce to Indian Dahl to Brazilian Feijoada. By the year 2001, a cable channel devoted exclusively to food—*The Food Network*—was available to 67 million American subscribers, heralding forth a new religion whose followers call themselves "foodies." Meanwhile, the joys of cooking and eating became a subject for art, film, and novels, and women began writing their memoirs in the form of cookbooks—mingling recipes, nostalgia, art, and food.

From all this, it would seem that the American food revolution had fully arrived and was a stunning success.

Perhaps.

But it takes only one open-eyed walk through any nonmetropolitan supermarket to see that America is an extremely diverse society, one in which home cooking—there is simply no way around it—is harder to come by.

To travel to the heart of women's cooking in America is no simple thing, here at the beginning of the twenty-first century, when many culinary viewpoints seem to coexist and clash at once.

We know there is conflict. We see the lines of stress in women's faces, especially beneath the glare of florescent lights at the supermarket, their carts loaded

No cooking for this career mom. Detail from fashion advertisement, 1997. PHOTO BY PAMELA HANSON.

high with Hamburger Helper and frozen pizzas. How great the contrast with those beautiful scenes in cookbooks and magazines.

Social class explains much. The United States is a nation of culinary haves and culinary have-nots. This has always been true and in recent years has become more so as economic expansion broadened the gulf between rich and poor. The wealthier and better educated can afford better foods than the poor, while minorities suffer from higher levels of obesity, diabetes, and blood pressure.

And yet, the inability to find time to cook seems to cut across class. The working poor may choose the cheapest and least-healthy options: fast-food burgers and pizza. The wealthier may eat "gourmet" frozen dinners, organic mesculun salad out of a bag, or Asian take-out food. In 2001, the *New York Times* reported on Jewish families paying mightily to have Passover catered in a Florida hotel. The grandmothers preferred to play with their grandkids rather than labor over gefilte fish. That same year, even Williams-Sonoma—that high-fallutin' store for "serious cooks"—was selling jars of gravy and cranberry sauce along with instant boxed stuffing mix for Thanksgiving dinner.

"Increasingly, consumers lack the time, energy and know-how to prepare a meal," reported the Food Marketing Institute in 2001. "This creates a lifestyle dilemma that they want others to solve."

During the last twenty years, convenience foods have gone to an extreme unthinkable even in the synthetic 1950s. Entire dinners now come in microwavable and disposable containers, obviating the need for a single pan or plate. Pastries are replacing cereal because they can be eaten with one hand while driving a car or while working at the office. Salads come already washed in resealable bags. Freshly cooked rotisserie chickens are bagged hot off the spit. And even that old American love, JELL-O brand gelatin, comes ready made and shelf stable, for those who lack the time to add boiling water and chill.

"As everyone in the packaged-food world knows, three square meals are going the way of the horse and buggy, replaced in our fast-paced lives by an endless loop of vending machines, doughnut stands and coffee breaks," reported Suein L. Hwang, in the *Wall Street Journal* in 2002.

Today, the American diet contains more vegetables and fruit than thirty years ago. But it also contains more sugar, fat, and meat—generally more of everything, with gigantic portions becoming the norm. The health food movement has been fully co-opted by American food corporations. And so, in a sad irony, Americans have become increasingly overweight, while an inescapable $30 billion chorus of advertising tells us that candy, cookies, and chips are good because they are low fat, low salt, high fiber, and vitamin- and calcium-enriched. The goal, of course, is to make Americans feel less guilty about eating, often overeating, commercial food products.

In her book *Food Politics*, the nutritionist Marion Nestle documents with staggering precision how the dairy, meat, and other food businesses shape our lives and our diets. Though research repeatedly concludes that the best diet is a low-fat one based on plant rather than animal sources, lobbyists have successfully pressured our government from issuing clear nutritional standards. If Americans suddenly ate fewer calories, and less dairy and meat, food corporations would make a lot less money.

As it is, food marketers already compete fiercely for profits because our nation makes more food than it can consume. Seeking new avenues of income, food companies have turned their marketing efforts increasingly to minorities and children. Though Americans should eat less and move their bodies more, the message of food advertising can be boiled down to a single command: eat more.

Americans are receptive to this message in part because we live in a culture that has come to demand lots of food at low cost, relative to our nation's affluence. In America, we have come to expect that we will pay four dollars for a package of meat that will make seven hamburgers. Foodmakers and government go to extremes to keep costs low while still maintaining profits.

Whereas, for example, it used to take a cow four to five years to be ready for slaughter, now it only takes fourteen to sixteen months, reported Michael Pollen in the *New York Times* in 2002. This speedup has become possible mainly because of growth hormones and antibiotic-laced feed—whose residues reach our bodies as well. Inexpensive commercial bakery goods get their long shelf life from hydrogenated oils—known for clogging arteries. Our agribusinesses provide flavorless but low-cost fruits, vegetables, and corn sugar thanks to farm subsidies, pesticides, and a tide of seasonal workers who make low wages, usually with no health benefits.

Now if all this seems quite depressing, well, I'd have to agree. This is the dark side of our food culture.

But it is the truth, and if we care about food, we must look at it. And once we do, we must also see the hopefulness in the fact that we can make choices, and

industries will respond. The unassailable proof of this is our current $7.7 billion organic industry, which has grown up in just two decades simply because consumers demanded better quality and were willing to pay more.

But perhaps the real question **is** *why* have Americans been willing to sacrifice quality? Why has food come to have such little value in our lives that we expect it be so cheap, abundant, fast, and convenient?

There is no simple answer. But our constant lack of time would have to be high on the list.

We know that the United States is in the midst of an immense economic transition in which the very nature of family, work, and community is undergoing radical change. This change began gradually around the turn of the last century, when technology began bringing new kinds of jobs that were friendlier to women than the old kind of muscle-powered work.

Just as family farms once faded to be replaced by factories, we, living today, find ourselves thrust into a new economy that relies heavily on wage labor and domestic labor from both sexes. Women work out of the home. Men do more chores and childrearing. The old bargain of housework (provided by women) in exchange for money (provided by men) has become optional for some—and unattainable for others.

Today, under the pressures of the global marketplace, technology, and increased competition, a new business structure has emerged in the United States. Employees are now expected to work harder, be better skilled, and be willing to work longer hours, with less job security. Home is no longer a haven from the cruel and ugly business world. In fact, it is increasingly entangled with business— via the Internet, cell phones, pagers, and other technologies that keep men and women in constant connection with their jobs.

And yet, many women yearn for the old model, the "separate spheres," that is within such recent memories of our mothers. We wish we had time to cook but

PHOTO BY MARY FREY.
From her *"Real Life Dramas,"* 1984–1987.

"But how can you be certain?" she asked.
"You never can," was her reply.

somehow can only fit it into weekends and holidays—if that. As a result, a nostalgia for the lost culinary past seems boundless.

We cannot help but admire and envy people who have retained, or revived, home manufacturing skills. The ones who live amid acres of clean and natural land and grow huge gardens, canning and preserving foods for winter. The ones who make their own sausage or bring big containers of homemade pickles to summer picnics.

Do we envy them simply because their homemade and homegrown dishes taste a million times better than the stuff of supermarkets? Or is there something else, something more deeply rooted we are missing as well?

In fact, for many of us, there is no golden past—no happy day of yore when we were all back on the farm with our hungers satisfied by the delicious slow-cooked food of our grandmothers. As historian Rachel Laudan reminds us, we might be shocked if we were to actually encounter the truly "natural" food of our ancestors, the tough meat, the sour fruits, the fresh warm milk that was unmistakably a bodily excretion. "Natural" may be fashionable now, but it once meant unreliable. Seasons of plenty were followed by cold weather and hunger when hens stopped laying eggs and cows dried up. Local and natural were what you ate if you were poor—along with organ meat and pigs' ears.

The only constants of history, it seems, have been change and human adaptation. These go back to the days when the Ice Age ended and humans had to give up mastodon meat. Or—put more simply—one generation loves croquettes; the next, gelatin molds; the next, arugula salads with balsamic vinegar.

What really matters, I have come to believe, is not so much the food itself but the act of cooking and the act of caring for others.

The most important thing we can do is believe in food—not only in how it tastes in our own mouths but also in the larger sense. By caring about the act of cooking itself, by believing in it, we give food a higher meaning. Once we value food and cooking, from there other good things follow. We make good choices. We care about the animals and earth and other human beings involved in our food chain. We find nourishment. We take care of others, ourselves, and the planet.

If we believe food is important, then we as women also become aware of how powerful we are—not only on a personal level but also when we go to the grocery store and take out our wallets.

Sometimes it makes me annoyed that on top of everything women have done and must do, we still must be in charge of worrying about what everyone eats. Isn't this the government's job to regulate these things? Can't someone else do it?

But if we don't do it, who will?

In my most idealistic moments, when I go to the stove or cutting board, I try to think of myself connected to a long human story. Then, I know that a dinner of sandwiches or a fresh salad with the right amount of grace and love can be superior to the finest presentation of salmon or squab with saffron that is cooked with disregard.

We can be ashamed of our wars and flaws, our capacity for evil as human beings. But cooking and caring for one another—this is our bright side. In cooking, we find our creativity, ingenuity. And I believe women want to embrace this connection because of our special history with food. If men want to join us in the kitchen, I think that's great. We need all the hospitality and caring we can get.

On this note, I close with a final course—naturally a dessert. It is a peach pie recipe handed down through three generations—a mere drop in the giant pastry bowl of time. I have no illusions that it comes from any great culinary origins. Perhaps it originated in a manufacturer's little cookbook during the 1920s. It belonged to my husband's grandmother, Louise Schaffner, gone more than thirty years now. She didn't come from a farm. Her parents immigrated here from Germany and ran a candy store in New York City, then got tuberculosis and died. Louise, at around age nine, was sent to an orphanage in the Philadelphia area. She was a strong woman who put her life together through talent and a little luck. Though orphanage girls generally did not go to high school, for some reason, Louise was chosen as the only girl to go to Philadelphia High. And then, she was chosen again to receive a scholarship for college. After that, she became an English teacher, married a man she loved, and then set about raising children in the rural German farming area around Harrisburg, Pennsylvania, where—there's no doubt about it—people love their pies.

I am not a big pie person myself. But many years ago, when my father-in-law was still alive, I heard he loved peach pie, so I made one. Being a man of polite country manners, he said thank you and ate it all. He seemed to enjoy it, but I couldn't tell for sure. I had my doubts because I'd heard that nothing could ever measure up to his mother's pie.

Many years later, after he died, my mother-in-law, Corinne, produced a tattered old recipe card she had found in a drawer.

"This," she announced ceremoniously, "is the original peach pie recipe."

She entrusted it to my care, and I was a little awed because I knew—her marriage having ended in divorce—that this was a sensitive relic. The favorite pie recipe of her ex-husband, whose mother's approval she could never fully win. You can be sure I studied that card and was fascinated to find that it had undergone some revisions. During the seventies, Corinne had crossed out the shortening and replaced it with margarine—believing it to be healthier. She also crossed out her mother-in-law's proportions for flour. Here it was, that endless effort of one generation to correct the previous, the search to finally get things just right.

With a keen sense of responsibility, I immediately typed up the recipe and sent it around the Schaffner family. "Here's your grandmother's pie," I declared. People were grateful, but my husband and I were a bit surprised to see that some members of the family didn't seem to remember it very well. "Oh yes, peach pie. Well, perhaps there was one. . . ."

"I am sure," my husband insisted. "This is her famous pie. Oh yes."

My husband's aunt went ahead and made it. And she validated him, saying that indeed the memories of her mother came flooding back upon first bite. We were relieved, needless to say.

Naturally, when good juicy peaches came to the supermarket, I bought a bunch and set about to do the job myself. My husband waited impatiently as I rolled the dough and peeled the fruit and beat the eggs. He stood by the oven door. After all, it's not every day you get to eat your grandmother's pie after a few decades.

How was it?

It was delicious. It had an unexpected custard that brought the pie to a surprising place. (Of course, in my own interest of perfecting things, I left off a little sugar to retain some tartness. And I used butter, not shortening, in my crust.) My husband was thrilled. And I was very proud, promising to do it every year, when good peaches became ripe.

This all happened some years ago, and of course I got busy having children, and there were some summers, like the one two years ago, when I had an exhausting pregnancy and didn't make peach pie. And the summer last year, too, when I was busy making other kinds of things like fruit pudding or never got the right peaches in time and made angel food cake with strawberries instead.

Despite this, last winter at a family event, my husband was bragging to some Schaffner relatives that *every* summer when the local peaches are ripe, his wife makes this peach pie. A pie just like Grandma Louise's. Oh yes, every summer. Pie.

His cousin's wife, who never misses a beat, wryly asked, "Once a year? Just once a year? What is it, some kind of sacred act?"

Well, you can be the judge.

Fay Drawhorn makes biscuits at Army and Lou's restaurant in Chicago, 2000. PHOTO BY ERIC FUTRAN.

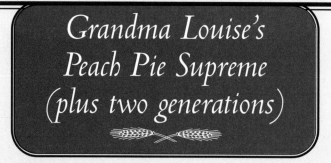

Grandma Louise's Peach Pie Supreme (plus two generations)

Use whatever basic single crust recipe you like. Or purchase one. Or try mine. (If you are inexperienced with pastry dough, you'll probably be glad if you consult a mentor or general reference cookbook with illustrations on rolling technique.)

For a Single Bottom Crust

1⅛ c flour
I t salt
 8 T very cold, unsalted butter, cut into small pieces
    A small bowl of ice water

- Sift flour and salt together.
- Work quickly to add your fat into the flour. Some people use their fingertips. For a long time I used a pastry blender (an inexpensive piece of equipment you can get at the supermarket). But now I prefer the food processor. If you do, process for about 10 to 15 seconds—until the mixture has a cornmeal texture.
- Place it in a bowl and sprinkle 3 to 5 tablespoons of the ice water lightly into the dough so that you can gather it up into a ball with your hands. If it's too dry, add more cold water, but use as little as possible. Shape into a flat round disk. Wrap in plastic and put your dough in the freezer for 10 minutes, or in the refrigerator if you have more time. This makes it easier to work with.

- Roll out your dough on a floured surface. Start in middle and roll outward. (I like to do this on a floured pastry cloth.) Roll it so it is thin, otherwise your bottom will remain raw.
- Use a wheel or knife to cut out a circle about 2 inches wider in circumference than your pie plate, then gently fold it in thirds, lift, and place it in. Make pretty edges by crimping with your fingers or indenting all around with the tines of a fork.

Pie Filling

2½ c fresh peaches, peeled and sliced (Don't even waste your time on this pie unless they are in season, beautifully ripe and juicy.)

¼ c peach juice (I use whatever is at the bottom of the bowl. If you don't have enough, squeeze juice from your left-over peach skins or a whole peach.)

- Fill unbaked pie shell with peaches and juice. Over the peaches, pour this "Supreme" mixture.

Supreme Mixture

½ c sugar (more or less depending on the sweetness of your peaches) and 2 T flour, mixed (If you're feeling like a perfectionist, sift together.)

2 large or extra large eggs, beat again

2 T melted butter

2 T whole milk

I t vanilla

- Bake at 400 degrees for 35 to 40 minutes. This is a custard filling, so you must take it out of the oven when the center is still a little jiggly. This requires a leap of faith. Take it, and enjoy.

Select Bibliography

There is no existing subject or library catalog entry known as "the history of women and food." To find materials, I consulted books on general history, women's history, culinary history, anthropology, and archaeology, as well as herbal guides, domestic manuals, cookbooks, and articles in the popular press. Here is a partial list of sources, chapter by chapter, based on those I depended on the most. Note that in older sources, the original dates of publication appear in parentheses. Also, with rare exceptions I did not list interviews, as these are not available to the reader. Finally, a number of works were extremely influential not just in one chapter, but the entire book. I list these first under "General."

GENERAL

American Social History Project. *Who Built America: Working People and the Nation's Economy, Politics, Culture and Society,* 2 vols. New York: Pantheon Books, 1992. A great work that provided me with many ideas, facts, and visual images.

Aresty, Esther B. *The Delectable Past.* New York: Bobbs-Merrill, 1964. Dated by useful overview of culinary history.

Cooks Illustrated. Various issues. Edited by Christopher Kimball. Brookline, MA. Helpful for classic American recipes, such as pot roast and fruit pudding.

Cott, Nancy, and Elizabeth H. Pleck. *A Heritage of Her Own: Toward a New Social History of American Women*. New York: Touchstone/Simon and Schuster, 1979.

Cowan, Ruth Schwartz. *More Work for Mother: The Ironies of Household Technology from the Open Hearth to the Microwave*. New York: Basic Books, 1983. A great one. Especially useful on the transformation of women's work after industrialism.

DuSablon, Mary Anna. *America's Collectible Cookbooks: The History, the Politics, the Recipes*. Athens: Ohio University Press, 1994. An underappreciated trove of cookbook history.

Food History News. Vols. 1–44, 1989–2001. Edited by Sandra Oliver. Isleboro, ME. Excellent quarterly covering diverse topics of serious culinary history.

Groveman, Carol, and Mary Beth Norton. *To Toil the Livelong Day: American Women at Work, 1780–1980*. Ithaca, NY: Cornell University Press, 1987.

Herbst, Sharon Tyler. *Food Lover's Companion: Comprehensive Definitions of over 4000 Food, Wine and Culinary Terms*. Hauppauge, NY: Barron's Educational Series, 1995.

Hess, Karen, and John. *Taste of America*. New York: Grossman/Viking, 1977. A beloved but polemical take of the decline of American food and cookery from colonial times to the 1970s.

Hine, Darlene Clark, and Kathleen Thompson. *A Shining Thread of Hope: The History of Black Women in America*. New York: Broadway Books, 1998. Beautifully written history.

Jones, Jacqueline. *Labor of Love, Labor of Sorrow*. New York: Vintage Books, 1995. Wonderful overview of African-American women's history.

Kerber, Linda, and Jane Sherron DeHart. *Women's America: Refocusing the Past*, 4th ed. New York: Oxford University Press, 1995. Extremely valuable overview of women's history.

Kirlin, Katherine S., and Thomas M. *Smithsonian Folklife Cookbook*. Washington, DC: Smithsonian Institution Press, 1991.

Levenstein, Harvey. *Revolution at the Table: The Transformation of the American Diet*. New York: Oxford University Press, 1988. The influence of science and industry on American eating, beginning with the turn of the last century. Good account of nineteenth-century milk scandals.

Longone, Janice B., and Daniel T. *American Cookbooks and Wine Books, 1797–1950*. Ann Arbor, MI: Clements Library, 1984. Invaluable exhibition catalog and accompanying notes.

Lowenstein, Eleanor. *Bibliography of American Cookery Books 1742–1860*. Based on *Waldo Lincoln's American Cookery Books, 1742–1860*. Worcester, MA: American Antiquarian Society, 1972.

http://memory.loc.gov. American Memory Historical Collections for the National Digital Library. This Library of Congress Web site is a gateway to a vast number of primary sources. A treasure.

Shapiro, Laura. *The Perfection Salad:. Women and Cooking at the Turn of the Century*. New York: Henry Holt, 1986. A fascinating account of the rise of home economics from a critic's perspective.

Theophano, Janet, curator. *Household Worlds: Women Write from and for the Kitchen*. Catalog from 1996 exhibit at University of Pennsylvania Library. Available on-line at www.library.upenn.edu/special. Choose "Exhibitions."

Traeger, James. *Food Chronology: A Food Lover's Compendium of Events and Anecdotes, from Prehistory to the Present*. New York: Henry Holt, 1996.

Weaver, William Woys. *America Eats: Forms of American Folk Art*. New York: Museum of American Folk Art and Harper and Row, 1989.

Witt, Doris. *Black Hunger: Food and the Politics of U.S. Identity*. New York: Oxford University Press, 1999. A fascinating look at the origins of Aunt Jemima, soul food, and the cookbook as a form of personal expression.

Wollach, Nancy. *Women and the American Experience*. New York: McGraw-Hill, 1984. Extremely useful overview.

INTRODUCTION: FROM HER HEAD GREW PUMPKIN VINES

Allen, Paula Gunn. *Sacred Hoop: Restoring the Feminine in American Indian Traditions*. Boston: Beacon Press, 1986.

Axtell, James, ed. *The Indian Peoples of Eastern America: A Documentary History of the Sexes*. Oxford: Oxford University Press, 1981.

Bruchac, Joseph, and Gale Ross. *The Girl Who Married the Moon: Tales from Native North America*. Mahwah, NJ: BridgeWater Books, 1994.

Coe, Sophie. *America's First Cuisines*. Austin: University of Texas Press, 1994.

Erdoes, Richard, and Alfonso Ortiz. *American Indian Myths and Legends*. New York: Pantheon, 1984.

Lankford, George E. *Native American Legends: Southeastern Legends—Tales from the Natchez, Caddo, Biloxi, Chickasaw, and Other Nations*. Little Rock, AR: August House, 1987.

Stone, Merlin. *Ancient Mirrors of Womanhood: A Treasury of Goddess and Heroine Lore from around the World*. Boston: Beacon Press, 1991.

Baily, Flora L. "Navaho Foods and Cooking Methods." *American Anthropologist,* vol.42, no. 2, April–June 1940.

Bataille, Gretchen M., and Kathleen M. Sands. *American Indian Women: A Guide to Research*. Hamden, CT: Garland, 1991. An excellent bibliography.

Claassen, Cheryl, and Rosemary A. Joyce, eds. *Women in Prehistory: North America and Mesoamerica*. Philadelphia: University of Pennsylvania Press, 1977.

Dahlberg, Frances, ed. *Woman the Gatherer*. New Haven: Yale University Press, 1981.

"De Gannes Memoir," in *The French Foundations, 1680–1693*. Vol. 23, French series, Vol. 1. Collections of the Illinois State Historical Library. Edited by Theodore C. Pease and Raymond C. Werner. Springfield, IL: Published by the Trustees of the Illinois State Historical Library, 1934. A riveting memoir including much on native food.

Densmore, Frances. *Chippewa Customs* (1929). St. Paul: Minnesota Historical Society Press, 1979. A legendary anthropologist attuned to women's stories.

Devens, Carol. "Separate Confrontations: Gender as a Factor in Indian Adaptation to European Colonization in New France." *American Quarterly,* vol. 38, no. 3, 1986. Quoting Jesuit Paul Le Jeune, *The Jesuit Relations and Allied Documents: Travels and Explorations of the Jesuit Missionaries in New France,* 1610–1791. Describes the impact of missionaries and fur traders on Montagnais Indians.

Fussel, Betty. *The Story of Corn*. New York: Alfred A. Knopf, 1992.

Gero, M. Joan, and Margaret W. Conkey, eds. *Engendering Archaeology: Women and Prehistory*. Oxford: Basil Blackwell, 1991. Especially useful chapters: "Gender, Shellfishing, and the Shell Mound Archaic," by Cheryl P. Claassen, as well as "The Development of Horticulture in the Eastern Woodlands of North America: Women's Role," by Patty Jo Watson and Mary C. Kennedy. Also "Weaving and Cooking: Women's Production in Aztec Mexico," by Elizabeth M. Brunfiel.

Giffen, Naomi Musmaker. *The Roles of Men and Women in Eskimo Culture*. Chicago: University of Chicago Press, 1930.

Green, Rayna. *Women in American Indian Society*. New York: Chelsea House, 1992.

Hughes, Phyllis. *Pueblo Indian Cookbook: Recipes from the Pueblos of the American Southwest*, 2nd ed. Santa Fe: Museum of New Mexico Press, 1977.

Jensen, Joan M., and Darlis A. Miller. *New Mexico Women, Intercultural Perspectives*. Albuquerque: University of New Mexico Press, 1986. Excellent academic articles ranging from prehistory to twentieth-century issues.

Josephy, Alvin, Jr. *Indian Heritage of America*. New York: Alfred A. Knopf, 1966.

———. *500 Nations: An Illustrated History of North American Indians*. New York: Alfred A. Knopf, 1994.

Klein, Laura F., and Lillian A. Ackerman, eds. *Women and Power in Native North America*. Norman: University of Oklahoma Press, 1995.

Mandryk, Carole A. S., Heiner Josenhans, Daryl W. Fedje, and Rolf W. Mathewes. "Late Quartenary Paleoenvironments of Northwestern North America: Implications for Inland versus Coastal Migration Routes." *Quaternary Science Reviews,* vol. 20, no. 1–3, 2001. Challenges the traditional migration route theories of first humans in North America.

Neithammer, Carolyn. *American Indian Food Lore*. New York: Macmillan, 1974. A popular work.

People of 'Ksan. *Gathering What the Great Nature Provided: Food Traditions of the Gitksan*. Vancouver: Douglas and McIntyre; Seattle: University of Washington Press, 1980. A beautiful book created by a tribal group.

Petit, Charles W. "Rediscovering America: The New World May Be 20,000 Years Older Than Experts Thought." *U.S. News and World Report*, October 12, 1998.

Reiter, Rayner, ed. *Toward an Anthropology of Women*. New York: Monthly Review Press, 1975. Especially helpful chapters: Sally Slocum's "Woman the Gatherer: Male Bias in Anthropology," and Judith K. Brown's "Iroquois Women: An Ethnohistoric Note."

Robbins, Wilfred William, John Peabody Harrington, and Barbara Friere-Marreco. *Ethnobotany of the Tewa Indians*. Washington, DC: Government Printing Office, 1916.

Roessel, Ruth. *Women in Navajo Society*. Rough Rock, Navajo Nation, AZ: Navajo Resource Center, 1981. Written from a Navajo's perspective.

Ruether, Rosemary Radford, and Rosemary Skinner Kellery. *Women and Religion in America,* vol. 2. San Francisco: Harper and Row, 1981.

Scarry, Margaret, ed. *Foraging and Farming in the Eastern Woodlands*. Gainesville: University Press of Florida, 1993. Includes time lines on the origins of farming.

Shoemaker, Nancy. *Negotiators of Change: Historical Perspectives on Native American Women*. New York: Routledge, 1995.

Spittal, William Guy, ed. *Iroquois Women: An Anthology*. Ohsweken, Ontario: Iroqrafts, 1990. Reprint of articles originally published from 1884 to 1989.

Stevenson, Matilda Coxe. *The Zuñi Indians and Their Uses of Plants* (1908–1909). Mineola, NY: Dover, 1993. An anthropologist's perspective.

Sturtevant, William C., gen. ed. *Handbook of North American Indians,* 11 vols. Washington, DC: Smithsonian Institution Press, 1986.

Ulmer, Mary. *Cherokee Cooklore: To Make My Bread, Museum of the Cherokee Indian.* Cherokee, NC: Museum of the Cherokee Indian, 1951. Authentic compendium of Cherokee recipes.

Vennum, Thomas, Jr. *Wild Rice and the Ojibway People.* St. Paul: Minnesota Historical Society Press, 1988. Quoting George W. Biddle. Essential reading.

Wagner, Gail E. " 'Their Women and Children do Continually Keepe it with Weeding,' Late Prehistoric Women and Horticulture in Eastern North America," in *The Influence of Women on the Southern Landscape.* Edited by Cornelia B. Wright. (Proceedings of the Tenth Conference on Restoring Southern Gardens and Landscapes.) Winston-Salem, NC: Old Salem, 1997.

Weatherford, Jack McIver. *Indian Givers, How the Indians of the Americas Transformed the World.* New York: Crown, 1988.

Wheat, Margaret M. *Survival Arts of the Primitive Paiutes.* Reno: University of Nevada Press, 1967.

Wilford, John Noble. "In Peru, Evidence of an Early Human Maritime Culture." *New York Times*, September 22, 1998. Popular article explains the battle of theoreticians.

Wilson, Gilbert L. *Buffalo Bird Woman's Garden: Agriculture of the Hidatsa Indians* (1917). St. Paul: Minnesota Historical Society Press, 1987.

———. *Waheenee* (1921). Lincoln: University of Nebraska Press, 1981.

Wrangham, Richard W., J. Jones, G. Laden, D. Pilbeam, and N. Conklin-Brittain. "The Raw and the Stolen: Cooking and the Ecology of Human Origins." *Current Anthropology*, vol. 40, no. 5., December 1999.

CHAPTER 2: SHE COOKED IN A NEW LAND

Anderson, Jay Allan. " 'A Solid Sufficiency': An Ethnography of Yeoman Foodways in Stuart England." Ph.D. dissertation, University of Pennsylvania, 1971.

Berkin, Carol. *First Generations: Women in Colonial America.* New York: Hill and Wang, 1996.

Booth, Sally Smith. *Hung, Strung and Potted: A History of Eating in Colonial America.* New York: C. N. Potter, 1971.

Bradford, William. *Of Plymouth Plantation, 1620–1657. The Complete Text, with Notes and an Introduction by Samuel Eliot Morison.* New York: Modern Library, 1967.

Bridenbaugh, Carl. *Jamestown, 1544–1699.* New York: Oxford University Press, 1980.

Carr, Lois Green, *Robert Cole's World.* Chapel Hill: University of North Carolina Press, 1991. The immigrant experience of one seventeenth-century planter's family in Maryland.

Carr, Lois Green and Lorena S. Walsh. "The Planter's Wife: The Experience of White Women in Seventeenth-Century Maryland." *William and Mary Collect Quarterly Historical Magazine*, 3rd series, vol. 34, 1977.

Carson, Jane. *Colonial Virginia Cookery.* Williamsburg, VA: Colonial Williamsburg Foundation, 1985.

Clark, Alice. *Working Life of Women in the Seventeenth Century* (England). New York: Routledge, 1992.

Deetz, James. *In Small Things Forgotten: The Archaeology of Early American Life.* Garden City, NY: Anchor Press/Doubleday, 1977.

Dexter, Elisabeth Anthony. *Colonial Women of Affairs: A Study of Women in Business and the Professions in America before 1776.* Boston: Houghton Mifflin, 1924. Includes information on women food merchants.

Dow, George Francis. *Every Day Life in the Massachusetts Bay Colony.* Boston: Society for the Preservation of New England Antiquities, 1935.

Earle, Alice Morse. *Home Life in Colonial Days.* Stockbridge, MA: Berkshire Traveller Press, 1974. Dated but useful.

Emerson, Everett. *Letters from New England.* Amherst: University of Massachusetts Press, 1976. My source for correspondence between John and Margaret Winthrop.

Gerard's Herbal. Reprint of 1636 edition, edited by Marcus Woodward. New York: Crescent Books, 1985.

Glasse, Mrs. Hannah. *The Art of Cookery Made Plain and Easy.* (First edition published 1747.) Reprint of 1805 edition, with historical notes by Karen Hess. Bedford, MA: Applewood Books, 1977. The most popular cookbook in eighteenth-century colonies and England.

Gould, Mary Earle. *The Early American House.* New York: M. McBride, 1949.

Hess, Karen, ed. *Martha Washington's Booke of Cookery.* New York: Columbia University Press, 1981. With copious annotations and insights from the great culinary historian.

Higginson, The Reverend Francis. *New England's Plantation: Or, a Short and True Description of the Commodoties And Discommodities of that Countrey* (1630). New York: New England Society, 1930.

Josselyn, John. *An Account of Two Voyages to England: made during the Years 1638 and 1663.* Boston: W. Veazie, 1865.

————. *New England Rarities Discovered in Birds, Beasts, Fishes, Serpents, and Plants of that Country.* London: Printed for G. Widdowes, 1672.

Marble, Annie Russel. *The Women Who Came in the Mayflower.* Boston: Pilgrim Press, 1920.

Markham, Gervase. *The English Housewife: Containing inward and outward virtues which ought to be in a complete woman; as her skill in physic, cookery, banqueting-stuff, distillation, perfumes, wool, hemp, flax, dairies, brewing, baking, and all other things belonging to a household* (1615). Edited by Michael R. Best. Montreal: McGill-Queen's University Press, 1986. Includes thorough introduction and great collection of images.

Morgan, Edmund S. *The Puritan Family: Essays on Religion and Domestic Relations in Seventeenth-Century New England* (1944). New York: Harper and Row, 1996.

Mourt's Relation: A Journal of the Pilgrims at Plymouth (1622). Edited by Dwight B. Heath. Bedford, MA: Applewood Books, 1963. A page-turning account of the arrival of pilgrims in Massachusetts. This unsigned journal was probably written mainly by Edward Winslow and John Bradford, but authorship is uncertain.

Norton, Mary Beth. *Founding Mothers and Fathers: Gendered Power and the Forming of American Society.* New York: Alfred A. Knopf, 1996.

Penn Family Recipes . . . With an Account of the Life of Gulielma Maria Springett Penn. Edited by Evelyn Abraham Benson. York, PA: George Shumway, 1966.

www.plimoth.org. The Web site for the Plimoth Plantation historical museum, an excellent beginning source for all matters of Plymouth Colony, including the "first" thanksgiving.

Ransome, David. "Wives for Virginia, 1621." *William and Mary Quarterly,* 3rd series, vol. 48, January 1991. All about the first group of imported wives.

Salley, Alexander S., Jr., ed. *Narratives of Early Carolina 1650–1708.* New York: Charles Scribner's Sons, 1911. Quoting letter "There are already all sorts of English fruit."

Schammas, Carole. "How Self-Sufficient Was Early America?" *Journal of Interdisciplinary History,* vol. XII, no. 2, Autumn 1982.

Smith, Abbot. *Colonists in Bondage: White Servitude and Convict Labor in Colonial America, 1607–1776.* Chapel Hill: Institute of Early American History and Culture/University of North Carolina Press, 1947.

Spruill, Julia Cherry. *Women's Life and Work in the Southern Colonies.* Chapel Hill: University of North Carolina Press, 1938. Still a breathtaking piece of work. Provided my sources on women merchants.

Tusser, Thomas. *Five Hundred Points of Good Husbandry* (1573). London: Lackington, Allen, 1812. Quoted in Anderson, above.

Ulrich, Laurel Thatcher. *Good Wives: Image and Reality in the Lives of Women in Northern New England, 1650–1750.* New York: Alfred A. Knopf, 1982. Essential reading.

Ulrich, Laurel. "Vertuous Women Found: New England Ministerial Literature, 1668–1735." *American Quarterly,* vol. 28, Spring 1976.

Aptheker, Herbert. *American Negro Slave Revolts*. New York: International Publishers, 1969.

Beoku-Betts, Josephine A. "She Made Funny Flat Cake She Called Saraka," in *Working toward Freedom: Slave Society and Domestic Economy in the American South*. Edited by Larry E. Hudson Jr. Rochester, NY: University of Rochester Press, 1994. Excellent article about transmigration of African food and culture to the low country.

Berlin, Ira. *Many Thousands Gone: The First Two Centuries of Slavery in North America*. Cambridge: Harvard University Press, 1998. Great book on American slavery as an evolving institution that varied from region to region.

The Carolina housewife, or House and home. By a lady of Charleston. Charleston, SC: W. R. Babcock, 1847. The author was Sarah Rutledge, though she preferred not to put her name on the book.

Channing, George G. *Early recollections of Newport, R.I., from the year 1793 to 1811*. Boston: Nichols and Noyes, 1868. In which Gibbes recalls Duchess Quamino, the family slave who helped raise him. My gratitude to Reverend Frank Carpenter for this and for generously sharing his extensive unpublished research regarding Duchess.

Davis, Angela. *Women Race and Class*. New York: Random House, 1981.

Egerton, John. *Southern Food: At Home, on the Road in History*. New York: Alfred A. Knopf, 1987. An opus including stories and recipes.

Eustis, Celestine. *Cooking in Old Créole Days. La cuisine créole à l'usage des petits ménages*, 2nd ed., 1904. Edited by Harry Worcester Smith. New York: Derrydale Press, 1928.

Fisher, Abby. *What Mrs. Fisher Knows About Southern Cooking* (1881). Reprint with introduction by Karen Hess. Bedford, MA: Applewood Books, 1995.

Fox-Genovese, Elizabeth. *Within the Plantation Household: Black and White Women of the Old South*. Chapel Hill: University of North Carolina Press, 1988.

Geraty, Virginia Mixson. *Gulla Fuh Oonu (Gullah for You): A Guide to the Gullah Language*. Orangeburg, SC: Sandlapper, 1997.

Harris, Jessica B. *Iron Pots and Wooden Spoons, Africa's Gifts to New World Cooking*. New York: Atheneum, 1989. From a leading culinary historian on African-American foodways. All her books are recommended.

Hess, Karen. *The Carolina Rice Kitchen: The African Connection*. Columbia: University of South Carolina Press, 1992. Extremely influential.

Hill, Anabella P. *Mrs. Hill's New Cook Book. Mrs. Hill's Southern Practical Cookery and Receipt Book* (1872). Columbia: University of South Carolina Press, 1995. Classic southern cooking that depended on slavery.

Jacobs, Harriet. *Incidents in the Life of a Slave Girl* (1861) in *The Classic Slave Narratives*. Edited by Henry Louis Gates, Jr. New York: Penguin, 1987.

Jones, Jacqueline. "Race, Sex, and Self-Evident Truths: The Status of Slave Women during the Era of the American Revolutions," in *Half Sisters of History: Southern Women and the American Past*. Edited by Catherine Clinton. Durham: Duke University Press, 1994.

Joyner, Charles. *Down by the Riverside, a South Carolina Slave Community*. Urbana: University of Illinois Press, 1984. A beautifully written and carefully researched account of the cultural connections of low-country blacks to Africa.

Littlefield, Daniel C. *Rice and Slaves: Ethnicity and the Slave Trade in Colonial South Carolina*. Baton Rouge: Louisiana State University Press, 1981.

Longone, Janice B. "Early Black-Authored American Cookbooks." *Gastronomica,* vol. 1, no.1, February 2001. An important overview of nineteenth-century cookbooks by African Americans, including a recent new find.

Morgan, Edmund. *American Slavery American Freedom: The Ordeal of Colonial Virginia*. New York: W. W. Norton, 1975.

Olwell, Robert. " 'Loose Idle and Disorderly': Slave Women in the Eighteenth Century Charleston Marketplace," in *More Than Chattel: Black Women and Slavery in the Americas*. Edited by David Barry Gaspar and Darlene Clark Hine. Bloomington: Indiana University Press, 1996.

Randolph, Mary. *Virginia Housewife* (1824). New York: Dover, 1993. A classic southern cookbook. Slave influences are apparent.

Rhett, Blanche, Lettie Gay, Helen Woodward, and Elizabeth Hamilton. *200 Years of Charleston Cooking*. New York: H. Smith and R. Haas, 1934.

Savannah Unit, Georgia Writers' Project, Work Projects Administration. *Drums and Shadows: Survival Studies among the Georgia Coastal Negroes* (1940). Garden City, NY: Anchor Books, 1972. Includes quotes from Shad Hall, as excerpted from Beoku-Betts (above).

Sterling, Dorothy. *We Are Your Sisters: Black Women in the Nineteenth Century*. New York: W. W. Norton, 1984.

Taylor, John Martin. *Hoppin' John's Lowcountry Cooking: Recipes and Ruminations from Charleston and the Carolina Coastal Plain*. New York: Bantam Books, 1992.

Witt, Doris. *Black Hunger*. See "General" section of bibliography.

Wood, Peter H. *Black Majority: Negroes in Colonial South Carolina from 1670 through the Stono Rebellion*. New York: W. W. Norton, 1974. Extremely influential.

CHAPTER 4: VIRTUOUS COOKERY

Abajian, James. *Blacks in Selected Newspapers, Censuses and Other Sources: An Index to Names and Subjects*. Boston: G. K. Hall, 1977. My source for African-American fund-raising events. See entry for "Food."

Appelbaum, Diana Karter. *Thanksgiving: An American Holiday, an American History*. New York: Facts on File, 1984.

Beecher, Catharine Esther. *A Treatise on Domestic Economy: For the Use of Young Ladies at Home and at School*. New York: Harper and Brothers, 1841.

————. *Miss Beecher's Domestic Receipt-Book*. New York: Harper and Brothers, 1846.

Beecher, Catharine Esther, and Harriet Beecher Stowe. *The American Woman's Home* (1869). Hartford, CT: Stowe-Day Foundation, 1994.

Boydston, Jeanne. *Home and Work: Housework, Wages, and the Ideology of Labor in the Early Republic*. New York: Oxford University Press, 1990. How women's work at home contributed to the rise of industrialism.

Bright, Mrs. M. *The Parish Cookery Book of the Ladies Aid Society of St. Peter's Church*. Hazelton, Pennsylvania, 1887.

Child, Lydia Maria. *The American Frugal Housewife: Dedicated to Those Who Are Not Ashamed of Economy*. Reprint of twelfth edition (1833). Bedford, MA: Applewood Books, n.d. Note: Originally published as *The Frugal Housewife* in 1829.

Christopher, Lasch. *Women and the Common Life: Love, Marriage, and Feminism*. Edited by Elisabeth Lasch-Quinn. New York: W. W. Norton, 1997.

Cook, Margaret. *America's Charitable Cooks: A Bibliography of Fund-Raising Cook Books Published in the United States, 1861–1915*. Kent, OH, 1971.

Cornelius, Mary Hooker. *The Young Housekeeper's Friend*. Boston: Taggard and Thompson, 1868.

Cott, Nancy. *The Bonds of Womanhood: "Woman's Sphere" in New England, 1780–1835*, 2nd ed. New Haven: Yale University Press, 1977.

Dann, John C. *The Revolution Remembered: Eyewitness Accounts of the War for Independence*. Chicago: University of Chicago Press, 1980. Includes Sarah Osborne's account quoted in the American Social History Project, *Who Built America*. (See "General" section of bibliography.)

DePaw, Linda Grant. *Founding Mothers: Women in America in the Revolutionary Era.* Boston: Houghton Mifflin, 1975.

Finley, Ruth Albright. *The Lady of Godey's: Sarah Josepha Hale.* Philadelphia: J. B. Lippincott, 1931.

Hale, Sarah Josepha. *The Good Housekeeper* (1841). Reprint with foreword by Jan Longone. Mineola, NY: Dover, 1996.

Howard, Mrs. B. C. *Fifty Years in a Maryland Kitchen.* Baltimore: Turnbull Brothers, 1873.

Karcher, Carolyn L. *The First Woman in the Republic: A Cultural Biography of Lydia Maria Child.* Durham: Duke University Press, 1994.

Kerber, Linda. *Women of the Republic: Intellect and Ideology in Revolutionary America.* Chapel Hill: University of North Carolina Press, 1980.

Lee, Mrs. N. K. M. *The Cook's Own Book, and Housekeeper's Register.* New York: C. S. Francis, 1854.

Longone, Janice Bluestein. " 'Tried Receipts': An Overview of America's Charitable Cookbooks," in *Recipes for Reading: Community Cookbooks, Stories, Histories.* Edited by Anne Bower. Amherst: University of Massachusetts Press, 1997. Provided the foundation for my section on charitable cookbooks.

Mann, Mrs. Horace. *Christianity in the Kitchen: A Physiological Cook Book.* Boston: Ticknor and Fields, 1857.

Moss, Maria J. *The Poetical Cookbook.* Philadelphia: Caxton Press of C. Sherman, 1864.

Norton, Mary Beth. *Liberty's Daughters: The Revolutionary Experience of American Women, 1750–1800.* Boston: Little, Brown, 1980.

Scott, Anne Firor. "Most Invisible of All: Black Women's Voluntary Associations." *Journal of Southern History,* vol. 56, February 1990.

Shaw, Stephanie. "Black Club Women and the Creation of the National Association of Colored Women." *Journal of Women's History*, vol. 3, no. 2, Fall 1991.

Simmons, Amelia. *American Cookery* (1796). Reprint of first edition, with an essay by Mary Tolford Wilson. New York: Oxford University Press. Also used reprint of second edition, 1796, with an introduction by Karen Hess. Bedford, MA: Applewood Books, 1996.

Sklar, Kathryn Kish. *Catharine Beecher: A Study in American Domesticity.* New York: W. W. Norton, 1973.

Sprigg, June. *Domestick Beings.* New York: Alfred A. Knopf, 1984. Quoting Abigail Adams.

Stowe, Harriet Beecher. *Uncle Tom's Cabin or, Life Among the Lowly* (1852). New York: Harper and Row, 1958.

Titus, Mary. "Food, Race, and Domestic Space in the Nineteenth-Century South," in *Haunted Bodies: Gender and Southern Texts*. Edited by Anne Goodwyn Jones and Susan V. Donaldson. Charlottesville: University Press of Virginia, 1997.

Turner, Bertha. *The Federation Cookbook: A Collection of Tested Recipes, Contributed by the Colored Women of the State of California*. Pasadena: author, 1910. This is the oldest or one of the oldest African-American charitable cookbooks, though more are certain to be discovered. My source is Witt, *Black Hunger*. (See "General" section of bibliography.)

Washington Women's Cook Book. Seattle: Washington Equal Suffrage Association, 1909.

The W.C.T.U Cook Book. Wenatchee, WA: Women's Christian Temperance Union, n.d.

Welter, Barbara. "The Cult of True Womanhood, 1820–1860." *American Quarterly*, vol. 18, no. 2, Summer 1966.

CHAPTER 5: A WOMAN'S WEST

Ackerman, Lillian. "The Effect of Missionary Ideals on Family Structure and Women's Roles in Plateau Indian Culture." *Idaho Yesterdays,* vol. 31, no. 1–2, 1987.

Amador, Adela. *Southwest Flavor: Tales from the Kitchen*. Santa Fe: New Mexico Magazine, 2000.

Bryan, Mrs. Lettice. *The Kentucky Housewife* (1839). Reprint. Paducah, KY: Image Graphics.

de Baca, Fabiola Cabeza. *We Fed Them Cactus*, 2nd ed. Introduction by Tey Diana Rebolledo. Albuquerque: University of New Mexico Press, 1994.

Deutsch, Sarah. *No Separate Refuge: Culture, Class, and Gender on an Anglo-Hispanic Frontier in the American Southwest, 1880–1940*. New York: Oxford University Press, 1987.

Faragher, John Mack. *Women and Men on the Overland Trail*. New Haven: Yale University Press, 1979. Quoting Rebecca Ketcham.

Fergusson, Erna. *Mexican Cookbook*. Santa Fe: Rydal Press, 1934.

Gilbert, Fabiola Cabeza de Baca. *The Good Life: New Mexico Traditions and Food* (1949). Santa Fe: Museum of New Mexico Press, 1982.

Goldman, Anne. *Take My Word: Autobiographical Innovations of Ethnic American Working Women*. Berkeley: University of California Press, 1996.

González, Deena J. *Refusing the Favor: The Spanish-Mexican Women of Santa Fe, 1820–1880*. New York: Oxford University Press, 1999.

James, Caroline. *Nez Perce Women in Transition, 1877–1990*. Moscow: University of Idaho Press, 1996. Quoting Pe-nah-we-non-mi from McWhorter Papers, 1926.

Jaramillo, Cleofas M. *The Genuine New Mexico Tasty Recipes* (1939). Reprint. Santa Fe: Ancient City Press, 1981.

Jeffrey, Julie Roy. *Frontier Women: "Civilizing" the West? 1840–1880*. New York: Hill and Wang, 1998.

A Lady of Philadelphia. *The National Cookbook*, 9th ed. Philadelphia: Hayes and Zell, 1856.

LeCompte, Janet. "The Independent Women of Hispanic New Mexico, 1821–1846." *Western Historical Quarterly*, vol. 12, January 1981.

Leslie, Eliza. *Miss Leslie's Directions for Cookery* (1837). Reprint of 1851 edition with introduction by Janice Bluestein Longone. Mineola, NY: Dover, 1999.

Limerick, Patricia. *Legacy of Conquest: The Unbroken Past of the American West*. New York: W. W. Norton, 1987.

Luchetti, Cathy. *Home on the Range: A Culinary History of the American West*. New York: Villard Books, 1993.

Myres, Sandra L. *Westering Women*. Albuquerque: University of New Mexico Press, 1982.

Nabokov, Peter, ed. *Native American Testimony: A Chronicle of Indian-White Relations from Prophecy to the Present, 1492–1992*. New York: Viking, 1991. Includes native accounts of reservation life.

Nurge, Ethel. "Dakota Diet: Traditional and Contemporary," in *The Modern Sioux: Social Systems and Reservation Culture*. Edited by Ethel Nurge. Lincoln: University of Nebraska Press, 1970.

Pancoast, Henry Spackman. *Impressions of the Sioux Tribes in 1882*. Philadelphia: Franklin Printing House, 1883.

Rubine, Erica. "La Comida y las Memorias: Food, Positionality, and the Problematics of Making One's Home." Ph.D. dissertation, University of Pennsylvania, 1998. An excellent source for continued importance of traditional foodways and farming methods among Hispanic farmers of the Southwest.

Schlissel, Lillian. *Women's Diaries of the Westward Journey*. New York: Schocken Books, 1992. Includes quotes from Cecelia Adams, Lucy Cooke, and Charlotte Sterns Pengra. A great book that was essential to this chapter.

Williams, Carey. *North from Mexico: The Spanish-Speaking People of the United States* (1948). Reprint. New York: Greenwood Press, 1968.

Williams, Jacqueline. *Wagon Wheels Kitchens: Food on the Oregon Trail*. Lawrence: University Press of Kansas, 1993. A fabulous culinary history.

Wilson, Luzena Stanley. *Luzena Stanley Wilson, Forty-Niner: memories recalled years later for her daughter, Correnah Wilson Wright*. Mills College, CA: Eucalyptus Press, 1937. Quoted in Schlissel, *Women's Diaries of Westward Journey*.

www.womenofthewest.org. Web site for the Women of the West Museum, Denver, CO. *"There Are No Renters Here": Women's Lives on the Sod House Frontier* (on-line exhibit, August 2002). Uriah W. Oblinger to Mattie V. Oblinger, April 6, 1873. Nebraska State Historical Society.

CHAPTER 6: SHE FED THE INDUSTRIAL GIANTS

Bliss, Mrs. *The Practical Cook Book Containing Upwards of One Thousand Receipts*. Philadelphia: Lippincott, Grambo, 1850.

Bolton, Sarah K. *Successful Women*. Boston: Lothrop, 1888. Includes an account of Juliet Corson.

Boorstein, Daniel J. *The Americans: The Democratic Experience*. New York: Vintage Books/Random House, 1973. My chief source for stories of Gail Borden and other food business leaders.

Boydston, Jeanne. *Home and Work*: See Chapter 4 bibliography.

"Come Butter Come: A Collection of Churning Chants from Georgia." *Foxfire*, vol. 3, 1966.

Corson, Juliet. *Fifteen Cent Dinners for Families of Six*. New York: author, 1877.

Cowan, Ruth Schwartz. *More Work for Mother*. See "General" section of bibliography.

The Cries of New York. New York: Harbor Press, 1931. Reprint edition including 1808 and 1814 editions. Street cries and illustrations of vendors.

Dublin, Thomas, ed. *Farm to Factory: Women's Letters, 1830–1860*. New York: Columbia University Press, 1981.

Duffy, John. *A History of Public Health in New York City*. New York: Russell Sage Foundation, 1968. Hard-hitting facts about real life for the urban nineteenth-century working class.

Eisler, Benita. *The Lowell Offering: Writings by New England Mill Women* (1977). New York: W. W. Norton, 1998. Source for Susan's quote.

Fisher, Abby. *What Mrs. Fisher Knows About Southern Cooking* (1881). See Chapter 3 bibliography.

Green, Harvey. *The Light of the Home: An Intimate View of the Lives of Women in Victorian America*. New York: Pantheon, 1983. Quoting diary of Almira MacDonald.

Kessler-Harris, Alice. *Out to Work: A History of Wage-Earning Women in the United States*. New York: Oxford University Press, 1982.

A Lady of Philadelphia. *The National Cook Book*. See Chapter 5 bibliography.

Lerner, Gerder. "The Lady and the Mill Girl: Changes in the Status of Women in the Age of Jackson 1800–1840." *Midcontinent American Studies Journal,* vol. 10, Spring 1969.

Leslie, Eliza. *Miss Leslie's Directions for Cookery*. See Chapter 5 bibliography.

Lincoln, Mrs. D. A. (Mary). *Mrs. Lincoln's Boston Cook Book: What To Do and What Not To Do in Cooking*. Boston: Roberts Brothers, 1883 and 1884 editions.

Lowell Historical Preservation Commission. "Mill Girls and Immigrants," a permanent exhibit at Lowell National Historic Park, Lowell, Massachusetts. Includes what the mill women ate for breakfast.

McMurry, Sally A. *Transforming Rural Life: Dairying Families and Agricultural Change, 1820–1885* (Revisiting Rural America). Baltimore: Johns Hopkins University Press, 1995. My source for Mrs. Allerton as well as quotes from *American Agriculturist* and *Harper's Weekly*.

Oliver, Sandra, ed. "Joy of Historical Cooking: Jumbles, Jumbals." *Food History News,* vol. 2, no. 1, June 1990. Isleboro, ME.

Randolph, Mary. *The Virginia Housewife* (1824). Reprint edition with introduction by Janice Bluestein Longone. New York: Dover, 1993.

Stansell, Christine. *City of Women: Sex and Class in New York, 1789–1860*. New York: Alfred A. Knopf, 1986. Great for working-class perspective.

Strasser, Susan. *Never Done*: *A History of American Housework*. New York: Pantheon Books, 1982.

Widdifield, Hannah. *Widdifield's New Cook Book*. Philadelphia: T. B. Peterson and Brothers, 1856.

Wright, Richardson Little. *Hawkers and Walkers in Early America*. Philadelphia: J. B. Lippincott, 1927.

Zinn, Howard. *A People's History of the United States: 1492 to present*. New York: Harper-Perennial, 1995.

CHAPTER 7: GIVE HER YOUR HUNGRY

Anderson, Margo J., ed. *Encyclopedia of the U.S. Census*. Washington, DC: CQ Press, 2000.

Chai, Alice Yun. "Picture Brides: Feminist Analysis of Life Histories of Hawai'i's Early Immigrant Women from Japan, Okinawa, and Korea," in *Seeking Common Ground: Multidisciplinary Studies of Immigrant Women in the United States*. Edited by Donna Gabaccia. Westport, CT: Greenwood Press, 1992.

Chang, K. C. *Food in Chinese Culture: Anthropological and Historical Perspectives.* New Haven: Yale University Press, 1977.

The Chinese Committee, International Institute, Y.W.C.A. *Chinese Home Cooking: Recipes of Cantonese Dishes.* Honolulu: author, 1941.

Cooper, John. *Eat and Be Satisfied: A Social History of Jewish Food.* Northvale, NJ: Jason Aronson, 1993.

Diner, Hasia R. *Erin's Daughters in America. Irish Immigrant Women in the Nineteenth Century.* Baltimore: The Johns Hopkins University Press, 1983.

————. *Hungering for America: Italian, Irish, and Jewish Foodways in the Age of Migration.* Cambridge: Harvard University Press, 2001. An extremely valuable book that helped shape this entire chapter in terms of hunger as a driving force of immigration, including quotes from Maria Torno and Calabrian contadino Francesco Saverio Nitti.

Dudden, Faye E. *Serving Women: Household Service in Nineteenth-Century America.* Middletown, CT: Wesleyan University Press, 1983.

Ewen, Elizabeth. *Immigrant Women in the Land of Dollars: Life and Culture on the Lower East Side, 1890–1925.* New York: Monthly Review Press, 1985.

Gabaccia, Donna R. *We Are What We Eat: Ethnic Food and the Making of Americans.* Cambridge, MA: Harvard University Press, 1998. Essential reading, especially for the rise of immigrant food businesses.

Kander, Mrs. Simon, and Mrs. Henry Schoenfeld, compilers. *The "Settlement" Cook Book: The Way to a Man's Heart.* Facsimile of 1903 edition. New York: Gramercy, 1987.

Kirshenblatt-Gimblett, Barbara. "The Kosher Gourmet." *Journal of Gastronomy,* vol. 2, no. 4, Winter 1986/87.

————. "Kitchen Judaism," in *Getting Comfortable in New York: The American Jewish Home, 1880–1950.* Edited by Susan L. Braunstein and Jenna Weissman. New York: Jewish Museum, 1990. Extremely influential in my discussion of Jewish cookbooks and assimilation.

Laudan, Rachel. *The Food of Paradise: Exploring Hawaii's Culinary Heritage.* Honolulu: University of Hawai'i Press, 1996. A fascinating book with much on the immigrant perspective.

Levy, Esther. *The Jewish Cookery Book: On Principles of Economy Adapted for Jewish Housekeepers* (1871). Reprint. Bedford, MA: Applewood Books.

Matsumoto, Valerie. *Farming the Home Place: A Japanese American Community in California, 1919–1982.* Ithaca, NY: Cornell University Press, 1993.

Mo, Fenn. *Chinese Recipes.* San Francisco: author, 1930.

Nathan, Joan. "Legacy of Egyptian Rose, In Time for Passover." *New York Times,* March 20, 2002.

National Japanese American Historical Society. *The Rice Cooker's Companion: Japanese American Food and Stories.* San Francisco: author, 2000. Quoting Julia Estrella.

Newman, Jacqueline M. "Chinese Community Cookbooks." *Flavor and Fortune Magazine*, vol. 6, no. 2, June 1999. My source for the earliest Chinese fund-raising cookbooks.

Ray, Krishnendu. "Meals, Migration and Modernity: Food and the Performance of Bengali-American Ethnicity." Ph.D. dissertation, Binghamton University, State University of New York, 2000. Valuable on food and immigrant women from turn of the twentieth century to today.

Ruiz, Vicky. *Cannery Women, Cannery Lives: Mexican Women, Unionization, and the California Food Processing Industry.* Albuquerque: University of New Mexico Press, 1987.

Schoener, Allon. *The Italian Americans.* New York: Macmillan, 1987.

Seller, Maxine Schwartz. *Immigrant Women.* Albany: State University of New York Press, 1994.

Simonds, Nina. "Food in Chinese Culture." *Journal of Gastronomy*, vol. 2, no. 3, Fall 1986.

Statue of Liberty National Monument/Ellis Island Immigration Museum, National Park Service. Oral History Program. Interview of Mary Nazaro Stracco, 1997, conducted by Janet Levine, Ph.D. Interview of Josephine Nardone Scola, 1997, conducted by Mindy Hapeman. Available at Ellis Island Research Library.

Taylor, David A. and John Alexander Williams, eds. *Old Ties, New Attachments: Italian-American Folklife in the West.* Washington, DC: Library of Congress, 1992

Tchen, John. *Photographs of San Francisco's Old Chinatown.* New York: Dover, 1984. Quoting handbill recruiting Chinese laborers.

Tutti a Tavola (Everyone to the Table): Italian Food in America. Ellis Island Immigration Museum, 1999–2000. Exhibition brochure available from Ellis Island Research Library.

Valle, Victor M., and Mary Lau Valle. *Recipe of Memory: Five Generations of Mexican Cuisine.* New York: New Press, 1995. Beautiful family story told with recipes.

Wong, Jade Snow. *Fifth Chinese Daughter.* New York: Harper, 1950. A great Chinese-American memoir.

Young, Grace. *The Wisdom of the Chinese Kitchen: Classic Family Recipes for Celebration and Healing.* New York: Simon and Schuster, 1999.

Yung, Judy. *Unbound Feet: A Social History of Chinese Women in San Francisco.* Berkeley: University of California Press, 1995. A fascinating account that provides extensive information for my chapter, from the Exclusion Act through assimilation.

Adams, David Wallace. *Education for Extinction: American Indians and the Boarding School Experience, 1875–1928.* Lawrence: University Press of Kansas, 1995.

Anonymous. Diary of 39-year-old Ohio woman, 1913. Schlesinger Library, Radcliffe Institute for Advanced Study. Cambridge, MA. A/A 615H.

Bethune, Mary McLeod. "How the Bethune-Cookman College Campus Started," in Kerber and DeHart, *Women's America.* See "General" section of bibliography.

Cooper, Gail. "Love, War, and Chocolate," in *His and Hers: Gender, Consumption, and Technology.* Edited by Roger Horowitz and Arwen Mohun. Charlottesville: University Press of Virginia, 1998.

Ellis, Peal Idelia. *Americanization through Homemaking.* Los Angeles: Wetzel, 1929.

Farmer, Fannie Meritt. *Boston Cooking-School Cook Book* (1896). Reprint with a new introduction by Janice Bluestein Longone. Mineola, NY: Dover, 1997.

———. *Fannie Farmer's Book of Good Dinners* (1905). Reprint of the 1905 title *What To Have for Dinner.* Princeton, NJ: Pyrne Press, 1972.

Francke, Maria. *Opportunities for Women in Domestic Science.* Prepared under the direction of Susan M. Kingsbury. Philadelphia: Association of Collegiate Alumnae, 1916.

Frederick, Christine. *Selling Mrs. Consumer.* New York: Business Bourse, 1929.

Glasse, Mrs. Hannah. *The Art of Cookery Made Plain and Easy.* See Chapter 2 bibliography.

Heath, Mrs. Julian. "The New Housekeeping." *Ladies' Home Journal,* February 1915.

Hooks, Janet M. *Women's Occupations through Seven Decades.* Women's Bureau Bulletin No. 218. Washington, DC: Zenger, 1947. Government statistics on women workers in canneries, confectioneries, and other food businesses.

Lincoln, Mrs. D. A. *Mrs. Lincoln's Boston Cook Book* See Chapter 6 bibliography.

Lincoln, Mary J. *The Boston School Kitchen Textbook: Lessons in Cooking and Domestic Science for the Use of Elementary Schools* (1887). Boston: Little, Brown, 1915.

Longone, Janice Bluestein. Telephone conversation in which Jan shared her extensive research on the culinary women of the 1893 World's Fair.

Manring, M. M. *Slave in a Box: The Strange Career of Aunt Jemima.* Charlottesville: University Press of Virginia, 1998. Everything you ever wanted to know about her.

Muccigrosso, Robert. *Celebrating the New World: Chicago's Columbian Exposition of 1893.* Chicago: I. R. Dee, 1993.

The New England Kitchen Magazine, April 1894. Describes the evolution of the New England Kitchen, the Boston Cooking School, the World's Fair of 1893, and the rise of the domestic science movement in general. Other issues of this magazine also helpful.

Proctor, Alice Adams. *Wonder Sandwich Suggestions.* Bakeries Service Co., 1930.

Prucha, Francis Paul. *Atlas of American Indian Affairs.* Lincoln: University of Nebraska Press, 1990.

Reed, Estelle. *Course of Study for the Indian Schools of the United States, Industrial and Literary.* Washington, DC: Government Printing Office, 1901. Lays out the government agenda for reeducating Indian girls in domestic science.

Richards, Ellen. *Plain Words about Food: The Rumford Leaflets.* Boston: Rockwell and Churchill Press, 1899. The leaflets handed out at the Rumford Kitchen at the 1893 World's Fair. Charts and scientific analysis of food.

Rockstroh, Bertha. "Fall Term, 1905." Unpublished manuscript, private collection.

Ruiz, Vicky. *Cannery Women, Cannery Lives.* See Chapter 7 bibliography.

Scanlon, Janet. *Inarticulate Longings: The Ladies' Home Journal, Gender, and the Promises of Consumer Culture.* New York: Routledge, 1995.

Shapiro, Laura. *The Perfection Salad.* (See "General" section of bibliography.) Very influential. Source of my quotes for Ellen Richards.

Shaw, Marian. *World's Fair Notes: A Woman Journalist Views Chicago's 1893 Columbian Exposition.* St. Paul, MN: Pogo Press, 1992.

The Silent Hostess Treasure Book. Cleveland: General Electric Company, 1930.

Vanek, Joann. "Time Spent in Housework." *Scientific American,* November 1974.

Weigley, Emma Seifrit. "It Might Have Been Euthenics: The Lake Placid Conferences and the Home Economics Movement." *American Quarterly,* vol. 26, no. 1, March 1974. An excellent account of the birth of home economics.

Weiman, Jeanne Madeline. *The Fair Women.* Introduction by Anita Miller. Chicago, IL: Academy of Chicago, 1981. Everything you wanted to know about the Board of Lady Managers and the Woman's Building.

Note: In addition I consulted numerous cookbooks and domestic science texts authored by Maria Parloa, Fannie Farmer, Mary Lincoln, Ellen Richards, Marion Harland, Sarah Tyson Rorer, and other home ec. leaders, from the 1870s through 1920s.

CHAPTER 9: RECIPES FOR TOUGH TIMES

Angelou, Maya. *I Know Why the Caged Bird Sings.* New York: Random House, 1969.

Anonymous. *A Red Triangle Girl in France.* New York: George H. Doran, 1918. My source for anonymous quote "I could not drop this work now. . . ."

Arnold, Eleanor, ed. *Voices of American Homemakers.* Bloomington, IN: National Association for Family and Community Education, 1985.

Baxandall, Rosalyn, and Linda Gordon with Susan Reverby. *America's Working Women: A Documentary History.* New York: W. W. Norton, 1995.

Beard, Mary R., ed. *America through Women's Eyes.* New York: Macmillan, 1933.

Berolzheimer, Ruth, ed. *The Wartime Cook Book.* Chicago: Consolidated Book, 1942.

Bird, Caroline. *The Invisible Scar.* New York: David McKay, 1966. Passionate account of the Great Depression.

Booth, Evangeline, and Grace Livingston Hill. *The War Romance of the Salvation Army.* Philadelphia: J. B. Lippincott, 1919. A fascinating account of the Salvation Army in Europe during World War I. My source for the doughnut story.

Campbell, D'Ann. *Women at War with America: Patriotic Lives in a Patriotic Era.* Cambridge: Harvard University Press, 1984.

Cuff, Robert D. "Herbert Hoover, the Ideology of Voluntarism and War Organization during the Great War." *The Journal of American History,* vol. 64, no. 2, September 1977.

"Do You Know Corn Meal?" U.S. Dept. of Agriculture, U.S. Food Administration, Leaflet No. 2. Washington, DC: Government Printing Office, 1917.

Fisher, M. F. K. *How to Cook a Wolf* (1942), in *The Art of Eating: The Collected Gastronomical Works of M.F.K. Fisher.* Cleveland: World Publishing, 1954.

"Food Demonstrations in New York." *Outlook,* March 7, 1917.

Gelhorn, Martha. *The Trouble I've Seen.* New York: Morrow, 1936. On the depression.

Greenbaum, Florence Kreisler. *The International Jewish Cook Book.* New York: Bloch, 1918.

Hartmann, Susan M. *The Home Front and Beyond: American Women in the 1940s.* Boston: Twayne, 1982.

Honey, Maureen. *Creating Rosie the Riveter.* Amherst: University of Massachusetts Press, 1984.

Hunton, Addie W., and Kathryn M. Johnson. *Two Colored Women with the American Expeditionary Forces* (1920). With introduction by Adele Logan Alexander. New York: G. K. Hall, 1997.

James, Bessie R. *For God, For Country, For Home.* The National League for Woman's Service. New York: G. P. Putnam's Sons, 1920. The role of home economics clubs, World War I.

Jones, Jacqueline. *Labor of Love, Labor of Sorrow.* See "General" section of bibliography. Quoting "Auntie Jane."

Le Sueur, Meridel. "Women on the Breadlines." *New Masses,* 1932.

Litoff, Judy Barret, ed. *Since You Went Away: World War II Letters from American Women on the Home Front.* Westport, CT: Greenwood Press, 1978. My source for letters from Edith Speert and Sonokou Iwata to their husbands.

Marsh, Dorothy. "Tips Busy Women Have Given Us on Managing their Meals." *Good Housekeeping Institute*, December 1943.

Mayo, Katherine. *That Damned Y: A Record of Overseas Service.* Boston: Houghton, 1920. My source for story of Ma Fitzgerald.

McCain, George Nox. *War Time Rations for Pennsylvanians.* Philadelphia: John C. Winston, 1920. Local account of food conservation, World War I.

Mead, Margaret. "Women in the War," in *While You Were Gone: A Report on Wartime Life in the United States.* Edited by Jack Goodman. New York: Simon and Schuster, 1946.

Mehlig, Madeline. *Kitchen Strategy: Food Planning for Victory.* Chicago: Wilcox and Folett, 1943.

Milkman, Ruth. "Women's Work and Economic Crisis: Some Lessons of the Great Depression." *Review of Radical Political Economics,* vol. 8, Spring 1976.

Moynihan, Ruth Barnes, Cynthia Russet, and Laurie Crumpacker. *Second to None: A Documentary History of American Women,* vol. II. Lincoln: University of Nebraska Press, 1993.

"National American Woman Suffrage Assoc. Rebuked for haste in offering services." *New York Times,* February 8, 1917. For more on suffragists who did and did not support the war effort, see *New York Times Index,* 1917, under "Woman Suffrage," including Alice Paul's hunger strike, November 8 and 9.

Ottilie, Juliet Gattuso, to President Truman. September 6, 1945. National Archives, College Park, MD. Records of the Women's Bureau, Record Group 86.

"Puschcarts Burned in Riots over Food." *New York Times,* February 20, 1917. Reports of riots and poultry boycotts continued through February and March. See *New York Times Index,* 1917, under "Foodstuffs."

Roosevelt, Mrs. Franklin D. *It's Up to the Women.* New York: Frederick A. Stokes, 1933.

Scheider, Dorothy, and Carl J. *Into the Breach: American Women Overseas in World War I.* New York: Viking, 1991. Quoting the YMCA volunteer, "We used to feed the men coming back from the front."

Schremp, Gerry. *Kitchen Culture: Fifty Years of Food Fads.* New York: Pharos Books, 1991.

Sternsher, Bernard, and Judith Sealander, eds. *Women of Valor: The Struggle against the Great Depression as Told in Their Own Life Stories.* Chicago: I. R. Dee, 1990.

Ware, Susan. *Holding Their Own: American Women in the 1930s.* Boston: Twayne, 1982.

Weatherford, Doris. *American Women and World War II.* New York: Facts on File, 1990. Includes Henry Kaiser's child care and carry-out food facilities.

Westin, Jeane. *Making Do: How Women Survived the 30s.* Chicago: Folett, 1976. Quoting recollections of Mary Grace McKenna Monahan.

CHAPTER 10: APRON STRINGS: DID SHE CUT THEM?

Beck, Simone, Louise Bertholle, and Julia Child. *Mastering the Art of French Cooking,* 2 vols. New York: Alfred A. Knopf, 1961–70.

Bracken, Peg. *The I Hate to Cook Book.* New York: Harcourt, Brace, 1960.

Branch, Taylor. *Parting the Waters: America in the King Years.* New York: Simon and Schuster, 1988.

Burros, Marion. "Missing: Great Woman Chefs in New York." *New York Times,* February 10, 1999. Good picture of challenges faced by women chefs nationally.

Carson, Rachel. *Silent Spring.* Boston: Houghton Mifflin, 1962.

Dahlin, Robert. "Stirring the Sales Pot." PublishersWeekly.com, July 24, 2000. Trends in cookbook marketplace.

Eig, Jonathan. "Food Industry Battles for Moms Who Want to Cook—Just a Little. Hamburger Helper Takes on New Competition in Race to Offer Homemade Feel: The Ideal: One Pan, 15 Minutes." *Wall Street Journal,* March 7, 2001.

Fitch, Noël Riley. *Appetite for Life: The Biography of Julia Child.* New York: Doubleday, 1997.

www.fmi.org/facts_figs/mealsolutions.pdf. Web site for the Food Marketing Institute. August 2002.

Fraser, J. *White-Collar Sweatshop: The Deterioration of Work and Its Rewards in Corporate America.* New York: W. W. Norton, 2001.

Freidan, Betty. *The Feminine Mystique.* New York: W. W. Norton, 1963.

Goodstein, Laurie. "Passover at Hotels Is Liberating Jewish Mothers." *New York Times,* April 27, 2000.

Harris, Jessica. Keynote address at "Grits & Greens," a conference on "soul food" held by Culinary Historians of Chicago, May 2000.

Hwang, Suein L. "What We Eat at Work Shows How Desperate We Can Be for Rewards." *Wall Street Journal,* April 17, 2002. The rise of processed foods.

Katzen, Mollie. *Moosewood Cookbook.* Berkeley, CA: Ten Speed Press, 1977.

Lam, Andrew. " 'Pho' Goes Global Thanks to Vietnamese Diaspora." *Jinn/Pacific Pulse,* www.pacificnews.org, April 28, 2000.

Lappé, Frances Moore. *Diet for a Small Planet.* New York: Ballantine Books, 1971.

Laudan, Rachel. "A Plea for Culinary Modernism. Why We Should Love New, Fast, Processed Food." *Gastronomica*, vol. 1, no. 1, February 2001. My thanks to Amy Besa for drawing this to my attention.

McFeely, Mary Drake. *Can She Bake a Cherry Pie?: American Women and the Kitchen in the Twentieth Century.* Amherst: University of Massachusetts, 2000.

Nestle, Marion. *Food Politics: How the Food Industry Influences Nutrition and Health.* Berkeley: University of California Press, 2002.

Neuhaus, Jessamyn. "The Way to a Man's Heart: Gender Roles, Domestic Ideology, and Cookbooks in the 1950s." *Journal of Social History*, vol. 32, no. 3, Spring 1999. Quoting Roland Barthes.

Ortiz, Yvonne. *A Taste of Puerto Rico.* New York: Dutton, 1994.

Poe, Tracey. *Food, Culture and Entrepreneurship among African Americans.* Baltimore: Johns Hopkins University Press, in press.

Pollen, Michael. "Naturally." *New York Times Magazine*, May 13, 2001. A look at America's evolving organic food industry.

———. "This Steer's Life: The Highly Unnatural Journey of No. 534, from Calf to Steak." *New York Times Magazine,* March 31, 2002.

Reardon, Joan. *M.F.K. Fisher, Julia Child and Alice Waters: Celebrating the Pleasures of the Table.* New York: Harmony Books, 1994.

Skolnick, Arlene. *A Time of Transition: Work, Family and Community in the Information Age.* New York: Families and Work Institute, February 1999.

Smart-Grosvenor, Vertamae. *Vibration Cooking; or, The Travel Notes of a Geechee Girl* (1970). New York: Ballantine Books Trade Edition, 1992.

Stewart, Martha. *Entertaining.* New York: Clarkson Potter, 1982.

Talbot, Margaret. "Les Très Riches Heures de Martha Stewart." *New Republic*, May 13, 1996.

Therrien, Melissa, and Roberto R. Ramirez. *The Hispanic Population in the United States*, March 2000. Current Population Reports, p20–535, U.S. Census Bureau, Washington, DC.

White, Deborah Gray. *Ar'n't I a Woman?: Female Slaves in the Plantation South*. New York: W. W. Norton, 1999.

Wyman, Carolyn. *JELL-O: A Biography.* New York: Harcourt, 2001.

Witt, Doris. *Black Hunger.* See "General" section of bibliography. Important account of soul food.

Resources for Historic Cooking

NATIVE AMERICAN INDIAN PRODUCTS

GREY OWL CANADIAN LAKE WILD RICE
510 11th Street, SE
Grand Rapids, MN 55744
(218) 327-2281
www.greyowlfoods.com
Wild rice of precontact times, harvested in large forest region of northern Saskatchewan.
A tribally owned company.

THE COOKING POST
The Pueblo of Santa Ana
2 Dove Road
Bernalillo, NM 87004
(888) 867-5198
(505) 771-6751/2
www.cookingpost.com
email: info@cookingpost.com
Reservation-grown blue corn meal, blue corn pancake mix, and chile sauce, beef and venison
sausage, fry bread mix, and food gifts. A consortium of Native-owned food companies.

NATIVE HARVEST
32033 East Round Lake Road
Ponsford, MN 56575
(888) 867-5198
(218) 573-3448
www.nativeharvest.com
Maple syrup, hand-harvested wild rice, buffalo sausage, and other native food products. A
nonprofit organization, part of the White Earth Land Recovery Project.

COLONIAL AND NINETEENTH-CENTURY RECIPES

GRAY'S GRIST MILL
PO Box 422
Adamsville, RI 02801
(508) 636-6075
Genuine flint corn, descended from the Narragansett Indians. Good for Amelia Simmons's
Federal Pancakes and any historic recipe for Johnny Cake.

HOPPING JOHN TAYLOR
PO Box 12775
Charleston, SC 29412
(843) 763-5252
(800) 828-4412
www.hoppinjohns.com
Stone-ground grits, cornmeal, and other low-country specialties.

JOHN F. MARTIN & SONS
55 Lower Hillside Road
Stevens, PA 17578
(717) 336-2804
Fresh, preservative-free lard, shipped to your doorstep by UPS.

SOUTHWESTERN INGREDIENTS

COYOTE CAFE GENERAL STORE
132 West Water Street
Santa Fe, NM 87501
(800) 866-HOWL (call for catalog)
(505) 982-2454
www.coyotecafe.com
Dried chile peppers, hominy, salsas, and tortilla mix.

TORTILLA PRESS
You can get a cast-iron tortilla press in many places. I ordered mine from www.texmex
.net for about $16 plus shipping. You can also order one from www.santafeschoolof
cooking.com.

FOR SPICES AND HERBS

PENZEYS, LTD.
PO Box 933
Muskego, WI 53150
(414) 679-7207

FOR CHEESEMAKING, SHOULD YOU BECOME INTERESTED

NEW ENGLAND CHEESEMAKING SUPPLY CO.
PO Box 85
Ashfield, MA 01330
(413) 628-3808
www.cheesemaking.com
email: info@cheesemaking.com
Rennet, both calf and vegetable, acids, starters, modern molds, presses, etc.

FOR THE NEW AMERICAN CHEESES, INCLUDING ARTISAN GOAT CHEESES HANDMADE BY WOMEN

CAPRIOLE INC.
(cheeses made by Judy Schad, mentioned in this book)
www.capriolegoatcheese.com

MURRAY'S CHEESE SHOP
257 Bleecker Street
New York, NY 10014
(888) 692-4339 (mail order)
(212) 243-3289
www.murrayscheese.com

ZINGERMAN'S MAIL ORDER
620 Phoenix Drive
Ann Arbor, MI 48108
(888) 636-8162
www.zingermans.com

FOR HISTORIC COOKBOOKS

A number of small presses such as Applewood Books and Dover reprint historic cookbooks in paperback editions. Thanks to them, you can have your own copy of *The Kentucky Houswife* (1839) or the *The Good Housekeeper* (1841) for a song. Food Heritage Press, a mail-order business run by Joe Carlin, carries a wide array of these in one worldwide Web spot: www.foodbooks.com. Phone: (800) 398-4474.

Acknowledgments

*T*o do this project, I needed a lot of help and a lot of time. I found both abundantly.

I thank my fabulous agent, Arielle Eckstut of James Levine Communications for sharing my vision from the start and offering creativity, energy, good humor, and the good judgment to steer me to Amy Cherry at W. W. Norton. Amy was extremely patient while I became pregnant, gave birth, raised young children, and slowly submitted chapters over the course of four years. She generously gave of her time and wisdom—listening, challenging, and encouraging me in just the right places, making the book a much better one. I am grateful to have had her as my editor.

My thanks, also, to the Schlesinger Library at Radcliffe for a grant that made it possible for me to travel there and use its wonderful collections, and to the New York Public Library for giving me space in the Allen Room, where I found sanctuary and camaraderie. My appreciation, also, to Wayne Furman.

This book and my life were greatly enriched by the precious personal stories and family recipes I encountered along the way. For these, I thank Helen Anglin, Amy Besa, Fabiana Chiou, Luigi Di Pasquale, Janet Black Eagle, Eleanor Howard, Mollie Katzen, Mary Lou Linyard, Fay Chew Matsuda, Lou Palma,

Ruth Roessel, Annie Ruth Smalls, and Connie Young Yu. A very special thanks to Nancy Henderson for sharing her grandmother's notebooks.

For a research project of this scope the list of professionals who helped me is necessarily long. Over the years, I consulted dozens of librarians, photo archivists, academics, food historians, and writers. Certain people extended themselves with unusual generosity. Among them, I thank Joshua Brown of the Social History Project at CUNY; Eric Byron at the Ellis Island Museum; the Reverend Frank Carpenter; Carolyn Kozo Cole of the Los Angeles Public Library; Kathleen Curtain and Paula Marcoux of Plimoth Plantation; Jennifer Cutting of the Folklife Center at the Library of Congress; writer Mary Anna Du Sablon; South Carolinian Ervina Falkner; historian Deena Gonzalez; Schlesinger Library Photo Curator Marie Helene Gold; Rayna Green of the Smithsonian Institution; Tom Lisanti of the New York Public Library; food historian and cookbook expert extraordinaire Jan Longone; Diane Mallickan of the Nez Perce National Historical Park; Carole Mandryk of Harvard University; Valerie Matsumoto of UCLA; Jacqueline Newman, editor of *Flavor and Fortune*; Barbara Oliver at the Library of Congress; Shelly Stanton of General Mills; Mark Thiel of Marquette University Archives; Gail Wagner of the University of South Carolina; and historian Judy Yung of USCS.

I also thank the following experts whom I contacted out of the blue with questions: Pat Albers, Ron Bryant, Marti Crippe De Montagne, John T. Edge, Harlan Graine, Harvey Green, Maria Guarnaschelli, Karen Hess, Denise Clark Hine, Joan Jensen, Linda Kerber, Mary Beth Norton, Sandra Oliver, Carole Shammas, John Martin Taylor, Kathleen Thompson, Jacqueline Williams, and Thomas Vennum. Their contributions were significant and greatly appreciated.

For his stellar research assistance and insights, my sincerest gratitude to Steve Froelich. I am also grateful to Regina Flanagan, who provided expert photo advice and permissions consulting when I needed it most, and to Mary Nash Babock, for her excellent copyediting job. My appreciation also to Andrew Marasia and Nomi Victor of W. W. Norton and designer Beth Tondreau.

Certain friends provided unusual encouragement and assistance. I thank Radha Bhatia, Daniella Diniz, Seth Grodofsky, Stacey Meyer, Joan Poole, Maria Ramos, and Eve Spencer. Special thanks to anthropologist and friend Erica Rubine who graciously answered my endless questions, and to Jennifer Liquori who gave me the last word.

I am grateful to my parents, Peter and Marcia Schenone, for countless good deeds and tactical assistance while I was writing (from old recipes and babysitting to electrical lines in my office) and to my beautiful sisters, Lisa and Andrea, with a special thanks to Lisa for going many, many extra miles. On my Schaffner side, I am grateful to Corinne for sharing her past, Heather for encouragement, Walter for the African food perspective, and my in-law primatologists Colleen and Filippo, who answered questions related to food and evolution.

I thank my precious boys, Gabriel and Simon, who have been adventurous eaters, helpers in the kitchen, beautiful children, and my source of inspiration each day.

And finally, above all, I thank my husband, Herb Schaffner, who loved and supported me from beginning to end and has been the best friend anyone could hope for. Despite the challenges of new babies and books being born at the same time, he remained steadfast and relentlessly encouraging. I thank him for reading every word, acting as my personal news clipping service, and for sharing this and all the other journeys—extending himself in all those private daily ways that no one can ever possibly know. This book is his as much as it is mine.

Additional Permissions Information and Credits

RECIPES AND TEXTS [IN ORDER OF APPEARANCE]:

The author is grateful for the right to reprint the following:

"Boiled Fully Dried Salmon" and "Toasted Seaweed" from *Gathering What Great Nature Provided* by the People of the 'Ksan River. Copyright © 1980. Reproduced here by permission.

"Tortillas de Maize" from *Pueblo Indian Cookbook,* edited by Phyllis Hughes. Copyright © 1972, 1977. Reproduced here by permission of the Museum of New Mexico Press.

"Red Rice" from *200 Years of Charleston Cooking,* recipes gathered by Blanche S. Rhett, edited by Lettie Gay. Copyright © 1934. Reproduced here by permission of the University of South Carolina Press.

"Mollettes" and "Salsa de Chile" from *The Good Life: New Mexico Traditions and Food* by Fabiola Cabeza de Baca. Copyright © 1949. Reproduced here by permission of the Museum of New Mexico Press.

"Frijoles" from *Mexican Cookbook* by Erna Fergusson. Copyright © 1934. Reproduced here by permission of the University of New Mexico Press.

"Posole" from *Southwest Flavor: Tales from the Kitchen, Recipes and Stories from New Mexico Magazine,* by Adela Amador. Copyright © 2000. Reproduced here by permission of Adela Amador and *New Mexico Magazine*.

"Mochi Soup" from *The Rice Cooker's Companion: Japanese American Food and Stories*. Copyright © 2000. Reproduced here by permission of the Japanese American Historical Society.

The cover image of *Crisco Recipes for the Jewish Housewife*. Copyright © 1935. Reprinted here courtesy of The J. M. Smucker Company. Crisco™ is a registered trademark of The J.M. Smucker Company.

"Made Dandy Cake . . ." excerpts from the unpublished diary of an anonymous Ohio woman. Reprinted here by permission of The Schlesinger Library, Radcliffe Institute, Harvard University. A/A 6151H.

"Wonder Bread Honeymoon Special" from *Wonder Sandwich Suggestions*. Copyright © 1930. Reproduced here by permission of the Interstate Brands Companies. Wonder Bread™ is a registered trademark of the Interstate Brands Companies.

"Fritatta of Zucchini" from "How to Cook a Wolf" in *The Art of Eating* by M. F. K. Fisher. Copyright © 1990 M. F. K. Fisher. All rights reserved. Reproduced here by permission of Wiley Publishing, Inc.

"Gypsy Soup" is reprinted with permission from *The Moosewood Cookbook* by Mollie Katzen. Copyright © 1977, 1992, 2000 by Tante Malka, Inc., Ten Speed Press, Berkeley, California, USA. Available from your local bookseller, or by calling 800-841-2665 or visiting www.tenspeed.com.

"Shrimp Stew (Camarones a La Criolla)" and "Recaíto" from *A Taste of Puerto Rico* by Yvonne Ortiz. Copyright © 1994. Reproduced here by permission of Dutton, a division of Penguin Putnam Inc.

p. xix (Hands with Carrots) Library of Congress, Folklife Center; **p. xxi** (Patriotic Celebration) Los Angeles Public Library, A-009-555; **p. xxviii** (Pottery Casa Grande Ruins) Library of Congress, Lot 3747; **p. xxxiv** (Corn Mother) Philbrook Museum of Art, 1947.63; **pp. 2 and 9** (Gatherers in Desert) Library of Congress, LC-USZ62-111943; **p. 16** (Smokehouses at Kisgegas) Canadian Museum of Civilization, image number: 49490; **p. 18** (Harvest Dance) Denver Art Museum, 1932.207; **p. 20** (Rice Gatherers) Library of Congress, LC-USA7-34115; **p. 26** (The Piki Maker) Library of Congress, LC-USZ62-115802; **p. 30** (Taos Women Winnowing Grain) Library of Congress, LC-USZ62-41784; **p. 31** (Seminole Women Grinding) National Anthropological Archives, Smithsonian Institution, 45331; **p. 33** (Making Fry Bread) Amon Carter Museum, P1979.228.274, copy print from original safety negative; **pp. 36 and 49** (Martha Washington's Recipe) Pennsylvania Historical Society, Am.003; **p. 38** (Colonial Women and Cow) Library of Congress, LC-USZ62-31133; **p. 70** (Woman Selling Food at Richmond Train Station) National Archives of Canada, 1986-7-232; **p. 75** (Separating Mother and Child) Library of Congress, LC-USZ62-33464; **p. 81** (Two Market Women with Baskets of Produce on their Heads) Library of Congress, LC-USZ62-43679; **p. 86** (Planting Sweet Potatoes) New Hampshire Historical Society, HP Moore #511; **p. 95** (Shaking the Rice from the Straw After Threshing) Gibbes Museum of Art, 37.09.23; **pp. 98 and 100** (Liberty. In the Form of the Goddess of Youth) Library of Congress, LC-USZ62-15369; **p. 108** (Lydia Maria Child) The Schlesinger Library, WRC-P18-1; **p. 120** (Catharine Beecher) The Schlesinger Library A-102-438; **p. 128** (Members of Christian Commission Working at White House Landing) Library of Congress, LC-B8171-2487; **p. 131** (The Ladies of Color) Clements Library, broadside ACQ: 13533; **pp. 134 and 162** (Women Eating Melon) Colorado Historical Society, CHS-B1033; **p. 139** (Spanish-American Woman Testing Oven) Library of Congress, LC-USF33-12421-M2; **p. 151** (Annie Yellowbear) Nez Perce National Historic Park, NEPE-HI-0773; **p. 166** (Woman Churning Butter) Colorado Historical Society, CHS-B1025; **pp. 168 and 195** (Women in Heinz Factory) Library of Congress, LC-USZ62-45; **p. 173** (Homes of the Poor) Library of Congress, LC-USZ62-75197; **p. 183 (**Dr. Chauncey's Stove) Library of Congress, LC-USZ62-20979; **p. 185** (Sterling Cookstove) The New-York Historical Society, 75339; **p. 188** (Dover Egg Beater) The New-York Historical Society, 75336; **p. 190** (You Don't Know Beans) The New-York Historical Society, 75337; **p. 192** (Lactated Food Babies) The New-York Historical Society, 75338; **p. 205** (Woman Drying Seaweed) Library of Congress LC-USZ62-87721;

Index

Page numbers in *italics* refer to illustrations.
Entries in **boldface** refer to recipes.

California (*continued*)
163, 208, 210, 216, 220–22, 224, 225,
332–34, *333*
California Gold Rush, 160, 161
Calvinism, 101
camarones a la criolla (shrimp stew), 338–39
camas roots, 150–54, *151, 202*
Cameron, Donaldina, 233
Campbell's Soup, 177, 274
Canada, xxx, 16, 17, 29
candlefish, 17
candy industry, 262, 265
canneries, 189, 190–91, 223, 228, *261,* 262
canning, *xix,* 287, *297, 303*
vacuum bottling, 190
canteeners, 287–92, *288,* 289, *290*
Caribbean, 80, 177
Carlisle Indian School, *255*
Carolina Gold rice, 96
Carolina Housewife, The, 79, 124
Carpenter, Reverend Frank, 69
Carson, Rachel, 329, *329*
Casa Grande Ruins, Arizona, xxviii
cast-iron cookstoves, 66, *183,* 184, 185, *185,*
186, 189
Catharine Market, 178–79
Catholicism, 25, 155, 130, 206, 214, 221
of Hispanic New Mexico, 138, 140, 142,
144, 145
cattails, xxviii, 8, 14
Cayugas, 29
cedar "knockers," 19, *20*
celery, stewed, 253
Cendrillon restaurant, 341
Central America, xxxi, *xxxii,* 22, 140
challah, 212, 216
Channing, John, 69
Channing, William, 69–71
Channing, William Ellery, 71
charitable cookbooks, 126–33, *128,* 230–32
advertising in, 133
African-American, 130–31
Chinese immigrant, 231–32, 233
recipes in, 127–28, 127, 129–30, 130
profitability of, 127, 128–29, 131–32
states represented in, 132–33
Tabasco "Hall of Fame" award for, 131–32
Charles II, King of England, 87

Charleston, S.C., 84
aristocratic cuisine of, 89, 90
food vendors in, 80, 81
cheesemaking, 38, 51, 197–98
modern handmade goat, 334–35, 342
process of, 197
redefined as men's work, 197–98
cheesemaking factories, 189, 197–98
inferior products of, 198
cheese peppers, 202, 203
chefs, 332–34, *333*
Chemistry of Cooking and Cleaning (Richards),
241
chenopod, 11
Cherokees, xxxiii, 34
cherry chutney, 197
Chesapeake Bay, 56–59
Chew, Fay, 223
Cheyennes, 149
Chez Panisse restaurant, 332–34, *333*
Chicago, Ill., 191, 218, 224, *351*
soul food restaurants in, 322–23
Chicago, Ill., Columbian Exposition at,
237–42, 244, 269
Board of Lady Managers at, 239, 241
cooking experts at, 240, 241
Electricity Building at, 238–39, 240, 265
labor-saving devices demonstrated at, 240–41
Woman's Building of, 239–42
chicken, *xiv,* 47, 110, 344, *346*
1917 boycott of, 280
chicken adobo, 341
chicken for the Sabbath (amastich), 281
Chief Joseph, 153–54
Child, Julia, 327–28
Child, Lydia Maria, 108–11, *108*
chile peppers, 15, 23–24, 77, 135, *136,* 139,
141, 144, 146, 147
Chincoteague, Va., 340–41
Chinese Exclusion Act (1882), 207–8
Chinese immigrants, 206, 207–8, 212, 216–17,
229
assimilation of, 227–28, 231–32
charitable cookbooks of, 231–32, 233
family-owned food businesses of, 223, 226
foot binding of, 222, 231
holidays and religious feasts of, 212,
214–15, 223, 226

women's occupations (*continued*)
    on Western frontier, 137, 160, 161, 163–67
women's rights, 127
    of Chinese immigrants, 207, 222, 226,
        231–32, 233
    in colonial period, 41, 53–55, 60, 63, 71, 72,
        106
    in Hispanic New Mexico, 144, 146
    of Native Americans, xxxv–xxxvi, 25–29,
        150, 155–56
    in Vietnam, 341
women's suffrage, 77, 107, *120,* 123, 129, 239,
    279, 285, 293
    World War I and, 287, 292
women's work, 120, 306–7
    of Chinese men, 222
    in colonial period, 38, 43, 50–55
Wonder Sandwich Suggestions (Proctor), *271*
Wong, Jade Snow, 227–28, 229
Woodward, Helen, 90
Work Progress Administration, 91–92
World War I, 129, 248, 269, 277–92, 295
    African-Americans in, 291–92, *292*
    canteeners in, 287–92, *288, 289, 290*
    food conservation campaign in, 282–86,
        286, 292
    food riots in, 277–81, *278, 282*
    women's suffrage and, 287, 292

World War II, 302–11, 317
    day care centers of, 308
    defense workers of, 304–11, *309*
    double-duty women of, 308–11
    gender roles and, 310–11
    postwar layoffs expected in, 308, 310, 311,
        317
    ration books of, 302
    victory gardens of, 302, *303, 307*
    women's magazines and, 308–10
wormwood, 44
Wyeth, N. C., 269
Wyoming, 163

yams, 76, 85
yeast, 79, *102,* 138, 139, 158–59, 186–87, 256
yin and yang, 214
Yorubas, 76
Yost, Nellie, 295
Young, Gumgee, 222
Young Housekeeper's Friend, The (Cornelius),
    114
Yu, Connie Young, 222
Yung, Judy, 207, 232

zucchini, frittata of, 304–5
Zunis, 22, 34